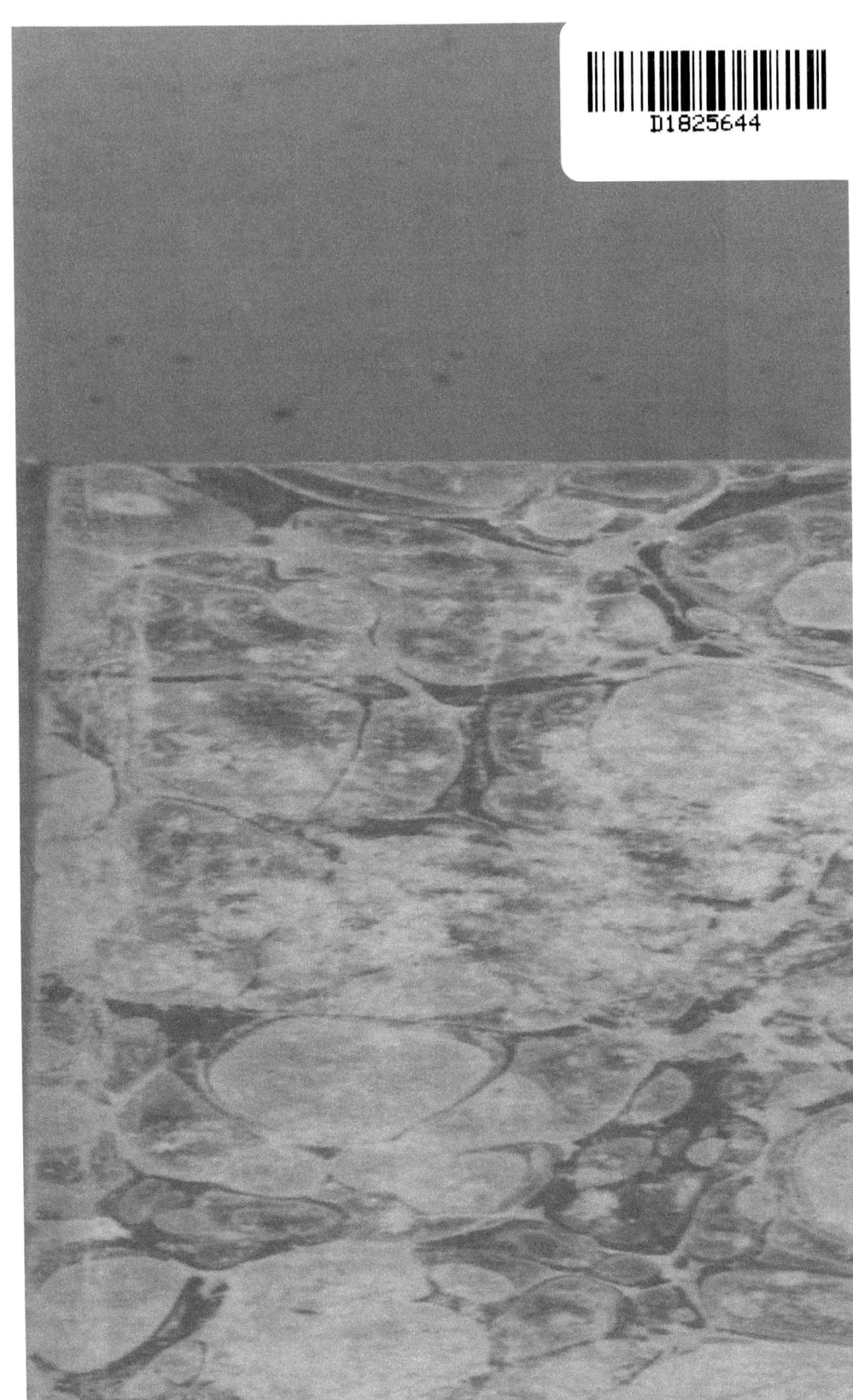

33.

200.

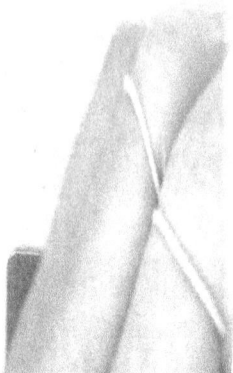

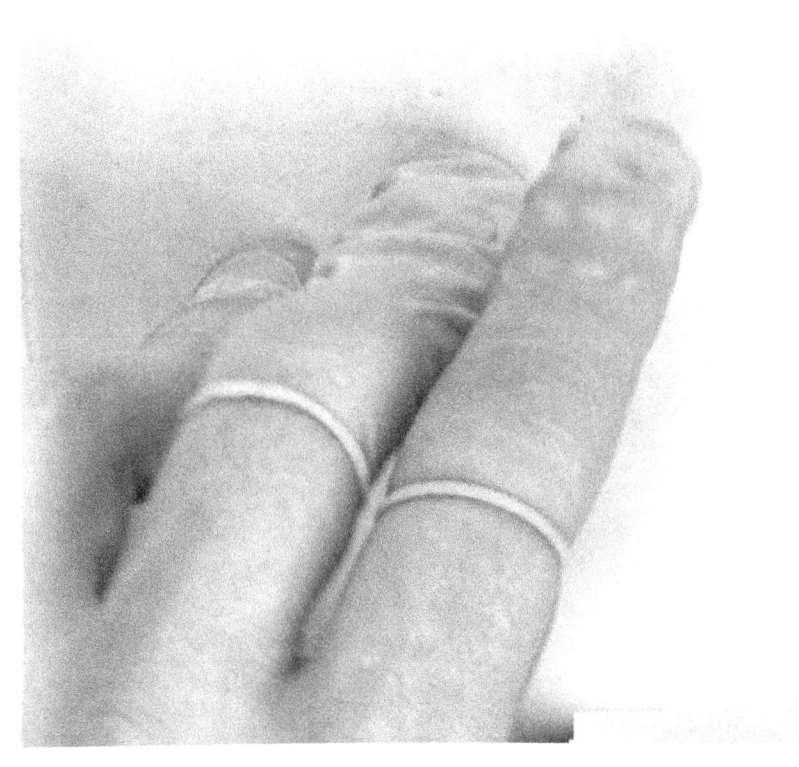

33.

200.

N S

L.

TRADITIONARY STORIES

OF

OLD FAMILIES,

AND

LEGENDARY ILLUSTRATIONS

OF

FAMILY HISTORY.

WITH NOTES, HISTORICAL AND BIOGRAPHICAL.

BY ANDREW PICKEN,

AUTHOR OF THE " DOMINIE'S LEGACY," &c. &c.

IN TWO VOLUMES.

VOL. I.

LONDON:

LONGMAN, REES, ORME, BROWN, GREEN, & LONGMAN, PATERNOSTER-ROW.

1833.

200.

LONDON :
Printed by A. SPOTTISWOODE,
New-Street-Square.

PREFACE.

It is seldom that the title-page of a new book conveys fully the meaning and aim of the author. As the plan of the present is something out of the common, and is intended to embrace and to bring before the general public many matters in the history of families and of individuals, which otherwise might have little chance of seeing the light, the author may, therefore, be permitted a few prefatory words.

Among those distinguished families in whom high descent and influential connections, running through the varieties of many generations, may cause a just pride in tracing lineage and history, there are, in numerous instances, preserved in private archives, or even through the medium of colloquial tradition, many interesting facts, or remarkable incidents, arising out of the characters or fortunes of the men of the past, which, if given to the public in the requisite form, before they are lost to the world by the rapid changing of taste, and the death of their remaining depositaries, might be most illustrative of the great subject of human nature, and even convey valuable moral instruction. Besides this, there are, in old books and scarce tracts — such as only the patient antiquary or the ardent literary enthusiast can plod through, — as well as among the quaint poetry of the olden time, occasional hints of life and manners which, when filled up by the fancy and illustrated by the judgment, or even unrolled from their original dryness, like a mummy of antiquity, are to us more interesting, from their basement in truth, than the most splendid illusions of mere invention.

If, in prosecuting a plan of this kind, and using the word " tradition " to designate our intent, it should be urged by any that we ought, in reference to family history, to amplify nothing, to extend nothing, but to confine ourselves to absolute recorded truth : — alas ! (for the objection draws from us a moralising exclamation) how little of human life is put upon actual record, or even told from our fathers in traditionary story ! The genealogists, if we are confined thus, are the true historians of the world. They say that we are born and die, marry and have children, inherit lands or titles, and transmit them to our posterity. But the tree of life hath a richer foliage than can be traced through the bald branches of a pedigree: it hath blooming flowers and mellow fruit; it stands lofty in the plain, spreading its roots abroad; or it struggles with its own nature on the barren face of the rock; a canker-worm eats out its sap and destroys its branches, or the storm from the mountains tears it up by the roots. Thus, even the oaks of the forest have a moral history, and man judgeth of man, and of his thoughts and deeds, because mind and feeling know all things.

If the plan of giving life and muscle, where it can be done satisfactorily, to the dry skeleton of tradition, or of filling up by the fancy the meagre outline of ill-recorded history, required any apology, after what has been done by the great magician of our age, it would be found in the fact, that the most interesting circumstances affecting conduct and happiness are often passed over altogether, among the names and dates of the re-

cords of exterior and showy events ; or
are handed down through generations, in
the shape of brief hints or recollections,
or treasured up as family secrets, or reach
the world, perhaps, in short anecdotes, or
mere surmises, where a world of anxiety,
joy, or grief, is compressed into the compass of half a page, or rhymed off in a
few stanzas of a forgotten ballad.

In turning our enquiries, then, into
the wide field of family history, and penetrating under the surface of generally
known fact, a mine is opened, but little
wrought as yet, of such richness and
variety as, particularly if aided by private
communication, will well repay the labours of the *con amore* enquirer, and not
be unworthy, as we think, of the encouragement of the public. Our plan, also,
offers, in future volumes, to the living
representatives of ancient families, and
others, an opportunity of bringing out

much curious and always instructive matter, which might have little chance, otherwise, of obtaining the attention of the public. In his little experience, the author has already found that the most interesting circumstances of domestic biography, particularly when they imply suffering or misfortune, are often those that individuals consider in the light of family secrets, which they are the most reluctant to have known ; and thus the world loses all the instruction of the warning or example of some painfully-earned experience. This delicacy, however, only adheres to certain minds; but where it does exist, it is easily provided for, in making use of its communications, by the simple plan of giving imaginary names and allusions where the nature of the case seems to require such concealment. The more modern fragments of family history, which may be chiefly of this sort, we put into the mouth of the simple Dominie, who would travel a score of miles any day to learn an interesting fact; yet would go twice the distance, if, by so doing, he might avoid giving any living mortal offence.

The stories in these two volumes are more confined to Scotland than the author had intended, could he have got his materials out of the hands of some to whom he unfortunately submitted them, in proper time for the present publication; or had the English and Irish families entered with the same readiness into his views, that was done by his more facile countrymen of the North. Should the present, nevertheless, be encouraged, — however imperfect as a first experiment, — future volumes will, he trusts, show how much it is his own wish to avoid the charge of any national partiality.

To the early friends of this work, and

its plan, who, by patronising it in private, or by supplying information for the present, or offering it for future volumes, have encouraged him to the publication, the author begs to offer his best thanks; and when he mentions, among these, the names of the DUKE OF HAMILTON, the DUKE OF BEDFORD, the DUKE OF BUCCLEUGH, the DUCHESS OF SUTHERLAND, the MARQUESS and MARCHIONESS OF HASTINGS, the EARL SPENCER, the EARL OF ERROL, the EARL OF GLASGOW, the EARL CADOGAN, the EARL MOUNTNORRIS, the LORD CHANCELLOR, the VISCOUNT MELBOURNE, the LORD ADVOCATE OF SCOTLAND, the LORD LEVESON GOWER, the VISCOUNT MAHON, LORD PANMURE, LORD CARBERRY, the late lamented LORD DOVER, SIR CHARLES FORBES, BART., SIR JOHN FORBES, BART., GENERAL NATHANIEL FORBES, MR. FORBES of Newe, SIR JOHN HAY, BART.,

M.P., Sir Michael Shaw Stewart, Bart., M.P., Patrick Maxwell Stewart, M.P., the Hon. D. G. Halliburton, M.P., Sir Andrew Halliday, Knt., M.D., Sir Daniel K. Sandford, Knt., Robert Wallace, M.P., Robert Gordon, M.P., J. H. Callander, M.P., Edward T. Bainbridge, M.P., John Maxwell, M.P., James Ewing, M.P., James Oswald, M.P., J. A. Murray, M.P., Mr. Gordon of Fyvie, Mr. Gordon of Cairnbulg, Mr. Lockhart, Mr. Southey, Mr. Thomas Campbell, Mr. Wordsworth, Mr. Moore, and others with whose names the public are hardly less familiar, he may be justified in anticipating some portion of success.

Many defects and " short comings " of his own conceptions are incident to an author's first step in any literary undertaking, however humble. But, not to be further egotistical where the sub-

ject will hardly bear it, we shall end
our preface by the quaint " excusation "
of the learned " prentar " of Boece's
black-letter chronicles : —

  " And in this wark that I have here assailzett
    To bring to lycht, maist humely I exhort
    Zow nobill reders, quhare that I have failzett,
    In letter, sillabe, poyntis lang, or schort,
    That ye will of your gentrice it support,
    And take *the present* the best wyse ze may,
I sall do better (will God) *maybe* ane other day."

MEN AND MANNERS

IN AMERICA.

CHAPTER I.

VOYAGE—NEW YORK.

On the morning of the 16th of October, I embarked at Liverpool, on board of the American packet ship, New York, Captain Bennet, bound for the port of the same name. There were twenty-six passengers on board, and though the accommodations were excellent, the cabin, as might be expected, was somewhat disagreeably crowded. Our party consisted of about fifteen or sixteen Americans, some half-dozen countrymen of my own, two or three English, a Swiss, and a Frenchman.

Though the elements of this assemblage were heterogeneous enough, I have great pleasure in remembering that the most perfect harmony prevailed on board.   To myself, the whole of my fellow-passengers were most obliging ; and for some I contracted a regard, which led me to regret that the period of our arrival in port, was likely to bring with it a lasting cessation of our intercourse.

The miseries of a landsman on board of ship, have afforded frequent matter for pen and pencil.   At *best*, a sea voyage is a confinement at once irksome and odious, in which the unfortunate prisoner is compelled for weeks, or months, to breathe the tainted atmosphere of a close and crowded cabin, and to sleep at night in a sort of box, about the size of a coffin for " the stout gentleman."   At *worst*, it involves a complication of the most nauseous evils that can afflict humanity,—an utter prostration of power, both bodily and mental,—a revulsion of the whole corporeal machinery, accompanied by a host of detestable diagnostics, which at once convert a well-dressed and well-favoured gentleman, into an object of contempt to himself, and disgust to those around him.

Such are a few of the joys that await a landsman, whom evil stars have led to "go down to the sea in ships, and occupy his business in the great waters." With regard to sailors, the case is different, but not much. Being seasoned vessels, they are, no doubt, exempt from some of those evils, and completely hardened to others, which are most revolting to a landsman. But their Pandora's box can afford to lose a few miseries, and still retain a sufficient stock of all sizes, for any reasonable supply. It may be doubted, too, whether the most ardent sailor was ever so hallucinated by professional enthusiasm, as to pitch his Paradise—wherever he might place his Purgatory—afloat.

On board of the New York, however, I must say, that our sufferings were exclusively those arising from the elements of air and water. Her accommodations were admirable. Nothing had been neglected which could possibly contribute to the comfort of the passengers. In another respect, too, we were fortunate. Our commander had nothing about him, of "the rude and boisterous captain of the sea." In truth, Captain Bennet was not only an adept in all professional accomplishment, but, in other respects, a person of extensive information; and I confess, it was even with some degree of pride, that I learned he had received his nautical education in the British navy. Partaking of the strong sense we all entertained, of his unvarying solicitude for the comfort of his passengers, I am happy also to profess myself indebted to him, for much valuable information relative to the country I was about to visit.

Among the passengers were some whose eccentricities contributed materially to enliven the monotony of the voyage. The most prominent of these was a retired hair-dresser from Birmingham, innocent of all knowledge unconnected with the wig-block, who, having recently married a young wife, was proceeding, accompanied by his fair rib, with the romantic intention of establishing themselves in "some pretty box," in the back-woods of America. As for the lady, she was good-looking, but, being somewhat gratuitously solicitous to barb the arrows of her charms, her chief occupation during the voyage, consisted in adorning her countenance with such variety of wigs of different colours, as unquestionably did excite the marvel, if not the admiration, of the passengers. The billing and cooing of this interesting couple, however, though sanctioned by the laws of Hymen, became at length so public and obtrusive, as, in the opinion of the other ladies, to demand repression; and a request was consequently made, that they would be so obliging for the future, as to reserve their mutual demonstrations of attachment, for the privacy of their own cabin.

Among the passengers too, was Master Burke, better known by the title of the Irish Roscius, who was about to cross the Atlantic with his father and a French music-master, to display his talents on a new field. Though not much given to admire those youthful prodigies, who, for a season or two, are puffed into notice, and then quietly lapse into very ordinary men, I think there can be no question that young Burke is a very wonderful boy. Barely eleven years old, he was already an accomplished and scientific musician, played the violin with first-rate taste and execution, and in his impersonations of character, displayed a versatility of power, and a perception of the deeper springs of human action, almost incredible in one so young. But independently of all this, he became, by his amiable and obliging disposition, an universal favourite on board ; and when the conclusion of our voyage brought with it a general separation, I am certain the boy carried with him the best wishes of us all, that he might escape injury or contamination in that perilous profession, to which his talents had been thus early devoted.

We sailed from Liverpool about one o'clock, and in little more than an hour, were clear of the Mersey. On the morning following we were opposite the Tuskar rocks, and a run of two days brought us fairly out into the Atlantic. Then bidding farewell to the bold headlands of the Irish coast, with a flowing sheet we plunged forward into the vast wilderness of waters, which lay foaming before us, and around.

For the first week, all the chances were in our favour. The wind, though generally light, was fair, and the New York—celebrated as a fast sailer—with all canvass set, ran down the distance gallantly.

But, on the seventh day, our good fortune was at an end. The wind came on boisterous and adverse, and our progress for the next fortnight was comparatively small. Many of the party became affected with sea-sickness, and the hopes, to which our early good fortune had given rise, of a rapid passage, were —as other dearer hopes have been by us all,—slowly, but unwillingly, relinquished.

We were yet some five hundred miles to the eastward of the banks of Newfoundland, when, on the 23d day, our spirits were again gladdened by a fair wind. Then it was that the New York gave unquestionable proof that her high character was not unmerited. In the six following days we ran down fifteen hundred miles, and the evening of the twenty-eighth day, found us off Sandy Hook, which forms the entrance to the Bay of New York.

Our misfortunes, however, were not yet at an end. When within a few hours' sail of port, our progress was arrested for four days, by a dense fog. Four more disagreeable days, I never passed. Sun, moon, stars, earth, and ocean, lay hid in impenetrable vapour, and it was only by the constant use of the lead, that the ship could move in safety. The air we breathed seemed changed into a heavier element; we felt like men suddenly smitten with blindness, and it almost seemed, as if the time of chaos had come again, when darkness lay brooding on the face of the deep. The effect of this weather on the spirits of us all, was very remarkable. Even the most jovial of the party became gloomy and morose. Conversation languished, and the mutual benevolence with which we had hitherto regarded each other, had evidently sustained a diminution.

At length, when our patience, hourly sinking, had nearly reached zero, a favourable change took place. About noon on the 17th of November, the mist suddenly rolled upward like a curtain, and with joyful eyes we beheld the coast of New Jersey outstretched before us. Towards evening, we received a pilot, and were visited by several boats employed by the proprietors of the New York newspapers, to procure the earliest intelligence from vessels in the offing. The avidity for news of all kinds, displayed both by these visitors and the American passengers, was rather amusing.

Numerous questions were interchanged, relative to politics and dry goods, shipping and shippers, freights and failures, corn, cotton, constitutions, and commissions. Though in this sort of traffic, as in all others, there was value given on both sides, yet it struck me, that a sincere desire to oblige was generally apparent. Every one seemed happy to enter on the most prolix details for the benefit of his neighbour; and the frequent repetition of the same question, appeared by no means to be attended with the usual consequences on the patience of the person addressed. I certainly could detect nothing of that dogged, and almost sullen brevity, with which, I take it, the communications of Englishmen, in similar circumstances, would have been marked. No one seemed to grudge the trouble necessary to convey a complete comprehension of facts or opinions to the mind of his neighbour, nor to circumscribe his communications, within the limits necessary to secure the gratification of his own curiosity.

We passed Sandy Hook in the night, and, on coming on deck in the morning, were greeted with one of the most beautiful prospects I had ever beheld. We were then passing the Narrows; Long Island on one side, Staten Island on the other, a finely undulating country, hills covered with wood, agreeably interspersed with villas and cottages, and New York on its island, with its vast forest of shipping, looming in the distance.

Such are some of the more prominent features of the scene, by which our eyes were first gladdened, on entering the American waters. A more glorious morning never shone from the heavens. All around was bathed in a flood of sunshine, which seemed brighter when contrasted with the weather under which we had so recently suffered.

I am not aware, that there is any thing very fine in the appearance of New York, when seen from the bay, but, taken in conjunction with the surrounding scenery, it certainly forms a pleasing feature in the landscape. The city stands on the southern extremity of York Island, and enlarging in latitude as it recedes from the apex of a triangle, stretches along the shores of the Hudson and East Rivers, far as the eye can reach. On the right are the heights of

Brooklyn, which form part of Long Island; and across the broad waters of the Hudson, the view is terminated on the left by the wooded shore of New Jersey.

But whatever may be the pictorial defects or beauties of New York, it is almost impossible to conceive a city, better situated for commerce. At no season of the year, can there be any obstruction in its communication with the ocean; and with a fine and navigable river, stretching for nearly two hundred miles into the interior of a fertile country, it possesses natural advantages of no common order. In extent of trade and population, I believe New York already exceeds every other city of the Union; and unquestionably it is yet very far from having gathered all its greatness.

The scene, as we approached the quay, became gradually more animated. Numerous steam-vessels, and boats of all descriptions, were traversing the harbour; and the creaking of machinery, and the loud voices which occasionally reached us from the shore, gave evidence of activity and bustle. About twelve o'clock the ship reached her mooring, and in half an hour I was safely housed in Bunker's Hotel, where I had been strongly recommended to take up my residence. A young American accompanied me to the house, and introduced me to the landlord, who, after some miscellaneous conversation, produced a book, in which I was directed to enrol my name, country, and vocation. This formality being complied with, a black waiter was directed to convey such of my baggage as I had been permitted to bring ashore, to an apartment, and I found myself at liberty to ramble forth, and gratify my curiosity by a view of the town.

In visiting a foreign city, a traveller—especially an English one—usually expects to find, in the aspect of the place and its inhabitants, some tincture of the barbaric. There is something of this, though not a great deal, at New York. The appearance of the population, though not English, is undoubtedly nearer to it than that of any city on the continent of Europe; and but for the number of blacks and people of colour, one encounters in the streets, there is certainly little to remind a traveller that the breadth of an ocean divides him from Great Britain.

The fashions of dress generally adopted by the wealthier classes are those of Paris and London; and the tastes and habits of the people, so far as these appear on the surface, bear a strong resemblance to those of his countrymen.   Minute differences, however, are no doubt apparent at the first glance.   The aspect and bearing of the citizens of New York, are certainly very distinguishable from any thing ever seen in Great Britain.   They are generally slender in person, somewhat slouching in gait, and without that openness of countenance and erectness of deportment to which an English eye has been accustomed.   Their utterance, too, is marked by a peculiar modulation, partaking of a snivel and a drawl, which, I confess, to my ear, is by no means laudable on the score of euphony.

Observations of a similar character, are as applicable to the city, as to its inhabitants.   The frequent intermixture of houses of brick and framework, was certainly unlike any thing I had ever seen in Europe; and the New-Yorkers have inherited from their Dutch ancestors the fashion of painting their houses of a bright colour, which produces an agree-

able effect, and gives to the streets an air of
gaiety and lightness which could not otherwise
have been attained. The prominent defect of the
city, is a want of consistency and compactness,
in the structure even of the better streets. There
are some excellent houses in them all, but these
frequently occur in alternation with mere hovels,
and collections of rubbish, which detract materially
from the general effect. But the general aspect of
New York is unquestionably pleasing. It is full,
even to overflow, of business and bustle, and crowded
with a population devoting their whole energies, to
the arts of money-getting. Such were the first impressions I received in New York.

Having gratified my curiosity with a cursory view
of the chief streets, my obliging companion conducted
me to the Custom-house, in order to procure a permit
for landing my baggage. On arriving there, I was
rather surprised to find, that the routine observed, in
such matters in this republican country, is in fact
more vexatious, than in England. In New York, you
are first required to swear that the specification
given of the contents of your boxes is true; and

then, as if no reliance were due to your oath, the officers proceed to a complete search. To the search, however troublesome, unquestionably no objection can be made ; but it does appear to be little better than an insulting mockery, to require an oath to which all credit is so evidently denied. The proverb says, that " at lovers' vows Jove laughs ;" and if, in America, the deity is supposed to extend his merriment to Custom-house oaths, it surely would be better to abolish a practice, which, to say nothing of the demoralizing influence it cannot fail to exert, is found to have no efficacy in the prevention of fraud. Certainly in no country of Europe is it usual to require an oath, in cases where it is not received as sufficient evidence of the fact deposed to ; and why the practice should be different, under a government so popular as that of the United States, it would be difficult to determine.

Custom-house regulations, however, are matters on which most travellers are given to be censorious. In truth, I know nothing so trying to the equanimity of the mildest temper, as the unpleasant ceremony of having one's baggage rummaged over by the rude fists of a revenue-officer. It is in vain reason tells us, that this impertinent poking into our portmanteaus is just and proper; that the privilege is reciprocal between nations, each of which necessarily enjoys the right, of excluding altogether articles of foreign manufacture, or of attaching such conditions to their importation, as it may see fit. All this is very true, but the sense of personal indignity cannot be got over. There is nothing of national solemnity at all apparent in the operation. The investigator of our property is undistinguished by any outward symbol of executive authority. It requires too great an effort of imagination, to regard a dirty Custom-house searcher, as a visible impersonation of the majesty of the law; and in spite of ten thousand unanswerable reasons to the contrary, we cannot help considering his rigid examination of our cloak-bag and shaving-case, rather as an act of individual audacity, than the necessary and perfunctory discharge of professional duty. In short, the *searcher* and *searchee* stand to each other in the relation of *plus* and *minus*, and the latter has nothing for it, but to put his pride in his pocket, and keep down his choler as best he can, with the complete knowledge that being *pro tem.* in the hands of the Philistines, the smallest display of either could only tend to make things worse. It is always my rule, therefore, when possible, to avoid being present at the scene at all; and having, on the present occasion, given directions to my servant, to await the business of inspection, and afterwards to convey the baggage to the hotel, I again committed myself to the guidance of some of my American friends, and commenced another ramble through the city.

As we passed, many of the signs exhibited by the different shops struck me as singular. Of these, " DRY GOOD STORE," words of which I confess I did not understand the precise import, was certainly the most prevalent. My companions informed me that the term *dry goods* is not, as might be supposed, generally applicable to merchandise devoid of moisture, but solely to articles composed of linen, silk, or woollen. " COFFIN WAREHOUSE," however, was sufficiently explanatory of the nature of the commerce carried on within; but had it been otherwise, the sight of some scores of these dismal commodities,

arranged in sizes, and ready for immediate use,
would have been comment enough. " FLOUR AND
FEED STORE," and " OYSTER REFECTORY," were
more grateful to the eye and the imagination.
" HOLLOW WARE, SPIDERS, and FIRE DOGS," seemed to indicate some novel and anomalous traffic, and
carried with it a certain dim and mystical sublimity,
of which I shall not venture to divest it, by any
attempt at explanation.

I was amused, too, with some of the placards which
appeared on the walls. Many of these were political, and one in particular was so unintelligible, as to
impose the task of a somewhat prolix commentary
on my friends. It ran thus, in sesquipedalian characters,

JACKSON FOR EVER.
GO THE WHOLE HOG !

When the sphere of my intelligence became
enlarged with regard to this *affiche*, I learned, that
" going the whole hog" is the American popular
phrase for Radical Reform, and is used by the Democratic party to distinguish them from the Federalists, who are supposed to prefer less sweeping mea-

sures, and consequently *to go* only *a part* of the interesting quadruped in question. The *Go-the-whole-hoggers*, therefore, are politicians determined to follow out Democratic principles to their utmost extent, and with this party, General Jackson is at present an especial favourite. The expression, I am told, is of Virginian origin. In that State, when a butcher kills a pig, it is usual to demand of each customer, whether he will " go the whole hog;" as, by such extensive traffic, a purchaser may supply his table at a lower price, than is demanded of him, whose imagination revels among *prime pieces*, to the exclusion of baser matter.

Before quitting the ship, it had been arranged among a considerable number of the passengers, that we should dine together on the day of our arrival, as a proof of parting in kindness and good-fellowship. Niblo's tavern, the most celebrated eating-house in New York, was the scene chosen for this amicable celebration. Though a little tired with my walks of the morning, which the long previous confinement on board of ship had rendered more than usually fatiguing, I determined to explore my

way on foot, and having procured the necessary
directions at the hotel, again set forth. On my way,
an incident occurred, which I merely mention to
show how easily travellers like myself, on their first
arrival in a country, may be led into a misconcep-
tion of the character of the people. Having proceeded some distance, I found it necessary to enquire
my way, and accordingly entered a small grocer's
shop. " Pray, sir," I said, " can you point out to me
the way to Niblo's tavern ?" The person thus addressed was rather a gruff-looking man, in a scratch-
wig, and for at least half a minute kept eyeing me
from top to toe without uttering a syllable. " Yes,
sir, I can," he at length replied, with a stare as
broad as if he had taken me for the great Katterfel-
to. Considering this sort of treatment, as the mere
ebullition of republican insolence, I was in the act
of turning on my heel and quitting the shop, when
the man added, " and I shall have great pleasure in
showing it you." He then crossed the counter, and
accompanying me to the middle of the street, pointed
out the land-marks by which I was to steer, and
gave the most minute directions for my guidance.

I presume that his curiosity in the first instance was excited by something foreign in my appearance; and that, having once satisfied himself that I was a stranger, he became on that account more than ordinarily anxious to oblige. This incident afforded me the first practical insight into the manners of the people, and was useful both as a precedent for future guidance, and as explaining the source of many of the errors of former travellers. Had my impulse to quit the shop been executed with greater rapidity, I should certainly have considered this man as a brutal barbarian, and perhaps have drawn an unfair inference with regard to the manners and character, of the lower orders of society in the United States.

The dinner at Niblo's,—which may be considered the London Tavern of New York,—was certainly more excellent in point of materiel, than of cookery or arrangement. It consisted of oyster soup, shad, venison,* partridges, grouse, wild ducks of diffe-

* In regard to game, I adopt the nomenclature in common use in the United States. It may be as well to state, however, that neither the partridges nor the grouse bear any very close resemblance to the birds of the same name in Europe. Their flesh is dry, and comparatively without flavour.

rent varieties, and several other dishes less notable. There was no attempt to serve this chaotic entertainment in courses, a fashion, indeed, but little prevalent in the United States. Soup, fish, flesh and fowl, simultaneously garnished the table; and the consequence was, that the greater part of the dishes were cold, before the guests were prepared to attack them. The venison was good, though certainly very inferior to that of the fallow-deer. The wines were excellent, the company agreeable in all respects, and altogether I do not remember to have passed a more pleasant evening, than that of my first arrival at New York.

CHAPTER II.

NEW YORK.

I HAD nearly completed my toilet on the morning after my arrival, when the tinkling of a large bell gave intimation, that the hour of breakfast was come. I accordingly descended as speedily as possible to the *salle à manger*, and found a considerable party engaged in doing justice to a meal, which, at first glance, one would scarcely have guessed to be a breakfast. Solid viands of all descriptions loaded the table, while, in the occasional intervals, were distributed dishes of rolls, toast, and cakes of buckwheat and Indian corn. At the head of the table, sat the landlady, who, with an air of complacent dignity, was busied in the distribution of tea and coffee. A large bevy of negroes were bustling about, ministering with all possible alacrity, to the many wants which were somewhat vociferously obtruded on their attention. Towards the upper end of the table, I observed about a dozen ladies, but by far the larger portion of the company were of the other sex.

The contrast of the whole scene, with that of an English breakfast-table, was striking enough. Here was no loitering nor lounging; no dipping into newspapers; no apparent lassitude of appetite; no intervals of repose in mastication; but all was hurry, bustle, clamour, and voracity, and the business of repletion went forward, with a rapidity altogether unexampled. The strenuous efforts of the company were of course, soon rewarded with success. Departures, which had begun even before I took my place at the table, became every instant more numerous, and in a few minutes the apartment had become, what Moore beautifully describes in one of his songs, " a banquet-hall deserted." The appearance of the table under such circumstances, was by no means gracious either to the eye or the fancy. It was strewed thickly with the *disjecta membra* of the entertainment. Here, lay fragments of fish, somewhat unpleasantly odoriferous; there, the skeleton of a chicken; on the right, a mustard-pot upset, and the cloth, *passim*, defiled with stains of eggs, coffee, gravy —but I will not go on with the picture. One nasty custom, however, I must notice. Eggs, instead of being eat from the shell, are poured into a wine-glass, and after being duly and disgustingly churned up with butter and condiment, the mixture, according to its degree of fluidity, is forthwith either spooned into the mouth, or drunk off like a liquid. The advantage gained by this unpleasant process, I do not profess to be qualified to appreciate, but I can speak from experience, to its sedative effect on the appetite of an unpractised beholder.

My next occupation was to look over my letters of introduction. Of these I found above thirty address-ed to New York, and being by no means anxious to become involved in so wide a vortex of acquaintance, I requested one of my American fellow-passengers to select such, as, from his local knowledge, he ima-gined might prove of more immediate service to a traveller like myself. In consequence of this ar-rangement, about half the letters with which the kindness of my friends had furnished me, were discarded, and I can truly say, that the very warm and obliging reception I experienced from those to whom I forwarded introductions, left me no room, to regret the voluntary limitation of their number.

Having despatched my letters, and the morning being wet, I remained at home, busied in throwing together a few memoranda of such matters, as appeared worthy of record. My labours, however, were soon interrupted. Several gentlemen who had heard of my arrival through the medium of my fellow-passengers, but on whose civility I had no claim, did me the honour to call, tendering a welcome to their city, and the still more obliging offer of their services. My letters, too, did not fail of procuring me a plentiful influx of visitors. Numerous invitations followed, and by the extreme kindness of my new friends, free admission was at once afforded me to the best society in New York.

The first impression made by an acquaintance with the better educated order of American gentlemen, is certainly very pleasing. There is a sort of republican plainness and simplicity in their address, quite in harmony with the institutions of their country. An American bows less than an Englishman; he deals less in mere conventional forms and expressions of civility; he pays few or no compliments; makes no unmeaning or overstrained professions; but he takes you by the hand with a cordiality which at once intimates, that he is disposed to regard you as a friend. Of that higher grace of manner, inseparable perhaps from the artificial distinctions of European society, and of which even those most conscious of its hollowness, cannot always resist the attraction, few specimens are of course to be found, in a country like the United States; but of this I am sure, that such a reception as I have experienced in New York, is far more gratifying to a stranger, than the farce of ceremony, however gracefully it may be performed.

Perhaps I was the more flattered by the kindness of my reception, from having formed anticipations of a less pleasing character. The Americans I had met in Europe had generally been distinguished by a certain reserve, and something even approaching to the offensive in manner, which had not contri-

buted to create a prepossession in their favour. It
seemed, as if each individual were impressed with
the conviction that the whole dignity of his country
was concentered in his person; and I imagined them
too much given to disturb the placid current of social
intercourse, by the obtrusion of national jealousies,
and the cravings of a restless and inordinate vanity.
It is indeed highly probable, that these unpleasant
peculiarities were called into more frequent display,
by that air of haughty repulsion, in which too
many of my countrymen have the bad taste to
indulge; but even from what I have already seen, I
feel sure that an American at home, is a very different person from an American abroad. With his foot
on his native soil, he appears in his true character;
he moves in the sphere, for which his habits and
education have peculiarly adapted him, and surrounded by his fellow-citizens, he at once gets rid of
the embarrassing conviction, that he is regarded as
an individual impersonation of the whole honour of
the Union.   In England, he is generally anxious to
demonstrate by indifference of manner, that he is
not dazzled by the splendour which surrounds him,

and too solicitously forward in denying the validity of all pretensions, which he fears the world may consider as superior to his own. But in his own country, he stands confessedly on a footing with the highest. His national vanity remains unruffled by opposition or vexatious comparison, and his life passes on in a dreamy and complacent contemplation of the high part, which, in her growing greatness, the United States is soon to assume, in the mighty drama of the world. His imagination is no longer troubled with visions of lords and palaces, and footmen in embroidery and cocked hats; or if he think of these things at all, it is in a spirit far more philosophical, than that with which he once regarded them. Connected with England by commercial relations, by community of literature, and a thousand ties, which it will still require centuries to obliterate, he cannot regard her destinies without deep interest. In the contests in which, by the calls of honour, or by the folly of her rulers, she may be engaged, the reason of an American may be against England, but his heart is always with her. He is ever ready to extend to her sons, the rites of kindness and hospitality, and is more flattered by their praise, and more keenly sensitive to their censure, than is perhaps quite consistent with a just estimate, of the true value of either.

I remember no city which has less to show in the way of *Lions* than New York. The whole interest attaching to it, consists in the general appearance of the place; in the extreme activity and bustle which is everywhere apparent, and in the rapid advances which it has made, and is still making, in opulence and population. In an architectural view, New York has absolutely nothing to arrest the attention. The only building of pretension is the State-House, or City-Hall, in which the courts of law hold their sittings. In form, it is an oblong parallelogram, two stories in height, exclusive of the basement, with an Ionic portico of white marble, which instead of a pediment, is unfortunately surmounted by a balcony. Above is a kind of lantern or pepper-box, which the taste of the architect has led him to substitute for a dome. From the want of simplicity, the effect of the whole is poor, and certainly not improved by the vicinity of a very ugly gaol, which might be advantageously removed to some less obtrusive situation.

The Exchange is a petty affair, and unworthy of a community so large and opulent as that of New York. With regard to churches, those frequented by the wealthier classes are built of stone, but the great majority are of timber. Their architecture in general is anomalous enough; and the wooden spires, terminating in gorgeous weathercocks, are as gay as the lavish employment of the painter's brush can make them.

But the chief attraction of New York is the Broadway, which runs through the whole extent of the city, and forms as it were the central line from which the other streets diverge to the quays on the Hudson and East River. It is certainly a handsome street, and the complete absence of regularity in the buildings,—which are of all sizes and materials, from the wooden cottage of one story, to the massive brick edifice of five or six,—gives to Broadway a certain picturesque effect, incompatible, perhaps, with greater regularity of architecture. The sides are skirted by a row of stunted and miserable-look-

ing poplars, useless either for shade or ornament,
which breaks the unity of the street without compensation of any sort.   The shops in Broadway are
the depots of all the fashionable merchandise of the
city, but somewhat deficient in external attractions,
to eyes accustomed to the splendour of display in
Regent Street, or Oxford Road.   About two o'clock,
however, the scene in Broadway becomes one of
pleasing bustle and animation.   The *trottoirs* are
then crowded with gaily dressed ladies, and that
portion of the younger population, whom the absence
of more serious employment enables to appear in the
character of beaux.   The latter, however, is small.
From the general air and appearance of the people,
it is quite easy to gather, that trade in some of its
various branches, is the engrossing object of every
one, from the youth of fifteen to the veteran of fourscore, who, from force of habit, still lags superfluous
on the Exchange.   There are no morning loungers
in New York; and the ladies generally walk unattended; but in the evening, I am told, it is different,
and the business of gallantry goes on quite as hope-
fully, as on our side of the water.

I have observed many countenances remarkable for beauty, among the more youthful portion of the fair promenaders. But unfortunately beauty in this climate is not durable. Like " the ghosts of Banquo's fated line," it comes like a shadow, and so departs. At one or two-and-twenty the bloom of an American lady is gone, and the more substantial materials of beauty follow soon after. At thirty the whole fabric is in decay, and nothing remains but the tradition of former conquests, and anticipations of the period, when her reign of triumph will be vicariously restored in the person of her daughter.

The fashions of Paris reach even to New York, and the fame of Madame Maradan Carson has already transcended the limits of the Old World, and is diffused over the New. I pretend to be something of a judge in such matters, and therefore pronounce *ex cathedrâ*, that the ladies of New York are well dressed, and far from inelegant. The average of height is certainly lower than among my fair countrywomen; the cheek is without colour, and the figure sadly deficient in *en-bon-point*. But with all these disadvantages, I do not remember to have seen more beauty than I have met in New York. The features are generally finely moulded, and not unfrequently display a certain delightful harmony, which reminds one of the *Belle Donne* of St Peter's and the Pincian Mount. The mouth alone is not beautiful; it rarely possesses the charm of fine teeth, and the lips want colour and fulness. The carriage of these fair Americans is neither French nor English, for they have the good sense to adopt the peculiarities of neither. They certainly do not paddle along, with the short steps and affected carriage of a Parisian belle, nor do they consider it becoming, to walk the streets with the stride of a grenadier. In short, though I may have occasionally encountered more grace, than has met my observation since my arrival in the United States, assuredly I have never seen less of external deportment, which the most rigid and fastidious critic could fairly censure.

One of my earliest occupations was to visit the courts of law. In the first I entered, there were two judges on the bench, and a jury in the box, engaged in the trial of an action of assault and battery, committed by one female on another. It is scarcely possible to conceive the administration of justice invested with fewer forms. Judges and barristers were both wigless and gownless, and dressed in garments of such colour and fashion, as the taste of the individual might dictate. There was no mace, nor external symbol of authority of any sort, except the staves which I observed in the hands of a few constables, or officers of the court. In the trial there was no more interest than what the quarrel of two old women, in any country, may be supposed to excite. The witnesses, I thought, gave their evidence with a greater appearance of phlegm and indifference than is usual in our courts at home. No one seemed to think, that any peculiar decorum of deportment was demanded by the solemnity of the court. The first witness examined, held the Bible in one hand, while he kept the other in his breeches pocket, and, in giving his evidence, stood lounging with his arm thrown over the bench. The judges were men about fifty, with nothing remarkable in the mode of discharging their duty. The counsel were younger, and, so far as I could judge, by no means deficient

either in zeal for the cause of their clients, or ingenuity in maintaining it.   The only unpleasant part
of the spectacle,—for I do not suppose that justice
could be administered in any country with greater
substantial purity,—was the incessant salivation going forward in all parts of the court. Judges, counsel, jury, witnesses, officers, and audience, all contributed to augment the mass of abomination; and the
floor around the table of the lawyers presented an
appearance, on which even now I find it not very
pleasant for the imagination to linger.

Having satisfied my curiosity in this court, I
entered another, which I was informed was the
Supreme Court of the state.   The proceedings here
were, if possible, less interesting than those I had
already witnessed. The court were engaged in hearing arguments connected with a bill of exchange,
and, whether in America or England, a speech on
such a subject must be a dull affair; I was therefore
on the point of departing, when a jury, which had
previously retired to deliberate, came into court,
and proceeded in the usual form to deliver their verdict.   It was not without astonishment, I confess,

that I remarked that three-fourths of the jurymen were engaged in eating bread and cheese, and that the foreman actually announced the verdict with his mouth full, ejecting the disjointed syllables during the intervals of mastication! In truth, an American seems to look on a judge, exactly as he does on a carpenter or coppersmith, and it never occurs to him, that an administrator of justice is entitled to greater respect than a constructor of brass knockers, or the sheather of a ship's bottom. The judge and the brazier are paid equally for their work; and Jonathan firmly believes, that while he has money in his pocket, there is no risk of his suffering from the want either of law or warming pans.

I cannot think, however, that with respect to these matters, legislation in this country has proceeded on very sound or enlightened principles. A very clever lawyer asked me last night, whether the sight of their courts had not cured me of my *John Bullish* predilection for robes, wigs, and maces, and all the other trumpery and irrational devices, for imposing on weak minds. I answered, it had not; nay, so far was the case otherwise, that had I before been disposed to question the utility of those forms to which he objected, what I had witnessed since my arrival in New York, would have removed all doubts on the subject. A good deal of discussion followed, and though each of us persisted in maintaining our own opinion, it is only justice to state, that the argument was conducted by my opponent with the utmost liberality and fairness. I refrain from giving the details of this conversation, because a " protocol" signed only by one of the parties is evidently a document of no weight, and where a casuist enjoys the privilege of adducing the arguments on both sides, it would imply an almost superhuman degree of self-denial, were he not to urge the best on his own, and range himself on the side of the gods, leaving that of Cato to his opponent.

It is a custom in this country to ask, and generally with an air of some triumph, whether an Englishman supposes there is wisdom in a wig; and whether a few pounds of horsehair set on a judge's skull, and plastered with pomatum and powder, can be imagined to bring with it any increase of knowledge to the mind of the person whose cranium is thus disagreeably enveloped? The answer is, No; we by no means hold, either that a head *au naturel*, or that garments of fustian or corduroy, are at all unfavourable to legal discrimination; and are even ready to admit, that in certain genial regions, a judge *in cuerpo*, and seated on a wooden stool, might be as valuable and efficient an administrator of law, as one wigged to the middle, and clad in scarlet and ermine. But whatever American is so deficient in dialectic, as to imagine that this admission involves a surrender of the question in debate, we would beg leave respectfully to remind him, that the schoolmaster is abroad, and recommend him to improve his logic with the least possible delay. If man were a being of pure reason, forms would be unnecessary. But he who should legislate on such an assumption, would afford ample evidence of his own unfitness for the task. Man is a creature of senses and imagination, and even in religion, the whole experience of the world has borne testimony to the necessity of some external rite, or solemnity of observance, to stimulate his devotion, and enable him to concentrate his faculties, for the worship of that awful and incomprehensible

Being, " whose kingdom is, where time and space are not." It is difficult to see on what principle, those who approve the stole of the priest, and cover their generals and admirals with gold lace, can condemn as irrational, all external symbols of dignity, on the part of the judge. Let the Americans at all events be consistent : While they address their judges by a title of honour, let them at least be protected from rudeness, and vulgar familiarity ; and they may, perhaps, be profitably reminded, that the respect exacted in a British court of justice, is homage not to the individual seated on the bench, but to the law, in the person of its minister. Law is the only bond by which society is held together ; its administration, therefore, should ever be marked out to the imagination, as well as to the reason of the great body of a nation, as an act of peculiar and paramount solemnity ; and when an Englishman sees the decencies of life habitually violated in the very seat of justice, he naturally feels the less disposed to dispense with those venerable forms with which, in his own country, it has been wisely encircled. Our answer therefore is, *that it is precisely to avoid such a state of things as now exists in the American courts*, that the solemnities which invest the discharge of the judicial office in England, were originally imposed, and are still maintained. We regard ceremonies of all sorts, not as things important in themselves, but simply as means conducing to an end. It matters not by what particular process; by what routine of observance; by what visible attributes, the dignity of justice is asserted, and its sanctity impressed on the memory and imagination. But at least let this end, by some means or other, be secured; and if this be done, we imagine there is little chance of our adopting many of the forensic habits, of our friends on this side of the Atlantic.

At New York, the common dinner hour is three o'clock, and I accordingly hurried back to the hotel. Having made such changes and ablutions as the heat of the court-rooms had rendered necessary, I descended to the *bar*, an apartment furnished with a counter, across which supplies of spirits and cigars are furnished to all who desiderate such luxuries. The bar, in short, is the lounging place of the establishment; and here, when the hour of dinner is at hand, the whole inmates of the hotel may be found collected. On the present occasion, the room was so full, that I really found it difficult to get farther than the door. At length a bell sounded, and no sooner did its first vibration reach the ears of the party, than a sudden rush took place towards the diningroom, in which—being carried forward by the crowd—I soon found myself. The extreme precipitation of this movement appeared somewhat uncalled for, as there was evidently no difficulty in procuring places; and on looking round the apartment, I perceived the whole party comfortably seated.

To a gentleman with a keen appetite, the *coup d'œil* of the dinner-table was far from unpleasing. The number of dishes was very great. The style of cookery neither French nor English, though certainly approaching nearer to the latter, than to the former. The dressed dishes were decidedly bad, the sauces being composed of little else than liquid grease, which, to a person like myself, who have an inherent detestation of every modification of oleaginous matter, was an objection altogether insuperable. On the whole, however, it would be unjust to complain. If, as the old adage hath it, " in the multitude of counsellors there is wisdom," so may it be averred, as equally consistent with human experience, that in the multitude of dishes there is good eating. After several unsuccessful experiments, I did discover unobjectionable viands, and made as good a dinner, as the ambition of an old campaigner could desire.

Around, I beheld the same scene of gulping and swallowing, as if for a wager, which my observations at breakfast had prepared me to expect. In my own neighbourhood there was no conversation. Each individual seemed to *pitchfork* his food down his gullet, without the smallest attention to the wants of his neighbour. If you asked a gentleman to help you from any dish before him, he certainly complied, but in a manner that showed you had imposed on him a disagreeable office; and instead of a *slice*, your plate generally returned loaded with a solid massive wedge of animal matter. The New York carvers had evidently never graduated at Vauxhall. Brandy bottles were ranged at intervals along the table, from which each guest helped himself as he thought proper. As the dinner advanced, the party rapidly diminished; before the second course, a considerable portion had taken their departure, and comparatively few waited the appearance of the dessert. Though brandy was the prevailing beverage, there were many also who drank wine, and a small knot of three or four (whom I took to be countrymen of my own) were still continuing the carousal when I left the apartment.

An American is evidently by no means a convivial being. He seems to consider eating and drinking as necessary tasks, which he is anxious to discharge as speedily as possible. I was at first disposed to attribute this singularity to the claims of business, which, in a mercantile community, might be found inconsistent with more prolonged enjoyment of the table. But this theory was soon relinquished, for I could not but observe, that many of the most expeditious bolters of dinner spent several hours afterwards, in smoking and lounging at the bar.

At six o'clock the bell rings for tea, when the party musters again, though generally in diminished force. This meal is likewise provided with its due proportion of solids. The most remarkable was raw hung beef, cut into thin slices, of which,—*horresco referens*,—I observed that even ladies did not hesitate to partake. The tea and coffee were both execrable. A supper, of cold meat, &c., follows at ten o'clock, and remains on the table till twelve, when eating terminates for the day. Such is the unvarying routine of a New York hotel.

On the first Sunday after my arrival, I attended divine service in Grace Church, which is decidedly the most fashionable place of worship in New York. The congregation, though very numerous, was composed almost exclusively of the wealthier class; and the gay dresses of the ladies,—whose taste generally leads to a preference of the brightest colours,—produced an effect not unlike that of a bed of tulips. Nearly in front of the reading desk, a comfortable chair and hassock had been provided for a poor old woman, apparently about fourscore. There was something very pleasing in this considerate and benevolent attention to the infirmities of a helpless and withered creature, who probably had outlived her friends, and was soon about to rejoin them in the grave.

The Episcopal church of America differs little in formula from that of England.   The liturgy is the same, though here and there an expression has been altered, not always, I think, for the better.   In the first clause of the Lord's Prayer, for instance, the word " which" has been changed into " who," on the score of its being more consonant to grammatical propriety.   This is poor criticism, for, it will scarcely be denied, that the use of the neuter pronoun carried with it a certain vagueness and sublimity, not inappropriate in reminding us, that our worship is addressed to a Being incomprehensible, infinite, and superior to all the distinctions applicable to material objects.   In truth, the grammatical anomaly so obnoxious to the American critics, is not a blemish, but a felicity.   A few judicious retrenchments have also been made in the service, and many of those repetitions which tend sadly to dilute the devotional feeling, by overstraining the attention, have been removed.

Trinity Church, in Broadway, is remarkable as

being the most richly endowed establishment in the Union, and peculiarly interesting, from containing in its cemetery the remains of the celebrated General Hamilton. I have always regarded the melancholy fate of this great statesman with interest. Hamilton was an American, not by birth, but by adoption. He was born in the West Indies, but claimed descent from a respectable Scottish family. It may be truly said of him, that with every temptation to waver in his political course, the path he followed was a straight one. He was too honest, and too independent, to truckle to a mob, and too proud to veil or modify opinions, which, he must have known, were little calculated to secure popular favour. Hamilton brought to the task of legislation, a powerful and perspicacious intellect, and a memory stored with the results of the experience of past ages. He viewed mankind not as a theorist, but as a practical philosopher, and was never deceived by the false and flimsy dogmas of human perfectibility, which dazzled the weaker vision of such men as Jefferson and Madison. In activity of mind, in soundness of judgment, and in the power of comprehensive induction, he unquestionably stood the first man of his age and country. While the apprehensions of other statesmen were directed against the anticipated encroachments of the executive power, Hamilton saw clearly that the true danger menaced from another quarter. He was well aware that democracy, not monarchy, was the rock on which the future destinies of his country were in peril of shipwreck. He was, therefore, desirous that the new Federal Constitution should be framed as much as possible on the model of that of England, which, beyond all previous experience, had been found to produce the result of secure and rational liberty. It is a false charge on Hamilton, that he contemplated the introduction of monarchy, or of the corruptions which had contributed to impair the value of the British constitution; but he certainly was anxious that a salutary and effective check should be found in the less popular of the legislative bodies, on the occasional rash and hasty impulses of the other. He was favourable to a senate chosen for life; to a federal government sufficiently strong to enforce its decrees in spite of party opposition, and the conflicting jealousies of the different States; to a representation rather founded on property and intelligence than on mere numbers; and perhaps of the two evils, would have preferred the tyranny of a single dictator, to the more degrading despotism of a mob.

Hamilton was snatched from his country, in the prime of life and of intellect. Had he lived, it is difficult to foresee what influence his powerful mind might have exercised on the immediate destinies of his country. By his talents and unrivalled powers as an orator, he might have gained fair audience, and some temporary favour, for his opinions. But this could not have been lasting. His doctrines of government in their very nature were necessarily unpopular. The Federalist party from the first occupied a false position. They attempted to convince the multitude of their unfitness for the exercise of political power. This of course failed. The influence they obtained in the period immediately succeeding the revolution, was solely that of talent and character. Being personal, it died with the men, and sometimes before them. It was impossible for human efforts to diminish the democratic impulse given by the revolution, or to be long successful in retarding its increase. In the very first struggle, the Federalists were defeated once and for ever, and the tenure of power by the Republican party has ever since, with one brief and partial exception, continued unbroken.

There is another tomb which I would notice before quitting the churchyard of Trinity. On a slab surmounting an oblong pile of masonry, are engraved the following words:

MY MOTHER.

THE TRUMPET SHALL SOUND AND THE DEAD SHALL ARISE.

This is the whole inscription; and as I read the words I could not but feel it to be sublimely affecting. The name of him who erected this simple monument of filial piety, or of her whose dust it covers, is unpreserved by tradition. Why should that be told, which the world cares not to know? It is enough, that the nameless tenant of this humble grave shall be known, "when the trumpet shall sound and the dead shall arise." Let us trust, that the mother and her child will then be reunited, to part no more.

One of the earliest occupations of a traveller in a strange city, is to visit the theatres. There are three in New York, and I am assured, that both actors and managers prosper in their vocation. Such a circumstance is not insignificant. It marks opulence and comfort, and proves that the great body of the people, after providing the necessaries of life, possess a surplus, which they feel at liberty to lavish on its enjoyments. I have already been several times to the Park Theatre, which is decidedly the most fashionable. The house is very comfortable, and well adapted both for seeing and hearing. On my first visit, the piece was Der Freischutz, which was very wretchedly performed. The farce was new to me, and, I imagine, of American origin. The chief character is a pompous old baronet, very proud of his family, and exceedingly tenacious of respect. In his old age he has the folly to think of marrying, and the still greater folly, to imagine the attractions of his person and pedigree irresistible. As may be anticipated, he is the laughing stock of the piece.

Insult and ridicule follow him in every scene; he is kicked and cuffed to the hearty content of the audience, who return home full of contempt for the English aristocracy, and chuckling at the thought that there are no baronets in America.

My curiosity was somewhat excited by the high reputation which an actor named Forrest has acquired in this country. As a tragedian, in the estimate of all American critics, he stands *primus sine secundo*. To place him on a level with Kean, or Young, or Kemble, or Macready, would here be considered as an unwarranted derogation from his merits. He is a Thespian without blemish and without rival.

I have since seen this *rara avis*, and I confess that the praise so profusely lavished on him does appear to me somewhat gratuitous. He is a coarse and vulgar actor, without grace, without dignity, with little flexibility of feature, and utterly commonplace in his conceptions of character. There is certainly some energy about him, but this is sadly given to degenerate into rant. The audience, however, were enraptured. Every increase of voice in the actor was followed by louder thunders from box, pit, and

gallery, till it sometimes became matter of serious
calculation, how much longer one's tympanum could
stand the crash. I give my impression of this gentleman's merits as an actor the more freely, because I
know he is too firmly established in the high opinion
of his countrymen, to be susceptible of injury from
the criticism of a foreigner, with all his prejudices,
inherent and attributive. Perhaps indeed he owes
something of the admiration which follows him on
the stage, to the excellence of his character in private
life. Forrest has realised a large fortune; and I hear
from all quarters, that in the discharge of every
moral and social duty, he is highly exemplary. His
literary talents, I am assured, are likewise respectable.

My fellow-passenger, Master Burke, draws full
houses every night of his performance. Each time
I have seen him, my estimate of his powers has been
raised. In farce he does admirably; but what must
be said of the taste of an audience, who can even
tolerate the mimicry of a child, in such parts as
Lear, Shylock, Richard, and Iago?

No one can be four-and-twenty hours in New

York without hearing the alarm of fire. Indeed, a conflagration here is so very ordinary an occurrence, that it is attended by none of that general anxiety and excitement which follow such a calamity in cities less accustomed to combustion. The New York firemen are celebrated for resolution and activity ; and as the exercise of these qualities is always pleasant to witness, I have made it a point to attend all fires since my arrival. The four first were quite insignificant, indeed three of the number were extinguished before my arrival, and I barely got up in time to catch a glimpse of the expiring embers of the fourth. But in regard to the fifth, I was in better luck. Having reached the scene, more than half expecting it would turn out as trumpery an affair as its predecessors, I had at length the satisfaction of beholding a very respectable volume of flame bursting from the windows and roof of a brick tenement of four stories, with as large an accompaniment of smoke, bustle, clamour, and confusion as could reasonably be desired. An engine came up almost immediately after my arrival, and loud cries, and the rattle of approaching wheels from either extremity of the street, gave notice that further assistance was at hand. Some time was lost in getting water, and I should think the municipal arrangements, in regard to this matter, might be better managed. In a few minutes, however, the difficulty was surmounted, and the two elements were brought fairly into collision.

The firemen are composed of young citizens, who, by volunteering this service,—and a very severe one it is,—enjoy an exemption from military duty. Certainly nothing could exceed their boldness and activity. Ladders were soon planted; the walls were scaled; furniture was carried from the house, and thrown from the windows, without apparent concern for the effects its descent might produce on the skulls of the spectators in the street. Fresh engines were continually coming up, and were brought into instant play. But as the power of water waxed, so unfortunately did that of the adverse element; and so far as the original building was concerned, the odds soon became Pompey's pillar to a stick of sealing-wax, on fire.

Day now closed, and the scene amid the darkness became greatly increased in picturesque beauty. At intervals human figures were seen striding through flame, and then vanishing amid the smoke. In the street, confusion became worse confounded. Had the crowd been composed of stentors, the clamour could not have been louder. The inhabitants of the adjoining houses, who, till now, seemed to have taken the matter very coolly, at length became alarmed, when the engines began to play on them, and ejected a torrent of chairs, wardrobes, feather-beds, and other valuable chattels from every available opening. The house in which the fire broke out was now a mere shell; the roof gone, and all the wooden-work consumed. The flames then burst forth in the roof of the house adjoining on the right, but the concentrated play of many engines soon subdued it. All danger was then at an end. The inhabitants began to reclaim the furniture which they had tumbled out into the street, and I have no doubt went afterwards to bed as comfortably as if nothing had happened. I saw several of the inmates of the house that had been burned, and examined their countenances with some curiosity. No external mark of excitement was visible, and I gave them credit for a degree of *nonchalance*, far greater than I should have conceived possible in the circumstances.

On the whole, I have no deduction to make from the praises so frequently bestowed on the New York firemen.   The chief defect that struck me, was the admission of the crowd to the scene of action.   This caused, and must always cause, confusion.   In England, barriers are thrown across the street at some distance, and rigorously guarded by the police and constables.   On suggesting this improvement to an American friend, he agreed it would be desirable, but assured me it was not calculated for the meridian of the United States, where exclusion of any kind is always adverse to the popular feeling.   On this matter, of course, I cannot judge, but it seems to me clear, that if the exclusion of an idle mob from the scene of a fire, increases the chance of saving property and life, the freedom thus pertinaciously insisted on, is merely that of doing private injury and public mischief.

With regard to the frequency of fires in New York, I confess, that after listening to all possible explanations, it does appear to me unaccountable.   I am convinced, that in this single city there are annually more fires than occur in the whole Island of Great Britain. The combustible materials of which the majority of the houses are composed, is a circumstance far from sufficient to account for so enormous a disparity. Can we attribute it to crime? I think not; at least it would require much stronger evidence than has yet been discovered to warrant the hypothesis. In the negligence of servants, we have surer ground. These are generally negroes, and rarely to be depended on in any way, when exempt from rigid *surveillance*. But I am not going to concoct a theory, and so leave the matter as I find it.

CHAPTER III.

NEW YORK—HUDSON RIVER.

THE 25th of November, being the anniversary of the evacuation of the city by the British army, is always a grand gala-day at New York. To perpetuate the memory of this glorious event, there is generally a parade of the militia, some firing of cannon and small arms, a procession of the different trades, and the day then terminates as it ought, in profuse and patriotic jollification. But on the present occasion it was determined, in addition to the ordinary cause of rejoicing, to get up a pageant of unusual splendour, in honour of the late Revolution in France. This resolution, I was informed, originated exclusively in the operative class, or *workies,* as they call themselves, in contradistinction to those who live in better houses, eat better dinners, read novels and poetry, and drink old Madeira instead of Yankee rum. The latter and more enviable class, however, having been taught caution by the results of the former French Revolution, were generally disposed to consider the present congratulatory celebration as somewhat premature, but finding it could not be prevented, prudently gave in, and determined to take part in the pageant.

It was arranged, that should the weather prove unfavourable on the 25th, the gala should be deferred till the day following. Nor was this precaution unwise. The morning of the appointed day was as unpropitious, as the prayers of the most pious advocate of legitimacy could have wished. The rain came down in torrents, the streets were flooded ankle deep, and I could not help feeling strong compassion for a party of militia, with a band of music, who with doleful aspect, and drenched to the skin, paraded past the hotel, to the tune of Yankee Doodle. But the morning following was of better promise : the rain had ceased, and though cold and cloudy, it was calm.

About ten o'clock, therefore, I betook myself to a house in Broadway, to which I had been obligingly invited to see the procession. During my progress, every thing gave note of preparation. The shops were closed, and men in military garb, and others decorated with scarfs and ribbons, were seen moving hastily along to their appointed stations. On approaching the route of the procession, the crowd became more dense, and the steps in front of the houses were so completely jammed up with human beings, that it was with difficulty I reached the door of that to which I was invited.

Having at length, however, effected an entrance, I enjoyed the honour of introduction to a large and very pleasant party assembled with the same object as myself, so that, though a considerable time elapsed before the appearance of the pageant, I felt no inclination to complain of the delay. At length, however, the sound of distant music reached the ear; the thunder of drums, the contralto of the fife, the loud clash of cymbals, and first and farthest heard, the spirit-stirring notes of the trumpet.

"Ἵππων μ' ἐκυπόδων ἀμφὶ κτύπος οὔατα βάλλει·

On they came, a glorious cavalcade, making

heaven vocal with sound of triumph, and earth beautiful with such colouring as nature never scattered from her pictured urn.

And first appeared, gorgeously caparisoned, a gallant steed bestrode by a cavalier, whose high and martial bearing bespoke him the hero of a hundred fights. The name of this chieftain I was not fortunate enough to learn. Next passed a body of militia, who, if they wished to appear as unlike soldiers as possible, were assuredly most successful. Then came the trades. Butchers on horseback, or drawn in a sort of rustic arbour or shambles, tastefully festooned with sausages. Tailors, with cockades and breast-knots of ribbon, pacing to music, with banners representative of various garments, waving proudly in the wind. Blacksmiths, with forge and bellows. Caravans of cobblers most seducingly apparelled, and working at their trade on a locomotive platform, which displayed their persons to the best advantage. And carpenters too,—but the rest must be left to the imagination of the reader; and if he throw in a few bodies of militia, a few bands of music, and a good many most *outré* and unmilitary looking officers, appareled in uniforms apparently of the last century, he will form a very tolerable idea of the spectacle.

I must not, however, omit to notice the fire engines, which formed a very prominent part of the procession, it fortunately happening that no houses were just at that moment in conflagration. These engines were remarkably clean and in high order, and being adorned with a good deal of taste, attracted a large share of admiration. Altogether, it really did seem as if this gorgeous pageant were interminable, and, like a dinner in which there is too large a succession of courses, it was impossible to do equal justice to all its attractions. In the latter case, the fervour with which we demonstrate our admiration of one dish, forces us to disregard the charms of another. If we are not unjust to venison, we must subsequently slight partridge, and then from a whole wilderness of sweets, our waning appetite demands that we should select but one. And thus it was, that I, fervent in my admiration of the butchers, was, in due course, charmed with the carpenters, and subsequently smitten with the singular

splendour of the saddlers. But another and another
still succeeded, till the eye and tongue of the spectator became literally bankrupt in applause. *Est
modus et dulci ;* in short, there was too much of it,
and one could not help feeling, after three hours
spent in gazing, how practicable it was to become
satiated with pomp, as well as with other good
things.

But tedious as the spectacle was, it did at length
pass, and I walked on to Washington Square, in
which the ceremonies of the day were to conclude
with the delivery of a public oration. On arriving,
I found that a large stage, or hustings, had been
erected in the square. From the centre of this stage
rose another smaller platform, for the accommodation of the high functionaries of the state and
city. As even the advanced guard of the procession had not yet given signal of its approach, it was
evident that some delay must occur, and I therefore
accepted an invitation to one of the houses in the
square, where I found a very brilliant concourse of
naval and military officers, and other persons of
distinction. Among these was the venerable Ex-

President Munroe. It was, of course, not without interest that I gazed on an individual who had played so distinguished a part during the most perilous epoch of American history. He was evidently bent down by the united inroads of age and infirmity; and it was with regret I learned, that to those afflictions, which are the common lot of humanity, had been added those of poverty. The expression of Mr Munroe's countenance was mild, though not, I thought, highly intellectual. His forehead was not prominent, yet capacious and well defined. His eye was lustreless, and his whole frame emaciated and feeble. It was gratifying to witness the respect paid to this aged statesman by all who approached him; and I was delighted to hear the loud demonstrations of reverence and honour, with which his appearance in the street was hailed by the crowd.

Mr Munroe being too feeble to walk even so short a distance, was conveyed to the hustings in an open carriage. His equipage was followed by a *cortège* of functionaries on foot; and accompanying these gentlemen, I was admitted without difficulty to the lower platform, which contained accommodation for

about a hundred.   Having arrived there, we had
still to wait some time for the commencement of the
performance, during which some vociferous mani-
festations of disapprobation were made by the mob,
who were prevented from approaching the hustings
by an armed force of militia.   At length, however,
a portly gentleman came forward, and read aloud
the address to the French inhabitants of New York,
which had been passed at a public meeting.   In
particular, I observed that his countenance and
gestures were directed towards a party of gentlemen
of that nation, who occupied a conspicuous station
on the stage beneath him.   The document was too
wordy and prolix, and written in a style of ambi-
tious elaboration, which I could not help considering
as somewhat puerile.

While all this was going forward on the hustings,
the crowd without were becoming every instant
more violent and clamorous; and a couple of boys
were opportunely discovered beneath the higher
scaffolding, engaged, either from malice or fun, in
knocking away its supports, altogether unembar-
rassed by the consideration, that had their efforts

been successful, they must themselves have been inevitably crushed in the fall of the platform.

Notwithstanding these *désagrémens*, the orator—a gentleman named Governor—came forward with a long written paper, which he commenced reading in a voice scarcely audible on the hustings, and which certainly could not be heard beyond its limits. The crowd, in consequence, became still more obstreperous. Having, no doubt, formed high anticipations of pleasure and instruction from the gifted inspiration of this gentleman's eloquence, it was certainly provoking to discover, that not one morsel of it were they destined to enjoy. The orator was, in consequence, addressed in ejaculations by no means complimentary, and such cries as—" Raise your voice, and be damned to you!" "Louder!"—" Speak out!"—" We don't hear a word!" were accompanied by curses which I trust were not deep, in proportion either to their loudness or their number. In vain did Mr Governor strain his throat, in compliance with this unreasonable requisition, but Nature had not formed him either a Hunt or an O'Connell, and the ill-humour of the multitude was not diminished.

At length order seemed at an end. A number of the mob broke through the barricade of soldiers, and, climbing up the hustings, increased the party there in a most unpleasant degree. But this was not all. The dissatisfied crowd below, thought proper to knock away the supports of the scaffolding, and just as Mr Governor was pronouncing a most emphatic period about the slavery of Ireland, down one side of it came with an alarming crash. Fortunately some gentlemen had the good sense to exhort every one to remain unmoved; and from a prudent compliance with this precaution, I believe little injury was sustained by any of the party. For myself, however, being already somewhat tired of the scene, the panic had no sooner ceased, than I took my departure.

Altogether, I must say that the multitude out of earshot had no great loss. The oration appeared a mere trumpery tissue of florid claptrap, which somewhat lowered my opinion with regard to the general standard of taste and intelligence in the American people. On the whole, the affair was a decided failure. What others went to see I know

not, but had I not anticipated something better
worth looking at, than a cavalcade of artisans mounted on cart-horses, and dressed out in tawdry finery,
or the burlesque of military display by bodies of
undrilled militia, I should probably have staid at
home. I do not say this is in allusion to any deficiency of splendour in the pageant itself. A republic can possess but few materials for display, and in
the present case I should not have felt otherwise,
had the procession been graced by all the dazzling
appendages of imperial grandeur. In truth, I had
calculated on a sight altogether different. I expected
to see a vast multitude animated by one pervading
feeling of generous enthusiasm; to hear the air rent
by the triumphant shouts of tens of thousands of
freemen, hailing the bloodless dawn of liberty, in a
mighty member of the brotherhood of nations. As
it was, I witnessed nothing so sublime. Throughout
the day, there was not the smallest demonstration of
enthusiasm on the part of the vast concourse of
spectators. There was no cheering, no excitement,
no general expression of feeling of any sort; and I
believe the crowd thought just as much of France

as of Morocco,—the Cham of Tartary, as of Louis
Philippe, King of the French.   They looked and
laughed indeed at the novel sight of their fellow
tradesmen and apprentices tricked out in ribbons
and white stockings, and pacing, with painted banners, to the sound of music.   But the *moral* of
the display, if I may so speak, was utterly overlooked.   The people seemed to gaze on the scene
before them with the same feeling as Peter Bell did
on a primrose; and it was evident enough—if, without irreverence, I may be permitted to parody the
fine words of the noblest of contemporary poets,—
that in the unexcited imagination of each spectator,

> A butcher on his steed so trim,
> A mounted butcher was to him,
> And he was nothing more.

Such was the source of my disappointment in
regard to this splendid festivity.   How far it was
reasonable, others may decide.   I can only say I
felt it.

One of the most pleasant evenings I have passed
since my arrival, was at a club composed of gentlemen of literary taste, which includes among its

members, several of the most eminent individuals of
the Union. The meetings are weekly, and take place
at the house of each member in succession. The
party generally assembles about eight o'clock; an
hour or two is spent in conversation; supper follows;
and after a moderate, though social potation, the
meeting breaks up. I had here the honour of being
introduced to Mr Livingston, lieutenant-governor of
the State, Mr Gallatin, Mr Jay, and several other
gentlemen of high accomplishment.

Mr Gallatin I regarded with peculiar interest.
His name was one with which I had been long familiar. Born in Switzerland, he became a citizen of
the United States, soon after the Revolution, and
found there a field, in which, it was not probable
that talents like his, would remain long without
high and profitable employment. I believe it was in
the cabinet of Mr Jefferson that Mr Gallatin commenced his career as a statesman. Since then, much
of his life has been passed either in high offices at
home, or as minister to some of the European
Courts; and the circumstance of his foreign birth
rendering him ineligible to the office of President,

this veteran statesman and diplomatist, wisely judging that there should be ' some space between the *cabinet* and grave,' has retired from political life, and finds exercise for his yet unbroken energies in the calmer pursuits of literature.

In his youth Mr Gallatin must have been handsome.   His countenance is expressive of great sagacity.   He is evidently an acute thinker, and his conversation soon discovered him to be a ruthless exposer of those traditionary or *geographical* sophisms, in politics and religion, by which the mind of whole nations has been frequently obscured, and from the influence of which, none perhaps are entirely exempt.   Mr Gallatin speaks our language with a slight infusion of his native accent, but few have greater command of felicitous expression, or write it with greater purity.

An evening passed in such company, could not be other than delightful.   There was no monopoly of conversation, but its current flowed on equably and agreeably.   Subjects of literature and politics were discussed with an entire absence of that bigotry and dogmatism, which sometimes destroy the pleasure of interchange of opinion, even between minds of high order. For myself, I was glad to enjoy an opportunity of observing the modes of thinking peculiar to intellects of the first class, in this new and interesting country, and I looked forward to nothing with more pleasure, than availing myself of the obliging invitation to repeat my visits at the future meetings of the Club.

Having already passed a fortnight in one unbroken chain of engagements in this most hospitable city, I determined to give variety to the tissue of my life, by accepting the very kind and pressing invitation of Dr Hosack, to visit him at his country-seat on the banks of the Hudson. The various works of this gentleman have rendered his name well known in Europe, and procured his admission to the most eminent Philosophical Institutions in England, France, and Germany. For many years, he enjoyed as a physician the first practice in New York, and has recently retired from the toilsome labours of his profession, with the reputation of great wealth, and the warm esteem of his fellow-citizens.

At eight o'clock in the morning, therefore, of a

G

At eight o'clock in the morning, therefore, of a day which promised to turn out more than usually raw and disagreeable, I embarked in the steam-boat North America, and proceeded up the river to Hyde-Park, about eighty miles distant. I had anticipated much enjoyment from the beautiful scenery on the Hudson, but the elements were adverse. We had scarcely left the quay, when the lowering clouds began to discharge their contents in the form of snow, and the wind was so piercingly cold that I found it impossible, even with all appliances of cloaks and great-coats, to remain long on deck. Every now and then, however, I reascended from below to see as much as I could, and when nearly half frozen, returned to enjoy the scarcely less interesting prospect of the cabin stove.

Of course, it was impossible, under such circumstances, to form any just estimate of scenery; but still the fine objects which appeared occasionally glimmering through the mist, were enough to convince me, that seen under more favourable auspices, my expectations, highly as they had been excited, were not likely to encounter disappointment. That portion of the scenery in particular, distinguished by the name of the Highlands, struck me, as combining the elements of the grand and beautiful, in a very eminent degree. I remember nothing on the Rhine at all equal to it. The river at this place has found a passage through two ranges of mountains, evidently separated by some convulsion of nature, and which, in beauty and variety of form, and grandeur of effect, can scarcely be exceeded.

But the vessel in which this little voyage was performed, demands some notice, even amid scenery fine as that along which it conducted us with astonishing rapidity. Its dimensions seemed gigantic. Being intended solely for river navigation, the keel is nearly flat, and the upper portion of the vessel is made to project beyond the hull to a very considerable distance on either side. When standing at the stern, and looking forward, the extent of accommodation appears enormous, though certainly not more than is required for the immense number of passengers who travel daily between New York and Albany. Among other unusual accommodations on deck, I was rather surprised at observing a barber's shop, in which,—judging from the state of the visages of my fellow-passengers,—I have no doubt that a very lucrative trade is carried on.

The accommodation below was scarcely less worthy of note. It consisted of two cabins, which I guessed, by pacing them, to be an hundred and fifty feet in length. The sternmost of these spacious apartments is sumptuously fitted up with abundance of mirrors, ottomans, and other appurtenances of luxury. The other, almost equally large, was very inferior in point of decoration. It seemed intended for a sort of tippling-shop, and contained a *bar*, where liquors of all kinds, from Champagne to small beer, were dispensed to such passengers as have inclination to swallow, and money to pay for them. The sides of both of these cabins were lined with a triple row of sleeping-berths; and as the sofas and benches were likewise convertible to a similar purpose, I was assured, accommodation could be easily furnished for about five hundred.

The scene at breakfast was a curiosity. I calculated the number of masticators at about three hundred, yet there was no confusion, and certainly no scarcity of provision. As for the waiters, their name might have been *Legion*, for they were many, and during the whole entertainment, kept skipping about with the most praiseworthy activity, some collecting money, and others engaged in the translation of cutlets and coffee. The proceedings of the party *in re* breakfast, were no less brief and compendious afloat, than I had observed them on shore. As for *eating*, there was nothing like it discoverable on board the North America. Each man seemed to *devour*, under the uncontrollable impulse of some sudden hurricane of appetite, to which it would be difficult to find any parallel beyond the limits of the Zoological Gardens. A few minutes did the business. The clatter of knives and voices, vociferous at first, speedily waxed faint and fainter, plates, dishes, cups, and saucers disappeared as if by magic, and every thing connected with the meal became so suddenly invisible, that but for internal evidence, which the hardiest sceptic could scarcely have ventured to discredit, the breakfast in the North America might have passed for one of those gorgeous, but unreal visions, which, for a moment, mock the eye of the dreamer, and then vanish into thin air.

The steamer made several brief stoppages at villages on the river, for the reception and discharge of goods or passengers. From the large warehouses which these generally contained, they were evidently places of considerable deposit for the agricultural produce of the neighbouring country. They were built exclusively of wood, painted of a white colour; and, certainly, for their population, boasted an unusual number of taverns, which gave notice of their hospitality, on signboards of gigantic dimensions. The business to be transacted at these places occasioned but little loss of time. Every arrangement had evidently been made to facilitate despatch, and by two o'clock I found myself fairly ashore at Hyde Park, and glad to seek shelter in the landing-house from the deluge of snow, which had already whitened the whole surface of the country.

I had just begun to question the landlord about the possibility of procuring a conveyance to the place of my destination, when Dr Hosack himself appeared, having obligingly brought his carriage for my conveyance. Though the drive from the landing-place led through a prettily variegated country, I was not much in the humour to admire scenery, and looked, I fear, with more indifference on the improvements past and projected, to which the Doctor directed my attention, than would have been consistent with politeness in a warmer and more comfortable auditor. The distance, however, was little more than a mile, and, on reaching the house, the disagreeables of the journey were speedily forgotten in the society of its amiable inmates, and the enjoyment of every convenience which wealth and hospitality could supply. Dr Hosack had received his professional education in Scotland, and passed a considerable portion of his early life there. I was fortunately enabled to afford him some information relative to the companions of his early studies, many of whom have since risen to eminence, while others, perhaps not less meritorious, have lived and died undistinguished. In return, the Doctor was good enough to favour me, by communicating much valuable knowledge on the state of science and the arts in the United States, which I must have found great difficulty in obtaining from other sources.

There is this advantage in the pursuit of science, that it tends to generate liberality of sentiment, and destroy those prejudices which divide nations far more effectually than any barrier of nature. Science is of no country, and its followers, wherever born, constitute a wide and diffusive community, and are linked together by ties of brotherhood and interest, which political hostility cannot sever. These observations were particularly suggested by my intercourse with Dr Hosack. Though our conversation was excursive, and embraced a vast variety of topics fairly debateable between an American and an Englishman, I could really detect nothing of national prejudice in his opinions. He uniformly spoke of the great names of Europe with admiration and respect, and his allusions to the achievements of his countrymen in arts, arms, science, or philosophy, betrayed nothing of that vanity and exaggeration, with which, since my arrival, I had already become somewhat familiar.

The following morning was bright and beautiful.

The snow, except in places where the wind had drifted it into wreaths, had entirely disappeared; and after breakfast, I was glad to accept the invitation of my worthy host, to examine his demesne, which was really very beautiful and extensive. Nothing could be finer than the situation of the house. It stands upon a lofty terrace, overhanging the Hudson, whose noble stream lends richness and grandeur to the whole extent of the foreground of the landscape. Above, its waters are seen to approach from a country finely variegated, but unmarked by any peculiar boldness of feature. Below, it is lost among a range of rocky and wooded eminences of highly picturesque outline. In one direction alone, however, is the prospect very extensive, and in that, (the southwest,) the Catskill Mountains, sending their bald and rugged summits far up into the sky, form a glorious framework for the picture.

We drove through a finely-undulating country, in which the glories of the ancient forest have been replaced by bare fields, intersected by hideous zigzag fences. God meant it to be beautiful, when He gave such noble varieties of hill and plain, wood and water; but man seemed determined it should be otherwise. No beauty which the axe could remove was suffered to remain; and wherever the tide of population reached, the havoc had been indiscriminate and unsparing.

Yet, of this, it were not only useless, but ridiculous to complain. Such changes are not optional, but imperative. The progress of population necessarily involves them, and they must be regarded only as the process by which the wilderness is brought to minister to the wants and enjoyments of civilized man. The time at length comes, when another and a higher beauty replaces that which has been destroyed. It is only the state of transition which it is unpleasant to behold; the particular stage of advancement in which the wild grandeur of nature has disappeared, and the charm of cultivation has not yet replaced it.

Dr Hosack was a farmer, and took great interest in the laudable, but expensive amusement of improving his estate. He had imported sheep and cattle from England, of the most improved breeds, and in this respect promised to be a benefactor to his neighbourhood. I am not much of a farmer, and found the Doctor sagacious about long horns and short legs, in a degree which impressed me with a due consciousness of my ignorance. The farm offices were extensive and well arranged, and contained some excellent horses. A pair of powerful carriage-horses, in particular, attracted my admiration. In this country these fine animals cost only two hundred dollars. In London, I am sure, that under Tattersall's hammer, they would not fetch less than three hundred guineas.

But America is not the place for a gentleman farmer. The price of labour is high, and besides, it cannot always be commanded at any price. The condition of society is not yet ripe for farming on a great scale. There will probably be no American Mr Coke for some centuries to come. The Transatlantic Sir John Sinclairs are yet *in ovo*, and a long period of incubation must intervene, before we can expect them to crack the shell. As things at present stand, small farmers could beat the great ones out of the field. What a man produces by his own labour, and that of his family, he produces cheaply. What he is compelled to hire others to perform, is done expensively. It is always the interest of the latter to get as much, and give as little labour in exchange for it as they can. Then arises the necessity of bailiffs and overseers, fresh mouths to be fed and pockets to be filled, and the owner may consider himself fortunate if these are content with devouring the profits, without swallowing the estate into the bargain.

Having passed two very pleasant days with my kind and hospitable friends, I again took steam on my return to New York. Dr Hosack was good enough to accompany me on board, and introduce me to a family of the neighbourhood, who were returning from their summer residence to pass the winter in the city. In its members, was included one of the most intelligent and accomplished ladies I have ever met in any country. The voyage, therefore, did not appear tedious, though the greater part of it was performed in the dark. About ten o'clock the steam-boat was alongside the quay, and I speedily found myself installed in my old quarters in Bunker's hotel.

CHAPTER IV.

NEW YORK.

PROFESSOR GRISCOMB, a member of the Society of Friends, was obliging enough to conduct me over a large seminary placed under his immediate superintendence. The general plan of education is one with which, in Scotland at least, we are familiar, and I did not remark that any material improvement had followed its adoption in the United States. To divide boys into large classes of fifty or a hundred, in which, of course, the rate of advancement of the slowest boy must regulate that of the cleverest and most assiduous, does not, I confess, appear a system founded on very sound or rational principles. On this plan of retardation, it is, of course, necessary to discover some employment for the boys, whose talents enable them to outstrip their fellows; and this is done by appointing them to the office of monitor, or teacher, of a subdivision of the class. This mode of communicating knowledge has its advantages and its faults. It is no doubt beneficial to the great body of the class, who are instructed with greater facility, and less labour to the master. But the monitors are little better than scapegoats, who, with some injustice, are made to pay the whole penalty of the comparative dulness of their companions. The system, however, I have been assured, both in this country and in England, is found to work well, and I have no doubt it does so in respect to the *average* amount of instruction imparted to the pupils. But the principle of sacrificing the clever few, for the advancement of the stupid many, is one, I still humbly conceive, to be liable to strong objections. Of establishments on this principle, I have seen none more successful than that of Professor Griscomb. Every thing which zeal and talent on the part of the master could effect, had obviously been done; and on the part of the scholars, there was assuredly no want of proficiency in any branch of knowledge adapted to their age and capacity.

A striking difference exists between the system of rewards and punishments adopted in the schools of the United States, and in those of England. In the former, neither personal infliction, nor forcible coercion of any kind, is permitted. How far such a system is likely to prove successful, I cannot yet form an opinion, but judging solely from the seminary under Dr Griscomb, I should be inclined to augur favourably of its results. It has always, however, appeared strange to me, that the Americans should betray so strong an antipathy to the system of the public schools of England. There are no other establishments, perhaps, in our country, so entirely republican both in principle and practice. Rank is there allowed no privileges, and the only recognised aristocracy is that of personal qualities. Yet these schools are far from finding favour in American eyes. The system of fagging, in particular, is regarded with abhorrence; and since my arrival, I have never met any one who could even speak of it with patience. The state of feeling on this matter

in the two countries presents this curious anomaly :
A young English nobleman is sent to Westminster
or Winchester to brush coats and wash tea-cups,
while the meanest American storekeeper would red-
den with virtuous indignation at the very thought of
the issue of his loins contaminating his plebeian
blood by the discharge of such functions.

This difference of feeling, however, seems to admit of easy explanation. In England, the menial
offices in question form the duties of *freemen;* in
America, even in those States where slavery has
been abolished, domestic service being discharged
by Negroes, is connected with a thousand degrading
associations. So powerful are these, that I have
never yet conversed with an American who could
understand that there is nothing intrinsically disgraceful in such duties ; and their being at all considered so, proceeds entirely from a certain confusion of thought, which connects the office with the
manners and character of those by whom it is discharged. In a country where household services
are generally performed by persons of respectable
character, on a level, in point of morals and acquire-

ment, with other handicraftsmen, it is evident that such prejudice could exist in no material degree. But it certainly could not exist *at all* in a country, where for a certain period such services were performed by *all*, including every rank below royalty. Let the idea of personal degradation, therefore, be wholly abstracted, and then the question will rest on its true basis, namely, whether such discipline as that adopted in our public schools, be favourable to the improvement of the moral character or not?

In England, the system is believed from long experience to work practically well. No man will say, that British gentlemen, formed under the discipline of these institutions, are deficient in high bearing, or in generous spirit; nor will it readily be considered a disadvantage, that those who are afterwards to wield the united influence of rank and wealth, should, in their early years, be placed in a situation, where their personal and moral qualities alone can place them even on an equality with their companions.

It is very probable, indeed, that a system suited to a country, in which gradation of ranks forms an integral part of the constitution, may not be adapted to another, which differs so widely in these respects, as the United States. Here, there is no pride of birth or station to be overcome; and whether, under circumstances so different, the kind of discipline in question might operate beneficially or otherwise, is a point on which I certainly do not presume to decide. I only assert my conviction, that in this country it has never yet been made the subject of liberal and enlightened discussion, and therefore that the value of Transatlantic opinion with regard to it is absolutely null. The conclusion adopted may be right, but the grounds on which it is founded are evidently wrong.

Having resolved to devote the day to the inspection of schools, I went from that under the superintendence of Professor Griscomb, to another for the education of children of colour. I here found about a hundred boys, in whose countenances might be traced every possible gradation of complexion between those of the swarthy Ethiop and florid European. Indeed several of the children were so fair, that I certainly never should have discovered the lurking taint of African descent. In person they were clean and neat, and though of course the offspring of the very lowest class of the people, there was nothing in their dress or appearance indicative of abject poverty. The master struck me as an intelligent and benevolent man. He frankly answered all my questions, and evidently took pride in the proficiency of his pupils.

It has often happened to me, since my arrival in this country, to hear it gravely maintained by men of education and intelligence, that the Negroes were an inferior race, a link as it were between man and the brutes. Having enjoyed few opportunities of observation on people of colour in my own country, I was now glad to be enabled to enlarge my knowledge on a subject so interesting. I therefore requested the master to inform me whether the results of his experience had led to the inference, that the aptitude of the Negroe children for acquiring knowledge was inferior to that of the whites. In reply, he assured me they had not done so; and, on the contrary, declared, that in sagacity, perseverance, and capacity for the acquisition and retention of knowledge, his poor despised scholars were equal to any boys he had ever known. "But alas, sir!" said he, " to what end are these poor creatures taught acquirement, from the exercise of which they are destined to be debarred, by the prejudices of society? It is surely but a cruel mockery to cultivate talents, when in the present state of public feeling, there is no field open for their useful employment. Be his acquirements what they may, a Negroe is still a Negroe, or, in other words, a creature marked out for degradation, and exclusion from those objects which stimulate the hopes and powers of other men."

I observed, in reply, that I was not aware that, in those States in which slavery had been abolished, any such barrier existed as that to which he alluded. "In the State of New York, for instance," I asked, " are not all offices and professions open to the man of colour as well as to the white ?"

" I see, sir," replied he, " that you are not a native of this country, or you would not have asked such a question." He then went on to inform me, that the exclusion in question did not arise from any legislative enactment, but from the tyranny of that prejudice, which, regarding the poor black as a being of inferior order, works its own fulfilment in making him so. There was no answering this, for it accorded too well with my own observations in society, not to carry my implicit belief.

The master then proceeded to explain the system of education adopted in the school, and subsequently afforded many gratifying proofs of the proficiency of his scholars. One class were employed in navigation, and worked several complicated problems with great accuracy and rapidity. A large proportion were perfectly conversant with arithmetic, and not a few with the lower mathematics. A long and rigid examination took place in geography, in the course of which questions were answered with facility, which I confess would have puzzled me exceedingly, had they been addressed to myself.

I had become so much interested in the little party-coloured crowd before me, that I recurred to our former discourse, and enquired of the master, what would probably become of his scholars on their being sent out into the world? Some trades, some description of labour of course were open to

them, and I expressed my desire to know what these
were. He told me they were few. The class study-
ing navigation, were destined to be sailors; but let
their talents be what they might, it was impossible
they could rise to be officers of the paltriest merchantman that entered the waters of the United
States. The office of cook or steward was indeed
within the scope of their ambition; but it was just as
feasible for the poor creatures to expect to become
Chancellor of the State, as mate of a ship. In other
pursuits it was the same. Some would become stone-
masons, or bricklayers, and to the extent of carrying
a hod, or handling a trowel, the course was clear
before them; but the office of master-bricklayer
was open to them in precisely the same sense as the
Professorship of Natural Philosophy. No white
artificer would serve under a coloured master. The
most degraded Irish emigrant would scout the idea
with indignation. As carpenters, shoemakers, or
tailors, they were still arrested by the same barrier.
In either of the latter capacities, indeed, they might
work for people of their own complexion, but no
gentleman would ever think of ordering garments of

any sort from a *schneider* of cuticle less white than his own.   Grocers they might be, but then who could conceive the possibility of a respectable household matron purchasing tea or spiceries from a vile " Nigger ?" As barbers, they were more fortunate, and in that capacity might even enjoy the privilege of taking the President of the United States by the nose.   Throughout the Union, the department of domestic service peculiarly belongs to them, though recently they are beginning to find rivals in the Irish emigrants, who come annually in swarms like locusts.

On the whole, I cannot help considering it a mistake to suppose, that slavery has been abolished in the Northern States of the Union. It is true, indeed, that in these States the power of compulsory labour no longer exists; and that one human being within their limits, can no longer claim property in the thews and sinews of another. But is this all that is implied in the boon of freedom? If the word mean any thing, it must mean the enjoyment of equal rights, and the unfettered exercise in each individual of such powers and faculties as God has given him. In this true meaning of the word, it may be safely asserted, that this poor degraded caste are still slaves. They are subjected to the most grinding and humiliating of all slaveries, that of universal and unconquerable prejudice. The whip, indeed, has been removed from the back of the Negro, but the chains are still on his limbs, and he bears the brand of degradation on his forehead. What is it but mere abuse of language to call him *free*, who is tyrannically deprived of all the motives to exertion which animate other men? The law, in truth, has left him in that most pitiable of all conditions, *a masterless slave*.

It cannot be denied, that the Negro population are still compelled, *as a class*, to be the hewers of wood, and drawers of water, to their fellow-citizens. *Citizens!* there is indeed something ludicrous in the application of the word to these miserable Pariahs. What privileges do they enjoy as such? Are they admissible upon a jury? Can they enroll themselves in the militia? Will a white man eat with them, or extend to them the hand of fellowship? Alas! if these men, so irresistibly manacled to degradation, are to be called *free*, tell us, at least, what stuff are slaves made of!

But on this subject, perhaps, another tone of expression—of thought, there can be no other—may be more judicious. I have already seen abundant proofs, that the prejudices against the coloured portion of the population, prevail to an extent, of which an Englishman could have formed no idea. But many enlightened men, I am convinced, are above them. To these I would appeal. They have already begun the work of raising this unfortunate race from the almost brutal state to which tyranny and injustice had condemned it. But let them not content themselves with such delusive benefits as the extension of the right of suffrage, recently conferred by the Legislature of New York.* The opposition

---

* The Legislature of New York, in 1829, extended the right of suffrage to men of colour, *possessed of a clear freehold estate, without encumbrance, of the value of* 250 *dollars.* A very safe concession no doubt, since to balance the *black interest,* the same right of suffrage was granted to *every* white male of twenty-one years, who has been one year in the State. It might be curious to know how many coloured voters became qualified by this enactment. They must indeed have been *rari nantes in gurgite vasto* of the election.

to be overcome, is not that of *law*, but of *opinion*. If in unison with the ministers of religion, they will set their shoulders to the wheel, and combat prejudice with reason, ignorance with knowledge, and pharisaical assumption with the mild tenets of Christianity, they must succeed in infusing a better tone into the minds and hearts of their countrymen. It is true, indeed, the victory will not be achieved in a day, nor probably in an age, but assuredly it will come at last. In achieving it, they will become the benefactors, not only of the Negro population, but of their fellow-citizens. They will give freedom to both; for the man is really not more free whose mind is shackled by degrading prejudice, than he who is its victim.

As illustrative of the matter in hand, I am tempted here to relate an anecdote, though somewhat out of place, as it did not occur till my return to New York in the following Spring. Chancing one day at the Ordinary at Bunker's, to sit next an English merchant from St Domingo; in the course of conversation, he mentioned the following circumstances. The son of a Haytian general, high in the favour of

Boyer, recently accompanied him to New York, which he came to visit for pleasure and instruction. This young man, though a mulatto, was pleasing in manner, and with more intelligence than is usually to be met with in a country in which education is so defective.   At home, he had been accustomed to receive all the deference due to his rank, and when he arrived in New York, it was with high anticipations of the pleasure that awaited him in a city so opulent and enlightened.

On landing, he enquired for the best hotel, and directed his baggage to be conveyed there.   He was rudely refused admittance, and tried several others with similar result.   At length he was forced to take up his abode in a miserable lodging-house kept by a Negro woman.   The pride of the young Haytian, (who, sooth to say, was something of a dandy, and made imposing display of gold chains and brooches,) was sadly galled by this, and the experience of every hour tended further to confirm the conviction, that, in this country, he was regarded as a degraded being, with whom the meanest white man would hold it disgraceful to associate.   In the evening he went to the theatre, and tendered his money to the box-keeper. It was tossed back to him, with a disdainful intimation, that the place for persons of his colour was the upper gallery.

On the following morning, my countryman, who had frequently been a guest at the table of his father, paid him a visit. He found the young Haytian in despair. All his dreams of pleasure were gone, and he returned to his native island by the first conveyance, to visit the United States no more.

This young man should have gone to Europe. Should he visit England, he may feel quite secure, that if he have money in his pocket, he will offer himself at no hotel, from Land's End to John O'-Groat's house, where he will not meet a very cordial reception. Churches, theatres, operas, concerts, coaches, chariots, cabs, vans, waggons, steam-boats, railway carriages and air balloons, will all be open to him as the daylight. He may repose on cushions of down or of air, he may charm his ear with music, and his palate with luxuries of all sorts. He may travel *en prince* or *en roturier*, precisely as his fancy dictates, and may enjoy even the honours of a crowned head, if he will only pay like one. In short, so long as he carries certain golden ballast about with him, all will go well. But, when that is done, God help him. He will then become familiar with the provisions of the vagrant act, and Mr Roe or Mr Ballantine will recommend exercise on the treadmill, for the benefit of his constitution. Let him but show his nose abroad, and a whole host of parish overseers will take alarm. The new police will bait him like a bull; and should he dare approach even the lowest eating-house, the master will shut the door in his face. If he ask charity, he will be told to work. If he beg work, he will be told to get about his business. If he steal, he will be found a free passage to Botany Bay, and be dressed gratis on his arrival, in an elegant suit of yellow. If he rob, he will be found a free passage to another world, in which, as there is no paying or receiving in payment, we may hope that his troubles will be at an end for ever.

CHAPTER V.

NEW YORK.

HAVING moved, since my arrival, in a tolerably wide circle, I now feel qualified to offer some observations on the state of society in New York. The houses of the better order of citizens, are generally of brick, sometimes faced with stone or marble, and in the allotment of the interior very similar to tenements of the same class in England. The dining and drawing-rooms are uniformly on the ground floor, and communicate by folding doors, which, when dinner is announced, are thrown open for the transit of the company. The former of these apartments, so far as my observation has carried me, differs nothing in appearance from an English one. But the drawing-rooms in New York certainly strike me as being a good deal more primitive in their appliances than those of the more opulent classes in the old country. Furniture in the United States is apparently not one of those articles in which wealth takes pride in displaying its superiority. Every thing is comfortable, but every thing is plain. Here are no buhl tables, nor or-molu clocks, nor gigantic mirrors, nor cabinets of Japan, nor draperies of silk or velvet; and one certainly does miss those thousand elegancies, with which the taste of British ladies delights in adorning their apartments. In short, the appearance of an American mansion is decidedly republican. No want remains unsupplied, while nothing is done for the gratification of a taste for expensive luxury.

This is as it should be. There are few instances of such opulence in America as would enable its owner, without inconvenience, to lavish thousands on pictures, ottomans, and china vases. In such a country, there are means of profitable outlay for every shilling of accumulated capital, and the Americans are too prudent a people to invest in objects of mere taste, that which, in the more vulgar shape of cotton or tobacco, would tend to the replenishing of their pockets. And, after all, it is better, perhaps, to sit on leather or cotton, with a comfortable balance at one's banker's book, than to lounge on damask, and tread on carpets of Persia, puzzling our brains about the budget and the ways and means.

One cause of the effect just noticed, is unquestionably the absence of the law, or rather the custom of primogeniture. A man whose fortune, at his death, must be divided among a numerous family in equal proportions, will not readily invest any considerable portion of it, in such inconvertible objects as the productions of the fine arts, and still less in articles of mere household luxury, unsuited to the circumstances of his descendants. It will rarely happen that a father can bequeath to each of his children enough to render them independent. They have to struggle into opulence as best they may; and assuredly, to men so circumstanced, nothing could be more inconvenient and distasteful, than to receive any part of their legacies, in the form of pictures, or scagliola tables, instead of Erie canal shares, or bills of the New York Bank.

Another circumstance, probably not without its effect in recommending both paucity and plainness of furniture, is the badness of the servants. These are chiefly people of colour, habituated from their cradle to be regarded as an inferior race, and consequently sadly wanting both in moral energy and principle. Every lady with whom I have conversed on the subject, speaks with envy of the superior comforts and facilities of an English establishment. A coloured servant, they declare, requires perpetual supervision. He is an executive, not a deliberative being. Under such circumstances the drudgery that devolves on an American matron, I should imagine to be excessive. She must direct every operation that is going on from the garret to the cellar. She must be her own housekeeper; superintend all the outgoings and comings in, and interfere in a thousand petty and annoying details, which, in England, go on like clock-work, out of sight and out of thought.

If it fare so with the mistress of an establishment, the master has no sinecure. A butler is out of the question. He would much rather know that the

keys of his cellar were at the bottom of the Hudson,
than in the pocket of black Cæsar, with a fair opportunity of getting at his *Marston* or his *Bingham*.
Few of the coloured population have energy to resist
temptation.   The dread of punishment has been removed as an habitual motive to exertion, but the
sense of inextinguishable degradation yet remains.

The torment of such servants has induced many
families in New York to discard them altogether, and
supply their places with natives of the Emerald Isle.
It may be doubted, whether the change has generally been accompanied by much advantage.   Domestic service in the United States, is considered as
degrading by all untainted by the curse of African
descent.   No native American could be induced to
it, and popular as the present President may be, he
would probably not find one of his constituents,
whom any amount of emolument would induce to
brush his coat, or stand behind his carriage.   On
their arrival in this country, therefore, the Scotch
and English, who are not partial to being looked
down upon by their neighbours, very soon get hold
of this prejudice; but he of that terrestrial paradise,

" first flower of the earth, and first gem of the sea," has no such scruples. Landing often at the quay of New York, without hat, shoes, and sometimes less dispensable garments, he is content to put his pride in his pocket, where there is always ample room for its accommodation. But even with him domestic service is only a temporary expedient. The moment he contrives to scrape together a little money, he bids his master good morning, and, fired with the ambition of farming or storekeeping, starts off for the back country.

The nuisance of this is, that no white servant is ever stationary in a place. He comes a mere clod-pole, and is no sooner taught his duty, and become an useful member of the house, than he accepts the Chiltern Hundreds, and a new writ must forthwith be issued for a tenant of the pantry. Now, though annual elections may be very good things in the body *politic*, the most democratic American will probably admit, that in the body *domestic*, the longer the members keep their seats the better. Habits of office are of some value in a valet, as well as in a secretary of state, and how these are to be obtained

by either functionary, as matters are at present ordered in this country, I profess myself at a loss to
understand.

When you enter an American house, either in
quality of casual visitor or invited guest, the servant
never thinks of ushering you to the company; on
the contrary, he immediately disappears, leaving you
to explore your way, in a navigation of which you
know nothing, or to amuse yourself in the passage
by counting the hat-pegs and umbrellas. In a strange
house, one cannot take the liberty of bawling for
assistance, and the choice only remains of opening
doors on speculation, with the imminent risk of intruding on the bedroom of some young lady, or of
cutting the gordian knot by escaping through the
only one you know any thing about. I confess, that
the first time I found myself in this unpleasant predicament, the latter expedient was the one I adopted,
though I fear not without offence to an excellent
family, who, having learned the fact of my admission, could not be supposed to understand the motive
of my precipitate retreat.

On the whole, the difference is not striking, I

should imagine, between the social habits of the people of New York, and those prevalent in our first-rate mercantile cities.   In both, the faculties are exerted in the same pursuits; in both, the dominant aristocracy is that of wealth; and in both, there is the same grasping at unsubstantial and unacknowledged distinctions.

It is the fashion to call the United States the land of liberty and equality.   If the term equality be understood simply as implying, that there exists no privileged order in America, the assertion, though not strictly true,* may pass.   In any wider acceptation it is mere nonsense.   There is quite as much practical equality in Liverpool as New York.   The magnates of the Exchange do not strut less proudly in the latter city than in the former; nor are their wives and daughters more backward in supporting their pretensions.   In such matters legislative enactments can do nothing.   Man's vanity, and the desire of distinction inherent in his nature, cannot be

* Not strictly true, because in many of the States the right of suffrage is made dependent on a certain qualification in property.   In Virginia, in particular, this qualification is very high.

repressed. If obstructed in one outlet, it will only gush forth with greater vehemence at another. The most contemptible of mankind has some talent of mind or body, some attraction—virtue—accomplishment—dexterity—or gift of fortune,—in short, something real or imaginary, on which he arrogates superiority to those around him. The rich man looks down upon the poor, the learned on the ignorant, the orator on him unblessed with the gift of tongues, and " he that is a true-born gentleman, and stands upon the honour of his birth," despises the *roturier*, whose talents have raised him to an estimation in society perhaps superior to his own.

Thus it is with the men, and with the fairer sex assuredly it is not different. No woman, conscious of attraction, was ever a republican in her heart. Beauty is essentially despotic—it uniformly asserts its power, and never yet consented to a surrender of privilege. I have certainly heard it maintained in the United States, that all men were equal, but never did I hear that assertion from the lips of a lady. On the contrary, the latter is always conscious of the full extent of her claims to preference and admiration, and is never satisfied till she feels them to be acknowledged. And what zephyr is too light to fill the gossamer sails of woman's vanity! The form of a feature, the whiteness of a hand, the shade of a ringlet, a cap, a feather, a trinket, a smile, a motion—all, or any of these, or distinctions yet finer and more shadowy, if such there be—are enough, here as elsewhere, to constitute the sign and shibboleth of her fantastic supremacy. It is in vain, therefore, to talk of female republicans; there exists, and can exist, no such being on either side of the Atlantic, for human nature is the same on both.

In truth, the spirit of aristocracy displays itself in this commercial community in every variety of form. One encounters it at every turn. T'other night, at a ball, I had the honour to converse a good deal with a lady, who is confessedly a star of the first magnitude in the hemisphere of fashion. She enquired what I thought of the company. I answered, " that I had rarely seen a party in any country in which the average of beauty appeared to me to be so high."

" Indeed !" answered my fair companion, with an

expression of surprise; " it would seem that you English gentlemen are not difficult to please; but does it strike you, that the average is equally high as regards air, manner, fashion?"

" In regard to such matters," I replied, " I certainly could not claim for the party in question any remarkable distinction; but that, in a scene so animated, and brilliant with youth, beauty, and gaiety of spirit, I was little disposed to play the critic."

" Nay," replied my opponent, for the conversation had already begun to assume something of the form of argument, " it surely requires no spirit of rigid criticism, to discriminate between such a set of vulgarians, as you see collected here, and ladies who have been accustomed to move in a higher and better circle. Mrs ———— is an odd person, and makes it a point to bring together at her balls all the riff-raff of the place—people whom, if you were to remain ten years in New York, you would probably never meet any where else. I assure you, there are not a dozen girls in this room that I should think of admitting to my own parties."

Thus driven from the field, I ventured to direct

her notice to several elegant and pretty girls, about whom I asked some questions. Their attractions, however, were either not admitted, or when these were too decided to allow of direct negation, the subject was ingeniously evaded. If I talked of a pretty foot, I was told its owner was the daughter of a tobacconist. If I admired a graceful dancer, I was assured (what I certainly should not have discovered) that the young lady was of vulgar manners, and without education. Some were so utterly unknown to fame, that the very names, birth, habits, and connexions, were buried in the most profound and impenetrable obscurity. In short, a Count of the Empire, with his sixteen quarterings, probably would not have thought, and certainly would not have spoken, with contempt half so virulent of these fair plebeians. The reader will perhaps agree, that there are more *exclusives* in the world than the lady-patronesses of Almack's.

I shall now give an instance of the estimation in which wealth is held in this commercial community. At a party a few evenings ago, the worthy host was politely assiduous in introducing me to the more prominent individuals who composed it. Unfortunately, he considered it necessary to preface each repetition of the ceremony with some preliminary account of the pecuniary circumstances of the gentleman, the honour of whose acquaintance was about to be conferred on me. " Do you observe," he asked, " that tall thin person, with a cast in his eye, and his nose a little cocked? Well, that man, not three months ago, made an hundred thousand dollars by a single speculation in tallow. You must allow me to introduce you to him."

The introduction passed, and my zealous cicerone again approached, with increased importance of aspect—" A gentleman," he said, " worth at least half a million, had expressed a desire to make my acquaintance." This was gratifying, and, of course, not to be denied. A third time did our worthy entertainer return to the charge, and before taking my departure, I had the honour of being introduced to an individual, who was stated to be still more opulent than his predecessors. Had I been presented to so many bags of dollars, instead of to their possessors, the ceremony would have been quite as interesting, and perhaps less troublesome.

The truth is, that in a population wholly devoted to money-getting, the respect paid to wealth is so pervadingly diffused, that it rarely occurred to any one, that it was impossible I should feel the slightest interest in the private circumstances of the gentlemen with whom I might chance to form a transient acquaintance. It is far from my intention, however, to assert, that many of the travelled and more intelligent order of Americans could be guilty of such *sottises* as that to which I have alluded. But it is unquestionably true, that the tone of conversation, even in the best circles, is materially lowered by the degree in which it is engrossed by money and its various interests. Since my arrival, I have received much involuntary instruction in the prices of corn, cotton, and tobacco. I am already well informed as to the reputed pecuniary resources of every gentleman of my acquaintance, and the annual amount of his disbursements. My stock of information as to bankruptcies and dividends is very respectable; and if the manufacturers of Glasgow and Paisley knew only half as well as I do, how thoroughly the New York market is glutted with their goods, they assuredly would send out no more on speculation.

The usual dinner hour at New York is three o'clock, and as the gentlemen almost uniformly return to the discharge of business in the evening, it may be presumed that dinner parties are neither convenient to the entertainer nor the guests. Though not uncommon, therefore, they are certainly less frequent than among individuals of the same class in England. This circumstance has, perhaps, wrought some change in their character, and deprived them of that appearance of easy and habitual hospitality, for the absence of which, additional splendour or profusion can afford but imperfect compensation. When a dinner party is given in this country, it is always on a great scale. Earth, and air, and ocean, are ransacked for their products. The whole habits of the family are deranged. The usual period of the meal is postponed for several hours; and considering the materials of which an American *ménage* is composed, it is not difficult to conceive the bustle and confusion participated by each member of the establishment, from Peter, the saffron-coloured groom of the chambers, to Silvia, the black kitchen wench.

In the ordinary routine, therefore, of American intercourse, visiting seldom commences till the evening, when the wealthier members of the community almost uniformly open their houses for the reception of company. Of this hospitable arrangement I have frequently taken advantage. On such occasions little ceremony is observed. Each guest enters and departs when he thinks proper, without apology or explanation. Music and conversation are the usual entertainments—some slight refection is handed round, and before midnight the party has broken up.

This facility of intercourse is both pleasant and convenient to a stranger like myself. It affords valuable opportunities for the observation of manners; and it is pleasing to be admitted within the charmed circle, which many of my predecessors have found it difficult, if not impossible, to overpass.

The formalities of a New York dinner do not differ much from those of an English one. Unfortunately, it is not here the fashion to invite the fairer part of creation to entertainments so gross and substantial, and it rarely happens that any ladies are present on such occasions, except those belonging to the family of the host. The party, however, is always enlivened by their presence at the tea-table, and then comes music, and perhaps dancing, while those who, like myself, are disqualified for active participation in such festivities, talk with an air of grave authority, of revolutions in Europe, the prospects of war or peace, Parliamentary Reform, and other high and interesting matters.

Before dinner, the conversation of the company assembled in the drawing-room is here, as elsewhere, generally languid enough; but a change suddenly comes over the spirit of their dream: The folding-doors which communicate with the dining-room are thrown open, and all paradise is at once let in on the soul of a gourmand. The table, instead of displaying, as with us, a mere beggarly account of fish and soup, exhibits an array of dishes closely wedged in triple column, which it would require at least an acre of mahogany to deploy into line. Plate, it is true, does not contribute much to the splendour of the prospect, but there is quite enough for comfort, though not perhaps for display. The lady of the mansion is handed in form to her seat, and the entertainment begins. The domestics, black, white, snuff-coloured, and nankeen, are in motion; plates vanish and appear again as if by magic; turtle, cold-blooded by nature, has become hot as Sir Charles Wetherell, and certainly never moved so rapidly before. The flight of ham and turkey is unceasing; venison bounds from one end of the table to the other, with a velocity never exceeded in its native forest; and the energies of twenty human beings are all evidently concentrated in one common occupation.

During soup and fish, and perhaps the first slice of the haunch, conversation languishes, but a glass or two of Champagne soon operates as a corrective. The eyes of the young ladies become more brilliant, and those of elderly gentlemen acquire a certain benevolent twinkle, which indicates, that for the time being they are in charity with themselves and all mankind.

At length the first course is removed, and is succeeded by a whole wilderness of sweets. This, too, passes, for it is impossible, alas! to eat for ever. Then come cheese and the dessert; then the departure of the ladies: and Claret and Madeira for an hour or twain are unquestioned lords of the ascendant.

The latter is almost uniformly excellent. I have never drank any Madeira in Europe at all equalling what I have frequently met in the United States. *Gourmets* attribute this superiority partly to climate, but in a great measure to management. Madeira, in this country, is never kept as with us, in a subterranean vault, where the temperature throughout the year is nearly equal. It is placed in the attics, where it is exposed to the whole fervour of the summer's heat, and the severity of winter's cold. The effect on the flavour of the wine is certainly remarkable.

The Claret is generally good, but not better than in England; Port is used by the natives only as a medicine, and is rarely produced at table except in compliment to some English stranger, it being a settled canon, here as elsewhere, that every Englishman drinks Port. I have never yet seen fine Sherry, probably because that wine has not yet risen into esteem in the United States.

The gentlemen in America pique themselves on their discrimination in wine, in a degree which is not common in England. The ladies have no sooner risen from table, than the business of winebibbing commences in good earnest. The servants still remain in the apartment, and supply fresh glasses to the guests as the successive bottles make their appearance. To each of these a history is attached, and the vintage, the date of importation, &c., are all duly detailed; then come the criticisms of the company, and as each bottle produced contains wine of a different quality from its predecessor, there is no chance of the topic being exhausted. At length, having made the complete tour of the cellar, proceeding progressively from the commoner wines to those of finest flavour, the party adjourns to the drawing-room, and, after coffee, each guest takes his departure without ceremony of any kind.

It would be most ungrateful were I not to declare, that I have frequently found these dinner parties extremely pleasant. I admit that there is a plainness and even bluntness in American manners, somewhat startling at first to a sophisticated European. Questions are asked with regard to one's habits, family, pursuits, connexions, and opinions, which are never put in England, except in a witness box, after the ceremony of swearing on the four Evangelists. But this is done with the most perfect *bonhomie*, and evidently without the smallest conception, that such examination can possibly be offensive to the patient. It is scarcely fair to judge one nation by the conventional standard of another; and travellers who are tolerant enough of the peculiarities of their continental neighbours, ought in justice, perhaps, to make more allowance than they have yet done, for those of Brother Jonathan. Such questions, no doubt, would be sheer impertinence in an Englishman, because, in putting them, he could not but be aware, that he was violating the established courtesies of society. They are not so in an American, because he has been brought up with different ideas, and under a social *régime* more tolerant of individual curiosity, than is held in Europe to be compatible with good manners. Yet, after all, it must be owned, that it is not always pleasant, to feel yourself the object of a scrutiny, often somewhat coarsely conducted, and generally too apparent to be mistaken. I do assert, however, that in noo ther country I have ever visited, are the charities of life so readily and so profusely opened to a stranger as in the United States. In no other country will he receive attentions so perfectly disinterested and benevolent; and in none, when he seeks acquaintances, is it so probable that he will find friends.

It has been often said,—indeed said so often as to have passed into a popular apophthegm, that a strong prejudice against Englishmen exists in America. Looking back on the whole course of my experience in that country, I now declare, that no assertion more utterly adverse to truth, was ever palmed by prejudice or ignorance, on vulgar credulity. That a prejudice exists, I admit, but instead of being *against* Englishmen, as compared with the natives of other countries, it is a prejudice in *their favour*. The Americans do not weigh the merits of their foreign visitors in an equal balance. They are only too apt to throw their own partialities into the scale of the Englishman, and give it a preponderance to which the claims of the individual have probably no pretensions.

I beg, however, to be understood. Of the vast multitude of English whom the extensive commercial intercourse between the countries draws to the United States, few, indeed, are persons of liberal acquirement, or who have been accustomed to mix in good society in their own country. Coming to the United States on the pursuits of business, they are, of course, left to the attentions of those gentlemen with whom their professional relations bring them more particularly in contact. Admitting, for argument's sake, that all those persons were entirely unexceptionable both in manners and morals, their mere number, which is very great, would, in itself, operate as an exclusion. That they are hospitably received, I have no doubt, nor have I any that they meet with every attention and facility which commercial men can expect in a commercial community.

But when an English gentleman, actuated by motives of liberal curiosity, visits their country, he is received in a different manner, and with very different feeling. Once assured of his respectability, he is admitted freely into society, and I again assert that he will meet a benevolent interest in promoting his views, which a traveller may in vain look for in other countries. I should be wrong in saying, however, that all this takes place without some scrutiny. Of whatever solecisms of deportment they are themselves guilty, the Americans are admirable, and, perhaps, not very lenient, judges of manners in others. They are quite aware of high breeding when they see it, and draw conclusions with regard to the pretensions of their guests from a thousand small circumstances apparent only to very acute observation. With them vulgar audacity will not pass for polished ease; nor will fashionable exterior be received for more than it is worth. I know of no country in which an impostor would have a more difficult game to play in the prosecution of his craft, and should consider him an accomplished deceiver, were he able to escape detection amid observation so vigilant and acute.

In admitting that the standard of manners in the United States is somewhat lower than in England, I wish to be understood as speaking exclusively of the higher circles in the latter country.   I am not aware, that bating a few peculiarities, the manners of the first-rate merchants of New York, are at all inferior to those either of Liverpool or any other of our great commercial cities.   I am certain that they are not inferior to any merchants in the world, in extent of practical information, in liberality of sentiment, and generosity of character.   Most of them have been in England, and from actual observation have formed notions of our national character and advantages, very different from the crude and ignorant opinions, which, I must say, are entertained by the great body of their countrymen.   Were it admissible to form general conclusions of the American character, from that of the best circle in the greater Atlantic cities of the Union, the estimate would be high indeed.

Unfortunately, however, the conclusions drawn from premises so narrow, would be sadly erroneous. The observations already made are applicable only to a very small portion of the population, composed almost entirely of the first-rate merchants and lawyers. Beyond that, there is a sad change for the worse. Neither in the manners nor in the morals of the great body of traders, is there much to draw approbation from an impartial observer. Comparing them with the same classes in England, one cannot but be struck with a certain resolute and obtrusive cupidity of gain, and a laxity of principle as to the means of acquiring it, which I should be sorry to believe formed any part of the character of my countrymen. I have heard conduct praised in conversation at a public table, which in England would be attended, if not with a voyage to Botany Bay, at least with total loss of character. It is impossible to pass an hour in the bar of the hotel, without being struck with the tone of callous selfishness which pervades the conversation, and the absence of all pretension to pure and lofty principle. The only restraint upon these men is the law, and he is evidently considered the most skilful in his vocation, who contrives to overreach his neighbour, without incurring its penalties.

It may probably be urged, that in drawing these
harsh conclusions, I judge ignorantly, since, having
no professional connexion with trade or traders, I
cannot be supposed to know from experience any
thing of the actual character of their commercial
transactions.   To this I reply, that my judgment
has been formed on much higher grounds than the
experience of any individual could possibly afford. If
I am cheated in an affair of business, I can appeal but
to a single case of fraud.   I can only assert, that a
circumstance has happened in America, which
might have happened in any country of Europe.
But when a man publicly confesses an act of fraud,
or applauds it in another, two conclusions are fairly
deducible.   First, that the narrator is a person
of little principle ; and, second, that he believes his
audience to be no better than himself.   Assuredly,
no man will confess any thing, which he imagines
may, by possibility, expose him to contempt ; and
the legitimate deduction from such details extends
not only to the narrator of the anecdote, but to the
company who received it without sign of moral indignation.

It may be well, however, to explain, that the preceding observations have not been founded exclusively on the population of New York. The company in a hotel, is generally composed of persons from all States in the Union; and it may be, that the standard of probity is somewhat higher in this opulent and commercial city, than in the poorer and more remote settlements. For the last three weeks I have been daily thrown into the company of about an hundred individuals, fortuitously collected. A considerable portion of these are daily changing, and it is perhaps not too much to assume that, as a whole, they afford a fair average specimen of their class. Without, therefore, wishing to lead the reader to any hasty or exaggerated conclusion, I must in candour state, that the result of my observations has been to lower considerably the high estimate I had formed of the moral character of the American people.

Though I have unquestionably met in New York with many most intelligent and accomplished gentlemen, still I think the fact cannot be denied, that the average of acquirement resulting from education is a good deal lower in this country than in

standing of a schoolboy, to suppose that he could entertain a doubt. Enquire their reasons for the inbred faith, of which they are the dark though vehement apostles, and you get nothing but a few shallow truisms, which absolutely afford no footing for the conclusions they are brought forward to establish. The Americans seem to imagine themselves imbued with the power of *feeling* truth, or, rather, of getting at it by intuition, for by no other process can I yet discover that they attempt its attainment. With the commoner and more vulgar truths, indeed, I should almost pronounce them too plentifully stocked, since in these, they seem to imagine, is contained the whole valuable essence of human knowledge. It is unquestionable, that this character of mind is most unfavourable to national advancement; yet it is too prominent not to find a place among the features which distinguish the American intellect from that of any other people with whom it has been my fortune to become acquainted.

To-morrow it is my intention to proceed to Boston; I shall leave the public establishments, &c.

of New York unvisited till my return; being anxious, during the first period of my residence, to confine my attention to the more prominent and general features which distinguish this interesting community.

CHAPTER VI.

VOYAGE—PROVIDENCE—BOSTON.

At four o'clock, P. M. on the 8th of December, I embarked on board the steam-boat Chancellor Livingstone, and in a few minutes the vessel was under weigh. Her course lay up the East River, and along the channel which divides Long Island from the mainland. I had heard much of a certain dangerous strait, called Hell Gate, formed by the projection of huge masses of rock, which obstruct the passage of the river, and diverting the natural course of the current, send its waters spinning round in formidable eddies and whirlpools. At high water— as it happened to be when we passed it—this said portal had no very frightful aspect. The stream was rapid, to be sure, but a double engine of ninety horse power was more than a match for it; and the Chancellor, in spite of its terrors, held on his course rejoicing, with little apparent diminution of velocity. Vessels, however, have been wrecked here, and a canal is spoken of, by which its dangers may be avoided.

The accommodations on board were such, as to leave the most querulous traveller no excuse for grumbling. The cabin, to be sure, with two huge red-hot stoves in it, was of a temperature which a salamander must have admired exceedingly, but the atmosphere, composed of the discarded breath of about an hundred passengers, still retained a sufficient portion of oxygen to support life. The hour of tea came, and all the appetite on board was mustered on the occasion. The meal passed speedily as heart could desire; but the mingled odour of fish, onions, and grease, was somewhat more permanent. Whether it improved the atmosphere, or not, is a point which I could not settle to my own satisfaction at the time, and must now, I fear, remain for ever undecided.

It was impossible, in such circumstances, to think of bed. The very thought of blankets was distressing. I had no book; and as for conversation, I could hear none in which I was at all qualified to bear a part. I therefore ordered my writing-box, adjusted a new Bramah, and of the words that flowed from it, he that has read the preceding pages is already in possession.

If I wrote in bad humour there was really some excuse for it. Close to my right were two loud polemics, engaged in fierce dispute on the Tariff bill. On my left was an elderly gentleman, without shoes or slippers, whose cough and expectoration were somewhat less melodious than the music of the spheres. In the berth immediately behind, lay a passenger, whose loud snoring proclaimed him as happy as a complete oblivion of all worldly cares could make him. Right opposite was a gentleman without breeches, who, before jumping into bed, was detailing to a friend the particulars of a lucky hit he had just made in a speculation in train oil. And beside me, at the table, sat a Baptist clergyman, reading, *sotto voce*, a chapter of Ezekiel, and casting, at the conclusion of each verse, a glance of furtive curiosity at my paper.

It may be admitted, that such are not the items which go to the compounding of a paradise. But the enjoyment of travelling, like other pleasures, must be purchased at some little expense; and he whose good-humour can be ruffled by every petty inconvenience he may chance to encounter, had unquestionably better remain at home. For myself, I beg it therefore to be understood, that in detailing the petty and transient annoyances connected with my journey, I do so, not as matters by which my tranquillity was materially affected, but as delineations naturally belonging to a picture of society, and without which it would be incomplete. A tourist in the United States, will find no occasion for the ardour, the perseverance, or the iron constitution of a Lander; and yet he will do well to remember, that travellers, like players at bowls, must occasionally expect rubbers.

But I have dwelt too much on the disagreeables of the voyage, without giving the *per contra* side of the account. There was a fair breeze and a smooth sea; and an Irish steward, who was particularly active in my behalf, and made my berth very comfortable, by the fraudulent abstraction of sundry pillows from those of my American neighbours. This he has done—he told my servant so—because I am from the old country; and yet one would suppose, that on such a man the claim of mere national affinity could have little influence. I talked a good deal with him about his former circumstances, and soon collected, that what is called *living* in Ireland, is usually entitled *starving* in other countries. Though rather chary of confession, I gathered, too, that the world was not his friend, nor the world's laws, and that he came to the United States to avoid a gaol, and without a shilling in his pocket. The day on which he left Ireland should be marked in his annals with a white stone. He now enjoys a comfortable situation—confesses he can save money; eats and drinks well; is encased in warm clothing; is troubled very little with the tax-gatherer, and not at all with the tithe-proctor. And what is there in the countenance of an Englishman, that it should excite in such a man the feeling of benevolence and kindred? In his memory, one would suppose, the past would be linked only with suffering, while the present is undoubtedly associated with the experience of a thousand comforts, to which, in his days of vassalage and white-boyism, his imagination never ventured to soar. Yet, believe the man, and he regrets having left home! He thinks he could have done as well in Ireland. He has no fault to find with America—it is a good country, enough for a poor man. Whisky is cheaper here, and so is bread and *mate*; but then his *ould* mother,—and his sisters,—and Tim Regan, he would like to see them again; and, please God, if he ever can afford it, he will return, and have his bones laid in the same churchyard with theirs.

But if Pat ever get back to Ireland, I venture to prophesy that his stay will not be long there. At present, his former privations are more than half-forgotten; but let him once again encounter them, and the difference between the country of his birth and that of his adoption, will become more apparent than argument could now make it. On the whole, it was pleasing to observe, that while time and distance obliterate the misfortunes of life, their tendency is to strengthen its charities.

On the following morning, about eleven o'clock,

we reached Providence, and found eight or ten stage-coaches waiting on the quay to convey the passengers to Boston. Though I carried letters of introduction to several gentlemen in Providence, it had not been my intention to remain there, and I had accordingly, before landing, secured places in one of these vehicles. But in the hurry and bustle of scrambling for seats and coaches, and with the sight of eight large human beings already cooped up in that by which I must have travelled, I began to waver in my resolution, and at length resolved to sacrifice the money I had paid, and take the chances of better accommodation, and a more agreeable party, on the day following. Besides, the weather was raw and gusty, and I had been drenched from the knee downward in wading through the masses of half-melted snow, which covered the landing-place. The idea, therefore, of a comfortable Providence hotel, naturally found more favour in my imagination, than an eight hours' journey to Boston, in such weather, such company, and such conveyance as I could reasonably anticipate.

On reaching the hostelry, however, its external ap-

pearance was far from captivating. There was no sign-
board, nor did the house display any external symbol
of the hospitality within. Below was a range of
shops, and the only approach was by a narrow stair,
which might have passed for clean in Rome, but
would have been considered dirty in England. On
entering, I stood for some time in the passage, and
though I enquired at several members of the establishment, who brushed past me, whether I could
have accommodation, no answer was vouchsafed. At
length, advancing to the bar, I observed the landlord, who was evidently too busily engaged in mixing brandy and water for a party of smokers, to have
any attention to bestow on a stranger like myself. I,
therefore, addressed a woman whom I observed to
look towards me with something of cold enquiry in
her expression, and again begged to know whether I
could be accommodated for the night. The question was not more fortunate than its predecessors
in drawing forth a response, nor was it till some
minutes had elapsed, that, during a fortunate inter-
mission of the demand for spirits, my enquiries were
at length attended to, and satisfactorily answered.

Matters now went on more promisingly. I found that I could not only be supplied, with every thing within the scope of reasonable expectation, but with a luxury I had not ventured to anticipate,—a private parlour, communicating with a very comfortable bed-room, and accompanied with the privilege of commanding my own hours.

Having changed my dress, and given a few directions about dinner, I sallied forth to view the city. Providence is the capital of the State of Rhode Island, and contains about 25,000 inhabitants. It stands at the foot and on the brow of a hill, which commands a complete view of the fine bay. The great majority of the houses are built of wood, interspersed, however, with tenements of brick, and a few which are at least fronted with stone. It contains considerable cotton manufactories, which—boasting no knowledge of such matters—I was not tempted to visit. The college appears a building of some extent, and is finely situated on the summit of a neighbouring height. The roads were so obstructed by snow, as to render climbing the ascent a matter of more difficulty than I was in the humour to encounter; and so it was decreed, that Brown's College should remain by me unvisited.

The first settlement of Providence is connected with a melancholy instance of human inconsistency. The Pilgrim Fathers, as they are called, had left their country, to find in the wilds of the New World that religious toleration which had been denied them in the Old. But no sooner had these victims of persecution established themselves in New England, than, in direct and flagrant violation, not only of all moral consistency, but of the whole scope and spirit of the Christian religion, they became *persecutors* in their turn. Socinians and Quakers,—all, in short, who differed from them in opinion, were driven forth with outrage and violence. Among the number was Roger Williams, a Puritan clergyman, who ventured to expose what he considered " evidence of backsliding" in the churches of Massachusetts. The clergy at first endeavoured to put him down by argument and remonstrance; the attempt failed, and it was then determined that the civil authority should free the orthodox population from the dangerous presence of so able and sturdy a polemic. Roger Williams was banished, and, followed by a few of his people, continued to wander in the wilderness, till, coming to a place called by the Indians Mooshausic, he there pitched his tabernacle, and named it Providence.

Such are a few of the circumstances connected with the first establishment of the State of Rhode Island.   The light in which they exhibit human nature is not flattering; yet they only afford another proof, if such were wanted, of the natural connexion between bigotry and persecution, and that the victims of political or religious oppression, too often want only the power to become its ministers.

The only building which makes any pretension to architectural display is the arcade, faced at either extremity with an Ionic portico.   Judging by the eye, the shaft of the columns is in the proportion of the Grecian Doric, an order beautiful in itself, but which, of course, is utterly barbarized by an Ionic entablature.   By the way, I know not any thing in which the absence of taste in America is more signally displayed than in their architecture.   The country residences of the wealthier citizens are generally

2

adorned with pillars, which often extend from the basement to the very top of the house, (some three or four stories,) supporting, and pretending to support, nothing. The consequence is, that the proportions of these columns are very much those of the stalk of a tobacco-pipe, and it is difficult to conceive any thing more unsightly. Even in the public buildings, there is often an obtrusive disregard of every recognised principle of proportion, and clamorous demands are made on the admiration of foreigners, in behalf of buildings which it is impossible to look upon without instant and unhesitating condemnation.

In a seaport one generally takes a glance at the harbour, to draw some conclusions, however uncertain, with regard to the traffic of the place. The guide-books declare, that Providence has a good deal of foreign commerce. It may be so, but in the bay I could only count two square-rigged vessels, and something under a score of sloops and schooners.

I must not forget to mention, having witnessed to-day the progress of an operation somewhat singular in character. This was nothing less than raising a large tenement, for the purpose of introducing another story below. The building was of frame-work, with chimneys of brick, and consisted of two houses connected by the gable. The lower part of one was occupied as a warehouse, which seemed well filled with casks and cotton-bags. I stood for some time to observe the progress of the work. The process adopted was this: The building was first raised by means of a succession of wedges inserted below the foundation. Having thus gained the requisite elevation, it was maintained there by supports at each corner, and by means of screws pressing laterally on the timbers. At the time I saw it, the building had been raised about five feet into the air, and the only mode of ingress or egress was by ladders. On looking with some curiosity at the windows, I soon gathered enough to convince me that the inhabitants were engaged in their usual domestic avocations, without being at all disturbed by their novel position in the atmosphere. As for the warehouse, the business of buying and selling had apparently encountered no interruption. On the whole, the operation, though simple, struck me as displaying a very considerable degree of mechanical ingenuity.

Having finished my ramble, I returned to the inn, where a very tolerable dinner awaited my appearance. It was the first time I had dined alone since leaving England, and, like my countrymen generally, I am disposed to attach considerable importance to the privilege of choosing my dinner, and the hour of eating it. It is only when alone that one enjoys the satisfaction of feeling that he is a distinct unit in creation, a being *totus, teres, atque rotundus.* At a public ordinary he is but a fraction, a decimal at most, but very probably a centesimal of a huge masticating monster, with the appetite of a Mastodon or a Behemoth. He labours under the conviction, that his meal has lost in dignity what it has gained in profusion. He is consorted involuntarily with people to whom he is bound by no tie but that of temporary necessity, and with whom, except the immediate impulse of brutal appetite, he has probably nothing in common. A man, like an American, thus diurnally mortified and abased from his youth upwards, of course knows nothing of the high thoughts which visit the imagination of the solitary, who, having finished a good dinner, reposes with a full consciousness of the dignity of his nature, and the high destinies to which he is called. The situation is one which naturally stimulates the whole inert mass of his speculative benevolence. He is at peace with all mankind, for he reclines on a well-stuffed sofa, and there are wine and walnuts on the table. He is on the best terms with himself, and recalls his own achievements in arms, literature, or philosophy, in a spirit of the most benign complacency. If he look to the future, the prospect is bright and unclouded. If he revert to the past, its " written troubles," its failures and misfortunes, are erased from the volume, and his memories are exclusively those of gratified power. He is in his slippers, and comfortable *robe-de-chambre*, and what to him, at such a moment, are the world and its ambitions? I appeal to the philosopher, and he answers—Nothing!

It was in such condition of enjoyment, physical and intellectual, that I was interrupted by the entrance of my servant, to inform me that he had just met Captain Bennet on the stair, who, learning that I was at dinner, had obligingly expressed his intention of favouring me with a visit at the conclusion of my meal. I immediately returned assurance, that nothing could afford me greater pleasure; and in a few minutes I had the satisfaction of exchanging a friendly grasp with this kind and intelligent sailor. In the course of our *tête-à-tête*, he informed me that he was travelling from his native town, New Bedford, to Boston, in company with Mrs Bennet, to whom he was good enough to offer me the privilege of an introduction. I accordingly accompanied the Captain to his apartment, where I passed a pleasant evening, and retired, gratified by the intelligence that they were to proceed on the following morning by the same vehicle in which I had already secured places. To travel with Captain Bennet was, in truth, not only a pleasure, but an advantage, for being a New Englander, he was enabled, in the course of our journey, to communicate many particulars with regard to his native province, which, though most useful in directing the opinions of a traveller, could scarcely, perhaps, have fallen within the immediate sphere of his observations.

On the following morning we were afoot betimes, and after a tolerable breakfast at a most unchristian hour, left Providence at seven o'clock, and I enjoyed my first introduction to an American stage-coach. Though what an Englishman accustomed to the luxuries of " light-post coaches," and Macadamised roads, might not unreasonably consider a wretched vehicle, the one in question was not so utterly abominable as to leave a Frenchman or an Italian any fair cause of complaint.   It was of ponderous proportions, built with timbers, I should think about the size of those of an ordinary waggon, and was attached by enormous straps to certain massive irons, which nothing in the motion of the carriage could induce the traveller to mistake for *springs*. The sides of this carriage were simply curtains of leather, which, when the heat of the weather is inconvenient, can be raised to admit a freer ventilation. In winter, however, the advantages of this contrivance are more than apocryphal.   The wind penetrates through an hundred small crevices, and with the thermometer below zero, this freedom of circulation is found not to add materially to the pleasures of a journey. The complement of passengers inside was nine, divided into three rows, the middle seat being furnished with a strap, removable at pleasure, as a back support to the sitters. The driver also receives a companion on the box, and the charge for this place is the same as for those in the interior. The whole machine indeed was exceedingly clumsy, yet perhaps not more so, than was rendered necessary by the barbarous condition of the road on which it travelled. The horses, though not handsome, were strong, and apparently well adapted for their work, yet I could not help smiling, as I thought of the impression the whole *set out* would be likely to produce on an English road. The flight of an air balloon would create far less sensation. If exhibited as a specimen of a fossil carriage, buried since the Deluge, and lately discovered by Professor Buckland, it might pass without question as the family-coach in which Noah conveyed his establishment to the ark. Then the Jehu! A man in rusty black, with the appearance of a retired grave-digger. Never was such a coachman seen within the limits of the four seas.

Though the distance is only forty miles, we were eight hours in getting to Boston. The road, I remember to have set down at the time, as the very worst in the world, an opinion, which my subsequent experience as a traveller in the United States, has long since induced me to retract It abounded in deep ruts, and huge stones which a little exercise of the hammer might have converted into excellent material. English readers may smile when one talks seriously of the punishment of being jolted in a stage-coach, but to arrive at the end of a journey with bruised flesh and aching bones, is, on the whole, not particularly pleasant. For myself, I can truly say, that remembering all I have occasionally endured in the matter of locomotion on the American continent, the martyr to similar sufferings shall always enjoy my sincere sympathy. On the present occasion, to say nothing of lateral concussion, twenty times at least was I pitched up with violence against the roof of the coach, which, being as ill provided with stuffing as the cushions below, occasioned a few changes in my phrenological developements. One of the passengers, however,—a grave valetudinarian—assured me, that such unpleasant exercise was an admirable cure for dyspepsy, and that when suffering under its attacks, he found an unfailing remedy in being jolted over some forty or fifty miles of such roads as that we now travelled. At the moment, I certainly felt more inclined to pity him for the remedy than the disease.

There had been thaw during the night, and the greater part of the snow had disappeared. The country through which we passed was prettily varied in surface, but the soil was poor and stony, and the extent to which wood had been suffered to grow on land formerly subjected to the plough, showed it had not been found to repay the cost of tillage. About four miles from Providence, we passed the village of Pawtucket. It is one of the chief seats of the cotton manufacture in the United States. The aspect of the place was not unpleasing, and I counted about a dozen factories of considerable size. The houses of the workmen had a clean and comfortable appearance. I was informed, however, by my fellow-travellers, that, within the last eighteen months, every establishment in the place had become bankrupt; a proof, I should imagine, that the success of the Tariff system has not been very brilliant.

During our journey there was a good deal of conversation in the coach, in which, I was physically too uneasy to bear any considerable part. I was amused, however, at the astonishment of a young Connecticut farmer, when Captain Bennet informed him, that in England, the white birch-tree—which, in this part of the world, is regarded as a noxious weed—is protected in artificial plantations with great care. He was evidently incredulous, though he had before made no difficulty in believing the numerous absurdities, in law, polity, and manners attributed, whether with truth or otherwise, to my countrymen. But to plant the white birch-tree ! This, indeed, was beyond the limits of belief.

The road, as we approached Boston, lay through a more populous country, and we passed a height, which commanded a fine view of the bay. At length, entering on a long street, I found myself again surrounded by the busy hum of a great city.   The first impression was decidedly favourable. There is in Boston less of that rawness of outline, and inconsistency of architecture, which had struck me in New York. The truth is, that the latter has increased so rapidly, that nine-tenths of the city have been built within the last thirty years, and probably one half of it within a third of the period. In Boston, both wealth and population have advanced at a slower pace. A comparatively small portion of the city is new, and the hand of time has somewhat mellowed even its deformities, contributing to render that reverend which was originally rude.

There is an air of gravity and solidity about Boston; and nothing gay or flashy, in the appearance of her streets, or the crowd who frequent them. New York is a young giantess, weighing twenty stone, and yet frisky withal. Boston, a matron of stayed and demure air, a little past her prime perhaps, yet showing no symptom of decay. The former is brisk, bustling, and annually outgrowing her petticoats. The latter, fat, fair, and forty, a great breeder, but turning her children out of doors, as fast as she produces them. But it is an old and true apophthegm, that similes seldom run on all fours, and therefore it is generally prudent not to push them too far.

Most gratifying is it to a traveller in the United States, when, sick to death of the discomforts of the road, he finds himself fairly housed in the Tremont Hotel. The establishment is on a large scale, and admirably conducted. I had no difficulty in procuring a small but very comfortable suite of apartments, deficient in nothing which a single gentleman could require. What is more, I enjoyed the blessing of rational liberty, had command of my own hours and motions, in short, could eat, drink, or sleep, at what time, in what manner, and on what substances I might prefer.

The truth is, that instead of being free, a large proportion of the American people live in a state of the most degrading bondage. No liberty of tongue can compensate for vassalage of stomach. In their own houses, perhaps, they may do as they please, though I much doubt whether any servants would consent to live in a family who adopted the barbarous innovation of dining at six o'clock, and breakfasting at eleven. But on the road, and in their hotels, they are assuredly any thing but freemen. Their hours of rest and refection are there dictated by Boniface, the most rigorous and iron-hearted of despots. And surely never was monarch blessed with more patient and obedient subjects! He feeds them in droves like cattle. He rings a bell, and they come like dogs at their master's whistle. He places before them what he thinks proper, and they swallow it without grumbling. His decrees are as those of fate, and the motto of his establishment is, "Submit or starve."

No man should travel in the United States without one of Baraud's best chronometers in his fob. In no other country can a slight miscalculation of time be productive of so much mischief. Woe to him whose steps have been delayed by pleasure or business, till the fatal hour has elapsed, and the dinner-cloth been removed. If he calculate on the emanation from the kitchen of smoking chop or spatchcock, he will be grievously deceived. Let him not look with contempt on half-coagulated soup, or fragments of cold fish, or the rhomboid of greasy pork, which has been reclaimed from the stock-barrel for his behoof. Let him accept in meekness what is set before him, or be content to go dinnerless for the day. Such are the horns of the dilemma, and he is free as air to choose on which he will be impaled.*

On the morning following my arrival, I despatched my letters of introduction, and walked out to see the city. Of its appearance, I have already said something, but have yet a little more to say. Boston stands on an undulating surface, and is surrounded

---

* It is fair, however, to state, that in the hotels in the greater cities, private apartments can generally be obtained. The charge for these is about as high as in London, and the privilege of separate meals is also to be paid for. To give the reader some idea of the expense of such mode of living in the United States, I may state, that in New York, with nothing but an inferior bedroom, and living at the public table, the charge for myself and servant was eighteen dollars a-week. At Boston, with three excellent rooms, and the privilege of private meals, it amounted, including every thing except wine, to thirty-five. At Philadelphia, I paid twenty-six dollars; at Baltimore, twenty-eight; at Washington, forty; the extent of accommodation nearly equal in all.

It is the invariable custom in the United States to charge by the day or week; and travellers are thus obliged to pay for meals whether they eat them or not. For a person who, like myself, rarely dined at home, I remember calculating the charge to be higher than in Long's, or the Clarendon.

on three sides by the sea. The harbour is a magnificent basin, encircled by a beautiful country, rising in gentle acclivities, and studded with villas. There is nothing very handsome about the town, which is rather English in appearance, and might in truth be easily mistaken for one of our more populous seaports. A considerable number of the buildings are of granite, or, more properly speaking, of sienite, but brick is the prevailing material, and houses of framework are now rarely to be met with in the streets inhabited by the better orders. The streets are narrow, and often crooked, yet, as already stated, they exhibit more finish and cleanliness than are to be found in New York. In architecture, I could discover little to admire. The State-house stands on an eminence commanding the city; it is a massive square building, presenting in front a piazza of rusticated arches, surmounted by a gratuitous range of Corinthian columns, which support nothing. The building in front has a small attic with a pediment, and from the centre rises a dome, the summit of which is crowned by a square lantern.

The Tremont hotel, and a church in the same

street, are likewise pointed out to strangers as worthy
of all the spare admiration at their disposal.   The
latter is a plain building, rather absurdly garnished,
along its whole front, with a row of Ionic columns,
stuck in close to the wall, which they are far from
concealing; and, to increase the deformity, above
these columns rises a naked square tower, intended,
I presume, for a belfry.

An anecdote connected with this place of worship,
however, is worth preserving : It was formerly called
the King's Chapel, and belonged to a congregation
holding the tenets of the Church of England.   In
this state of things a rich old gentleman died, be-
queathing, by his last testament, a considerable sum,
to be expended in defraying the charge of a certain
number of annual discourses "on the Trinity." The
testator having lived and died in the communion of
the Church of England, of course no doubt could be
entertained of his intention in the bequest; but the
revolution took place, and, at the restoration of
peace, the congregation of the King's Chapel were
found to have cast off both king and creed, and become not only Republicans in politics, but Unita-

rians in religion. Under these circumstances, what was to be done with the legacy? This did not long remain a moot point. It was discovered that an Unitarian could preach sermons on the Trinity as well as the most orthodox Athanasian that ever mounted a pulpit; and the effect of the testator's zeal for the diffusion of pure faith, has been to encourage the dissemination of doctrines, which of course he regarded as false and damnable! The old gentleman had better have left his money to his relations.

I have been too well satisfied with the good living of the Tremont hotel, not to feel grieved to be compelled to speak disparagingly of its architecture. I beg to say, however, that I allude to it only because I have heard its construction gravely praised by men of talent and intelligence, as one of the proudest achievements of American genius. The edifice is of fine sienite, and I imagine few parts of the world can supply a more beautiful material for building. In front is a Doric portico of four columns, accurately proportioned, but, as usual, without pediment. These have not sufficient projection, and seem as if they had been thrust back upon the walls of the building by the force of some gigantic steam-engine. The dining-hall, which is here the chief object of admiration, is defective, both in point of taste and proportion. The ceiling, in the first place, is too low ; and then the ranges of Ionic columns, which extend the whole length of the apartment, are mingled with Antæ of the Composite order ; thus defacing, by the intermixture of a late Roman barbarism, the purer taste of Greece. But it were mere waste of time and patience to enlarge on such matters.

My letters of introduction soon fructified into a plentiful harvest of visits and invitations. I discerned, or thought I discerned, some difference of manner between the gentlemen of Boston and those of New York. For the first five minutes, perhaps, the former seemed less pleasing, but my opinion in this respect soon changed, and I certainly now class many of my Boston friends, not only among the most liberal and enlightened, but among the most agreeable men, I had the good fortune to encounter in my tour.

My first visit was to a club, not professedly literary, but which numbered among its members many of the most eminent individuals of the State. Nothing could exceed the kindness of my reception. Several gentlemen, on learning my objects in visiting their city, obligingly professed their readiness to promote them by every means in their power, and I soon found that hospitality to strangers was by no means an exclusive attribute of New York.

The day following being Sunday, I attended morning service in one of the Episcopal churches. It was performed with great propriety to a congregation generally composed of the better orders. In the evening I accompanied an amiable family to a church, of which the celebrated Dr Channing is the pastor. The Doctor, I learned, was then at Havannah, where he had accompanied Mrs Channing, whose health required a milder winter climate than that of New England. The tenets of the congregation are Unitarian, and the service is that of the Church of England, with the omission of all expressions which attribute divinity to our Saviour. Yet this, if not asserted, is not denied. It seems to have been the object to establish a service in which all

sects and classes of Christians may conscientiously
join, and which affirms nothing in regard to those
points which afford matter of controversy to Theolo-
gians.

Though the intentions of the framers of this service were obviously good, I am not sure that they
have been guided by very just or philosophical views
of the infirmities of human nature. The great benefit to be derived from public worship, is connected
with the feeling of fellowship with those by whom
we are surrounded, and that diffusive sentiment of
charity and brotherhood, arising from community of
faith. In the presence of God it is indeed proper
that all minor differences should be forgotten; but
when these differences extend beyond a certain limit,
and embrace the more sacred points of belief, I can
understand no benefit which can arise from the common adoption of a liturgy so mutilated, as to exclude
all expression of that faith and those doctrines, which
Christians in general regard as the very keystone of
their hope. The value of prayer, perhaps, consists
less in any influence it can be supposed to have on
the decrees of an eternal and immutable Being, than

in that which it exercises over the heart and feelings of the worshipper. To exert this influence, it must be felt to be appropriate to our individual wants and necessities. It must not deal in vague generalities, nor petition only for those blessings in which the great body of mankind possess an equal interest. Like material objects, the human feelings become uniformly weakened by extension. We cannot pray for the whole of our species with the same earnestness that we petition for the prosperity of our country, and our supplications in behalf of our family are yet more ardent. There is a gradation of fervour for each link of the chain as it approaches nearer to ourselves, and it is only, perhaps, in imploring mercy for some one individual, that our feelings reach their climax of intensity. I have no faith in the efficacy of a system of devotion founded on the abstract principles of philosophy. The religious worship of mankind must be accommodated to their infirmities. The prayer which is adapted to all sects can evidently express the faith or sentiments of none.

The liturgy was plainly, but effectively, read by the Rev. Mr Greenwood, whom I had the pleasure of ranking among my acquaintance. The sermon was elegant, but somewhat cold and unemphatic. Indeed, how could it be otherwise? An Unitarian is necessarily cut off from all appeals to those deeper sources of feeling, which, in what is called Evangelical preaching, are found to produce such powerful effects. No spirit was ever strongly moved by a discourse on the innate beauty of virtue, or arguments in favour of moral purity drawn from the harmony of the external world. The inference that man should pray, because the trees blossom and the birds sing, is about as little cogent in theory as the experience of mankind has proved it in practice. The *sequitur* would be quite as good, were it asserted that men should wear spectacles because bears eat horse-flesh, and ostriches lay eggs in the sand. But, admitting the conclusion to be clear as the daylight, the disease of human depravity is too strong to be overcome by the administration of such gentle alteratives. Recourse must be had to stronger medicines, and these, unfortunately, the chest of the Unitarian does not furnish.

Boston is the metropolis of Unitarianism. In no

other city has it taken root so deeply, or spread its branches so widely. Fully half of the population, and more than half of the wealth and intelligence of Boston, are found in this communion. I was at one time puzzled to account for this; but my journey to New England has removed the difficulty. The New Englanders are a cold, shrewd, calculating, and ingenious people, of phlegmatic temperament, and perhaps have in their composition less of the stuff of which enthusiasts are made, than any other in the world. In no other part of the globe, not even in Scotland, is morality at so high a premium. Nowhere is undeviating compliance with public opinion so unsparingly enforced. The only lever by which people of this character can be moved, is that of argument. A New Englander is far more a being of reason than of impulse. Talk to him of what is high, generous, and noble, and he will look on you with a vacant countenance. But tell him of what is just, proper, and essential to his own well-being or that of his family, and he is all ear. His faculties are always sharp; his feelings are obtuse.

Unitarianism is the democracy of religion. Its

creed makes fewer demands on the faith or the imagination, than that of any other Christian sect.   It appeals to human reason in every step of its progress, and while it narrows the compass of miracle, enlarges that of demonstration.   Its followers have less bigotry than other religionists, because they have less enthusiasm.   They refuse credence to the doctrine of one grand and universal atonement, and appeal to none of those sudden and preternatural impulses which have given assurance to the pious of other sects.   An Unitarian will take nothing for granted but the absolute and plenary efficacy of his own reason in matters of religion.   He is not a fanatic, but a dogmatist; one who will admit of no distinction between the incomprehensible and the *false.*

With such views of the Bostonians and their prevailing religion, I cannot help believing, that there exists a curious felicity of adaptation in both.   The prosperity of Unitarianism in the New England States, seems a circumstance, which a philosophical observer of national character, might, with no great difficulty, have predicted.   Jonathan chose his religion, as one does a hat, because it fitted him.   We believe, however, that his head has not yet attained its full size, and confidently anticipate that its speedy enlargement will erelong induce him to adopt a better and more orthodox covering.

One of my first morning's occupations was to visit Cambridge University, about three miles distant. In this excursion I had the advantage of being accompanied by Professor Ticknor, who obligingly conducted me over every part of the establishment. The buildings, though not extensive, are commodious; and the library—the largest in the United States—contains about 30,000 volumes; no very imposing aggregate. The academical course is completed in four years, at the termination of which the candidates for the degree of Bachelor of Arts are admitted to that honour, after passing the ordeal of examination. In three years more, the degree of Master may—as in the English Universities—be taken as matter of course. There are three terms in the year, the intervals between which amount to about three months. The number of students is somewhat under two hundred and fifty. These have the option of either living *more academico* in the college, or of boarding in houses in the neighbourhood. No religious tenets are taught; but the regnant spirit is unquestionably Unitarian. In extent, in opulence, and in number of students, the establishment is not equal even to the smallest of our Scottish Universities.

On leaving Cambridge, we drove to Bunker's Hill, celebrated as the spot on which the first collision took place between the troops of the mother-country and her rebellious colonists. It is a strong position, and if duly strengthened by intrenchments, might be defended against an enemy of much superior force. On the summit of this height, a monument to the memory of Washington was in progress. A more appropriate site could not have been selected. But tributes of stone or brass are thrown away upon Washington. *Si monumentum quæris, circumspice.*

Our next visit was to the navy-yard, an establishment of considerable extent. There were two seventy-fours on the stocks, and, if I remember rightly, a frigate and a sloop. A dry-dock had nearly been completed of size sufficient to receive the largest line-of-battle ship. Commodore Morris, the commandant, was obligingly communicative, and, in the course even of a short conversation, afforded abundant proof, that his acquirements were very far from being exclusively professional.

On the day following, I went, accompanied by a very kind friend, to see the State-prison at Charleston. The interesting description given by Captain Hall of the prison at Sing-Sing had raised my curiosity, and I felt anxious to inspect an establishment, conducted on the same general principle, and with some improvements in detail. It was difficult to conceive, that a system of discipline so rigid could be maintained, without a degree of severity, revolting to the feelings. That hundreds of men should live together for years in the daily association of labour, under such a rigorous and unbroken system of restraint, as to prevent them during all that period from holding even the most trifling intercourse, seemed a fact so singular, and in such direct opposition to the strongest propensities of human nature, as to require strong evidence to establish its credibility. I was glad to take advantage, therefore, of the first opportunity to visit the prison at Charleston, and the scene there presented, was unquestionably one of the most striking I have ever witnessed. Pleasant it was not, for it cannot be so to witness the degradation and sufferings of one's fellow-creatures.

In no part of the establishment, however, was there any thing squalid or offensive. The gaoler— one expects hard features in such an official—was a man of mild expression, but of square and sinewy frame. He had formerly been skipper of a merchantman, and it was impossible to compliment him on the taste displayed in his change of profession. Before proceeding on the circuit of the prison, he communicated some interesting details in regard to its general management, and the principles on which it was conducted.

The prisoners amounted to nearly three hundred; the keepers were only fourteen. The disparity of force, therefore, was enormous; and as the system adopted was entirely opposed to that of solitary confinement, it did, at first sight, seem strange that the convicts—the greater part of whom were men of the boldest and most abandoned character—should not take advantage of their vast physical superiority, and, by murdering the keepers, regain their liberty. A cheer, a cry, a signal, would be enough; they had weapons in their hands, and it required but a momentary effort of one-tenth of their number, to break the chains of perhaps the most galling bondage to which human beings were ever subjected.

In what then consisted the safety of the goaler and his assistants? In one circumstance alone. In a *surveillance* so strict and unceasing, as to render it physically impossible, by day or night, for the prisoners to hold the slightest communication, without discovery. They set their lives upon this cast. They knew the penalty of the slightest negligence, and they acted like men who knew it.

The buildings enclose a quadrangle of about two hundred feet square. One side is occupied by a building, in which are the cells of the prisoners. It contains three hundred and four solitary cells, built altogether of stone, and arranged in four stories. Each cell is secured by a door of wrought iron. On the sides where the cell-doors present themselves, are stone galleries, three feet wide, supported by cast-iron pillars. These galleries extend the whole

length of the building, and encircle three sides of
these ranges of cells. The fourth presents only
a perpendicular wall, without galleries, stairs, or
doors. Below, and exterior to the cells and galleries,
runs a passage nine feet broad, from which a complete view of the whole can be commanded.

The cells have each a separate ventilator. They are
seven feet long, three feet six inches wide, and contain each an iron bedstead. On one side considerably elevated, is a safety watch-box, with an alarum-
bell, at the command only of the gaoler on duty. In
front of the building, or rather between the building
and the central quadrangle, is the kitchen, communicating, by doors and windows, with a passage,
along which the prisoners must necessarily travel
in going to, or returning from their cells. Adjoining
is a chapel, in which the convicts attend prayers
twice a-day.

In regard to the system of discipline enforced in
this interesting establishment, it may be better described in other words than my own. The following
is an extract from the annual report of the Boston
Prison Discipline Society :—" From the locking up

at night till daylight, all the convicts, except an average of about five in the hospital, are in the new building, in separate cells, and in cells so arranged, that a sentinel on duty can preserve entire silence among three hundred. The space around the cells being open from the ground to the roof, in front of four stories of cells, in a building two hundred feet in length, furnishes a perfect sounding gallery, in which the sentinel is placed, who can hear a whisper from the most distant cell. He can, therefore, keep silence from the time of locking up at night to the time of unlocking in the morning, which, at some seasons of the year, makes more than one half of all the time, which is thus secured from evil communication. From the time of unlocking in the morning, about twelve minutes are occupied in a military movement of the convicts, in companies of thirty-eight, with an officer to each company, in perfect silence, to their various places of labour. At the end of that period, it is found that there is a place for every man, and every man in his place. This is as true of the officers as of the convicts. If an officer have occasion to leave his place, the system requires that a substitute be called ; if a convict have occasion to leave his place, there is a token provided for each shop, or for a given number of men, so that from this shop or number only one convict can leave his place at a time.   The consequence is, that with the exception of those who have the tokens in their hands, any officer of the institution may be certain of finding, during the hours of labour, a place for every man, and every man in his place.   There is, however, a class of men, consisting of ten or twelve, called *runners* and *lumpers*, whose duty consists in moving about the yard.   But even their movements are in silence and order.   Consequently, during the hours of labour, the convicts are never seen moving about the yard promiscuously, or assembled in little groups, in some hiding-places of mischief, or even two and two in common conversation.   All is order and silence, except the busy noise of industry during the hours of labour.

"The hours of labour in the morning vary a little with the season of the year, but amount at this season to nearly two hours, from the time of unlocking in the morning till breakfast.   When the hour for breakfast comes, almost in an instant the convicts are all seen marching in solid and silent columns, with the lock-step, under their respective officers, from the shops to the cells. On their way to the cells they pass the cookery, where the food, having been made ready, is handed to them as they pass along; and at the end of about twelve minutes, from the time of ringing the bell for breakfast, all the convicts are in their cells eating their breakfasts, silently and alone. One officer only is left in charge to preserve silence, and the others are as free from solicitude and care, till the hour for labour returns, as other citizens.

" When the time of labour again returns, which is at the end of about twenty-five minutes, almost in an instant the whole body of convicts are again seen marching as before to their places of labour. On their way to the shops, they pass through the chapel and attend prayers. The time from breakfast till dinner passes away like the time for labour before breakfast, all the convicts being found in their places industriously employed, in silence. The time assigned for dinner is filled up in the same manner as the time assigned for breakfast; and the time for labour in the afternoon in the same manner as the time for labour in the morning; and when the time for evening prayers has come, at the ringing of the bell, all the convicts, and all the officers not on duty elsewhere, are seen marching to the chapel, where the chaplain closes the day with reading the Scriptures and prayer. After which the convicts march with perfect silence and order to their cells, taking their supper as they pass along. In about five-and-twenty minutes from the time of leaving their labour, the convicts have attended prayers in the chapel, taken their supper, marched to their cells with their supper in their hands, and are safely locked up for the night. This is the history of a day at Charleston; and the history of a day is the history of a year, with the variations which are made on the Sabbath, by dispensing with the hours of labour, and substituting the hours for instruction in the Sabbath-School, and the hours for public worship."

We had hardly time to examine the arrangement of the cells when the dinner-bell sounded, and issuing out into the quadrangle, the whole prisoners

marched past in imposing military array.   In passing the kitchen, each man's dinner was thrust out
on a sort of ledge, from which it was taken without
any interruption of his progress.   In less than two
minutes they were in their " deep solitudes and awful cells," and employed in the most agreeable duty
of their day—dinner.   I again entered the building,
to listen for the faintest whisper.   None was to be
heard; the silence of the desert could not be deeper.
In about half an hour another bell rang, and the
prisoners were again a-foot.   The return to labour
differed in nothing from the departure from it; but
the noise of saws, axes, and hammers, soon showed
they were now differently employed.

The gaoler next conducted us through the work-
shops.   Each trade had a separate apartment.   The
masons were very numerous; so were the carpenters
and coopers.   The tailors were employed in making
clothes for their companions in misfortune, and the
whole establishment had the air rather of a well-
conducted manufactory than of a prison.   There
was nothing of deep gloom, but a good deal of callous indifference generally observable in the counte-

nances of the convicts.   In some, however, I thought
I did detect evidence of overwhelming depression.
Yet this might be imagination, and when I pointed
out the individuals to the gaoler, he assured me I was
mistaken.

The prisoners are allowed to hold no intercourse
of any kind, with the world beyond the walls which
enclose them.   It is a principle invariably adhered to,
that they shall be made to feel, that during their confinement—and many are confined for life—they are
beings cut off even from the commonest sympathies
of mankind.   I know not but that severity in this
respect has been carried too far.   If they are again
to be turned out upon society, is it not injudicious,
as it is cruel policy, to trample on the affections
even of these depraved and guilty beings, and to
send them forth with every tie broken which might
have acted as a motive to reformation ?   What can
be expected from men so circumstanced, but that
they will renew their former courses, or plunge into
guilt yet deeper.   On the other hand, if they are to
be immured for life, the punishment can be considered little better than a gratuitous barbarity.   But

the great evil is, that on the utterly abandoned it falls lightly. It is the heart guilty, yet not hardened in guilt, which is still keenly alive to the gentler and purer affections, that it crushes with an oppression truly withering. And can no penalty be discovered more appropriate for the punishment of the sinner, than one which falls directly and exclusively on the only generous sympathies which yet link him to his fellow-men? Why should he be treated like a brute, whose very sufferings prove him to be a man?

The whole produce of the labour of the prisoners belongs to the state. No portion of it is allowed to the prisoner on his discharge. This regulation may be judicious in America, where the demand for labour is so great, that every man may, at any time, command employment; but in Great Britain it is different, and there to turn out a convict on the world, penniless, friendless, and without character, would be to limit his choice to the alternative of stealing or starving.

Of course, a system of discipline so rigorous could not be enforced without a power of punishment, almost arbitrary, being vested in the gaoler. The slightest infraction of the prison rules, therefore, is uniformly followed by severe infliction. There is no pardon, and no impunity for offenders of any sort; and here, as elsewhere, the certainty of punishment following an offence is found very much to diminish the necessity for its frequency. There is great evil, however, in this total irresponsibility on the part of the gaoler. There is no one to whom the convict, if unjustly punished, can complain, and a power is intrusted to an uneducated man, possibly of strong passions, which the wisest and best of mankind would feel himself unfit to exercise. I cannot help thinking, therefore, that a board of inspectors should assemble at least monthly at the prison, in order to hear all complaints that may be made against the gaoler. There is no doubt that this unpopular functionary would be subject to many false and frivolous accusations. The latter, however, may always be dismissed without trouble of any sort, but all plausible charges should receive rigid and impartial examination. The circumstances connected with the Charleston prison are precisely the most favourable for the attainment of truth. There can be no concert among the witnesses to be examined, no system of false evidence got up, no plotting, no collusion. Here coincidence of testimony could be explained only on the hypothesis of its truth; and this circumstance must be quite as favourable to the gaoler as to the prisoners. The former could never want the means of vindication, if falsely impeached.

I had a good deal of conversation with the gaoler in regard to the effects produced by the system on the morals of the convicts. He at once admitted that any material improvement of character in full-grown offenders was rarely to be expected, but maintained that the benefit of the Charleston system, even in this respect, was fully greater than had been found to result from any other plan adopted in the United States. His experience had not led him to anticipate much beneficial consequence from the system of solitary confinement. He had seen it often tried, but the prisoners on their liberation had almost uniformly relapsed into their former habits of crime. One interesting anecdote which occurred under his own observation, I shall here record.

Many years ago, long before the establishment of the present prison system, a man of respectable connexions, but of the most abandoned habits, was convicted of burglary, and arrived at Charleston jail, under sentence of imprisonment for life. His spirit was neither humbled by the punishment nor the disgrace. His conduct towards the keepers was violent and insubordinate, and it was soon found necessary, for the maintenance of discipline, that he should be separated from his fellow-prisoners, and placed in solitary confinement. For the first year he was sullen and silent, and the clergyman who frequently visited him in his cell, found his mind impervious to all religious impression. But by degrees a change took place in his deportment. His manner became mild and subdued; he was often found reading the Scriptures, and both gaoler and chaplain congratulated themselves on the change of character so manifest in the prisoner. He spoke of his past life, and the fearful offences in which it had abounded, with suitable contrition, and expressed his gratitude to God, that, instead of being snatched away in the midst of his crimes, time had been afforded him for repentance, and the attainment of faith in that grand and prevailing atonement, by the efficacy of which even the greatest of sinners might look for pardon.

Nothing in short could be more edifying than this man's conduct and conversation. All who saw him became interested in the fate of so meek a Christian, and numerous applications were made to the Governor of the State for his pardon. The Governor, with such weight of testimony before him, naturally inclined to mercy, and in a few weeks the man would have been undoubtedly liberated, when one day, in the middle of a religious conversation, he sprang upon the keeper, stabbed him in several places, and having cut his throat, attempted to escape.

The attempt failed. The neophyte in morality was brought back to his cell, and loaded with heavy irons. In this condition he remained many years, of course without the slightest hope of liberation. At length, his brother-in-law, a man of influence and fortune in South Carolina, made application to the authorities of Massachusetts on his behalf. He expressed his readiness to provide for his unfortunate relative, and, if liberated, he promised, on his arrival in Charleston, to place him in a situation above all temptation to return to his former crimes.

This offer was accepted; the prisoner was set at liberty, and the goaler, who told me the anecdote, was directed to see him safely on board of a Charleston packet, in which due provision had been made for his reception. His imprisonment had extended to the long period of twenty years, during which he had never once breathed the pure air of heaven, nor gazed on the sun or sky. In the interval, Boston, which he remembered as a small town, had grown into a large city. Its advance in opulence had been still more rapid. In every thing there had been a change. The appearance, manners, habits, thoughts, prejudices, and opinions of the generation then living, were different from all to which he had been accustomed. Nor was the aspect of external objects less altered. Streets of framework cottages had been replaced by handsome squares, and stately edifices of brick. Gay equipages, such as he never remembered, met his observation at every turn. In short, he felt like the inhabitant of another planet, suddenly cast into a world of which he knew nothing.

My informant—I wish I could give the story in his own words—described well and feelingly the progress of the man's impressions. A coach had been provided for his conveyance to the packet. On first entering it he displayed no external symptom of emotion; but as the carriage drove on, he gazed from the window, endeavouring to recognise the features of the scenery. But in vain; he looked for marsh and forest, and he beheld streets; he expected to cross a poor ferry, and the carriage rolled over a magnificent bridge; he looked for men as he had left them, and he saw beings of aspect altogether different. Where were the great men of the State-house and the Exchange—the aristocracy of the dollar bags—the Cincinnati of the Revolution, who brought to the counting-house the courtesies of the camp and the parade, and exhibited the last and noblest specimens of the *citizen gentleman?* They had gone down to their fathers full of years and of honour, and their descendants had become as the sons of other men. Queues, clubs, periwigs, shoe-buckles, hair-powder, and cocked hats, had fled to some other and more dignified world. The days of dram-drinking and tobacco-chewing, of gaiters, trowsers, and short crops, had succeeded. The latter circumstances, indeed, might not have occasioned the poor relieved convict any great concern, but the whole scene was too much for him to bear unmoved. His spirit was weighed down by a feeling of intense solitude, and he burst into tears.

The remainder of the story may be told in a few words. He reached Charleston, where his brother placed him in a respectable boarding-house, and supplied him with necessaries of every kind. His conduct for the first year was all that could be desired. But at length in an evil hour he was induced to visit New York. He there associated with profligate companions, and relapsing into his former habits, was concerned in a burglary, for which he was tried and convicted. He is now in the prison at Sing-Sing, under sentence of imprisonment for life, and from death only can he hope for liberation.

The gaoler told me this anecdote, as a proof how little amendment of the moral character is to be ex-

pected from solitary confinement. The case undoubtedly is a strong one, yet, of all the systems of punishment hitherto devised, the entire isolation of the criminal from his fellow-men,—if judicious advantage
be taken of the opportunities it affords, and the state
of mind which it can scarcely fail to produce,—
seems that which is most likely to be attended with
permanent reformation.   The great objection to the
Auburn and Charleston system, is, that the prisoners are treated like brutes, and any lurking sense of
moral dignity is destroyed.   Each individual is not
only degraded in his own eyes, but in those of his
companions; and it appears impossible that a criminal, once subjected to such treatment, should ever
after be qualified to discharge, with advantage to his
country, the duties of a citizen.   Solitary confinement, on the other hand, has necessarily no such
consequence; it at once obviates all occasion for
corporal punishment, and for the exercise of arbitrary and irresponsible power on the part of the
gaoler.   The prisoner, on his liberation, is restored
to society, humbled, indeed, by long suffering, yet

not utterly degraded below the level of his fellow-creatures.

On the whole, the system of discipline I have witnessed at Charleston must be considered as a curious experiment, illustrating the precise degree of coercion necessary to destroy the whole influence of human volition, and reduce man to the condition of a machine. How far it accomplishes the higher objects contemplated in the philosophy of punishment, is a question which demands more consideration than I have at present time or inclination to bestow on it. I anticipate, however, having occasion to return to the subject, in narrating my visit to the Penitentiary at Philadelphia.

CHAPTER VII.

BOSTON.

THE New England States are the great seat of manufactures in the Union; and in Boston especially, it is impossible to mix at all in society without hearing discussions on the policy of the Tariff Bill. I was prepared to encounter a good deal of bigotry on this subject, but on the whole found less than I expected. Of course, here, as elsewhere, men will argue strenuously and earnestly on the policy of a measure, with which they know their own interests to be inseparably connected; but both the advocates and opponents of the Tariff are to be found mingled very sociably at good men's feasts, and I have not been able to discover that antagonism of opinion has been in any degree productive of hostility of feeling.

On this question, as on many others, the weight of numbers is on one side, and that of sound argument on the other. It is the observation, I think, of Hobbes, that were it to become the interest of any portion of the human race to deny the truth of a proposition in Euclid, by no power of demonstration could it ever after command universal assent. This may be going too far, but we know how difficult it is, in the less certain sciences, to influence the understanding of those in favour of a conclusion, whose real or imagined interests must be injuriously affected by its establishment. Truths cease to be palpable when they touch a man's prejudices or his pocket, and patriotism is generally found at a premium or a discount, precisely as it happens to be connected with profit or loss.

It was not to be expected, therefore, that a question affecting the various and conflicting interests of different classes of men should be discussed in a very calm or philosophical spirit. " The American system," as it is called, was strenuously supported by the rich northern merchants, who expected to find in manufactures a new and profitable investment for

2

their capital; and by the farmers, who expected to realize better prices for their wool and corn than could be commanded in the English market. It was opposed with at least equal vehemence by the planters of the Southern States, who regarded England as their best customer, and who must have been the chief sufferers had these measures of restriction been met by retaliation.   Of course, as no manufactures of any kind exist south of the Potomac, the inhabitants of that extensive region were by no means satisfied of the justice of a policy, which, by increasing the price of all foreign commodities, had the effect of transferring money from their pockets to those of the New England monopolists.   The Tariff Bill encountered strong opposition in both houses of the Legislature, but the representatives of the Western States having declared in its favour, it eventually passed, though by narrow majorities, and became law.

The passing of this bill inflicted a deep wound on the stability of the Union.   The seeds of dissension among the different States had long been diffused, and now began to exhibit signs of rapid and luxuriant growth. The inhabitants of the Southern States were almost unanimous against the law. Their representatives not only protested loudly against its injustice, but declared, that in imposing duties, not for the sake of revenue but protection, Congress had wantonly exceeded its powers, and violated one of the fundamental principles of the constitution. Thus arose the celebrated doctrine of *nullification*, or, in other words, the assertion of an independent power in each State of the Union, to decide for itself on the justice of the measures of the Federal government, and to declare null, within its own limits, any act of the Federal Congress which it may consider as an infraction of its separate rights.

To this great controversy, affecting in its very principle the cohesion of the different states, I shall not at present do more than allude. It does, however, appear abundantly clear, that if there ever was a country in which it is injudicious to trammel industry with artificial restrictions, that country is the United States. Covering a vast extent of fertile territory, and advancing in wealth and population with a rapidity altogether unparalleled, it seems only necessary to the happiness and prosperity of this favoured people, that they should refrain from counteracting the beneficence of nature, and tranquilly enjoy the many blessings which she has placed within their reach.   But this, unfortunately, is precisely what American legislators are not inclined to do. They seem determined to have a prosperity of their own making; to set up rival Birminghams and Manchesters; and in spite of " nature and their stars," to become, without delay, a great manufacturing, as well as a great agricultural nation.

But such things as Birmingham and Manchester are not to be created by an act of Congress.   They can arise only under a vast combination of favourable circumstances, the approach of which may be retarded, but cannot possibly be accelerated, by a system of restrictions.   They would undoubtedly have arisen far sooner in England, but for the ignorant adoption of the very policy which the Americans have now thought it expedient to imitate. But there is this excuse at least for our ancestors : The policy they adopted was in the spirit of their age.   They

did not seek to revive the exploded dogmas of a
country or a period less enlightened than their own ;
and it can only be charged against them, that in
seeking to gain a certain object, with but few and
scattered lights to guide their footsteps, they went
astray.

But to such palliation the conduct of the American legislators has no claim. With the path before
them clear as daylight, they have preferred entangling
themselves in thickets and quagmires. Like children, they have closed their eyes, and been content
to believe that all is darkness. Living in one age,
they have legislated in the spirit of another, and
their blunders want even the merit of originality.
They have exchanged their own comfortable clothing
for the cast-off garments of other men, and strangely
appeal to their antiquity as evidence of their value.

The appeal to English precedent may have some
weight as an *argumentum ad hominem*, but as an *argumentum veritatis* it can have none. We cheerfully
admit, that there is no absurdity so monstrous, as to
want a parallel in the British statute-book. We only
hope that we are outgrowing our errors, and profit-

ing, however tardily, by our own experience and
that of the world.   But even this praise the advocates of American monopoly are not inclined to
allow us. They charge us with bad faith in our commercial reforms ; with arguing on one side, and act-
ing on the other; and allege, that our statesmen,
with the words *free trade* constantly on their lips, are
still guided in their measures, by the spirit of that
antiquated policy, which they so loudly condemn.

Enough of allowance, however, has not been made
for the difficulties of their situation.   Our legislators, it should be remembered, had to deal with vast
interests, which had grown up under the exclusive
system so long and rigidly adhered to.   Any great
and sudden change in our commercial policy would
have been ruinous and unjust. It was necessary that
the transition should be gradual, even to a healthier
regimen ; that men's opinions should be conciliated,
and that time should be afforded for the adjustment
of vested interests to the new circumstances of competition which awaited them.   The question was far
less as to the truth or soundness of certain abstract
doctrines of political economy, than by what means

changes affecting the disposition of the whole capital
of the country, could be introduced with least injury
and alarm.

Those only who have minutely followed the public life of Mr Huskisson during the last ten years,
can duly estimate the magnitude of the obstacles
with which at every step of his progress he had to
contend.   In truth, we know not any portion of
history which would better repay the study of American statesmen.   They will there acquire some
knowledge of the difficulties, which assuredly, sooner
or later, they will be compelled to encounter. They
will learn, that a system of prohibition cannot be
abandoned with the same ease with which it was originally assumed.   Their first advance in the course
on which they have entered may be prosperous,
but their retreat must necessarily be disastrous.
They will have to endure the reproaches of the bankrupt manufacturers. They will have the punishment
of beholding a large proportion of the capital of their
country irrecoverably lost. They will be assailed by
the clamour and opposition of men of ruined fortunes and disappointed hopes, and while they

lament the diminution of their country's prosperity, even their self-love will scarcely secure them from the conviction of its being attributable solely to their own selfish and ignorant policy.

In no country in the world, perhaps, could the prohibitory system be tried with less prospect of success than in the United States. The vast extent of territory alone presents an insuperable obstacle to its enforcement. The statesmen of England had no such difficulty to struggle with. They had to legislate for a small, compact, and insular country, in which there existed no such diversity of climate or of interest as to create much inequality of pressure in any scheme, however unreasonable, of indirect taxation. In England, there are no provincial jealousies to be reconciled, no rivalries or antipathies between different portions of the kingdom, and the facilities of communication are already so great as to give promise that the word *distance* will be speedily erased from our vocabulary.

But in America all this is different. Those err egregiously who regard the population of the United States as an uniform whole, composed throughout of similar materials, and whose patriotic attachment embraces the whole territory between the Mississippi and the Penobscot. An American is not a being of strong *local* attachments, and the slightest temptation of profit is always strong enough to induce him to quit his native State, and break all the ties which are found to operate so powerfully on other men. Entire disparity of circumstances and situation between the Northern and Southern States have, besides, produced considerable alienation of feeling in their inhabitants; and disputes, arising from differences of soil and climate, are evidently beyond the control of legislative interference. The Georgian or Carolinian, therefore, lives in a state of the most profound indifference with regard to the prosperity of New England, or rather, perhaps, is positively jealous of any increase of wealth or population, by which that portion of the Union may acquire additional influence in the national councils. To the people of the Southern States, therefore, any indirect taxation, imposed for the benefit of the Northern, must be doubly odious. The former wish only to buy where they can buy cheapest, and to sell where they can find the best market for their produce. Besides, they are violent and high-spirited, strong republicans, and averse from any unnecessary exercise of power on the part of the Federal government. England is their great customer, and the planter can entertain no reasonable hope of opulence which is not founded on her prosperity. Such are the discordant materials with which Congress has to deal, and which visionary legislators have vainly attempted to unite in cordial support of " the American system."

It is obvious, that a legislature which enters on a system of protection-duties, assumes the exercise of a power with which no wise men would wish to be intrusted, and which it is quite impossible they can exercise with advantage. They, in fact, assume the direction of the whole industry and capital of the country; dictate in what channels they shall flow; arbitrarily enrich one class at the expense of another; tax the many for the benefit of the few, and, in short, enter on a policy, which, if followed by other countries, would necessarily put a stop to all commerce, and throw each nation on its individual resources. There can be no *reductio ad absur-dum* more complete. The commercial intercourse of nations would be annihilated were there a dozen governments in the world actuated by a cupidity so blind and uncalculating. It is, besides, impossible that any system of protection can *add* any thing to the productive industry of a people. The utmost it can effect is the transference of labour and capital from one branch of employment to another. It simply holds out a bribe to individuals to divert their industry from the occupations naturally most profitable, to others which are less so. This cannot be done without national loss. The encouragement which is felt in one quarter, must be accompanied by at least equal depression in another. The whole commercial system is made to rest on an insecure and artificial foundation, and the capital of the country, which has been influenced in its distribution, by a temporary and contingent impulse, may, at any moment, be paralysed by a change of system.

It is impossible, therefore, as matters now stand in America, that the manufacturing capitalists can look with any feeling of security to the future. They know, that the sword which is suspended over them hangs only by a hair, and may fall at any time. A large portion of the Union are resolutely, and almost unanimously, opposed to the continuance of the system. The monopolists, therefore, can ground their speculations on no hope but that of large and *immediate* profits, and the expectation, that should the present Tariff continue in force but a few years, they will, in that period, not only have realized the original amount of their investments, but a return sufficiently large to compensate for all the hazards of the undertaking. It is from the pockets of their fellow-subjects that they look for this enormous reimbursement; and, in a general point of view, perhaps, it matters little how much of the wealth of Virginia and the Carolinas may be transferred to New England, since the aggregate of national opulence would continue unchanged. One great and unmitigated evil of the Tariff-tax, however, consists in this, that while it is unjust and oppressive in its operation, it destroys far more capital than it sends into the coffers either of the Government or of individuals. All that portion of increased price which proceeds from increased difficulty of production in any article, is precisely so much of the national capital annihilated without benefit of any sort.

But, in truth, the exclusion of British goods from the Union is impossible.   The extent of the Canadian frontier is so great, that the vigilance of a million of custom-house officers could not prevent their introduction.   A temptation high in exact proportion to the amount of the restrictive duty, is held out to every trader; or in other words, the government which enforces the impost, offers a premium for its evasion.   If Jonathan,—which we much doubt,—is too honest to smuggle, John Canadian is not; and the consequence simply is, that the United States are supplied with those goods from Montreal, which, under other circumstances, would have been directly imported.   I remember walking through some warehouses in New York with an eminent merchant of that city; and on remarking the vast profusion of British manufactures everywhere apparent, he significantly answered, " Depend upon it, you have seen many more goods to-day than ever passed the Hook."   In this matter, therefore, there exists no discrepancy between reason and experience.   The trade between the countries still goes on with little, if any diminution.   It has only been diverted from its natural and wholesome channel ; taken from the respectable merchant, and thrown into the hands of the smuggler.

Among the body of the people there exists more ignorance as to the nature and effects of commerce, than might have been expected in a nation so generally commercial.   I believe the sight of the vast importations from Britain, which fill the warehouses in every seaport, is accompanied with a feeling not unallied to envy.   They would pardon us for our king and our peers, our palaces and our parade, far sooner than for our vast manufactories, which deluge the world with their produce.   Such feelings are the consequence of ignorant and narrow views. In truth, every improvement in machinery which is made in Leeds or Manchester is a benefit to the world.   By its agency the price of some commodity has been lowered, and an article, perhaps essential to comfort, is thus brought within the reach of millions to whom it must otherwise have been inaccessible.

Any sentiment of jealousy arising from the diffusion of British manufactures in their own country is no less absurd. Every increase of importation is, in fact, an evidence of increased opulence and prosperity in the importing country. Not a bale of goods is landed at the quay of New York, without an equal value of the produce of the country being exported to pay for it. Commerce is merely a barter of equivalents, and carries this advantage, that both parties are enriched by it. Thus, a piece of muslin may be more valuable in America than a bag of cotton; while, in England, the superiority of value is on the side of the latter. It is evident, therefore, that if these two articles be exchanged, both parties are gainers; both receive a greater value than they have given, and the mass of national opulence, both in England and America, has received a positive increase. A commerce which is not mutually advantageous cannot be continued. No Tariff bill, no system of restriction, is required to put a stop to it. Governments have no reason to concern themselves about the balance of trade. They may safely leave that to individual sagacity, and devote their attention to those various interests in which legislation may at least possibly be attended with benefit.

But formidable as the difficulties are which surround the supporters of the prohibitory system, another is approaching, even of greater magnitude. In two years the national debt will be extinguished, and the Federal government will find itself in possession of a surplus revenue of 12,000,000 of dollars, chiefly the produce of the Tariff duties. The question will then arise, how is this revenue to be appropriated. If divided among the different states, the tranquillity of the Union will be disturbed by a thousand jealousies, which very probably would terminate in its dissolution. Besides, such an appropriation is confessedly unconstitutional, and must arm the government with a power never contemplated at its formation. To apply the surplus in projects of general improvement, under direction of Congress, would increase many of the difficulties, while it obviated none. In short, there is no escaping from the dilemma; and, singular as it may seem to an Englishman, the Tariff will probably be extinguished by a sheer plethora of money. The most enlightened statesmen unite in the conviction, that there is but one course to be pursued, and that is, to reduce the duties to a fair system of revenue; to extract from the pockets of the people what is sufficient for the necessary expenses of the government, and no more. It is singular, that the wealth of a nation, which in other countries is found to generate corruption, should, in the United States, be the means of forcing the government to return to the principles of sound and constitutional legislation.

I am aware there is nothing new in all this, nor is it possible perhaps to be very original on a subject which has been so often and so thoroughly discussed. It ought perhaps in justice to be stated, that the majority of the gentlemen among whom I moved in Boston, were opposed to the Tariff, and that I derived much instruction both from their conversation and writings. The great majority of the mercantile population, however, are in favour of the prohibitory system, though I could not discover much novelty in

3

the arguments by which they support it. To these, however, I shall not advert, and gladly turn from a subject, which I fear can possess little interest for an English reader.

A traveller has no sooner time to look about him in Boston, than he receives the conviction that he is thrown among a population of a character differing in much from that of the other cities of the Union. If a tolerable observer, he will immediately remark that the lines of the forehead are more deeply indented; that there is more hardness of feature; a more cold and lustreless expression of the eye; a more rigid compression of the lips, and that the countenance altogether is of a graver and more meditative cast. Something of all this is apparent even in childhood; as the young idea shoots, the peculiarities become more strongly marked; they grow with his growth and strengthen with his strength, and it is only when the New Englander is restored to his kindred dust that they are finally obliterated. Observe him in every different situation; at the funeral, and the marriage-feast; at the theatre, and the conventicle; in the ball-room, and on the ex-

change, and you will set him down as of God's creatures the least liable to be influenced by circumstances appealing to the heart or imagination.

The whole city seems to partake of this peculiar
character, and a traveller coming from New York is
especially struck with it.   It is not that the streets
of Boston are less crowded, the public places less
frequented, or that the business of life is less energe-
tically pursued. In all these matters, to the eye of a
stranger there is little perceptible difference.   But
the population is evidently more orderly; the conventional restrictions of society are more strictly
drawn, and even the lower orders are distinguished
by a solemnity of demeanour, not observable in their
more southern neighbours.   A shopkeeper weighs
coffee or measures tape with the air of a philosopher ;
makes observations on the price or quality with an
air of sententious sagacity; subjects your coin to a
sceptical scrutiny, and as you walk off with your
parcel in your pocket, examines you from top to toe,
in order to gain some probable conclusion as to your
habits or profession.

Boston is quiet, but there is none of the torpor of

still life about it. Nowhere are the arts of money getting more deeply studied or better understood. There is here less attempt than elsewhere to combine pleasure and business, simply because to a New Englander business *is* pleasure—indeed the only pleasure he cares much about. An English shopkeeper is a tradesman all morning, but a gentleman in the evening. He casts his slough like a snake, and steps into it again, only when he crosses the counter. Tallow, *dry goods*, and tobacco are topics specially eschewed in the drawing-rooms of Camberwell and Hackney, and all talk about sales and bankruptcies is considered a violation of the *bienséances* at Broadstairs and Margate. In short, an English tradesman is always solicitous to *cut the shop* whenever he can do so with impunity, and it often happens that an acute observer of manners can detect a man's business rather by the topics he betrays anxiety to avoid, than those on which he delivers his opinion.

There is some folly in all this, but there is likewise some happiness. Enough, and too much, of man's life is devoted to business and its cares, and it is well that at least a portion of it should be given to enjoyment, and the cultivation of those charities, which constitute the redeeming part of our nature. The follies of mankind have at least the advantage of being generally social, and connected with the happiness of others as well as with our own. But the pursuits of avarice and ambition are selfish; their object is the attainment of solitary distinction, and the depression of competitors is no less necessary to success, than the positive elevation of the candidate. The natural sympathies of humanity are apt to wither in the hearts of men engrossed by such interests. Even the vanities and follies of life have their use in softening the asperities of contest, and uniting men in their weakness, who would willingly stand apart in their strength. It is good, therefore, that the lawyer should sometimes forget his briefs, and the merchant his " argosies," and his money-bags; that the poor man should cast off the memory of his sweat and his sufferings, and find even in frivolous amusements, a Sabbath of the sterner passions.

But such Sabbath the New Englander rarely knows. Wherever he goes the coils of business are

around him. He is a sort of moral Laocoon, differing
only in this, that he makes no struggle to be free.
Mammon has no more zealous worshipper than your
true Yankee. His homage is not merely that of the
lip, or of the knee ; it is an entire prostration of the
heart ; the devotion of all powers, bodily and mental,
to the service of the idol. He views the world but
as one vast exchange, on which he is impelled, both
by principle and interest, to over-reach his neighbours if he can. The thought of business is never
absent from his mind. To him there is no enjoyment
without traffic. He travels snail-like, with his shop
or his counting-house on his back, and, like other
hawkers, is always ready to open his budget of little
private interests for discussion or amusement. The
only respite he enjoys from the consideration of his
own affairs, is the time he is pleased to bestow on
prying into yours. In regard to the latter, he evidently considers that he has a perfect right to unlimited sincerity. There is no baffling him. His curiosity seems to rise in proportion to the difficulty of
its gratification : He will track you through every
evasion, detect all your doublings, or, if thrown out,

will hark back so skilfully on the scent, that you are
at length fairly hedged in a corner, and are tempted
to exclaim, in the words of the most gifted of female
poets,—

> " The devil damn thy question-asking spirit ;
> For when thou takest a notion by the skirt,
> Thou, like an English bull-dog, keepest thy hold,
> And wilt not let it go."

Their puritan descent has stamped a character on
the New Englanders, which nearly two centuries
have done little to efface.   Among their own countrymen they are distinguished for their enterprise,
prudence, frugality, order, and intelligence.   Like
the Jews, they are a marked people, and stand out
in strong relief from the population which surrounds
them.   I imagine attachment to republicanism is
less fervent in this quarter of the Union than in any
other.   The understanding of a Yankee is not likely
to be run away with by any political plausibilities,
and concerns itself very little about evils which are
merely speculative.   He is content when he feels a
grievance to apply a remedy, and sets about the
work of reform, with none of that revolutionary fury,

which has so often marred the fairest prospects of the philanthropist. Since the establishment of their independence, the representatives of these States have almost uniformly advocated in Congress the principles of Washington, Hamilton, and Adams, and rather regarded with apprehension the democratic tendencies of the constitution, than the dangers which might result from increase of power on the part of the executive.

This is the more remarkable, as the constitutions of most of the New England States are in truth republican in a degree verging on democracy. In New Hampshire, the governor, council, senators, and representatives are all elected annually by the people. In Vermont, there is only one Legislative Body, which, along with the governor and council, and *judges*, is chosen annually. Rhode Island, strange to say, has no written constitution at all, and the inhabitants find it very possible to live in perfect comfort and security without one. The custom is, however, to have a governor, senate, and representatives, who are chosen annually. The appointment of judges is likewise annual. In Massachusetts, the governor and Legislative Bodies are annually chosen — the judges, however, hold their offices *ad vitam aut culpam.* In the States of Maine and Connecticut, the Executive and Legislative Bodies are appointed annually; the Judiciary, however, is permanent. In all these states, the right of suffrage, with some few restrictions in regard to paupers, &c. is universal.

In contrast with this, it may be curious to take a glance at the constitution of Virginia, the native state of Washington, Jefferson, Madison, and Munroe, which has always been remarkable in the Federal Congress for the assertion of the highest and purest principles of republicanism. It must be observed, however, that until 1829, the right of suffrage depended on a much higher territorial qualification than at present. In that year, the constitution was remodelled and liberalized by a convention of the inhabitants.

There are in Virginia two Legislative Bodies. The members of the Lower House are chosen annually, the senators every *four* years. These houses, by a joint vote, elect the governor, who remains in office *three* years. The judges are during good behaviour, or until removed by a concurrent vote of both houses, two-thirds being required to constitute the necessary majority. The right of suffrage is vested in every citizen possessed of a freehold of the value of twenty-five dollars, or who has a life-interest in land of the value of fifty dollars, or who shall own or occupy a leasehold estate of the annual value of two hundred dollars, &c.

There is thus presented the anomaly of the most democratic state of the Union adhering to a constitution comparatively aristocratic, and appending to the right of suffrage a high territorial qualification; while the New England States, with institutions more democratic than have ever yet been realized in any other civilized community, are distinguished as the advocates of a strong federal legislature, a productive system of finance, the establishment of a powerful navy, and such liberal expenditure at home and abroad, as would tend to ensure respect and influence to the government.

The truth seems to be, that the original polity of these States partook of the patriarchal character, and has not yet entirely lost its hold on the feelings of the people.   It was easy to maintain order in a country where there was little temptation to crime ; where, by a day's labour, a man could earn the price of an acre of tolerable land, and becoming a territorial proprietor, of course, immediately partook of the common impulse, to maintain the security of property.   Add to this the character of the people ; their apathetic temperament, their habits of parsimony, the religious impressions communicated by their ancestors, and, above all, the vast extent of fertile territory which acted as an escape-valve for the more daring and unprincipled part of the population, and we shall have reasons enough, I imagine, why the New Englanders could bear, without injury, a greater degree of political liberty than perhaps any other people in the world.

But though the New Englanders had little apprehension of glaring violations of law within their own territory, they had evidently no great confidence in the wisdom and morality of their neighbours.   They were, therefore, in favour of a federal legislature, strong enough to command respect, and maintain order throughout the Union.   Forming a small minority of the confederated States, yet for long subsequent to the Revolution, possessing by far the greater share of the national capital, they felt that they had more to lose than those around them, and were consequently more solicitous to strengthen the guarantees of public order. They would, therefore, have been better satisfied had greater influence been given to property, and would gladly have seen the senate so constituted, as to act as a check on the hasty impulses of the more popular chamber. Within their own limits there was no risk of domestic disturbance. The most wealthy capitalist felt, that from the citizens of his own province, he had nothing to apprehend. But it was to the federal legislature alone, that they could look for security from without, and they were naturally anxious that this body should be composed of men with a deep interest in the stability of the Union, and representing rather the deliberate opinions of their more intelligent constituents, than the hasty and variable impressions of the ignorant and vulgar.

The New England states have something approaching to a religious establishment. In Massachusetts,

Vermont, New Hampshire, and Connecticut, the
law requires each town to provide, by taxation, for
the support of the *Protestant* religion, leaving, however, to every individual, the choice of the particular sect to which he will contribute.   In the other
States of the Union, every person is at liberty to act
as he pleases in regard to religion, which is regarded
solely as a relation between man and his Maker,
and any compulsory contribution would be considered a direct encroachment on personal liberty.
But if Christianity be a public benefit; if it tend to
diminish crime and encourage the virtues essential
to the prosperity of a community, it is difficult to
see on what grounds its support and diffusion should
not form part of the duties of a legislature.

In these States, the education of the people is likewise the subject of legislative enactment.   In Massachusetts, public schools are established in every
district, and supported by a tax levied on the public.
In Connecticut they are maintained in another manner.   By the charter of Charles the Second, this
colony extended across the Continent to the Pacific,
within the same parallels of latitude which bound it

on the East. It therefore included a large portion of the present States of Pennsylvania and Ohio, which being sold, produced a sum amounting to L.270,000 sterling, the interest of which is exclusively devoted to the purposes of education throughout the State. This fund is now largely increased, and its annual produce, I believe, is greater than the whole income of the State arising from taxation.

In these public schools every citizen has not only a right to have his children educated, but, as in some parts of Germany, he is compelled by law to exercise it. It is here considered essential to the public interest that every man should receive so much instruction as shall qualify him for a useful member of the State. No member of society can be considered as an isolated and abstract being, living for his own pleasure, and labouring for his own advantage. In free States, especially, every man has important political functions, which affect materially not only his own well-being but that of his fellow-citizens; and it is surely reasonable to demand that he shall at least possess such knowledge as shall render it possible for him to discharge his duties with advantage to the community. The policy which attempts to check crime by the diffusion of knowledge, is the offspring of true political wisdom. It gives a security to person and property, beyond that afforded by the law, and looks for the improvement of the people, not to the gibbet and the prison, but to increased intelligence, and a consequently keener sense of moral responsibility.

Speaking generally, it may be said that every New Englander receives the elements of education. Reading and writing, even among the poorest class, are universally diffused; arithmetic, I presume, comes by instinct among this guessing, reckoning, expecting, and calculating people. The school-master has long been abroad in these States, deprived, it is true, of his rod and ferule, but still most usefully employed. Up to a certain point he has done wonders; he has made his scholars as wise as himself, and it would be somewhat unreasonable to expect more. If it be considered desirable, however, that the present range of popular knowledge should be enlarged, the question then arises, who shall teach the schoolmaster? Who shall impress a pedagogue (on the best terms with himself, and whose only wonder is, " that one small head should carry all he knows,") with a due sense of his deficiencies, and lead him to admit that there are more things between heaven and earth than are dreamt of in his philosophy? A New Englander passes through the statutory process of education, and enters life with the intimate conviction that he has mastered, if not the *omne scibile*, at least every thing valuable within the domain of intellect. It never occurs to him as possible, that he may have formed a wrong conclusion on any question, however intricate, of politics or religion. He despises all knowledge abstracted from the business of the world, and prides himself on his stock of practical truths. In mind, body, and estate, he believes himself the first and noblest of God's creatures. The sound of triumph is ever on his lips, and, like a man who has mounted the first step of a ladder, it is his pride to look down on his neighbours, whom he overtops by an inch, instead of directing his attention to the great height yet to be surmounted.

This folly, indeed, is not peculiar to the New Englander, though in him it is more strongly marked than in the inhabitants of the other States. It enters into the very essence of his character; it is part and parcel of him, and its eradication would involve an entire change of being. " A blessing be on him who first invented sleep," says Sancho Panza, " for it covers a man all over like a cloak." And even so Jonathan may bless his vanity. He is encased in it from top to toe; it is a panoply of proof, which renders him invulnerable equally to ridicule and argument

If to form a just estimate of ourselves and others, be the test of knowledge, the New Englander is the most ignorant of mankind. There is a great deal that is really good and estimable in his character, but, after all, he is not absolutely the ninth wonder of the world. I know of no benefit that could be conferred on him equal to convincing him of this truth. He may be assured that the man who knows nothing, and is aware of his ignorance, is a wiser and more enviable being than he who knows a little, and imagines that he knows all. The extent of our ignorance is a far more profitable object of contemplation than that of our knowledge. Discontent with our actual amount of acquirement is the indispensable condition of possible improvement. It is to be wished that Jonathan would remember this. He may rely on it, he will occupy a higher place in the estimation of the world, whenever he has acquired the wisdom to think more humbly of himself.

The New England free-schools are establishments happily adapted to the wants and character of the people. They have been found to work admirably, and too much praise cannot be bestowed on the enlightened policy which, from the very foundation of the colony, has never once lost sight of the great object of diffusing education through every cottage within its boundaries. It will detract nothing from the honour thus justly due, to mention that the establishment of district schools was not an original achievement of New England intelligence. The parish-schools of Scotland (to say nothing of Germany) had existed long before the pilgrim fathers ever knelt in worship beneath the shadows of the hoary forest trees. The principle of the establish-

ments in both countries is the same, the only difference is in the details.   In Scotland the land-own-
ers of each parish contribute the means of education for the body of the people.   The schoolhouse
and dwelling-house of the master are provided and
kept in repair by an assessment on the land, which
is likewise burdened with the amount of his salary.

It has been an object, however, wisely kept in
view, that instruction at these seminaries shall not be
wholly gratuitous.   There are few even of the poorest
order in Scotland who would not consider it a degradation to send their children to a charity school, and
the feeling of independence, is perhaps the very last
which a wise legislator will venture to counteract.   It
is to be expected, too, that when the master depends
on the emolument to be derived from his scholars, he
will exert himself more zealously than when his
remuneration arises from a source altogether independent of his own efforts.   The sum demanded from
the scholars, however, is so low, that instruction is
placed within the reach of the poorest cottager ; and
instances are few indeed, in which a child born
in Scotland is suffered to grow up without sufficient

instruction to enable him to discharge respectably the duties of the situation he is destined to fill.

When Mr Brougham, however, brought forward in the British Parliament his plan of national education, which consisted mainly in the establishment throughout the kingdom of parish-schools, similar to those in Scotland, one of the most eminent individuals of the Union* did not hesitate to arrogate the whole merit of the precedent for New England. I have more than once since my arrival heard Mr Brougham accused of unworthy motives, in not publicly confessing that his whole project was founded on the example set forth for imitation in this favoured region. It was in vain that I pleaded the circumstances above stated, the company were evidently determined to believe their own schools without parallel in the world, and the Lord Chancellor will assuredly go down to his grave unabsolved from this weighty imputation.

In character there are many points of resemblance between the Scotch and New Englanders. There is

* Mr Webster, in his speech delivered at Plymouth, in commemoration of the first settlement of New England.

the same sobriety, love of order, and perseverance in both; the same attachment to religion, mingled with more caution in Sanders, and more enterprise in Jonathan. Both are the inhabitants of a poor country, and both have become rich by habits of steady industry and frugality. Both send forth a large portion of their population to participate in the wealth of more favoured regions. The Scot, however, never loses his attachment to his native land. It has probably been to him a rugged nurse, yet, wander where he will, its heathy mountains are ever present to his imagination, and he thinks of the bleak muirland cottage in which he grew from infancy to manhood, as a spot encircled by a halo of light and beauty. Whenever fortune smiles on him, he returns to his native village, and the drama of his life closes where it commenced.

There is nothing of this local attachment about the New Englander. His own country is too poor and too populous to afford scope for the full exercise of his enterprise and activity. He therefore shoulders his axe, and betakes himself to distant regions; breaks once and for ever all the ties of kindred and connexion, and without one longing lingering look, bids farewell to all the scenes of his infancy.

In point of morality, I must be excused for giving the decided preference to my countrymen. The Scotch have established throughout the world a high character for honesty, sobriety, and steady industry. Jonathan is equally sober and industrious, but his reputation for honesty is at a discount. The whole Union is full of stories of his cunning frauds, and of the impositions he delights to perpetrate on his more simple neighbours. Whenever his love of money comes in competition with his zeal for religion, the latter is sure to give way. He will insist on the scrupulous observance of the Sabbath, and cheat his customer on the Monday morning. His life is a comment on the text, *Qui festinat ditescere, non erit innocens.* The whole race of Yankee pedlars, in particular, are proverbial for dishonesty. These go forth annually in thousands to lie, cog, cheat, swindle, in short, to get possession of their neighbour's property, in any manner it can be done with impunity. Their ingenuity in deception is confess-

edly very great.   They warrant broken watches to
be the best time-keepers in the world; sell pinch-
beck trinkets for gold; and have always a large
assortment of wooden nutmegs, and stagnant baro-
meters.   In this respect they resemble the Jews, of
which race, by the by, I am assured, there is not a
single specimen to be found in New England.   There
is an old Scotch proverb, " Corbies never pick out
corbies' een."

The New Englanders are not an amiable people.
One meets in them much to approve, little to admire,
and nothing to love.   They may be disliked, however, but they cannot be despised.   There is a degree
of energy and sturdy independence about them, incompatible with contempt.   Abuse them as we may,
it must still be admitted they are a singular and
original people.   Nature, in framing a Yankee, seems
to have given him double brains, and half heart.

Wealth is more equally distributed in the New
England states, than perhaps in any other country
of the world.   There are here no overgrown fortunes.   Abject poverty is rarely seen, but moderate
opulence everywhere.   This is as it should be.   Whe

would wish for the introduction of the palace, if it must be accompanied by the Poor's-house ?*

There are few beggars to be found in the streets of Boston, but some there are, both there and at New York. These, however, I am assured, are all foreigners, or people of colour, and my own observations go to confirm the assertion. Nine-tenths of those by whom I have been importuned for charity, were evidently Irish. The number of negroes in Boston is comparatively small. The servants, in the better houses at least, are generally whites, but I have not been able to discover that the prejudices which, in the other States, condemn the poor African to degradation, have been at all modified or diminished by the boasted intelligence of the New Englanders.

* The observations on the New England character in the present chapter, would perhaps have been more appropriately deferred till a later period of the work. Having written them, however, they must now stand where chance has placed them. I have only to beg they may be taken, not as the hasty impressions received during a few days or weeks residence in Boston, but as the final result of my observations on this interesting people, both in their own states, and in other portions of the Union.

This observation is equally applicable to the opinions expressed in different parts of these volumes, and I must request the reader to be good enough to bear it in mind.

Though the schoolmaster has long exercised his vocation in these States, the fruit of his labours is but little apparent in the language of his pupils. The amount of bad grammar in circulation is very great; that of barbarisms enormous.   Of course, I do not now speak of the operative class, whose massacre of their mother-tongue, however inhuman, could excite no astonishment; but I allude to the great body of lawyers and traders: the men who crowd the exchange and the hotels; who are to be heard speaking in the courts, and are selected by their fellow-citizens to fill high and responsible offices. Even by this educated and respectable class, the commonest words are often so transmogrified as to be placed beyond the recognition of an Englishman. The word *does* is split into two syllables, and pronounced *do-es*.   *Where*, for some incomprehensible reason, is converted into *whare*, *there* into *thare*; and I remember, on mentioning to an acquaintance that I had called on a gentleman of taste in the arts, he asked, "Whether he *shew* (showed) me his pictures." Such words as oratory and dilatory, are pronounced with the penult syllable, long and accented; missionary becomes *missionairy*, angel, *angel*, danger, *danger*, &c.

But this is not all. The Americans have chosen arbitrarily to change the meaning of certain old and established English words, for reasons which they cannot explain, and which I doubt much whether any European philologist could understand. The word *clever* affords a case in point. It has here no connexion with talent, and simply means pleasant or amiable. Thus a good-natured blockhead in the American vernacular, is a *clever* man, and having had this drilled into me, I foolishly imagined that all trouble with regard to this word at least, was at an end. It was not long, however, before I heard of a gentleman having moved into a *clever* house, of another succeeding to a *clever* sum of money, of a third embarking in a *clever* ship, and making a *clever* voyage, with a *clever* cargo ; and of the sense attached to the word in these various combinations, I could gain nothing like satisfactory explanation.

With regard to the meaning intended to be conveyed by an American in conversation, one is sometimes left utterly at large. I remember, after conversing with a very plain, but very agreeable lady, being asked whether Mrs —— was not *a very fine woman*. I believe I have not more conscience than my neighbours in regard to a compliment, but in the present case there seemed something so ludicrous in the application of the term, that I found it really impossible to answer in the affirmative. I therefore ventured to hint, that the personal charms of Mrs —— were certainly not her principal attraction, but that I had rarely enjoyed the good fortune of meeting a lady more pleasing and intelligent. This led to an explanation, and I learned that in the dialect of this country, the term *fine woman* refers exclusively to the intellect.

The privilege of barbarizing the King's English is assumed by all ranks and conditions of men. Such words as *slick*, *kedge*, and *boss*, it is true, are rarely used by the better orders; but they assume unlimited liberty in the use of " expect," " reckon," " guess," "calculate," and perpetrate conversational anomalies with the most remorseless impunity. It were easy to accumulate instances, but I will not go on with this unpleasant subject; nor should I have alluded to it, but that I feel it something of a duty to express the natural feeling of an Englishman, at finding the language of Shakspeare and Milton thus gratuitously degraded. Unless the present progress of change be arrested, by an increase of taste and judgment in the more educated classes, there can be no doubt that, in another century, the dialect of the Americans will become utterly unintelligible to an Englishman, and that the nation will be cut off from the advantages arising from their participation in British literature. If they contemplate such an event with complacency, let them go on and prosper ; they have only to " *progress* " in their present course, and their grandchildren bid fair to speak a jargon as novel and peculiar as the most patriotic American linguist can desire.

CHAPTER VIII.

NEW ENGLAND.

HAVING directed the attention of the reader to some of the more prominent defects of the New England character, it is only justice to add, that in Boston at least, there exists a circle almost entirely exempt from them. This is composed of the first-rate merchants and lawyers, leavened by a small sprinkling of the clergy, and, judging of the quality of the ingredients, from the agreeable effect of the mixture, I should pronounce them excellent. There is much taste for literature in this circle ; much liberality of sentiment, a good deal of accomplishment, and a greater amount, perhaps, both of practical and speculative knowledge, than the population of any other mercantile city could supply. In such society it is possible for an Englishman to express his opinions without danger of being misunderstood, and he enjoys the advantage of free interchange of thought, and correcting his own hasty impressions by comparison with the results of more mature experience and sounder judgment.

It certainly struck me as singular, that while the great body of the New Englanders are distinguished above every other people I have ever known by bigotry and narrowness of mind, and an utter disregard of those delicacies of deportment which indicate benevolence of feeling, the higher and more enlightened portion of the community should be peculiarly remarkable for the display of qualities precisely the reverse. Nowhere in the United States will the feelings, and even prejudices of a stranger, meet with such forbearance as in the circle to which I allude. Nowhere are the true delicacies of social intercourse more scrupulously observed, and nowhere will a traveller mingle in society, where his errors of opinion will be more rigidly detected or more charitably excused. I look back on the period of my residence in Boston with peculiar pleasure. I trust there

are individuals there who regard me as a friend, and
I know of nothing in the more remote contingencies
of life, which I contemplate with greater satisfaction,
than the possibility of renewing in this country, with
at least some of the number, an intercourse which I
found so gratifying in their own.

In externals, the society of Boston differs little
from that of New York.   There is the same routine
of dinners and parties, and in both the scale of expensive luxury seems nearly equal.   In Boston, however, there is more literature, and this circumstance
has proportionally enlarged the range of conversation.   An Englishman is a good deal struck in America with the entire absence of books, as articles of
furniture.   The remark, however, is not applicable
to Boston.   There, works of European literature,
evidently not introduced for the mere purpose of display, are generally to be found, and even the drawing-room sometimes assumes the appearance of a
library.

The higher order of the New Englanders offers no
exception to that grave solemnity of aspect, which is
the badge of all their tribe. The gentlemen are more

given than is elsewhere usual, to the discussion of abstract polemics, both in literature and religion. There is a moral pugnacity about them, which is not offensive, because it is never productive of any thing like wrangling, and is qualified by a very large measure of philosophical tolerance. The well-informed Bostonian is a calm and deliberative being. His decision, on any point, may be influenced by interest, but not by passion. He is rarely contented, like the inhabitants of other states, with taking the plain and broad features of a case; he enters into all the refinements of which the subject is capable, discriminates between the plausible and the true, establishes the precise limits of fact and probability, and with unerring accuracy fixes on the weak point in the argument of his opponent. Of all men he is the least liable, I should imagine, to be misled by any general assertion of abstract principle. He uniformly carries into the business of common life a certain practical good sense, and never for a moment loses sight of the results of experience. In politics he will not consent to *go the whole hog*, or, in other words, to hazard a certain amount of present benefit, for the

promise, however confident, of new and untried advantages.

Of the ladies of Boston I did not see much, and
can therefore only speak in doubtful terms of the
amount of their attractions. Unfortunately it is still
less the fashion, than at New York, to enliven the
dinner-table with their presence, and, during my
stay, I was only present at one ball. But the impression I received was certainly very favourable.
These fair New Englanders partake of the endemic
gravity of expression, which sits well on them, because it is natural. In amount of acquirement, I
believe they are very superior to any other ladies of
the Union. They talk well and gracefully of novels
and poetry, are accomplished in music and the living
languages, and though the New York ladies charge
them with being *dowdyish* in dress, I am not sure
that their taste in this respect is not purer, as it certainly is more simple, than that of their fair accusers.

The habits of the Bostonians are, I believe, more
domestic than is common in the other cities of the
Union. The taste for reading contributes to this,
by rendering both families and individuals less de-

pendent on society. A strong aristocratic feeling is apparent in the families of older standing. The walls of the apartments are often covered with the portraits of their ancestors, armorial bearings are in general use, and antiquity of blood is no less valued here than in England. The people, too, display a fondness for title somewhat at variance with their good sense in other matters. The governor of Massachusetts receives the title of Excellency. The President of the United States claims no such honour. The members of the Federal Senate are addressed generally in the northern states, with the prefixture of Honourable, but the New Englanders go further, and extend the same distinction to the whole body of representatives, a practice followed in no other part of the Union.

Such trifles often afford considerable insight to the real feelings of a people. Nowhere are mere nominal distinctions at so high a premium as in this republican country. Military titles are caught at with an avidity, which to an Englishman appears absolutely ridiculous. The anomaly of learned majors at the bar addressing learned colonels or generals on the bench is not uncommon, and as the privates of militia enjoy the privilege of electing their officers, of course the principle of choice is by no means the possession of military knowledge.   In a thinly-peopled country, where candidates of a better class are not to be had, it must often happen, that the highest military rank is bestowed on men of the very lowest station in society. This circumstance, it might be expected, would bring this class of honours into disrepute, and that, like the title of knight-bachelor in England, they would be avoided by the better order of citizens.   This, however, is by no means the case. Generals, colonels, and majors, swarm all over the Union, and the titular distinction is equally coveted by the President and the senator, the judge on the bench and the innkeeper at the bar.

There is far more English feeling in Boston than I was prepared to expect. The people yet feel pride in the country of their forefathers, and even retain somewhat of reverence for her ancient institutions. At the period of my visit, the topic of Parliamentary Reform was naturally one of peculiar interest.   The revolution in France had communicated a strong impulse to opinion in England, and the policy to be adopted by the ministry in regard to this great question, was yet unknown. The subject, therefore, in all its bearings, was very frequently discussed in the society of Boston. It was one on which I had anticipated little difference of opinion among the citizens of a republic. Admitting that their best wishes were in favour of the prosperity of Britain, and the stability of her constitution, I expected that their judgment would necessarily point to great and immediate changes in a monarchy confessedly not free from abuse. For myself, though considered, I believe, as something of a Radical at home, I had come to the United States prepared to bear the imputation of Toryism among a people whose ideas of liberty were carried so much further than my own.

In all these anticipations I was mistaken. Strange to say, I found myself quite as much a Radical in Boston, and very nearly as much so in New York, as I had been considered in England. It was soon apparent that the great majority of the more enlightened class in both cities, regarded any great and sudden change in the British institutions as pregnant with the most imminent danger. In their eyes the chance of ultimate advantage was utterly insignificant, when weighed against the certainty of immediate peril. " You at present," they said, " enjoy more practical freedom than has ever in the whole experience of mankind been permanently secured to a nation by any institutions. Your government, whatever may be its defects, enjoys at least this inestimable advantage, that the habits of the people are adapted to it. This cannot be the case in regard to any change, however calculated to be ultimately beneficial. The process of moral adaptation is ever slow and precarious, and the experience of the world demonstrates that it is far better that the intelligence of a people should be in advance of their institutions, than that the institutions should precede the advancement of the people. In the former case, however theoretically bad, their laws will be practically modified by the influence of public opinion ; in the latter, however good in themselves, they cannot be secure or beneficial in their operation. We speak as men whose opinions have been formed from experience, under a government, popular in the widest sense of the term. As friends, we caution you to beware. We pretend not to judge whether change be necessary. If it be, we trust it will at least be gradual ; that your statesmen will approach the work of reform, with the full knowledge that every single innovation will occasion the necessity of many. The appetite for change in a people grows with what it feeds on. It is insatiable. Go as far as you will, at some point you must stop, and that point will be short of the wish of a large portion—probably of a numerical majority—of your population. By no concession does it appear to us that you can avert the battle that awaits you. You have but the choice whether the great struggle shall be for reform or property."

I own I was a good deal surprised by the prevalence of such opinions among the only class of Americans whose judgment as to matters of government, could be supposed of much value. As it was my object to acquire as much knowledge as possible with regard to the real working of the American constitution on the habits and feelings of the people; I was always glad to listen to political discussion between enlightened disputants. This carried with it at least the advantage of affording an indication to the prevailing tone of thought and opinion, in a condition of society altogether different from any within the range of European experience. At present I have only alluded to the subject of politics at all, as illustrative of a peculiar feature in the New England character. At a future period, I shall have occasion to view the subject under a different aspect.

The comparative diffusion of literature in Boston, has brought with it a taste for the fine arts. The better houses are adorned with pictures; and in the Athenæum—a public library and reading-room—is a collection of casts from the antique. Establishments for the instruction of the people in the higher branches of knowledge, are yet almost unknown in the United States, but something like a Mechanics' Institute has at length been got up in Boston, and I went to hear the introductory lecture. The apartment, a large one, was crowded by an audience whose appearance and deportment were in the highest degree orderly and respectable. The lecture was on the steam-engine, the history, principle, and construction of which were explained most lucidly by a lecturer, who belonged, I was assured, to the class of operative mechanics.

Boston can boast having produced some eminent artists, at the head of whom is Mr Alston, a painter, confessedly of fine taste, if not of high genius. His taste, however, unfortunately renders him too fastidious a critic on his own performances, and he has now been upwards of ten years in painting an historical subject, which is yet unfinished. This surely is mere waste of life and labour. Where a poet or painter has a strong grasp of his subject, he finds no difficulty in embodying his conceptions. The idea which requires years of fostering, and must be cherished and cockered into life, is seldom worth the cost of its nurture. Mr Alston should remember that a tree is judged by the quantity as well as by the quality of its fruit. Had Raphael, Rubens, or Titian, adopted such a process of elaboration, how many of the noblest specimens of art would have been lost to the world !

I had the pleasure of becoming acquainted with Mr Harding, a painter of much talent, and very considerable genius. His history is a singular one. During the last war with Great Britain, he was a private soldier, and fought in many of the battles on the frontier. At the return of peace, he exchanged the sword for the pallet, and without instruction of any kind, attained to such excellence, that his pictures attracted much notice, and some little encouragement. But America affords no field for the higher walks of art, and Harding, with powers of the first order, and an unbounded enthusiasm for his profession, is not likely, I fear, to be appreciated as he deserves. Some years ago he visited England, where his talents were fast rising into celebrity, but the strength of the *amor patriæ* unfortunately determined him to return to his native land. I say unfortunately, because in England he could scarcely have failed of attaining both wider fame, and more liberal remuneration, than can well be expected in America. The modesty of this artist is no less remarkable than his genius. He uniformly judges his own performances by the highest standard of criticism, and is far rather disposed to exaggerate than extenuate their defects. Such a character of mind holds out high hopes of future achievement. In truth, even now, he is deficient in nothing, but a certain softness and finish, which time and a little practice will undoubtedly supply.

The better society of Boston, I imagine, is somewhat more exclusive than that of New York. Both pride of family, and pride of knowledge, contribute to this, though there is no public or apparent assertion of either. It is the custom on every Sunday evening for the different branches of a family to assemble at the house of one or other of its members. This generally produces a very social and agreeable party, and though a stranger, I was sometimes hospitably permitted to join the circle. It certainly at first appeared rather singular, that the Bostonians, who are strict observers of the Sabbath, should select that day for any festive celebration, however innocent. I learned, however, that on the literal interpretation of the assertion in Genesis, that " the evening and the morning were the first day," the Sabbath is not observed, as with us, from midnight to midnight,

but from sunset to sunset.   In conformity with this
doctrine, the shops are generally closed at twilight
on Saturday evening, and all business is suspended.
Of course, after sunset on the day following, they
consider themselves discharged from further religious observance, and the evening is generally devoted to social intercourse.

Having passed nearly three weeks in Boston, it
became necessary that I should direct my steps to
the southward. I determined to return to New York
by land, being anxious to see something of the country, and more than I had yet done of its inhabitants.
The festivities of Christmas, therefore, were no sooner
over, than I quitted Boston, with sentiments of deep
gratitude for a kindness, which, from the hour of my
arrival, to that of my departure, had continued
unbroken.

I have already described an American stage-coach.
The one in which I now travelled, though distinguished by the title of " mail-stage," could boast
no peculiar attraction.   It was old and rickety, and
the stuffing of the cushions had become so conglo-
merated into hard and irregular masses, as to im-

press the passengers with the conviction of being seated on a bag of pebbles. Fortunately it was not crowded, and the road, though rough, was at least better than that on which I had been jolted on my journey from Providence. It was one o'clock before we got fairly under way, and it is scarcely possible, I imagine, for a journey to commence under gloomier auguries. The weather was most dismal. The wind roared loudly among the branches of the leafless trees, and beat occasionally against the carriage in gusts so violent, as to threaten its overthrow. At length the clouds opened, and down came a storm of snow, which, in a few minutes, had covered the whole surface of the country, as with a winding-sheet.

The first night we slept at Worcester, a town containing about 3000 inhabitants, which the guide-book declares to contain a bank, four printing-offices, a court-house, and a gaol, assertions which I can pretend neither to corroborate nor deny. Its appearance, however, as I observed on the following morning, was far from unprepossessing; the streets were clean, and round the town stood neat and pretty-looking villas, which might have been still prettier, had they displayed less gaudy and tasteless decoration.

As the county court,—or some other,—was then sitting, the inn was crowded with lawyers and their clients, at least fifty of whom already occupied the public *salon*, which was certainly not more than twenty feet square. The passengers were left to scramble out of the coach as they best could in the dark, and afterwards to explore their way without the smallest notice, beyond that of a broad stare from the master of the house. On entering the room, I stood for some time, in the hope that a party who engrossed the whole fire, would compassionate our half-frozen condition, and invite our approach. Nothing, however, was farther from their thoughts than such benevolence. " Friend, did you come by the stage ?" asked a man immediately in my front, " I guess you found it tarnation cold." I assured him his conjecture was quite correct, but the reply had not the effect of inducing any relaxation of the blockade. I soon observed, however, that my fellow-travellers elbowed their way without ceremony, and by adopting Rodney's manœuvre of cutting the line, had already gained a comfortable position in rear of the *cordon*. I therefore did not hesitate to follow their example, and pushing resolutely forward, at length enjoyed the sight and warmth of the blazing embers.

In about half an hour, the ringing of a bell gave welcome signal of supper, and accompanying my fellow-passengers to the eating-room, we found a plentiful meal awaiting our appearance. On the score of fare there was certainly no cause of complaint. There were dishes of beef-steaks—which in this country are generally about half the size of a news-paper,—broiled fowl, ham, cold turkey, toast—not made in the English fashion, but boiled in melted butter,—a kind of crumpet called waffles, &c. &c. The tea and coffee were poured out and handed by a girl with long ringlets and ear-rings, not remarkable for neatness of apparel, and who remained seated, unless when actually engaged in the discharge of her functions. Nothing could exceed the gravity of her expression and deportment, and there was an air of cool indifference about her mode of ministering to the wants of the guests, which was certainly far from prepossessing. This New England Hebe, however, was good-looking, and with the addition of a smile would have been pleasing.

Having concluded the meal, I amused myself on our return to the public room, by making observations on the company. The clamour of Babel could not have been much worse than that which filled the apartment. I attempted to discriminate between lawyer and client, but the task was not easy. There was in both the same keen and callous expression of worldly anxiety; the same cold selfishness of look and manner. The scene altogether was not agreeable; many of the company were without shoes, others without a cravat, and compared with people of the same class in England, they were dirty both in habit and person. It is always unpleasant to mingle in a crowd, with the consciousness that you have no sympathy or fellow-feeling with the individuals that compose it. I therefore soon desisted from my task of observation, and having fully digested the contents of a Worcester newspaper, determined on retiring for the night.

The process in England in such circumstances, is

to ring for the chamber-maid, but in America there
are no bells, and no chamber-maids.   You therefore walk to the bar, and solicit the favour of being
supplied with a candle, a request which is ultimately,
though by no means immediately, complied with.
You then explore the way to your apartment unas-
sisted, and with about the same chance of success as
the enterprising Parry in his hunt after the north-
west passage.   Your number is 63, but in what part
of the mansion that number is to be found, you are
of course without the means of probable conjecture.
Let it be supposed, however, that you are more fortunate than Captain Parry, and at length discover
the object of your search.   If you are an Englishman, and too young to have roughed it under Wellington, you are probably, what in this country is
called "mighty particular;" rejoice in a couple of
comfortable pillows, to say nothing of a lurking prejudice in favour of multiplicity of blankets, especially with the thermometer some fifty degrees below
the freezing point.   Such luxuries, however, it is
ten to one you will not find in the uncurtained crib
in which you are destined to pass the night.   Your

first impulse, therefore, is to walk down stairs and make known your wants to the landlord. This is a mistake. Have nothing to say to him. You may rely on it, he is much too busy to have any time to throw away in humouring the whimsies of a foreigner; and should it happen, as it does sometimes in the New England States, that the establishment is composed of natives, your chance of a comfortable sleep for the night, is about as great as that of your gaining the Thirty Thousand pound prize in the lottery. But if there are black, and, still better, if there are Irish servants, your prospect of comfort is wonderfully improved. A douceur, judiciously administered, generally does the business, and when you at length recline after the fatigues of the day, you find your head has acquired at least six inches additional elevation, and the superincumbent weight of woollen has been largely augmented.

It was at Worcester that I received this most useful information. Being in want of the above-mentioned accommodations, I deputed my servant to make an humble representation of my necessities to the landlord. The flinty heart of Boniface, however,

6

was not to be moved. The young lady with the ringlets and ear-rings was no less inexorable, but, luckily for me, a coloured waiter was not proof against the eloquence of a quarter dollar. In five minutes the articles were produced, and as sailors say, " I tumbled in" for the night, with a reasonable prospect of warmth and comfort.

After a good breakfast on the following morning, I felt again fortified for the perils and disagreeables of the mail-stage. Mr Harding, to whose merits as an artist I have already alluded, was fortunately a fellow-passenger, being on his way to join his family at Springfield. The only other passenger was a young lady, with an enormous band-box on her knee, to whom Mr Harding introduced me. There was something in this fair damsel and her band-box peculiarly interesting. She sat immediately opposite to me, but nothing of her face or person was visible, except a forehead, a few dark ringlets, and a pair of the most beautiful eyes in the world, which, like the sun just peeping above the horizon, sent the brightest flashes imaginable, along the upper level of this Brobdignag of a band-box.

The snow had continued to fall during the night, and the jolting of the " mail-stage " was certainly any thing but agreeable. When out of humour, however, by the united influence of the weather and the road, I had only to direct a single glance towards the beautiful orbs scintillating in my front, to be restored to equanimity. When any thing at all jocular was said, one could read a radiant laughter in this expressive feature, though her lips gave utterance to no sound of merriment. For about five hours the fair oculist continued our fellow-traveller, and I had at length come to think of her as some fantastic and preternatural creation; such a being as one sometimes reads of in a German romance, half band-box, and half eye.

At length she left the coach. When her band-box was about to be removed from its position, I remember averting my face, lest a view of her countenance might destroy the fanciful interest she had excited. She departed, therefore, unseen; but those eyes will live in my memory, long after all record of her fellow-traveller shall have faded from hers.

After her departure, Harding told me her story;

she was a young lady of respectable connexions, and with the consent of her family, had become engaged to a young man, who afterwards proved false to his vows, and married a wealthier bride. She had suffered severely under this disappointment, and was then going on a visit to her aunt at Northampton, in the hope that change of scene might contribute to the restoration of her tranquillity. That this result would follow I have no doubt. Those eyes were too laughing and brilliant, to belong permanently to a languishing and broken-hearted maiden.

We dined at a tolerable inn, and proceeded on our journey. The snow had ceased; there was a bright sun above, but I never remember to have felt cold so intense. It was late before we reached Springfield, where I had determined on making a day's halt. The inn was comfortable, and I succeeded in procuring private apartments. On the following morning I took a ramble over the village, which is by far the gayest I had yet seen in the course of my tour. It abounds with white framework villas, with green Venetian blinds, and porticoes of Corinthian or Ionic columns sadly out of proportion.   It appears to me, however, that massive columns—and columns not *apparently* massive at least, must be absurd—are sadly out of place when attached to a wooden building.   When such fragile materials are employed, *lightness* should be the chief object of the architect, but these transatlantic Palladios seem to despise the antiquated notions of fitness and proportion which prevail in other parts of the world.   They heap tawdry ornament upon their gingerbread creations, and you enter a paltry clapboard cottage, through—what is at least meant for—a splendid colonnade.

In the country through which I passed, the houses are nearly all of the class which may be called comfortable. The general scenery at a more favourrable season I can easily conceive to be pretty. The chief defect is the utter flimsiness of the houses, and the glaring effect arising from the too profuse use of the paint-brush. They are evidently not calculated to last above fifteen or twenty years, and this extreme fragility renders more glaring the absurdity of that profusion of gewgaw decoration in which the richer inhabitants delight to indulge.

The country is too new for a landscape painter. With variety of surface, and abundance of wood and water, an artist will certainly find many scenes worthy of his pencil, but the worm fences, and the freshness and regularity of the houses, are sadly destructive of the picturesque. Had the buildings been of more enduring materials, time, the beautifier, would have gradually mellowed down their hardness of outline, and diminished the unpleasant contrast which is here so obtrusively apparent between the works of man and those of nature. But at present there is no chance of this. Each generation builds for itself, and even the human frame is less perishable than the rickety and flimsy structures erected for its comfort.

The advantages of a country, however, are not to be measured by the degree of gratification it may administer to the taste or imagination of a traveller. Where plenty is in the cottage, it matters but little what figure it may make on the canvass of the painter. I have travelled in many countries, but assuredly never in any, where the materials of happiness were so widely and plentifully diffused as in

these New England States. And yet the people are
not happy, or if they be, there is no faith in Lavater.
Never have I seen countenances so furrowed by care
as those of this favoured people. Both soul and
body appear to have been withered up by the anxieties of life; and with all appliances of enjóyment
within their reach, it seems as if some strange curse
had gone forth against them, which said, " Ye shall
not enjoy." One looks in vain here for the ruddy
and jovial faces which in England meet us on every
hand. The full, broad, and muscular frame; the
bold serenity of aspect; the smile, the laugh, the song,
the dance,—let not a traveller seek these, or any indications of a light heart and a contented spirit in the
New England States.

Let me not, however, be misunderstood. The distinction I would draw is simply this. The Englishman has the inclination to be happy, though not
always the means of happiness at command. The
New Englander, with a thousand blessings, is deficient in what outvalues them all, the disposition to
enjoyment. He is *inter opes inops.*

Something of this misfortune, I have no doubt, is

attributable to climate, but I cannot help believing it in a great degree hereditary. The pilgrim fathers were certainly not men of a very enviable temperament. Full of spiritual pride, needy, bigoted, superstitious, ignorant and despising knowledge, intolerant, fleeing from persecution in the Old World, and yet bringing it with them to the New; such were the men to whom this people may trace many of their peculiarities. That they were distinguished by some of these qualities, was their misfortune; that they were marked by others, was their crime. They and their descendants spread through the wilderness, and solitude had not the effect of softening the asperities of faith or feeling. The spirit of social dependence became broken; and as ages passed on, and the increase of population, and the pursuits of gain, induced them to collect in masses, the towns and villages became peopled with men of solitary habits, relying on their own resources, and associating only for the purposes of gain. Such, doubtless, the New Englanders were; and such they are now, to the observation of a stranger, who is conscious of no temptation to misrepresent them.

The character of the New Englanders is a subject on which I confess I feel tempted to be prolix. In truth, it seems to me so singular and anomalous, so compounded of what is valuable and what is vile, that I never feel certain of having succeeded in expressing the precise combination of feeling which it inspires. As a philanthropist, I should wish them to be less grasping and more contented with the blessings they enjoy, and would willingly barter a good deal of vanity, and a little substantial knavery, for an additional infusion of liberal sentiment, and generous feeling.

Springfield is the seat of one of the chief arsenals and manufactories of arms in the United States. An officer of artillery was good enough to conduct me over these. Every thing seemed well managed, and the machinery at all points very complete. About twelve or thirteen thousand muskets are produced annually. My conductor was a particularly well-informed and obliging person, who had lately returned from Europe, where he had been sent to receive instruction in regard to the recent improvements in gunnery.

The officers of the United States army are better paid than the English. A captain receives about L.400 a-year, or about L.100 more than a lieutenant-colonel in our service. But there is this difference between the British army and that of the United States; no one can enter the latter for pleasure, or to enjoy the enviable privilege of wearing an epaulet and an embroidered coat. The service is one of real and almost constant privation. The troops are scattered about in forts and garrisons in remote and unhealthy situations, and are never quartered, as with us, in the great cities. The principal stations are on the Canadian and Indian frontiers, and on the Mississippi, and I imagine the sort of life they lead there would not be greatly relished by his Majesty's Coldstream Guards or the Blues. I confess I was rather surprised at the smallness of the United States army. It amounts only to 6000 men including all arms, and I was certainly not less astonished at the enormous proportion of desertions, which are no less than 1000 annually, or one-sixth of the whole numbers. Desertions in the British army do not exceed one in a hundred.

On the following day the snow was so deep as to render the road impassable for coaches, so with the thermometer fifteen degrees below zero, I took a sleigh for Hartford, where, after a journey of five hours, we were deposited in safety. Hartford is a small and apparently a very busy town on the Connecticut river. It is rather remarkable as being the seat of the celebrated convention, which, during the late war with Britain, threatened the dissolution of the Union.

I slept at Hartford. The inn was dirty, but this disadvantage was more than counterbalanced by its possession of an Irish waiter, to whom nothing was impossible, and who bustled about in my behalf with an activity and good-will which fortunately it was not difficult to repay. The stage for Newhaven did not start till late on the following day, and I had all the morning on my hands. What to make of it I did not know; so I wandered about the town, saw the College and the New Exchange Buildings, and a church, and a gaol, and a school, and the Charter Oak, and peeped into all the shops, and then returned to the inn with the assured conviction that

Hartford is one of the stupidest places on the surface of the globe.   I may as well, however, relate a circumstance which happened here, since it may perhaps throw some light on the New England character.

I had returned from my ramble, and was sitting near the stove in the public room, engaged in the dullest of all tasks, reading an American newspaper, when a woman and a girl, about ten years old, entered, cold and shivering, having just been discharged from a Boston stage-coach.   The woman was respectable in appearance, rather good-looking, and evidently belonging to what may in this country be called the middling class of society.   She immediately enquired at what hour the steam-boat set off for New York, and, on learning that owing to the river being frozen up, it started from Newhaven, some thirty miles lower, she was evidently much discomposed, and informed the landlord, that calculating on meeting the steam-boat that morning at Hartford, her pocket was quite unprepared for the expense of a further land journey, and the charges of different sorts necessarily occasioned by a day's delay on the road.

The landlord shrugged up his shoulders and walked off; the Irish waiter looked at her with something of a quizzical aspect, and an elderly gentleman, engaged like myself in reading a newspaper, raised his eyes for a moment, discharged his saliva on the carpet, and then resumed his occupation. Though evidently without a willing audience, the woman continued her complaints; informed us she had left her husband in Boston to visit her brother in New York; explained and re-explained the cause of her misfortune, and a dozen times at least concluded by an assurance,—of the truth of which the whole party were quite satisfied,—that she was sadly puzzled what to do.

In such circumstances, I know not whether it was benevolence, or a desire to put a stop to her detestable iteration, or a mingled motive compounded of both, that prompted me to offer to supply her with any money she might require. However, I did so, and the offer, though not absolutely refused, was certainly very ungraciously received. She stared at me, expressed no thanks, and again commenced the detail of her grievances, of which, repetition had something staled the infinite variety. I therefore left the apartment. Shortly after the sleigh for Newhaven drove up, and I had entirely forgotten the amiable sufferer and her pecuniary affliction, when she came up, and said, without any expression of civility, "You offered me money, I'll take it." I asked how much she wished. She answered, sixteen dollars, which I immediately ordered my servant to give her. Being a Scotchman, however, he took the prudent precaution of requesting her address in New York, and received a promise that the amount of her debt should be transmitted to Bunker's on the following day.

Weeks passed after my arrival in New York, and I heard no more either of the dollars or my fellow-traveller, and being curious to know whether I had been cheated, I at length sent to demand repayment. My servant came back with the money. He had seen the woman, who expressed neither thanks nor gratitude; and on being asked why she had violated her promise to discharge the debt, answered that she could not be at the trouble of sending the money, for she supposed it was my business to ask for it. It should be added, that the house in which she resided, was that of her brother, a respectable shop-keeper in one of the best streets in New York, whose establishment certainly betrayed no indication of poverty.

The truth is, that the woman was very far from being a swindler. She was only a Yankee, and troubled with an indisposition—somewhat endemic in New England—to pay money. She thought, perhaps, that a man who had been so imprudent as to lend to a stranger, might be so negligent as to forget to demand repayment. The servant might have lost her address; in short, it was better to take the chances, however small, of ultimately keeping the money, than to restore it unasked. All this might be very sagacious, but it certainly was not very high-principled or very honest.

It was late before we reached Newhaven, and the greater part of the journey was performed in the dark. The inn was so crowded, that the landlord told me fairly he could not give me a bed. I then requested a sofa and a blanket, but with no greater success. However, he proved better than his word. I was shown to a sort of dog-hole without plaster, which I verily believe was the dormitory of the black waiter, who was displaced on my account. The smell of the bed was most offensive, the sheets were dirty, and the coverlid had the appearance of an old horse-cloth. The only other furniture in the apartment was a table and a wooden chair; no glass, no washing-stand, no towels. These articles were promised in the morning, but they never came, though most importunately demanded. The heat of the crowded sitting-room was intense; the temperature of the bed-room was in the opposite extreme. At length, driven from the former, I wrapped myself in my cloak, and sought slumber on the filthy mass of flock from which its usual sable occupant had been expelled.

Cold weather and strong odours are not favourable to sleep. In about two hours I arose, and exploring my way to the sitting-room, now untenanted, passed the rest of the night in a chair by the fire. The steam-boat was to start at five in the morning, and at half past four several coaches drove up to convey the passengers to the quay. I saw nothing of Newhaven, and its associations in my memory are certainly far from pleasant. It was with satisfaction I reached the steam-boat, and bade farewell to it for ever.

The night concluded, however, more fortunately than it commenced. I procured a berth in the steam-boat, and was only roused from a comfortable snooze by the announcement of breakfast, and the clatter of knives and plates which immediately succeeded it. Under such circumstances, I had experience enough to know that no time was to be lost. There is a tide in the affairs of steam-passengers in America, which must be taken at the flood in order to lead either to breakfast or dinner. A minute, therefore, was enough to find me seated at the table, and contributing my strenuous efforts to the work of destruction. Breakfast was succeeded by the still greater luxury of basin and towel, and when I went on deck, a few whiffs of a cigar, and the fine scenery of Long Island Sound, had the effect of obliterating all trace of the disagreeables of the night.

The voyage was pleasant and prosperous; the weather, though still cold, was clear, and before day closed, I again found myself at New York.

CHAPTER IX.

NEW YORK.

On the day after my arrival at New York, the city was thrown into a bustle by the intelligence that a packet from Liverpool had been telegraphed in the offing.   Owing to the prevalence of contrary winds, an unusual period had elapsed without an arrival from Europe, and the whole population seemed agog for news.   I dined that day with a friend; and as there was no party, and we were both anxious to receive the earliest intelligence, he proposed our walking to the News-room, and afterwards returning to wine and the dessert.   On approaching the house, we found some thousands of people collected about the door, and in the window was exhibited a placard of the following import:—" Duke of Wellington and Ministry resigned; Lord Grey, Premier; Brougham, Lord Chancellor," &c.

It was impossible not to be struck with the extreme interest this intelligence excited. Here and there were groups of quidnuncs engaged in earnest discussion on the consequences of this portentous intelligence. Some anticipated immediate revolution; a sort of second edition of the Three Days of. Paris. Others were disposed to think that Revolution, though inevitable, would be more gradual. A third party looked forward to the speedy restoration of the Duke of Wellington to power. But all partook of the pervading excitement, and the sensation produced by these changes in the government, could scarcely have been greater in Liverpool than in New York.

On the last night of the year there was a public assembly, to which I received the honour of an invitation. The ball-rooms were very tolerable, but the entrance detestable. It led close past the bar of the City Hotel, and the ladies, in ascending the stair, which, by the by, was offensively dirty, must have been drenched with tobacco smoke. Within, how-

ever, I found assembled a great deal of beauty. At
seventeen, nothing can be prettier than a smiling
damsel of New York.   At twenty-two, the same
damsel, metamorphosed into a matron, has lost a good
deal of her attraction.   I had never been in so large
and miscellaneous a party before.   I looked about
for solecisms of deportment, but could detect none
on the part of the ladies.   There was, however, a
sort of *Transatlanticism* about them ; and even their
numerous points of resemblance to my fair countrywomen, had the effect of marking out certain shadowy differences, to be felt rather than described.

There was certainly an entire absence of what the
French call *l'air noble*,—of that look of mingled elegance and distinction which commands admiration
rather than solicits it. Yet the New York ladies are
not vulgar.   Far from it.   I mean only to say that
they are not precisely European ; and with the possession of so much that is amiable and attractive,
they may safely plead guilty to want of absolute
conformity to an arbitrary standard, the authority of
which they are not bound to acknowledge.

But what shall be said of the gentlemen ?   Why,

simply that a party of the new police, furnished
.orth with the requisite *toggery*, would have played
their part in the ball-room, with about as much
grace. There is a certain uncontrollable rigidity of
muscle about an American, and a want of sensibility
to the lighter graces of deportment, which makes
him perhaps the most unhopeful of all the votaries
of Terpsichore. In this respect the advantage is
altogether on the side of the ladies. Their motions
are rarely inelegant, and never grotesque. I leave it
to other travellers to extend this praise to the gentlemen.

An American dandy is a being *sui generis*. He has
probably travelled in Europe, and brought back to
his own country, a large stock of second-rate fopperies, rings, trinkets, and gold chains, which he
displays, evidently with full confidence in their
powers of captivation. For a season after his return
he is all the fashion. He suggests new improvements in quadrille dancing, and every flourish of his
toe becomes the object of sedulous imitation. Tailors
wait on him to request the privilege of inspecting his
wardrobe. His untravelled companions regard with

envy his profusion of jewellery and waistcoats of figured velvet. He talks of "Dukes and Earls, and all their sweeping train; and garters, stars and coronets, appear" in his conversation, as if such things had been familiar to him from his infancy. In short, he reigns for a time the *Magnus Apollo* of his native town, and his decrees in all matters of taste are received as the oracles of the god.

But time passes on. The traveller has returned to the vulgar drudgery of the counting-house; his coats, like his affectations, become threadbare, and are replaced by the more humble productions of native artists; later tourists have been the heralds of newer fashions and fopperies; his opinions are no longer treated with deference; he sinks to the level of other men, and the vulgar dandy is gradually changed into a plain American citizen, content with the comforts of life, without concerning himself about its elegancies.

The ball was very pleasant, and one of its chief *agrémens* undoubtedly was an excellent supper. The oyster-soup, a favourite dish in this part of the world, was all that Dr Kitchiner could have desired.

Turkey, ham, terrapin—a sort of land crab, on which I have not ventured—jellies, creams, ices, fruit, hot punch, and cold lemonade, were in profusion. Having afterwards remained to witness some badly danced quadrilles, and the perpetration of the first gallopade ever attempted on the American continent, I returned to take "my pleasure in mine inn."

It is the custom in New York, on the first day of the year, for the gentlemen to visit all their acquaintances; and the omission of this observance in regard to any particular family, would be considered as a decided slight. The clergy, also, hold a levee on this day, which is attended by their congregation. For my own part, I confess, I found the custom rather inconvenient, there being about thirty families, whose attentions rendered such an acknowledgment indispensable. Determined, however, to fail in nothing which could mark my sense of the kindness of my friends, I ordered a coach, and set forth at rather an early hour on this task of visit-paying.

The first person on whom I waited was Dr Wainwright, the clergyman of Gracechurch, in whose society I had often experienced much pleasure. I found him attired in full canonicals, with a table displaying a profusion of wine and cake, and busied in conversing and shaking hands with his parishioners. Having paid my compliments, I proceeded on my progress, and in the course of about four hours had the satisfaction of believing that I had discharged my duty, though not,—as I afterwards remembered, —without some omissions, which I trust my friends were good enough to forgive.

The routine is as follows : The ladies of a family remain at home to receive visits ; the gentlemen are abroad, actively engaged in paying them. You enter, shake hands, are seated, talk for a minute or two on the topics of the day, then hurry off as fast as you can. Wine and cake are on the table, of which each visitor is invited to partake. The custom is of Dutch origin, and, I believe, does not prevail in any other city of the Union. I am told its influence on the social intercourse of families, is very salutary. The first day of the year is considered a day of kindness and reconciliation, on which petty differences are forgotten, and trifling injuries forgiven. It sometimes happens, that between friends

5

long connected, a misunderstanding takes place. Each is too proud to make concessions, alienation follows, and thus are two families, very probably, permanently estranged. But on this day of annual amnesty, each of the offended parties calls on the wife of the other, kind feelings are recalled, past grievances overlooked, and at their next meeting they take each other by the hand, and are again friends.

In company with a most intelligent and kind friend, who was lately mayor of the city, I visited the Navy yard at Brooklyn. Commodore Chauncey, the commander, is a fine specimen of an old sailor of the true breed. He has a good deal of the *Benbow* about him, and one can read in his open and weatherbeaten countenance, that it has long braved both the battle and the breeze. He took us over several men-of-war, and a frigate yet on the stocks, which appeared the most splendid vessel of her class I had ever seen. American men-of-war are built chiefly of live oak, the finest and most durable material in the world.

Every thing in these navy yards is conducted with admirable judgment, for the plain reason, as the

Americans themselves assure me, that the management of the navy is a department in which the mob, everywhere else triumphant, never venture to interfere. There is good sense in this abstinence. The principles of government, which are applicable to a civil community, would make sad work in a man-of-war. The moment a sailor is afloat, he must cast the slough of democracy, and both in word and action cease to be a free man. Every ship is necessarily a despotism, and the existence of any thing like a deliberative body, is utterly incompatible with safety. The necessity of blind obedience is imperious, though it is not easy to understand how those accustomed to liberty and equality on shore, can readily submit to the rigours of naval discipline.

In the same excellent company I made the round of the most interesting public institutions of the city —the House of Refuge for juvenile delinquents, the Deaf and Dumb Asylum, and the Asylum for Lunatics. All are conducted with exemplary judgment, and benevolence exerted with an ardent but enlightened zeal for the general interests of humanity. The first of these institutions is particularly laudable, both as respects its objects and management. It is an asylum for juvenile offenders of both sexes, who, by being thrown into the depraved society of a common gaol, would, in all probability, grow up into hardened and incorrigible criminals. In this institution, they are taught habits of regular industry; are instructed in the principles of religion, and when dismissed, they enter the world with ample means at command of earning an honest livelihood.

The girls are generally bred up as sempstresses or domestic servants; and on quitting the institution, are uniformly sent to a part of the country, where their previous history is unknown. By this judicious arrangement they again start fair, with the full advantage of an unblemished character. The establishment seemed a perfect hive of industry. The taste and talent of the boys is consulted in the choice of a trade. There were young carpenters and blacksmiths, and tailors and brushmakers, and Lilliputian artificers of various kinds, all busily engaged in their peculiar handicraft. Though looking at the details of the establishment with a critical eye, I could detect no fault in any department. There can be no doubt, I think, that the benevolence to which this institution is indebted for its origin and support, is of the most enlightened kind.

I have not yet spoken of the political parties in this country, and, in truth, the subject is so complicated with opinions continually varying, and interests peculiar to particular districts, and includes the consideration of so many topics, apparently unconnected with politics altogether, that I now enter on it with little expectation of making it completely intelligible to an English reader.   Of course, all the world knows that the population of the Union is, or was, divided into two great parties, entitled Federalist and Republican.   These terms, however, by no means accurately express the differences which divide them.   Both parties are Federalist, and both Republican, but the former favour the policy of granting wider powers to the Federal legislature and executive; of asserting their control over the State governments; of guarding the Constitution against popular encroachment; in short, of strengthening the bonds of public union, and maintaining a presiding power of sufficient force and energy, to overawe turbulence at home, and protect the national honour and interests abroad.

The Democratic Republican, on the other hand, would enlarge to the utmost extent the political influence of the people. He is in favour of universal suffrage; a dependent judiciary; a strict and literal interpretation of the articles of the Constitution, and regards the Union simply as a voluntary league between sovereign and independent States, each of which possesses the inalienable right of deciding on the legality of the measures of the general government. The Federalist, in short, is disposed to regard the United States as one and indivisible, and the authority of the United government as paramount to every other jurisdiction. The Democrat considers the Union as a piece of mosaic, tesselated with stones of different colours, curiously put together, but possessing no other principle of cohesion than that of mutual convenience. The one regards the right of withdrawing from the national confederacy as indefeasible in each of its members; the other denies the existence of such right, and maintains the Federal government to be invested with the power of enforcing its decrees within the limits of the Union.

During the period succeeding the Revolution, New England, pre-eminent in wealth, population, and intelligence, gave her principles to the Union. The two first presidents were both Federalists, but their political opponents were rapidly increasing both in numbers and virulence, and even the services, the high name, and unsullied character of Washington, were not sufficient to protect him from the grossest and most slanderous attacks. Adams succeeded him, and certainly did something to merit the imputations which had been gratuitously cast on his predecessor. His sedition law was bad ; the prosecutions under it still worse, and in the very first struggle he was driven from office, to return to it no more.*

It is evident that a constitution, however precisely defined, must differ in its practical operation, ac-

---

* Carey in the Olive Branch mentions a prosecution under this act, in which a New Jersey man was tried and punished for expressing a desire, that the wadding of a gun discharged on a festival day, "had singed or otherwise inflicted damage on" a certain inexpressible part of Mr Adams! After such a prosecution, one is only tempted to regret that the efficiency of the wish was not equal to its patriotism.

cording to the principles on which it is administered. From the period of Jefferson's accession to power, a change in this respect took place. The government was then administered on democratic principles; a silent revolution was going forward; the principles, opinions, and habits of the people, all tended towards the wider extension of political rights; and at the conclusion of the war with England, the Federalists became at length convinced, that the objects for which they had so long strenuously been contending, were utterly unattainable. Farther contention, therefore, was useless. The name of Federalist had become odious to the people; it was heard no more. No candidate for public favour ventured to come forward and declare his conviction, that a government, which looked for support to the prejudices of the populace, was necessarily less secure and beneficial than one which represented the deliberate convictions of the wealthier and more enlightened.

The result of all this was, an apparent harmony of political principle throughout the Union. Open differences of opinion were no longer expressed, as to the broad and fundamental doctrines of government.

The ascendency of numbers, in opposition to that of property and intelligence, had been firmly established; the people, in the widest sense of the term, had been recognised as the only source of power and of honour; and the government, instead of attempting to control and regulate the passions and prejudices of the multitude, were forced, by the necessity of their situation, to adopt them as the guide and standard of their policy. They were compelled, in short, to adopt the measures, and profess the principles most palatable to the people, instead of those which wider knowledge and keener sagacity might indicate as most for their advantage.

I remember one of my first impressions in the United States was that of surprise, at the harmony in regard to the great principles of government, which seemed to pervade all classes of the community. In every thing connected with men and measures, however, all was clamour and confusion. The patriot of one company was the scoundrel of the next, and to an uninterested observer, the praise and the abuse seemed both to rest on a foundation too narrow to afford support to such disproportionate superstructures. Parties there evidently were, but it was not easy to become master of the distinctions on which they rested. I asked for the Federalists, and was told, that like the mammoth and the megatherion, they had become extinct, and their principles delighted humanity no longer. I asked for the Democrats, and I was desired to look on the countenance of every man I met in the street. This puzzled me, for the principles of this exploded party, appeared, in my deliberate conviction, to be those most in accordance with political wisdom, and I had little faith in the efficacy of sudden conversions, either in politics or religion.

In such circumstances, instead of attempting to grope my way to a conclusion, by any dark and doubtful hypothesis, I determined to demand information from those best calculated to afford it. I therefore explained my difficulties to one of the most eminent individuals of the Union, whom I knew at least to have been formerly a Federalist. "How comes it," I asked, "that the party which you formerly adorned by your talents and eloquence, is no longer to be found? Is it, that the progress of

events, increased experience, and more deliberate
and enlightened views, have induced you to relinquish your former tenets; or, that still entertaining
the same opinions, you are simply withheld by policy
from expressing them?" His answer—in substance
as follows—was too striking to be forgotten. " My
opinions, and I believe those of the party to which
I belonged, are unchanged; and the course of events
in this country has been such, as to impress only a
deeper and more thorough conviction of their wisdom. But, in the present state of public feeling, we
dare not express them. An individual professing
such opinions, would not only find himself excluded
from every office of public trust, within the scope of
his reasonable ambition, but he would be regarded
by his neighbours and fellow-citizens with an evil
eye. His words and actions would become the objects of jealous and malignant scrutiny, and he would
have to sustain the unceasing attacks of a host of
unscrupulous and ferocious assailants. And for what
object is his life to be thus embittered, and he is to
be cut off from the common objects of honourable
ambition? Why, for the satisfaction of expressing

his adherence to an obsolete creed, and his persuasion of the wisdom of certain doctrines of government, which his judgment assures him, are utterly impracticable in the present condition of society."

When the Americans do agree, therefore, their unanimity is really *not* very wonderful, seeing it proceeds from the observance of the good old rule, of punishing all difference of opinion. The consequence, however, has been, not the eradication of federal principles, but a discontinuance of their profession. The combatants fight under a new banner, but the battle is not less bitter on that account. There is no longer any question with regard to increase of power on the part of the general government; that has long since been decided; but the point of contention now is, whether it shall keep that authority with which it is at present understood to be invested. But even this substantial ground of difference is rarely brought prominently forward in debate. The struggle generally is with regard to particular measures, involving many collateral interests, but which are felt to have a tendency to one side or the other.

Thus one great subject of discussion relates to the

power of the government to expend a portion of the national funds in internal improvements. In 1830, a bill which had passed the legislature for the construction of a national road, was returned with the veto of the President. By the articles of the constitution, the federal legislature are invested with the power of " establishing post-offices and post-roads." The doubt is, whether the word *establish* gives the privilege to *construct*, or is to be understood as simply granting authority to convert into post-roads, thoroughfares already in existence. A principle of great importance is no doubt involved in this question, since by it must be decided whether the federal government have the power of adopting any general system of improvements, or of executing public works with a view to the national advantage. The existence of such a power would no doubt materially tend to strengthen its influence, and this, which is a recommendation with one party, constitutes the chief objection with the other. General Jackson is the leading champion on the one side; Mr Clay, his opponent for the Presidency, on the other. The latter is backed by the northern and a considerable portion of the Central States; the former by the Southern and Western.

There can be no doubt, I imagine, that the Federalists, in supporting the affirmative of this question, are influenced by the *tendency* of the opinions they advocate, to enlarge and strengthen the power of the executive, but the grounds on which they attempt to gain proselytes are entirely collateral. They urge the general expediency of such a power; the impossibility of inducing the legislatures of the different States to concur heartily in any one project for the benefit of the whole; the necessity of unity of execution, as well as unity of design; and the probability, that if such improvements are not undertaken by the federal government, they will never be executed at all.

Of course, such questions as the Tariff, and that of which I have just spoken, are not exclusively decided by political principle. Private interest steps in; many of the democratic party adopt the views of their opponents on some single question of policy, and where that is of great importance, range themselves under the same banner. Thus, a candidate for

Congress is often supported by men differing on many questions, and agreeing only in one. Commercial men are usually in favour of the system of internal improvements, because these must generally bring with them increased facilities for commerce. A new road may open a new market; the deepening of a harbour may change the whole aspect of a province; and those, who by their local position or pursuits are more immediately interested in these benefits, may be pardoned, if, on an occasion of such moment, they lay aside their principles, and act on the narrower and stronger motive of personal advantage.

In a country of such extraordinary extent as the United States, there are of course a vast number of local interests, which modify the application of theoretical principle. In the representative of each district, some peculiarity of creed is commonly necessary to secure the support of his constituents. Conformity on leading points of opinion is not enough; there is almost always some topic, however unconnected with politics, on which coincidence of sentiment is demanded. I may quote a striking instance of this in the State of New York.

Some years ago a man of the name of Morgan, who wrote a book revealing the secrets of Free-Masonry, was forcibly seized in his own dwelling-house, carried off, and murdered. Of the latter fact there is no direct proof, but it is impossible to account for the circumstances on any other supposition. He is known to have been conveyed to the neighbourhood of Niagara, and there is evidence of his having passed a night there; but from that period to the present, no traces of the unfortunate man have ever been discovered. Of course the vigilance of justice was aroused by this outrage. The public prosecutor was long unsuccessful in his attempts to bring the criminals to trial. At length, however, strong circumstantial evidence was obtained, which went to fix participation in the crime on two individuals. They were brought to trial. A majority of the jury had no doubt of their guilt, but the minority thought otherwise, and the men were acquitted.

The circumstance of the jurymen who procured the acquittal being Free-Masons, contributed to inflame the public indignation, already strongly excited by the original outrage. The principles of this secret society had not only caused crime to be committed, but justice to be denied. Unquestionably Free-Masonry had given rise to murder, and as unquestionably, in the opinion of many, its influence had secured impunity to the offenders. The question thus arose,—is a society which produces such consequences to be tolerated in a Christian community? A large portion of the people banded together in hostility to all secret and affiliated societies. They pronounced them dangerous and unconstitutional, and pledged themselves to exert their utmost efforts for their suppression.

The Masons, on the other hand, were a widely ramified and powerful body, embracing in their number nearly half the population of the State. Their constitution gave them the advantage of unity of purpose and of action. The keenness of contest, of course, excited the passions of both parties. The public press ranged itself on different sides; every candidate for office was compelled to make confession of his creed on this important subject, and to fight under the banner of one party or the other; and the distinction of Mason or Anti-Mason superseded, if it did not extinguish, those arising from differences more legitimately political. In the late elections the Masonic party were triumphant; but the struggle is still carried on with vigour, and there is no doubt that the votes in the next presidential election will be materially affected by it. Indeed the mania on this subject is daily spreading. It was at first exclusively confined to the State of New York; it is now becoming diffused over the New England States and Pennsylvania.

It is such collateral influences which puzzle an Englishman, when he attempts to become acquainted with the state of parties in this country. He looks for the broad distinction of political principle, and he finds men fighting about Masonry, or other matters which have no apparent bearing on the great doctrines of government. He finds general opinions modified by local interests, and seeks in vain to discover some single and definite question which may serve as a touchstone of party distinctions. It is only by acute and varied observation, and by conversation with enlightened men of all parties, that he is enabled to make due allowance for the variations of the political compass, and judge accurately of the course which the vessel is steering.

The Americans have a notion that they are a people not easily understood, and that to comprehend their character requires a long apprenticeship of philosophical observation, and more both of patience and liberality than are usually compatible with the temper and prejudices of foreign travellers. This is a mistake. The peculiarities of the Americans lie more on the surface than those of any people I have ever known. Their features are broad and marked; there exists little individual eccentricity of character, and it is in their political relations alone that they are difficult to be understood. One fact, however, is confessed by all parties, that the progress of democratic principles from the period of the Revolution has been very great. During my whole residence in the United States, I conversed with no enlightened American, who did not confess, that the constitution now, though the same in letter with that established in 1789, is essentially different in spirit. It was undoubtedly

the wish of Washington and Hamilton to counterpoise, as much as circumstances would permit, the
rashness of democracy by the caution and wisdom
of an aristocracy of intelligence and wealth.   There
is now no attempt at counterpoise.   The weight is
all in one scale, and how low, by continued increase
of pressure, it is yet to descend, would require a
prophet of some sagacity to foretell.   I shall state a
few circumstances which may illustrate the progress
and tendency of opinion among the people of New
York.

In that city a separation is rapidly taking place
between the different orders of society.   The operative class have already formed themselves into a
society, under the name of " *The Workies*," in direct
opposition to those who, more favoured by nature or
fortune, enjoy the luxuries of life without the necessity of manual labour.   These people make no secret
of their demands, which to do them justice are few
and emphatic.   They are published in the newspapers, and may be read on half the walls of New
York.   Their first postulate is " EQUAL AND UNI-
VERSAL EDUCATION."   It is false, they say, to main-

tain that there is at present no privileged order, no practical aristocracy, in a country where distinctions of education are permitted. That portion of the population whom the necessity of manual labour cuts off from the opportunity of enlarged acquirement, is in fact excluded from all the valuable offices of the State. As matters are now ordered in the United States, these are distributed exclusively among one small class of the community, while those who constitute the real strength of the country, have barely a voice in the distribution of those loaves and fishes, which they are not permitted to enjoy. There does exist then—they argue—an aristocracy of the most odious kind,—an aristocracy of knowledge, education, and refinement, which is inconsistent with the true democratic principle of absolute equality. They pledge themselves, therefore, to exert every effort, mental and physical, for the abolition of this flagrant injustice. They proclaim it to the world as a nuisance which must be abated, before the freedom of an American be something more than a mere empty boast. They solemnly declare that they will not rest satisfied, till every citizen in the United

States shall receive the same degree of education, and start fair in the competition for the honours and the offices of the state. As it is of course impossible —and these men know it to be so—to educate the labouring class to the standard of the richer, it is their professed object to reduce the latter to the same mental condition with the former; to prohibit all supererogatory knowledge; to have a maximum of acquirement beyond which it shall be punishable to go.

But those who limit their views to the mental degradation of their country, are in fact the MODE-RATES of the party. There are others who go still further, and boldly advocate the introduction of an AGRARIAN LAW, and a periodical division of property. These unquestionably constitute the *extrême gauche* of the Worky Parliament, but still they only follow out the principles of their less violent neighbours, and eloquently dilate on the justice and propriety of every individual being equally supplied with food and clothing; on the monstrous iniquity of one man riding in his carriage while another walks on foot, and after his drive discussing a bottle of

Champagne, while many of his neighbours are shamefully compelled to be content with the pure element. Only equalize property, they say, and neither would drink Champagne or water, but both would have brandy, a consummation worthy of centuries of struggle to attain.

All this is nonsense undoubtedly, nor do I say that this party, though strong in New York, is yet so numerous or so widely diffused as to create immediate alarm. In the elections, however, for the civic offices of the city, their influence is strongly felt; and there can be no doubt that as population becomes more dense, and the supply of labour shall equal, or exceed the demand for it, the strength of this party must be enormously augmented. Their ranks will always be recruited by the needy, the idle and the profligate, and like a rolling snowball it will gather strength and volume as it proceeds, until at length it comes down thundering with the force and desolation of an avalanche.

This event may be distant, but it is not the less certain on that account. It is nothing to say, that the immense extent of fertile territory yet to be occupied by an unborn population will delay the day of ruin. It will delay, but it cannot prevent it. The traveller, at the source of the Mississippi, in the very heart of the American Continent, may predict with perfect certainty, that however protracted the wanderings of the rivulet at his foot, it must reach the ocean at last. In proportion as the nearer lands are occupied, it is very evident that the region to which emigration will be directed must of necessity be more distant. The pressure of population therefore will continue to augment in the Atlantic States, and the motives to removal become gradually weaker. Indeed, at the present rate of extension, the circle of occupied territory must before many generations be so enormously enlarged, that emigration will be confined wholly to the Western States. Then, and not till then, will come the trial of the American constitution ; and until that trial has been passed, it is mere nonsense to appeal to its stability.

Nor is this period of trial apparently very distant. At the present ratio of increase, the population of the United States doubles itself in about twenty-four years, so that in half a century it will amount to about fifty millions, of which ten millions will be slaves, or at all events a degraded caste, cut off from all the rights and privileges of citizenship. Before this period it is very certain that the pressure of the population, on the means of subsistence, especially in the Atlantic States, will be very great. The price of labour will have fallen, while that of the necessaries of life must be prodigiously enhanced. The poorer and more suffering class, will want the means of emigrating to a distant region of unoccupied territory. Poverty and misery will be abroad; the great majority of the people will be without property of any kind, except the thews and sinews with which God has endowed them; they will choose legislators under the immediate pressure of privation; and if in such circumstances, any man can anticipate security of property, his conclusion must be founded, I suspect, rather on the wishes of a sanguine temperament, than on any rational calculation of probabilities.

It is the present policy of the government to encourage and stimulate the premature growth of a manufacturing population. In this it will not be

2

successful, but no man can contemplate the vast internal resources of the United States,—the varied productions of their soil,—the unparalleled extent of river communication,—the inexhaustible stores of coal and iron which are spread even on the surface, —and doubt that the Americans are destined to become a great manufacturing nation. Whenever increase of population shall have reduced the price of labour to a par with that in other countries, these advantages will come into full play; the United States will then meet England on fair terms in every market of the world, and in many branches of industry at least, will very probably attain an unquestioned superiority. Huge manufacturing cities will spring up in various quarters of the Union, the population will congregate in masses, and all the vices incident to such a condition of society will attain speedy maturity. Millions of men will depend for subsistence on the demand for a particular manufacture, and yet this demand will of necessity be liable to perpetual fluctuation. When the pendulum vibrates in one direction, there will be an influx of wealth and prosperity; when it vibrates in the other, misery, discontent, and turbulence will spread through the land. A change of fashion, a war, the glut of a foreign market, a thousand unforeseen and inevitable accidents are liable to produce this, and deprive multitudes of bread, who but a month before were enjoying all the comforts of life. Let it be remembered that in this suffering class will be practically deposited the whole political power of the state; that there can be no military force to maintain civil order, and protect property; and to what quarter, I should be glad to know, is the rich man to look for security, either of person or fortune?

There will be no occasion however for convulsion or violence. The *Worky* convention will only have to choose representatives of their own principles, in order to accomplish a general system of spoliation, in the most legal and constitutional manner. It is not even necessary that a majority of the federal legislature should concur in this. It is competent to the government of each state to dispose of the property within their own limits as they think proper, and whenever a *numerical* majority of the people shall be in favour of an Agrarian law, there exists no counteracting influence to prevent, or even to retard its adoption.

I have had the advantage of conversing with many of the most eminent Americans of the Union on the future prospects of their country, and I certainly remember none who did not admit that a period of trial, such as that I have ventured to describe, is according to all human calculation inevitable. Many of them reckoned much on education as a means of safety, and unquestionably in a country where the mere power of breathing carries with it the right of suffrage, the diffusion of sound knowledge is always essential to the public security. It unfortunately happens, however, that in proportion as poverty increases, not only the means but the desire of instruction are necessarily diminished. The man whose whole energies are required for the supply of his bodily wants, has neither time nor inclination to concern himself about his mental deficiencies, and the result of human experience does not warrant us in reckoning on the restraint of individual cupidity, where no obstacle exists to its gratification, by any deliberate calculation of its consequences on society.   There can be no doubt, that if men could be made wise enough to act on an enlarged and enlightened view of their own interest, government might be dispensed with altogether; but what statesman would legislate on the probability of such a condition of society, or rely on it as a means of future safety?

The general answer, however, is, that the state of things which I have ventured to describe, is very distant.   "It is enough," they say, "for each generation to look to itself, and we leave it to our descendants some centuries hence to take care of their interests as we do of ours.   We enjoy all manner of freedom and security under our present constitution, and really feel very little concern about the evils which may afflict our posterity."   I cannot help believing, however, that the period of trial is somewhat less distant than such reasoners comfort themselves by imagining; but if the question be conceded that democracy necessarily leads to anarchy and spoliation, it does not seem that the mere length of road to be travelled is a point of much importance.   This, of course, would vary according to the peculiar circumstances of every country in which the experiment might be tried. In England the journey would be performed with railway velocity. In the United States, with the great advantages they possess, it may continue a generation or two longer, but the termination is the same. The doubt regards time, not destination.

At present the United States are perhaps more safe from revolutionary contention than any other country in the world. But this safety consists in one circumstance alone. *The great majority of the people are possessed of property ;* have what is called a stake in the hedge ; and are therefore, by interest, opposed to all measures which may tend to its insecurity. It is for such a condition of society that the present constitution was framed ; and could this great bulwark of prudent government, be rendered as permanent as it is effective, there could be no assignable limit to the prosperity of a people so favoured. But the truth is undeniable, that as population increases, another state of things must necessarily arise, and one unfortunately never dreamt of in the philosophy of American legislators. The majority of the people will then consist of men without property of any kind, subject to the immediate pressure of want, and then will be decided the great struggle between property and numbers; on the one side hunger, rapacity, and physical power; reason, justice, and helplessness on the other. The weapons of this fearful contest are already forged; the hands will soon be born that are to wield them. At all events, let no man appeal to the stability of the American government as being established by experience, till this trial has been overpast. Forty years are no time to test the permanence, or, if I may so speak, the vitality of a constitution, the immediate advantages of which are strongly felt, and the evils latent and comparatively remote.

It may be well to explain, that what I have hitherto said has rather been directed to the pervading democracy of the institutions of the different States than to the federal government. Of the latter it is difficult to speak, because it is difficult to ascertain with any precision, the principles on which it is founded. I think it was a saying of Lord Eldon, that there was no act of Parliament so carefully worded that he could not drive a coach and six through it. The American lawyers have been at least equally successful with regard to their federal constitution. No man appears precisely to understand what it is, but all agree that it is something very wise. It is a sort of political gospel, in which every man finds a reflection of his own prejudices and opinions. Ask a New England statesman what is the constitution, and he will tell you something very different from a Georgian or South Carolinian. Even the halls of Congress yet echo with loud and bitter disputation as to the primary and fundamental principle on which it is based. Ask the President of the United States, what is the nature of the government he administers with so much honour to himself and advantage to his country, and General Jackson will tell you that it is a government of *consolidation*, possessing full power to enforce its decrees in every district of the Union. Ask the Vice-president, and he will assure you that the government is merely *confederative*, and depends for its authority on the free consent of the individual States. Ask Mr Clay or Mr Webster what are the powers of this apparently unintelligible constitution, and they will probably include in their number the privilege of taxing at discretion the commerce of the country, and expending the money so raised in projects of internal improvement. Put the same question to General Hayne or Mr Van Buren, and they will assert that such doctrine is of the most injurious tendency, and proceeds altogether on a false interpretation; and yet all will agree that the federal constitution is the highest, most perspicuous, and faultless achievement of human legislation! It may be so, but till this masterpiece of polity becomes something more definite and intelligible, a foreigner may perhaps be excused for holding his admiration in abeyance.

At all events, it is abundantly clear, that the seeds of discord are plentifully scattered throughout the Union. Men of different habits, different interests, different modes of thought; the inhabitants of different climates, and agreeing only in mutual antipathy, are united under a common government, whose powers are so indefinite as to afford matter for interminable and rancorous disputation. Does such a government bear the impress of permanence? Or does it not rather seem, in its very structure, to concentrate all the scattered elements of decay?

When we contemplate the political relations of this singular people, the question naturally arises whether unity of government be compatible with great diversities of interest in the governed. There may possibly be reasoners who are prepared to answer this question in the affirmative, and to these we may look for instruction as to the advantages such a government as that of the United States possesses over others of smaller extent, and therefore capable of closer adaptation to the peculiar wants and interests of a people. To me it certainly appears that there can be no firm adhesion without homogeneity in a population. Let men once feel that their interests are the same; that they are exposed to the same dangers; solicitous for the same objects, partaking of the same advantages, and connected by some reasonable degree of geographical propinquity, and in such a community there is no fear of separation or dismemberment. The population in such circumstances forms one uniform and firmly-concatenated

whole, whereas a Union on other principles re-
sembles that of a bag of sand, in which the separate
particles, though held together for a time, retain
their original and abstract individuality.

Let us look for a moment at this Union. In
Florida and Louisiana they grow sugar; in Maine
there is scarcely sun enough to ripen a crop of maize.
The people of these States are no less different than
the productions of their soil. They are animated by
no sentiment of brotherhood and affinity. Nature has
divided them by a distance of two thousand miles;
the interests of one are neither understood nor cared
for in the other. In short, they are connected by
nothing but a clumsy and awkward piece of machinery most felicitously contrived to deprive both of
the blessing of self-government. What is gained by
this? A certain degree of strength, undoubtedly,
but not more than might be produced by an alliance
between independent States, unaccompanied by that
jealousy and conflict of opposing interests, which is
the present curse of the whole Union.

I remember, when at Washington, stating my impressions on this subject to a distinguished mem-

ber of the House of Representatives, who admitted that the ends of good government would most probably be better and more easily attainable were the Union divided into several republics, firmly united for purposes of defence, but enjoying complete legislative independence. " And yet," he continued, " the scheme could not possibly succeed. The truth is, the Union is necessary to prevent us from cutting each other's throats." Nor is this to be considered as the singular opinion of some eccentric individual. I have often conversed on the subject with men of great intelligence in different parts of the Union, and found a perfect harmony of opinion as to the results of separation. The northern gentlemen, in particular, seemed to regard the federal government as the ark of their safety from civil war and bloodshed. In such circumstances it might charitably be wished, that their ark was a stronger seaboat, and better calculated to weather the storms to which it is likely to be exposed.

In truth, every year must increase the perils of this federal constitution. Like other bubbles, it is at any time liable to burst, and the world will then

discover that its external glitter covered nothing but
wind. It may split to-morrow on the Tariff question, or it may go on, till, like a dropsical patient, it
dies of mere extension, when its remains will probably be denied even the decent honours of Christian
burial. It was near giving up the ghost at the time
of the Hartford Convention, and is now in a state of
grievous suffering from the Carolina fever. It will
probably survive this attack as it did the former,
since the great majority of the States are at present
in favour of its continuance. But, with the prevalence of the doctrine of nullification, it is impossible it can ever gain much strength or vigour. If
each State is to have the privilege of sitting in
judgment on the legality of its measures, the range
of its legislation must necessarily be very confined. It will puzzle the ingenuity of American
statesmen, to discover some policy which will prove
palatable to the various members of the Union, and
which all interpreters of the Constitution will confess to be within the narrow limits of its power.

Let us suppose in England that every county asserted the privilege of nullifying, when it thought

proper, the acts of the British Parliament. Leicestershire would summon her population in convention to resist any reduction of the foreign wool-duty. Kent and Surry would nullify the hop-duty. Lay a rude finger on kelp, and a distant threat of separation would be heard from the Orkneys. Dorset and Wilts would insist on the continuance of the corn-laws, and woe to the Chancellor of the Exchequer who should venture to raise the Highland war-slogan by an impost on horned cattle ! Yet in Great Britain there exist no provincial jealousies, and the interests of the whole kingdom are far more intimately amalgamated than can ever be the case in the United States.

Amid the multitude of events which threaten the dissolution of the Union, I may venture to specify one. The influence of each State in the election of the President is in the exact ratio of the amount of its population. In this respect the increase in some States is far greater than in others. The unrivalled advantages of New York have already given it the lead, and the same causes must necessarily still continue to augment its comparative superiority. Ohio—,

a State also rich in natural advantages—has recently been advancing with astonishing rapidity, and the
time is apparently not far distant when three States
(New York, Pennsylvania, and Ohio) must possess
a numerical majority of the whole population, and of
course the power of electing the President, independently of the other twenty-one States.   Will the
States thus virtually excluded, tamely submit to
this, or will they appeal to Congress for an amendment of the constitution ? There can be no prospect
of redress from this quarter.   The same superiority
of population which gave those three States the
power of electing the President, has of course also
given them the majority of the House of Representatives, and no amendment of the constitution can take
place without the concurrence of two-thirds of both
houses.   Besides, the principle of election by numerical majority is fundamental throughout the Union,
and could not be abrogated without a total violation
of consistency.   It does appear, therefore, that in no
great distance of time the whole substantial influence of the federal government may be wielded by
three States, and that whenever these choose to com-

bine, it will be in their power to carry any measure, however obnoxious, to the rest of the Union. The Senate, it is true, which consists of delegates in equal number from each State, would be free from this influence, but in any struggle with the more popular house, it must of course prove the weaker party, and be compelled to yield.

Those know little of the character of the American people, who imagine that the great majority of the States would tolerate being reduced to the condition of political ciphers. Their jealousy of each other is very great, and there can be no doubt, that should the contingency here contemplated occur, it must occasion a total disruption of the bonds of union. I believe it is the probability of such an event, joined to the apprehension of some interference with the condition of the slave population, which makes the people of the Southern States so anxious to narrow the power of the general government. At all events, it will be singular indeed if the seeds of civil broil, disseminated in a soil so admirably fitted to bring them to maturity, should not

its exercise. In densely peopled countries the test of property in reference to moral qualities is fallible, —perhaps too fallible to be relied on with much confidence. In the United States it is *unerring*, or at least the possible exceptions are so few, and must arise from circumstances so peculiar, that it is altogether unnecessary they should find any place in the calculations of a statesman. But American legislators have thought proper to cast away this inestimable advantage. Seeing no immediate danger in the utmost extent of suffrage, they were content to remain blind to the future. They took every precaution that the rights of the poor man should not be encroached on by the rich, but never seem to have contemplated the possibility that the rights of the latter might be violated by the former. American protection, like Irish reciprocity, was all on one side. It was withheld where most needed ; it was profusely lavished where there was no risk of danger. They put a sword in the hand of one combatant, and took the shield from the arm of the other.

The leader who gave the first and most powerful

impulse to the democratic tendencies of the constitution was unquestionably Jefferson. His countrymen call him great, but in truth he was great only when compared with those by whom he was surrounded. In brilliance and activity of intellect he was inferior to Hamilton; but Hamilton in heart and mind was an aristocrat, and too honourable and too proud to shape his political course to catch the flitting gales of popular favour. Death, fortunately for Jefferson, removed the only rival, by whom his reputation coul dhave been eclipsed, or his political principles successfully opposed. Adams he encountered and overthrew. Federalism, never calculated to secure popular favour, dwindled on, till in the termination of the late war it received its death-blow, and the democratic party remained undisputed lords of the ascendant.

We seek in vain in the writings of Jefferson for indications of original or profound thought. When in France, he had been captivated by that shallow philosophy of which Diderot and Condorcet were the apostles, and he returned to America, the zealous partisan of opinions, which no subsequent experience could induce him to relinquish or modify. During by far the greater portion of his life, the intellect of Jefferson remained stationary. Time passed on ; generations were gathered to their fathers ; the dawn of liberty on the continent of Europe had terminated in a bloody sunset ; but the shadow on the dial of his mind remained unmoved. In his correspondence we find him to the very last, complacently putting forth the stale and flimsy dogmas, which, when backed by the guillotine, had passed for unanswerable in the Jacobin coteries of the Revolution.

The mind of Jefferson was essentially unpoetical. In his whole works there is no trace discoverable of imaginative power. His benevolence was rather topical than expansive. It reached France, but never ventured across the channel. Had Napoleon invaded England, the heart and prayers of Jefferson would have followed him in the enterprise. He would have gloated over her fallen palaces, her conflagrated cities, her desolate fields. Her blood, her sufferings, her tears, the glorious memory of her past achievements, would in him have excited no feeling of compassionate regret. Jefferson had little enthusiasm

of character.   Nor was he rich in those warm charities and affections, in which great minds are rarely
deficient.   He has been truly called a good hater.
His resentments were not vehement and fiery ebul-
litions, burning fiercely for a time, and then subsi-
ding into indifference or dislike.   They were cool,
fiendlike, and ferocious ; unsparing, undying, unap-
peaseable. The enmities of most men terminate with
the death of their object.   It was the delight of Jefferson to trample even on the graves of his political
opponents.   The manner in which he speaks of
Hamilton in his correspondence, and the charges by
which he vainly attempts to blast his reputation, will
attach an indelible tarnish to his own memory.   He
never forgave the superior confidence which Washington reposed in the wisdom and integrity of Hamilton.   The only amiable feature in the whole life
of Jefferson was his reconciliation with Adams, and
there the efficient link was community of hatred.
Both detested Hamilton.

The moral character of Jefferson was repulsive.
Continually puling about liberty, equality, and the
degrading curse of slavery, he brought his own chil-

dren to the hammer, and made money of his debaucheries. Even at his death, he did not manumit his numerous offspring, but left them, soul and body, to degradation, and the cart-whip. A daughter of Jefferson was sold some years ago, by public auction, at New Orleans, and purchased by a society of gentlemen, who wished to testify, by her liberation, their admiration of the statesman,

" Who dreamt of freedom in a slave's embrace."

This single line gives more insight to the character of the man, than whole volumes of panegyric. It will outlive his epitaph, write it who may.

Jefferson was succeeded by Madison, a mere reflex of his political opinions. If he wanted the harsher points of Jefferson's character, he wanted also its vigour. The system he pursued was indistinguishable from that of his predecessor, and during his Presidency the current of democracy flowed on with increased violence and velocity. Munroe came next, and becoming at length aware of the prevailing tendencies of the constitution, was anxious to steer a middle course. He organized a piebald cabinet, composed of men of different opinions, and the result of their conjunction was a sort of hybrid policy, half federalist and half democratic, which gave satisfaction to no party.

At the termination of Mr Monroe's second period of office, Mr John Quincy Adams became his successor, by a sort of electioneering juggle which occasioned a universal sentiment of disgust. What the principles of this statesman were, or are, seems a matter not very intelligible to his own countrymen, and of course is still less so to a foreigner. All that is necessary to be known is, that at the expiration of four years Mr Quincy Adams was turned out to the great satisfaction of the whole Union, and that though he still continues in the healthy enjoyment of all corporeal and mental functions, there is assuredly no chance that he will ever again be promoted to any office of political trust and importance.

General Jackson, the present President, has always been an eminent member of the democratic party. His accession to office however, united to the experience of a long life, is understood to have induced a change in some of his opinions, and a modification of others. His policy is as moderate as the circumstances of the times will permit. On the Tariff question his opinions are not precisely known, but he decidedly opposes the application of the public money, under direction of the federal government, to projects of internal improvement.

General Jackson was certainly indebted for his present elevation, to the reputation he acquired in the successful defence of New Orleans. In truth, I believe his popularity is rather military than political, since even those—and they are many—who dislike him as a politician, extol him as the first general of the age, whose reputation beggars the fame of the most celebrated modern strategists.

It is excusable to smile at this, but scarcely fair to visit it with the severity of ridicule. New Orleans, —for want of a better,—is the American Waterloo; and while the loss to England occasioned by this disaster is a fixed quantity neither to be increased nor diminished, why should we object to the display of a little harmless vanity, or demand that our successful opponents should measure the extent of their achievement rather by our standard than by their own?

When talking of American statesmen, I may as well detail a few circumstances connected with one, who has certainly played a very conspicuous part in the politics of his country. I allude to the celebrated Colonel Burr, formerly Vice-President of the United States, and who, in 1800, was within a vote of becoming President in opposition to Jefferson and Adams. It is well known, that strong political differences with General Hamilton, embittered by a good deal of personal dislike, led to a duel, in which Hamilton lost his life. To this misfortune is attributable the entire ruin of Colonel Burr's prospects as a statesman. Hamilton was admired by all parties, and the voice of lamentation was heard from the whole Union on the premature extinction of the highest intellect of the country. There arose a general and powerful feeling of indignation against the author of this national calamity; but Burr was not a man to shrink from the pelting of any tempest, however vehement. He braved its violence, but at once knew that his popularity was gone for ever.

Subsequently he was concerned in some conspiracy to sieze on part of Mexico, of which he was to become sovereign, by the style and title—I suppose—of Aaron the First, King or Emperor of the Texas. Colonel Burr was likewise accused of treason to the commonwealth, in attempting to overthrow the constitution by force of arms. But a veil of mystery hangs around this portion of American history. I have certainly read a great deal about it, and left off nearly as wise as when I began. A conspiracy of some sort did undoubtedly exist. Preparations were in progress to collect an armament on the Ohio, and there was some rumour of its descending the Mississippi and seizing on New Orleans. Some of Burr's followers were tried, but—unless my memory deceives me—acquitted. At all events, materials could not be discovered for the conviction of the Great Catiline, whose projects, whether defensible or not, were original, and indicative of the fearless character of the man.

His acquittal, however, by two juries, was not sufficient to establish his innocence in the opinion of his countrymen. He was assailed by hatred and

execration; his name was made a by-word for every
thing that was odious in morals, and unprincipled in
politics. It was under such circumstances that Burr
became an exile from his country for several years.
During that period he visited England, where he
attracted the jealous observation of the ministry,
and his correspondence with France being more frequent than was quite agreeable, and of a cast somewhat too political, he received a polite invitation
to quit the country with the least possible delay.
Colonel Burr now lives in New York, secluded from
society, where his great talents and extensive professional knowledge, still gain him some employment as a consulting lawyer.

A friend of mine at New York enquired whether
I should wish an interview with this distinguished
person. I immediately answered in the affirmative,
and a note was addressed to Colonel Burr, requesting permission to introduce me. The answer contained a polite assent, and indicated an hour when
his avocations would permit his having sufficient
leisure for the enjoyment of conversation. At the
time appointed, my friend conveyed me to a house

in one of the poorer streets of the city. The Colonel received us on the landing place, with the manners of a finished courtier, and led the way to his little library, which—judging from the appearance of the volumes—was principally furnished with works connected with the law.

In person, Colonel Burr is diminutive, and I was much struck with the resemblance he bears to the late Mr Percival. His physiognomy is expressive of strong sagacity. The eye keen, penetrating, and deeply set; the forehead broad and prominent; the mouth small, but disfigured by the ungraceful form of the lips; and the other features, though certainly not coarse, were irreconcilable with any theory of beauty. On the whole, I have rarely seen a more remarkable countenance. Its expression was highly intellectual, but I imagined I could detect the lines of strong passion mingled with those of deep thought. The manners of Colonel Burr are those of a highly bred gentleman. His powers of conversation are very great, and the opinions he expresses on many subjects marked by much shrewdness and originality.

When in England he had become acquainted with many of the Whig leaders, and I found him perfectly versed in every thing connected with our national politics.

It would be an unwarrantable breach of the confidence of private life, were I to publish any particulars of the very remarkable conversation I enjoyed with this eminent person. I shall, therefore, merely state, that having encroached perhaps too long, both on the time and patience of Colonel Burr, I bade him farewell, with sincere regret that a career of public life, which had opened so brilliantly, should not have led to a more fortunate termination.

CHAPTER X.

PHILADELPHIA.

On the 8th of January I again bade farewell to New York, and embarked on board of a New Brunswick steamer on my way to Philadelphia. Our course lay up the Raritan river, which has nothing interesting to display in point of scenery, and the morning being raw and gusty, the voyage was not particularly agreeable. It occupied about four hours, and on reaching Brunswick we found a cavalcade of nine stage-coaches, drawn up for the accommodation of the passengers. In these we were destined to cross the country between the Raritan and Delaware, which forms part of the State of New Jersey. In theory nothing could be easier than this journey. The distance was only twenty-seven miles;

and in a thoroughfare so much travelled as that between the two great cities of the Union, it was at least not probable that travellers would be subjected to much inconvenience.

But theory and experience were at variance in this case, as in many others. We changed coaches at every stage, and twice had the whole baggage of the party to be unpacked and reloaded. The road was detestable; the jolting even worse than what I had suffered on my journey from Providence to Boston. For at least half the distance the coach was axle-deep in mud, and once it fairly stuck in a rut, and might have continued sticking till doomsday, had the passengers not dismounted to lighten the vehicle. I enquired the reason of the disgraceful neglect of this important line of communication, and was answered, that as it was intended at some future period to have a railway, it would be mere folly to go to any expense in repairing it. Thus are this intelligent people content to sacrifice a great present benefit, to a mere speculative, and probably remote contingency.

The scenery through which our route lay was devoid of beauty, and the soil wretchedly poor. The whole country had evidently at one time been under cultivation, but in much of it the plough had long ceased from labour, and the forest had already resumed its ancient rights. The weather added to the bleakness of the landscape, and though the coach crept on with the velocity of a tortoise, it was not till long after dark that we reached Bristol. Here we took boat again, and our troubles were at an end. A plentiful dinner contributed to beguile the distance, and the city clocks were in the act of chiming ten as we landed on the quay of Philadelphia.

Having procured a coach, I drove to Head's hotel, which had been recommended to me as one of the best houses in the Union. Here I could only procure a small and nasty bedroom, lighted by a few panes of glass fixed in the wall, some eight or ten feet from the floor. On the following morning, therefore, I removed to the United States Hotel, where I found the accommodation excellent. My letters of introduction were then despatched, with the result which my experience of American kindness had led me to anticipate.

Philadelphia stands on an isthmus about two miles wide, between the Delaware and the Schuylkill. Below the city, both rivers are navigable for vessels of any class, but the severity of the winter climate generally causes an interruption to the communication with the sea, of considerable duration. As a great seat of commerce the advantage is altogether on the side of New York. Philadelphia has but trifling extent of river communication with the interior. The Delaware is navigable only for about thirty miles above the city, and the Schuylkill is too full of shoals and rapids to be practicable for any thing but small craft. To remedy this inconvenience there are several canals, and others are in progress, which must contribute largely to the prosperity of the State.

There is nothing striking in the appearance of Philadelphia when seen from the river. It stands on a flat surface, and presents no single object of beauty or grandeur to arrest the attention. Spires may be monsters in architecture, but they are beautiful monsters, and the eye feels a sad want of them, as it wanders over the unvaried extent of dull uniform building presented by Philadelphia. When one enters the city the scene is certainly improved, but not much. The streets are rather respectable than handsome, but there is everywhere so much appearance of real comfort, that the traveller is at first delighted with this Quaker paradise. He looks from the carriage windows prepared to see every thing *couleur de rose.* The vehicle rolls on; he praises the cleanness and neatness of the houses, and every street that presents itself seems an exact copy of those which he has left behind. In short, before he has got through half the city, he feels an unusual tendency to relaxation about the region of the mouth, which ultimately terminates in a silent but prolonged yawn.

Philadelphia is mediocrity personified in brick and mortar. It is a city laid down by square and rule, a sort of habitable problem,—a mathematical infringement on the rights of individual eccentricity,—a rigid and prosaic despotism of right angles

and parallelograms. It may emphatically be called a *comfortable* city, that is, the houses average
better than in any other with which I am acquainted. You here see no miserable and filthy streets,
the refuge of squalid poverty, forming a contrast to
the splendour of squares and crescents. No Dutch
town can be cleaner, and the marble stairs and window sills of the better houses, give an agreeable relief to the red brick of which they are constructed.

The public buildings are certainly superior to
any I have yet seen in America. Some of the
churches are handsome, and the United States Bank,
with its marble portico of Grecian Doric, gives evidence, I trust, of an improving taste. I confess,
however, that my hopes on this matter are not very
strong. Even persons of information are evidently
unable to appreciate the true merit of the building
or the architect, and connect ridicule with both by
declaring the former to be " the finest building in
the world !" Is a poor traveller in the United States,
when continually beset by such temptation, to be
held utterly inexcusable, if he sometimes venture to
indulge in a sneer ?

The Bank of Pennsylvania is another structure entitled to applause. Its front presents a flight of steps sustaining an Ionic portico of six columns, with an entablature and pediment. The banking-house of Mr Girard,—the Coutts of the Union,—is likewise handsome. Like the two buildings I have already mentioned its whole front is of marble, but in taste it is far less chaste, and presents more faults than I have time or inclination to enumerate. There are likewise two buildings of some pretension, in the Gothic style. Both are contemptible.

The State House, from which issued the declaration of American independence, is yet standing. It is built of brick, and consists of a centre and two wings, without ornament of any sort. There is something appropriate, and even imposing in its very plainness. Above is a small cupola with a clock, which at night is illuminated by gas.

The Philadelphians, however, pride themselves far more on their waterworks than on their State House. Their *Io Pæans* on account of the former, are loud and unceasing, and I must say, the annoyance which these occasion to a traveller, is very considerable. A dozen times a-day was I asked whether I had seen the waterworks, and on my answering in the negative, I was told that I positively must visit them; that they were unrivalled in the world; that no people but the Americans could have executed such works, and by implication, that no one but an Englishman, meanly jealous of American superiority, would omit an opportunity of admiring their unrivalled mechanism.

There is no accounting for the eccentricities of human character. I had not heard these circumstances repeated above fifty times, ere I began to run restive, and determined not to visit the waterworks at all. To this resolution I adhered, in spite of all annoyance, with a pertinacity worthy of a better cause. Of the waterworks of Philadelphia, therefore, I know nothing, and any reader, particularly solicitous to become acquainted with the principle of this remarkable piece of machinery, must consult the pages of other travellers.

I had the honour of being present at an annual celebration of the American Philosophical Society. About a hundred members sat down to a most excellent supper, and the wine and punch were equally unimpeachable. The President, Mr Du Ponceau, then made a speech, in which he gave a very interesting account of the rise and progress of the Society to its present flourishing condition. It was originally established by Franklin, and a few of his fellow-tradesmen, who met in some back-room of an obscure tavern, and having supped on bread and cheese, enjoyed the feast of reason over a pot of London Particular. The Society now includes in its members all that America can boast of eminence in literature or science.

On the following evening, I passed an hour or two very agreeably at one of a series of meetings, which are called " Wistar Parties," from the name of the gentleman at whose house they were first held. Their effect and influence on society must be very salutary. These parties bring together men of different classes and pursuits, and promote the free interchange of opinion, always useful for the correction of prejudice. Such intercourse, too, prevents the narrowness of thought, and exaggerated estimate of the value of our own peculiar acquirements, which

devotion to one exclusive object is apt to engender
in those who do not mix freely with the world.

These meetings are held by rotation at the houses
of the different members. The conversation is generally literary or scientific, and as the party is usually
very large, it can be varied at pleasure. Philoso-
phers eat like other men, and the precaution of an
excellent supper is by no means found to be superfluous. It acts too as a gentle emollient on the acri-
mony of debate. No man can say a harsh thing
with his mouth full of turkey, and disputants forget
their differences in unity of enjoyment.

At these parties I met several ingenious men of a
class something below that of the ordinary members.
When an operative mechanic attracts notice by his
zeal for improvement in any branch of science, he
is almost uniformly invited to the Wistar meetings.
The advantage of this policy is obviously very
great. A modest and deserving man is brought into
notice. His errors are corrected, his ardour is sti-
mulated, his taste improved. A healthy connexion
is kept up between the different classes of society,
and the feeling of mutual sympathy is duly cherish-

ed. During my stay in Philadelphia I was present at several of these Wistar meetings, and always returned from them with increased conviction of their beneficial tendency.

Most of the great American cities have a peculiar character,—a sort of civic idiosyncracy, which distinguishes their population even to the eye of an unpractised observer. There is no mistaking that of Philadelphia ; it is Quaker all over. All things, animate and inanimate, seem influenced by a spirit of quietism as pervading as the atmosphere. The manners of the higher orders are somewhat more reserved than in other parts of the Union, and I must say that all ranks are particularly free from the besetting sin of curiosity. Fortunately for travellers, it is not here considered essential that they should disclose every circumstance connected with their past life and opinions.

Philadelphia is *par excellence* a city of mediocrity. Its character is republican not democratic. One can read the politics of its inhabitants in the very aspect of the streets. A coarse and vulgar demagogue would have no chance among a people so palpably observant of the proprieties, both moral and political. The Philadelphians are no traffickers in extremes of any sort, and were I to form my opinion of a government, from the impression made by its policy on some particular district of the Union, I should certainly take this enlightened and respectable city as the guide and standard of my creed.

The chief defect of Philadelphia is want of variety. It is just such a city as a young lady would cut out of a thread paper,—

Street answers street, each alley has a brother,
And half the city just reflects the other.

Something is certainly wanted to relieve that unbroken uniformity, which tires the eye and stupifies the imagination. One would give the world for something to admire or to condemn, and would absolutely rejoice, for the mere sake of variety, to encounter a row of log huts, or to get immersed in a congress of dark and picturesque *closes,* such as delight all travellers—without noses—in the old town of Edinburgh.

The Utilitarian principle is observed, even in

the nomenclature of the streets. Those running in one direction are denoted by the name of some particular tree,—such as vine, cedar, chestnut, spruce, &c. The cross-streets are distinguished by numbers, so that a stranger has no difficulty in finding his way, since the name of the street indicates its situation. Market Street is the great thoroughfare of the city, and stretches from one river to the other, an extent of several miles. The streets are generally skirted by rows of Lombardy poplars, for what reason I know not. They certainly give no shade, and possess no beauty.

Notwithstanding the attractions of Philadelphia, it was not my intention to have remained there longer than a week, but while engaged in preparation for departure, a deep fall of snow came on, and the communications of the city were at once cut off. A week passed without intelligence from the northward, and even the southern mails were several days in arrear. The snow lay deep on the streets, and wheeled carriages were of necessity exchanged for sledges, or, as they are usually called, sleighs. Of course, it would have been absurd for a traveller, with no motive for expedition, to commence a journey under such circumstances, and I determined to prolong my stay until the roads should be reported in such condition as to threaten no risk of detention in my route to Baltimore.

During this interval I visited the Penitentiary. It stands about two miles from the city, but owing to the depth of snow, the sleigh could not approach within a considerable distance of the building, and the pedestrian part of the excursion presented much difficulty. A thin icy crust had formed over the surface of the snow, which often gave way beneath the foot, and more than once I was immersed to the shoulders.

I did, however, reach the Penitentiary at last. It is a square granite building of great extent, with a tower at each angle, and the walls enclose a space of ten acres. In the centre of the area stands an observatory, from which it is intended that seven corridors shall radiate, but three only have been yet completed. The cells are arranged on either side of these corridors, with which they communicate by a square aperture, which may be opened at pleasure from without.   There is likewise a small eye-hole, commanding a complete view of the cell, and attached to each is a walled court, in which the prisoner may take exercise.   The only entrance to the cells lies through these court-yards.

The system pursued in this institution is entirely different from that which, in a former part of this volume, I have had occasion to describe.   No punishment is permitted within its walls but that of solitary confinement.   Nothing is left to the discretion of the gaoler, or his assistants, and all risk of abuse is thus obviated.   I cannot but consider this as an inestimable advantage.   If discretionary power be confessedly dangerous when exercised by a judge in open court, under the strong check of public opinion, what are we to say of it when confided to a gaoler, and exercised without responsibility of any sort, amid the secrecy of his prisonhouse?

The warder of the establishment struck me as a person of much enthusiasm and benevolence.   He evidently took pleasure in affording every information in regard to the practical operation of the system, though its introduction is too recent to afford room for any conclusive appeal to experience. The punishment originally contemplated in this prison was solitary confinement, unmitigated by labour. All experience is against the practicability of combining this system with the continuance of bodily health and mental sanity in the prisoners. It was therefore wisely given up, and of that adopted in its stead I shall now offer a few details.

A convict, on arriving at the prison, is blind-folded, and conveyed to a room, where his hair is cut, and after a complete personal ablution, he is led with the same precaution, to the cell destined for his reception. He is thus kept in ignorance of the localities of the prison, and the chances of escape are diminished. Each cell is provided with an iron bedstead, a comfortable mattrass, two blankets, and a pillow. There is likewise a water-cock and tin mug, so that the prisoner may supply himself *ad libitum* with the pure element. The cells are heated by pipes, and though I visited the prison in the very coldest weather, the temperature was very pleasant.

When a prisoner is first received, he is uniformly left to enjoy the full privilege of solitary idleness ;

but in the course of a short time he generally makes application for work, and for a Bible.   Each man is permitted to select his own trade, and those who understand none when they enter the prison are taught one. The allowance of food is good and plentiful, but those who refuse to work, are kept on a reduced allowance.   Their number, however, is exceedingly small, and the great majority consider even the temporary withdrawal of work as a severe punishment.

Having taken up rather strong opinions with regard to the injurious influence of solitary confinement, I was rather anxious to have an opportunity of conversing with a few of the prisoners.   To this no objection was made, and I was accordingly ushered into the cell of a black shoemaker, convicted of theft, whom I found very comfortably seated at his trade.   I asked him many questions, which he answered with great cheerfulness.   He had been confined—I think—for eighteen months, yet this long period of separation from his fellow-creatures had occasioned no derangement of his functions, bodily or mental.   I likewise conversed with two other prisoners, and the result of my observations certainly was the conviction, that solitary confinement, when associated with labour, is by no means liable to the objections which I have often heard urged to its adoption as a punishment. I have likewise the assurance of the warder, that during his whole experience, he has not known a single instance of the discipline adopted being found prejudicial to health, either of mind or body.

There is undoubtedly much that is admirable in this Penitentiary, but I am not sure that either the plan or the practice of the establishment is so perfect as to admit of no improvement. In the first place, I cannot but think that the Panopticon principle is on the whole preferable. Facility of supervision is always important, and there is no point in the present prison from which the keeper can command a general and complete view, either of the cells or of the exercise yards. The central observatory commands only the corridors. In the second place, it strikes me as a defect that there should be no entrance to the cells from the corridors, by which a far more ready and convenient access would be ob-

tained.   There is also a defect in the construction
of the exercise courts, in which it is quite possible
for the adjoining prisoners to hold conversation.

There is no chapel attached to this establishment,
and when divine service is performed, the clergyman takes his station at the head of the corridors;
the apertures communicating with the cells are
thrown open, and his voice I am assured, is distinctly audible, even by the most distant prisoner.
Strange to say, however—and I confess that in a
state so religious as Pennsylvania, the fact struck me
with astonishment—morning and evening prayers
are unknown in the Penitentiary.   Surely, it is both
wholesome and fitting that the days of these suffering criminals should be begun and ended by an appeal to the mercy of that Maker, whose laws they
have offended.   It is true, that divine service is performed once every Sunday, but this will scarcely be
held sufficient, either by the moralist who simply
regards the interest of society in the reformation of
a criminal, or by him whose philanthropy is connected with the higher hopes and motives of religion.

On the whole, I am inclined to prefer the system

of solitary confinement to that adopted in the prisons at Auburn and Charleston. The former obviates all necessity for punishment of any kind, beyond that inflicted by the execution of the sentence. Whatever be his sufferings, the prisoner has the distinct knowledge that they are not arbitrary or extrajudicial. Even amidst the solitude of his cell, he feels that he is in one sense a *free man.* He undergoes the sentence of the law, but he is not dependent on the capricious discretion of those by whom he is surrounded. In Charleston each prisoner knows himself to be a slave. His punishment is in truth unlimited, for its only measure is the conscience of his gaoler, an unknown and indeterminate quantity.

There is nothing humiliating in solitary confinement. The interests of society are protected by the removal of the criminal, while the new circumstances in which he is placed are precisely the most favourable to moral improvement. It is the numerous temptations of the world, the scope which it affords for the gratification of strong passion, that overpower the better principles implanted in the heart of the most depraved of mankind. Remove these temptations, place the criminal in a situation where there are no warring influences to mislead his judgment; let him receive religious instruction, and be taught the nature and extent of his moral obligations, and when, after such preparation, he is left to reflection, and communion with his own conscience, all that human agency can effect, has probably been done for his reformation.

Solitary confinement contributes to all this. It throws the mind of the criminal back upon itself. It forces him to think who never thought before. It removes all objects which can stimulate the evil passions of his nature. It restores the prisoner to society, if not " a wiser and a better man," at least undegraded by a course of servile submission. His punishment has been that of a man, not of a brute. He has suffered privation, but not indignity. He has submitted to the law, and to the law alone, and whatever debasement may still attach to his character, is the offspring of his crime, not of its penalty.

The other system is far less favourable I should imagine to moral improvement. The gaoler must necessarily appear to the prisoners in the light of an arbitrary tyrant. He is an object of fear and hatred. His inflictions are accompanied by none of the solemnities of justice, and they are naturally followed by smothered rancour and desire of revenge. Even where there is no abuse of authority, it is impossible for those subjected to it, to appreciate the motives for its rigid exercise. They cannot be supposed to discriminate between severity and cruelty.

All this is unfortunate. The character of the prisoners is rendered callous to shame, while their evil passions are in a state of permanent excitement. They are taught obedience like spaniels, and by the same means. They are forced down to the very lowest point of human debasement. Never again shall these men know the dignity of self-respect; never again can they feel themselves on a level with their fellow-men. Human endurance can extend no further than they have carried it, and it were well that American legislators should remember, that it is easy to degrade the freeman, but impossible to elevate the slave.

One great advantage belongs to the Philadelphia

3

system. A prisoner on being discharged enters the world without danger of recognition, and thus enjoys the benefit of starting with a fair character. If his confinement has been long, disease and the gibbet have probably disposed of the great majority of his former companions in crime, and in a country like the United States, nothing but honest industry is wanting to the attainment of independence. But a convict discharged from a prison like those of Charleston and Auburn, must continue through life a marked man. His face is known to thousands, and go where he will—unless he fly altogether from the haunts of men—the story of his past life will follow him. Excluded from communion with the more respectable portion of the community, he will probably again seek his associates among the dissolute. His former course of crime will then be renewed, and all hope of reformation will be at an end for ever.

It is impossible, however, to praise too highly that active benevolence which in America takes so deep an interest in the reformation of the objects of punishment. In their ameliorations of prison discipline, the people of this country have unquestion-

ably taken the lead of Europe.   In old established
communities the progress of improvement is necessarily slow, and there are difficulties to be overcome
which are fortunately unknown on this side of the
Atlantic. Let the Americans, therefore, continue as
they have begun, to lead the way in this important
department of practical philanthropy. By doing so,
they will earn a distinction for their country more
honourable than could result from the highest eminence in arts, or achievements in arms.

Of all the American colleges beyond the limits of
New England, that of Pennsylvania is perhaps the
most distinguished.   Its medical school is decidedly
so, and an Esculapian armed with a Philadelphia
diploma, is held to commit slaughter on his fellow-
creatures according to the most approved principles
of modern science.   Till within a few years, however, the scientific and literary departments of this
institution had fallen into comparative neglect. But
a revolution in an American college is an easier
affair than the introduction of the most trifling
change in such establishments as Oxford or Cambridge.   The statutes were revised by a board of

trustees appointed for the purpose. The system of education was corrected and enlarged, and men of competent talent and acquirements were invited to preside over the various departments of instruction. A new edifice was erected, and an extensive addition made to the former beggarly account of philosophical apparatus. The natural consequences followed. The number of students was considerably increased, and the benefits of the institution were augmented not only in magnitude, but in extent of diffusion.

In this establishment there is no discretion permitted in regard to the course of study to be followed by the student. Every one is compelled to travel in the same track, and to reach the same point, whatever may be his future destination in life. It is perhaps quite right that such portions of a university course should be considered imperative, as relate to the preparatory developement of the intellectual powers, but it does appear somewhat absurd to insist on cramming every boy with mathematics, chemistry, and natural philosophy. In America, the period devoted to education is so short, that there can be no folly greater than that of frittering it away in a variety of pursuits, which contribute little to the general elevation of the intellect. It is the certain result of attempting too much, that nothing will be accomplished. With such a system of education the standard of acquirement must of necessity be greatly lower than in other countries, where excellence in some one department constitutes the great object of individual ambition. The truth of this position is in perfect accordance with the state of knowledge in America. In illustration of it, I shall direct the attention of the reader to an extract from the report of the Board of Trustees of this very University of Pennsylvania. Alluding to the prescribed course of education, these gentlemen assure the public, that " Its object is to communicate *a profound* and *critical knowledge* of the *classics ;* an *extensive acquaintance* with the *different branches of mathematical science, natural philosophy*, and *chemistry*, combined with *all the varieties of knowledge* comprehended within the sphere of *moral philosophy, logic, rhetoric, metaphysics*, and the *evidences of Christianity. This course of instruction will occupy FOUR YEARS !*"

Had the number of years to be devoted to the acquisition of this vast mass of knowledge been *forty* instead of *four*, the promise of the Board of Trustees might still have been objectionable on the score of hyperbole.   In Europe no body of gentlemen connected with any public seminary durst have ventured on such a statement.   Respect for their own character, and the certainty of ridicule, would have prevented it.   But in America it is different.   The standard of knowledge being there infinitely lower, the Trustees promised nothing more than they might reasonably hope to accomplish.   On the Western shores of the Atlantic, a young man is believed to have "a profound and critical knowledge of the classics," when he can manage to construe a passage of Cæsar or Virgil, and—by the help of the lexicon—haply of Xenophon or Anacreon.   And so with the other branches of acquirement.   In mathematics, it is scarcely meant to be implied that the student shall have mastered the works of La Grange or La Place; nor in metaphysics, that he shall even understand the philosophy of Kant or Cousin, but simply that he shall have acquired enough to constitute, in the eyes of the American public, "an extensive acquaintance with the different branches of mathematical science, combined with all the varieties of knowledge comprehended within the sphere of moral philosophy, logic, rhetoric, and metaphysics."

It thus appears that what in one country would be nothing better than impudent quackery, becomes the language of sober truth in another. The same terms carry different meanings on different sides of the water, and the cause of the discrepancy is too obvious to be mistaken. Having alluded to this subject, I would willingly be permitted to offer a few observations on the interesting question, How far the condition of society in the United States, and the influence of its institutions are favourable, or otherwise, to the cultivation of philosophy and the higher literature ?

The termination of the Revolutionary war left the United States with a population graduating in civilisation from slaves to planters. The scale went low enough, but unfortunately not very high. The great mass of the white population, especially in the Northern States, were by no means deficient in such education as was suited to their circumstances. In a country to which abject poverty was happily a stranger, there existed few obstacles to the general diffusion of elementary instruction. But between the amount of acquirement of the richer and the poorer orders, little disparity existed. Where the necessity of labour was imposed on all, it was not probable that any demand should exist for learning not immediately connected with the business of life. To the grower of indigo or tobacco ; to the feller of timber, or the retailer of cutlery and dry goods, the refinements of literature were necessarily unknown. In her whole population America did not number a single scholar, in the higher acceptation of the term, and had every book in her whole territory been contributed to form a national library, it would not have afforded the materials from which a scholar could be framed.

It is true, that in several of the States there existed colleges, but these were little better than schools without the necessary discipline ; and had their pretensions been greater, it is very certain that such poor and distant establishments could offer no inducement to foreigners of high acquirement to exchange " the ampler ether, the diviner air," of their native universities, for the atmosphere of Yale or Harvard. At all events, the Americans had no desire to draw our men of letters from their learned retreats. In the condition of society I have described, it was impossible that learning should engross any portion of the public favour. Even to the present day, the value of education in the United States is estimated, not by its result on the mind of the student, in strengthening his faculties, purifying his taste, and enlarging and elevating the sphere of thought and consciousness, *but by the amount of available knowledge which it enables him to bring to the common business of life.*

The consequences of this error, when participated in by a whole nation, have been most pernicious. It has unquestionably contributed to perpetuate the very ignorance in which it originated. It has done its part, in connexion with other causes, in depriving the United States of the most enduring source of national greatness. Nor can we hope that the evil will be removed, until the vulgar and unworthy sophistry which has imposed on the judgment, even of the most intelligent Americans, shall cease to influence some wiser and unborn generation.

The education of the clergy differed in little from that of laymen. Of theological learning there was none, nor did there exist the means of acquiring it. It is probable, that within the limits of the United States, there was not to be found a single copy of the works of the Fathers. But this mattered not. Protestantism is never very amenable to authority, and least of all when combined with democracy. Neither the pastors nor their flocks were inclined to attach much value to primitive authority, and from the solid rock of the Scriptures, each man was pleased to hew out his own religion, in such form and proportions as were suited to the measure of his taste and knowledge. It was considered enough that the clergy could read the Bible in their vernacular tongue, and expound its doctrines to the satisfaction of a congregation, not more learned than themselves. To the present day, in one only of the colleges has any provision been made for clerical education. Many of the religious sects, however, have established theological academies, in which candidates for the Ministry may, doubtless, acquire such accomplishment as is deemed necessary for the satisfactory discharge of their high function.*

In short, the state of American society is such as to afford no leisure for any thing so unmarketable as abstract knowledge. For the pursuit of such studies, it is necessary that the proficient should " fit audience find though few." He must be able to calcu-

* The American Almanac for 1831 contains a list of all the theological establishments in the United States, with the number of students at each seminary, and of the volumes contained in its library. According to this document, the whole number of theological students is 657. The combined aggregate of volumes in possession of all the institutions is 43,450. The best furnished library in the list is that of the theological department of Yale College, which contains 8000 volumes. None of the others approach nearly to this amount. The institution of New Hampton possesses only 100 volumes, and is attended by fourteen students. Calculating each book to consist, on the average, of three volumes, the New Hampton library contains *thirty-three* works on theology. But this is not all. Seven of these establishments possess *no libraries at all*, so that the learning of the students must come by inspiration. Until the year 1808, no seminaries for religious instruction appear to have existed in the United States. One was founded in that year, another in 1812, but the great majority are of far more recent origin.

late on sympathy at least, if not encouragement, and assuredly he would find neither in the United States.

Whatever were the defects of Jefferson, he seems to have been impressed with a deep consciousness of the deficiencies of his countrymen. He saw that the elements of knowledge were diffused every where, but that all its higher fruits were wanting. He endeavoured, not only to rouse his countrymen to a sense of their intellectual condition, but to provide the means by which it might be improved. With this view he founded a university in his native State, and his last worldly anxieties were devoted to its advancement. Jefferson felt strongly, that while philosophy and literature were excluded from the fair objects of professional ambition, and the United States continued to be dependent for all advances in knowledge on importations from Europe, she was wanting in the noblest element of national greatness. Though the commerce of mind be regulated by loftier principles than more vulgar traffic, it should consist, unquestionably, of exchange of some kind. To receive, and not to give, is to subsist on charity ; to be a mute and changeling in the great family of nations.

The obstacles to success, however, were too great for the powers of Jefferson to overcome.   In a community where the gradations of opulence constitute the great distinction between man and man, the pursuits which lead most readily to its attainment will certainly engross the whole volume of national talent.   In England there are various coexistent aristocracies which act as mutual correctives, and by multiplying the objects of ambition, give amplitude and diffusion to its efforts. In America there exists but one, and the impulse it awakens is, of course, violent in proportion to its concentration. Jefferson, therefore, failed in this great object, towards the accomplishment of which his anxious efforts were directed. As a politician, he exercised a far greater influence over the national mind than any other statesman his country has produced. But in his endeavours to direct the intellectual impulses of his countrymen towards loftier objects, the very structure of society presented an insuperable barrier to success.

I am aware, it will be urged, that the state of things I have described is merely transient, and that when population shall become more dense, and increased competition shall render commerce and agriculture less lucrative, the pursuits of science and literature will engross their due portion of the national talent. I hope it may be so, but yet it cannot be disguised, that there hitherto has been no visible approximation towards such a condition of society. In the present generation of Americans, I can detect no symptom of improving taste, or increasing elevation of intellect. On the contrary, the fact has been irresistibly forced on my conviction, that they are altogether inferior to those, whose place, in the course of nature, they are soon destined to occupy. Compared with their fathers, I have no hesitation in pronouncing the younger portion of the richer classes to be less liberal, less enlightened, less observant of the proprieties of life, and certainly far less pleasing in manner and deportment.

In England every new generation starts forward into life with advantages far superior to its predecessor. Each successive crop—if I may so write—

of legislators, is marked by increase of knowledge and enlargement of thought. The standard of acquirement necessary to attain distinction in public life, is now confessedly higher than it was thirty years ago. The intellectual currency of the country, instead of being depreciated, has advanced in value, while the issue has been prodigiously enlarged. True, there are no giants in our days, but this may be in part at least accounted for, by a general increase of stature in the people. We have gained at least an inch upon our fathers, and have the gratifying prospect of appearing diminutive when compared with our children.

But if this be so in America, I confess my observation is at fault. I can discern no prospect of her soon becoming a mental benefactor to the world. Elementary instruction, it is true, has generally kept pace with the rapid progress of population; but while the steps of youth are studiously directed to the base of the mountain of knowledge, no facilities have been provided for scaling its summit. There is at this moment nothing in the United States worthy of the name of a library. Not only is there an entire absence of learning, in the higher sense of the term, but an absolute want of the material from which alone learning can be extracted. At present an American might study every book within the limits of the Union, and still be regarded in many parts of Europe—especially in Germany—as a man comparatively ignorant. And why does a great nation thus voluntarily continue in a state of intellectual destitution so anomalous and humiliating? There are libraries to be sold in Europe. Books might be imported in millions. Is it poverty, or is it ignorance of their value, that withholds America from the purchase?* I should be most happy to believe the former.

In one point of view at least, the strong—and I fear not to say, the insuperable prejudice against the

---

* The value of books imported from Europe during the year 1829-30 for public institutions, amounted only to 10,829 dollars! Even of this wretched sum, I am assured the greater part was expended in works strictly new. Of the old treasures of learning, America seems content to remain destitute.

In regard to science, it is a fact scarcely credible, that the second maritime power in the world does not at the present moment possess a single astronomical observatory, and is dependent on France and England for the calculations of an ephemeris by which her ships may be enabled in tolerable safety to navigate the ocean!

claims of primogeniture, is unfavourable to national advancement. It must continue to prevent any large accumulations of individual wealth, and the formation of a class which might afford encouragement to those branches of science and literature, which cannot be expected from their very nature to become generally popular. Nor is it likely that the impediments to which I have alluded, will be at all diminished by the character of the government, on which I shall hazard a few observations.

When we speak of a government being popular or otherwise, we mean that it is more or less influenced by the prevailing currents of opinion and feeling in those subjected to its action. A highly popular government, therefore, can neither be in advance of the average intelligence of a people, nor can it lag behind it. It is, and must be, the mere reflex of the public mind in all its strength and weakness; the representative not only of its higher qualities and virtues, but of all the errors, follies, passions, prejudices, and ignorances by which it is debased.

It is in vain, therefore, to expect from such a

government any separate and independent action. It cannot react upon, it is merely co-operative with, the people. It embodies no self-existent or countervailing influence. It is only when it ceases to be expressly representative, and stands on a firmer basis than mere popular favour, that a government can acquire a positive and determinate character, and be recognised as an influence distinct from that of national opinion.

Neither in the American legislative or executive, is there any thing of this latter character discernible. The institutions of the United States afford the purest specimen the world has yet seen, of a representative government; of an executive, whose duties are those of mere passive agency; of a legislative, which serves but as the vocal organ of the sole and real dictator, the people. Into whatever speculations, therefore, we may be induced to enter, either with regard to the present condition or further prospects of the United States, it would be mere folly to attribute influence of any kind to a government, which, in truth, is nothing more than a mere recipient of popular impulse.

To an American of talent, there exist no objects
to stimulate political ambition, save the higher
offices of the federal government, or of the individual States.   The latter, indeed, are chiefly valued
for the increased facilities they afford for the attainment of the former ; but to either, the only passport
is popular favour.   Acquirements of any sort, therefore, which the great mass of the people do not
value, or are incapable of appreciating, are of no
practical advantage, for they bring with them neither fame, nor more substantial reward.   But this
is understating the case.   Such knowledge, if displayed at all, would not merely be a dead letter in
the qualifications of a candidate for political power,
it would oppose a decided obstacle to his success.
The sovereign people in America are given to be
somewhat intolerant of acquirement, the immediate
utility of which they cannot appreciate, but which
they do feel has imparted something of mental superiority to its possessor.   This is particularly the case
with regard to literary accomplishment.   The cry
of the people is for " *equal and universal education ;*"
and attainments which circumstances have placed

beyond their own reach, they would willingly discountenance in others.

It is true, indeed, that with regard to mere professional acquirements, a different feeling prevails. The people have no objection to a clever surgeon or a learned physician, because they profit by their skill. An ingenious mechanic they respect. There is a fair field for a chemist or engineer. But in regard to literature, they can discover no practical benefit of which it is productive. In their eyes it is a mere appanage of aristocracy, and whatever mental superiority it is felt to confer, is at the expense of the self-esteem of less educated men. I have myself heard in Congress the imputation of scholarship bandied as a reproach; and if the epithet of " literary gentleman" may be considered as malignant, as it did sometimes appear to be gratuitous, there assuredly existed ample apology for the indignant feeling it appeared to excite. The truth I believe is, that in their political representatives, the people demand just so much knowledge and accomplishment as they conceive to be practically available for the promotion of their own interests. This, in their opinion, is enough.   More were but to gild refined gold, and paint the lily, operations which could add nothing to the value of the metal, or the fragrance of the flower.

The consequence of all this has been, that the standard of judgment, in regard to public men, is decidedly lower in the United States than in most countries of Europe.   It is perhaps natural, that the demand for political accomplishment should not precede its necessity, and I am far from wishing to assert, that American statesmen have not been hitherto found adequate to all the wants of the commonwealth.   But if it be the great object of enlightened institutions to encourage the development of the highest faculties, and, generally, to raise man in the scale of intellectual being ; if knowledge be confessedly power, and freedom from prejudice a nobler enfranchisement than mere physical liberty, then I fear that, in reference to this great and ultimate function, those of the United States will be found wanting.   I am far from arguing, that science and literature should be indebted for their promotion to a system of direct encouragement.   Such policy is always dubious, and has rarely proved successful. But I certainly regard as one most important standard of excellence in a government, the degree in which, *by its very constitution*, it tends to call into action the higher powers and qualities of the human mind. It is a poor policy, which, in matters of intellect, looks not beyond the necessities of the present hour. There is no economy so shortsighted, as that which would limit the expenditure of mind, and assuredly the condition of society cannot be desirable, in which great qualities of every sort do not find efficient excitement and ample field for display.

How far the influences, which have hitherto prevented the intellectual advancement of the Americans, may hereafter be counteracted by others more favourable to the cultivation of learning, I presume not to predict. There is certainly no deficiency of talent in the United States; no deficiency of men, stored even to abundance with knowledge, practically applicable to the palpable and grosser wants of their countrymen. But of those higher branches of acquirement, which profess not to minister to mere vulgar necessities, or to enlarge the sphere of physical enjoyment, and of which the only result is the elevation of the intellect, I fear it must be acknowledged she has not yet been taught even to appreciate the value.

CHAPTER XI.

PHILADELPHIA.

THE United States' hotel, where I had taken up my abode, was a favourite resort of American naval officers. An opportunity was thus afforded me, of forming acquaintance with several, to whom I was indebted for many kind and most obliging attentions. It must be confessed, that these republicans have carried with them their full share of " Old Albion's spirit of the sea," for better sailors, in the best and highest acceptation of the term, I do not believe the world can produce. During the course of my tour, I had a good deal of intercourse with the members of this profession; and I must say, that in an officer of the United States' navy, I have uniformly found, not only a well-informed gentleman, but a person

on whose kindness and good offices to a stranger, I
might with confidence rely. They betray nothing
of that silly spirit of bluster and bravado, so prevalent among other classes of their countrymen; and
even in conversing on the events of the late war,
they spoke of their successes in a tone of modesty
which tended to raise even the high impression I had
already received of their gallantry.

In company with one of these gentlemen I visited
the Navy Yard, and went over a splendid line-of-
battle ship, the Pennsylvania. She is destined to
carry a hundred and forty-four guns; and is, I
believe, the largest ship in the world. I likewise
inspected a magnificent frigate called the Raritan.
Both of these vessels are on the stocks, but I was
assured that a couple of months would suffice at any
time to make them ready for sea. They are completely covered in from the weather; and every
aperture of the wood is carefully filled with sea-salt
to prevent decay. Great faith is placed in the efficacy of this preservative.

Messrs Carey and Lea are the chief booksellers
of Philadelphia, and, I believe, of the Union. Their

establishment is very extensive, and they are evidently men of much sagacity and enterprise. The principal part of their business consists in issuing reprints of English works, which, either from their merit or their notoriety, may be expected to have a considerable circulation on this side of the water. Of original publications the number is comparatively small; though, I am told, of late years it has considerably increased.

The three great publishing cities of the Union are Boston, New York, and Philadelphia. From the first and last of these places I have seen some very respectable specimens of typography; but, in general, the reprints of English works are executed in the coarsest and most careless manner. It is quite a mistake to suppose that books are cheaper in the United States than in England. If there were no copyright, and the British public would be content to read books printed in the most wretched manner on whitey-brown paper, there can be no doubt that the English bibliopole would beat his American brother out of the field. A proof of this is, that the British editions of works of which the copyright has expired, are quite as cheap, and much superior in execution, to those produced in this country.

Copyright in the United States is not enjoyable by a foreigner, though an American can hold it in England. The consequence is, that an English author derives no benefit from the republication of his work in America, while every Englishman who purchases the work of an American, is taxed in order to put money in the pocket of the latter. There is no reciprocity in this; and it is really not easy to see why Mr Washington Irving or Mr Cooper should enjoy greater privileges in this country than are accorded to Mr Bulwer or Mr Theodore Hook in the United States. There is an old proverb, "What is good for the goose is good for the gander," which will be found quite as applicable to the policy of Parliament as the practice of the poultry-yard. It is to be hoped this homely apophthegm will not escape the notice of the Government, and that by an act of signal justice, (the abolition of American copyright in England,) it will compel the United States to adopt a wiser and more liberal system.

All novels, good, bad, and indifferent, which appear in England, seem to be reprinted in this country. Indeed, the American appetite in this respect is apparently quite as indiscriminate as our own. A good deal also of the more valuable British literature issues from the Philadelphia press, but in the most democratic form. I have been sometimes amused at observing the entire transmogrification undergone by one of Mr Murray's hot-pressed and broad-margined volumes under the hands of an American bookseller. It enters his shop a three guinea quarto; it comes out a four and twopenny duodecimo. The metamorphosis reminds one of a lord changing clothes with a beggar. The man is the same, but he certainly owes nothing to the toilet.

The Americans are as jealous on the subject of their literature as on other matters of national pretension. The continual importation of European books contributes to excite a consciousness of inferiority which is by no means pleasant. There are many projects afloat for getting rid of this mental bondage, and establishing intellectual independence. By one party it is proposed to exclude English works altogether, and forbid their republication under a high penalty. " Americans," say the advocates of this system, " will never write books, when they can be had so cheaply from England. Native talent is kept under ; it wants protection against the competition of foreign genius. Give it the monopoly of the home market ; deal with intellect as you do with calico and broad-cloth, and do not prematurely force our literary labourers into a contest with men enjoying the advantages of larger libraries, learning, and leisure." In short, what these gentlemen want is, that ignorance and barbarism should be established by legislative enactment, a policy which, till America has suffered more than she has yet done from the inroads of knowledge, will probably strike a foreigner as somewhat gratuitous.

If the American legislature, however, has not done this, it has certainly done what is something akin to it. A duty of thirty cents, or about fifteen pence a-pound, is charged on all imported books, which, in every point of view, is highly injudicious. In the first place, American books require no protection, because the expense of copyright, and of transport, is far more than enough to secure to native book-sellers the undisturbed possession of their own market. When a book is of a character to lead to republication in the United States, of course the only effect of the duty is to force those, who might wish handsomer and better copies, to furnish their libraries with inferior material. The number of these however, would be found very small. In this country, when a book is once read, it is cast aside and thought of no more. In comparatively few instances, is it bound and consigned to the shelves of the book-case, and therefore it is, that the purchasers of books almost uniformly prefer the very cheapest form. The injurious effect, however, of the duty on imported works, is felt with regard to those which, although valuable, are not of a character to repay the cost of republication. The duty in all such cases acts not as a protection—for when the book is not reprinted there is nothing to protect—but as *a tax upon know-ledge ;* or, in other words, a premium for the perpetuation of ignorance.

During my stay at Philadelphia, I frequently visited the courts of law. The proceedings I happened to witness were in nothing remarkable, and I have already described the externals of an American Court. It is not unusual among the lower orders in England, when any knotty point is proposed for discussion, to say it would "puzzle a Philadelphia lawyer." To do this, however, it must be knotty indeed, for I have never met a body of men more distinguished by acuteness and extensive professional information than the members of the Philadelphia bar.

In the American courts there is much tacit respect paid to English decisions, each volume of which is reprinted in this country as soon as it appears. Indeed, but for these, law in America would soon become an inextricable jumble. It is impossible to expect much harmony of decision from twenty-four independent tribunals, unless there exist some common land-marks to serve as guides to opinion. Even as it is, the most anomalous discrepancies occur between the decisions of the different State Courts; but without a constant influx of English authorities, the laws regarding property would be speedily overcast by such a mass of contradictory precedents as to be utterly irrevocable to any system.

The low salaries of the judges constitute matter of general complaint among the members of the bar, both at Philadelphia and New York. These are so inadequate, when compared with the income of a well-employed barrister, that the State is deprived of the advantage of having the highest legal talent on the bench. Men from the lower walks of the profession, therefore, are generally promoted to the office, and for the sake of a wretched saving of a few thousand dollars, the public are content to submit their lives and properties to the decision of men of inferior intelligence and learning.

In one respect, I am told the very excess of democracy defeats itself. In some States the judges are so inordinately underpaid, that no lawyer, who does not possess a considerable private fortune, can afford to accept the office. From this circumstance something of aristocratic distinction has become connected with it, and a seat on the bench is now more greedily coveted than it would be, were the salary more commensurate with the duties of the situation.

All lawyers with whom I have conversed agree, that the discrepancy between the laws of the different States is productive of much injury. The statutes of one State are often defeated in the tribunals of another, when not in accordance with the tone of public opinion in the latter. A laxity thus arises in the administration of municipal law incompatible with good government. The criminal codes are likewise highly discordant, and from the variety of jurisdictions, the probability of crime being followed by punishment is much diminished. When a man guilty of an offence in one State escapes into another, he can only be apprehended on the formal demand of the executive authority of the State having jurisdiction of the crime. Before the necessary machinery, however, can be set at work, he has generally time and opportunity for a second evasion, and it thus often happens that the ends of justice are entirely defeated.

There can be no doubt that the want of uniformity in the administration of justice, is injurious both to public morals and private security. But the evil is one naturally arising from the political subdivisions of the Union, and for which, with the jealousy which prevails of the jurisdiction of the federal government, it is perhaps impossible to devise a remedy. With so many co-existent and independent legislatures, uniformity of legislation is impossible, and we can only hope that in the growing political experience of American statesmen, the evil may be diminished, though there exist no prospect of its being entirely removed.

Philadelphia may be called the Bath of the United States, and many individuals who have amassed fortunes in other parts of the Union, select it as the place of their residence. Money-getting is not here the furious and absorbing pursuit of all ranks and conditions of men. On the contrary, every thing goes on quietly. The people seem to dabble in business, rather than follow it with that impetuous energy observable in other cities. The truth is, that a large portion of the capital of the Philadelphians is invested in New York, where there is ample field for its profitable employment. The extent of their own traffic is limited, and in this respect I should imagine it to be inferior even to Boston. But, in point of opulence, Philadelphia is undoubtedly first city of the Union. It is the great focus of American capital, the pecuniary reservoir which fills the various channels of profitable enterprise.

In Philadelphia it is the fashion to be scientific, and the young ladies occasionally display the *bas bleu*, in a degree, which in other cities would be considered rather alarming. I remember at a dinner party, being instructed as to the component parts of the atmosphere by a fair spinster, who anticipated the approach of a period when oxygen would supersede champagne, and young gentlemen and ladies would hob or nob in gas. The vulgar term *drunk* would then give place to *inflated*, certainly more euphonious to ears polite, and the coarser stimulants, such as alcohol and tobacco, in all their forms and uses, be regarded with contempt.

There is no American city in which the system of *exclusion* is so rigidly observed as in Philadelphia. The ascent of a *parvenu* into the aristocratic circle is slow and difficult. There is a sort of holy alliance between its members to forbid all unauthorized approach. Claims are canvassed, and pretensions weighed; manners, fortune, tastes, habits, and descent, undergo a rigid examination; and from the temper of the judges, the chances are, that the final oscillation of the scale, is unfavourable to the reception of the candidate. I remember being present at a party, of which the younger members expressed a strong desire to enliven the dulness of the city, by getting up a series of public balls. The practicability of this project became matter of general discussion, and it was at length given up, simply because there were many families confessedly so respectable as to afford no tangible ground for exclusion, and yet so unfashionable as to render their admission a nuisance of the first magnitude.

I have already alluded to the existence of this aristocratic feeling in New York, but it certainly is there far less prevalent than in Philadelphia. This may easily be accounted for. In the former city, the vicissitudes of trade, the growth and dissipation of opulence, are far more rapid. Rich men spring up like mushrooms. Fortunes are made and lost by a single speculation. A man may go to bed at night worth less than nothing, and pull off his nightcap in the morning with some hundred thousand dollars waiting his acceptance. There is comparatively no settled and permanent body of leading capitalists, and consequently less room for that sort of defensive league which naturally takes place among men of common interests and position in society.

In Philadelphia, on the other hand, the pursuits of commerce are confined within narrower limits. There is no field for speculation on a great scale, and the regular trade of the place is engrossed by old established houses, which enjoy a sort of prescriptive confidence, against which younger establishments, however respectable, find it in vain to contend. The keener, and more enterprising traders, therefore, generally remove to New York, and Philadelphia continues comparatively untroubled by those fluctuations of wealth, which impede any permanent and effective union among its aristocracy.

In society in Philadelphia, I had the good fortune to meet the Count de Survilliers, better known by the untitled name of Joseph Bonaparte. This personage has purchased an estate in the neighbourhood, and by his simplicity and benevolence of character, has succeeded in winning golden opinions from all classes of Americans. He often visits Philadelphia, and mingles a good deal in the society of the place. In the party where I first met him, a considerable time elapsed before I was aware of the presence of a person so remarkable. He was at length pointed out to my observation, with an offer of introduction which I thought proper to decline ; being aware, that in a work with which he was probably unacquainted, I had spoken of him in a manner, which, whether just or otherwise, made it indelicate that I should be obtruded on his notice.

Joseph Bonaparte, in person, is about the middle height, but round and corpulent. In the form of his head and features there certainly exists a resemblance to Napoleon, but in the expression of the countenance there is none. I remember, at the Pergola theatre of Florence, discovering Louis Bonaparte from his likeness to the Emperor, which is very striking. but I am by no means confident that I should have been equally successful with Joseph. There is nothing about him indicative of high intellect. His eye is dull and heavy ; his manner un-

graceful and deficient in that ease and dignity which
we vulgar people are apt to number among the necessary attributes of majesty.   But Joseph was not
bred to kingcraft, and seems to have been forced
into it rather as a sort of political stop gap, than from
any particular aptitude or inclination for the duties
of sovereignty.   I am told he converses without any
appearance of reserve on the circumstances of his
short and troubled reign—if reign, indeed, it can be
called—in Spain.   He attributes more than half his
misfortunes, to the jealousies and intrigues of the
unruly marshals, over whom he could exercise no
authority.   He admits the full extent of his unpo-
pularity, but claims credit for a sincere desire to
benefit the people.

One circumstance connected with his deportment
I particularly remember. The apartment was warm,
and the ex-king evidently felt it so ; for taking out
his pockethandkerchief, he deliberately mopped his
bald " discrowned head," with a hand which one
would certainly have guessed to have had more connexion with a spit than a sceptre.

I remained a fortnight waiting for a change of

weather, but it never came. The roads, however, had become quite practicable for travelling, and I at length determined on departure. At five o'clock in the morning I accordingly drove to Market Street, where I took possession of a place in a sleigh shaped like an omnibus, which contained accommodation for about as many passengers. The snow lay deep on the ground, and the weather was cold in the extreme. After some delay the vehicle got into motion, and when we reached the Schuylkill, which is crossed by a wooden bridge of very curious mechanism, I looked back on the Quaker city, yet glimmering in the distance, and bade farewell to it for ever.

END OF VOLUME ONE.

EDINBURGH: BALLANTYNE AND CO., PAUL'S WORK, CANONGATE.

TRADITIONARY STORIES,

&c.

VOLUME II.

LONDON :
Printed by A. SPOTTISWOODE,
New-Street-Square.

TRADITIONARY STORIES

OF

OLD FAMILIES,

AND

LEGENDARY ILLUSTRATIONS

OF

FAMILY HISTORY.

WITH NOTES, HISTORICAL AND BIOGRAPHICAL.

BY ANDREW PICKEN,

AUTHOR OF THE " DOMINIE'S LEGACY,"
&c. &c.

IN TWO VOLUMES.

VOL. II.

LONDON:

LONGMAN, REES, ORME, BROWN, GREEN, & LONGMAN,
PATERNOSTER-ROW.

1833.

TRADITIONARY STORIES,

&c.

THE HAYS,

AND

THE FIGHT OF LONCARTY.

CHAPTER I.

ALL true Scotsmen will firmly believe that Kenneth the Third, of thief-hunting memory, was the *eightieth* king, at least[1], who had dominion over their unparalleled country. How many hundreds of monarchs besides may have ruled and "rang"[2] in that ancient kingdom before tradition could remember or history

[1] See Note A. at the end of this Tradition.
[2] We like to resort to words that were in use before

could write, it is not for us now particularly to affirm.

It was in the course of those romantic days when fable was considered as good as truth, and Poetry and Prose walked hand in hand together, in the imaginative ignorance of the olden time, that the great family of the Hays first began to have an historical origin in Scotland. Every one has heard of the battle of Loncarty, and how the Scots fought, and the Danes fell; but every one has *not* heard all the veritable particulars thereof, which have been revealed to us by the sure word of black-letter history, and transmitted tradition, assisted, no doubt,

---

our language, if not our manners, fell into a decline, as in the well-known old ballad : —

> " In days when our king Robert *rang*,
>   His trews they cost him half-a-crown ;
> He swore they were a groat * o'er dear,
>   And ca'd the tailor thief and loon."

A specimen both of expression and economy, some-what in contrast with the practice of most monarchs who at present " *ring*."

---

* Fourpence.

where need is, by the ruminating gestations of fancy.

Denmark, at the time we speak of, was a warlike kingdom; although Scotland, of course, was much its superior; and it was after the crowning of Haco the Fourth, its puissant monarch (we would not be positive about these ancient historicals), that a grand council was summoned of the nobles of the land, concerning some weighty matter that was to be laid before them, and the worthy lieges of the northern snows wondered what was hatching for the coming time.

The day of summons at length arrived, and the king and nobles were assembled in a magnificent hall, built of chipped logs, and hung round with a drapery of bears' hides; and, a secret ambition having come with a swelling effect over the monarch's heart, his majesty rose from his stool to make a speech.

" Nobles of Denmark, and mighty puissances," he said, "we are, without doubt, a great people, and I am, as you know, a potent king. Nevertheless, it cannot be denied that we are exceedingly poor, and have neither gold nor silver to build palaces withal, nor stamped coin to buy fine stuffs, nor flocks to make feasts of, like the nations of the south, nor a sufficiency of generous liquor for this exceeding cold climate ; while these Saxon islanders, in the western ocean, have a thousand good things that we greatly desire, and verily that we ought to have. Let us, therefore, cross the sea in our ships, and invade them at once, and we will bring home a glorious booty !"

Never was a king's speech better received. We cannot pledge ourselves for the precise words, but we know it had an instantaneous effect. The council saw at once the justice of the suggestion, and were unanimous in its favour. Proclamations were issued for the repairing of ships, and the whole coast of Denmark resounded with the clang of active preparation. In three weeks' time [or thereabouts] the fleet was ready, and sailed forth from the shores of the Baltic; for the ravage and robbery so pleasingly contemplated had been undertaken on a scale that rendered it respectable.

When the news of all this reached Scotland, the consternation and anxiety were proportionate to the occasion. But King Kenneth himself was but a poor man; the wealth, such as it was, being in the hands of the nobles, who kept the king, as at present, in proper subjection. So that, having the usual trouble with his " barons bold," his majesty, though puissant over the lower order of thieves, found himself in no good condition to resist the threatened invasion in a manner becoming the high character of Scotland.

At length the Danish fleet was fairly descried from a cape land, called the Red-head, in Angus-shire, while the Scottish monarch himself was then

—— " at Stirling town
Drinking the blood red wine,"

or engaged in some similarly kingly occupation.

Learning the tidings, his majesty immediately despatched " letters " —— that is, messages by word of mouth, for real *letters* would have been of little use, supposing his majesty could read himself, which he could not—to all his nobles and chief men that could be reached, for them to come forth with their followers, and meet him near the east coast, to fight the Danes, before they should take the kingdom.

But the invading Danes, still lingering at sea, when they got a sight of the black hills and hard-featured shores of " auld Scotland," were considerably damped in their anticipations of a rich paradise, and, before they landed, held a grave deliberation as to future proceedings. They said, that though the Scots were undoubtedly their ancient foes, and ought to be murdered and robbed for their special advantage, as had been done before, nevertheless, as the present was in reality more an adventure for booty, a sort of commercial speculation, after the ancient fashion, than any actual project for warlike glory, it would be much better to sail on to the southern end of the island, where what they were in quest of was in far greater plenty ; and where they might not, after all, find such a desperate resistance, as was well known to be usually given by a hungry people, who had nothing to spare to strangers. This scheme, however, feasible as it was, and all the desirable prospects that it opened up to the chiefs, whose mouths watered at the description given of English wealth, fell to the ground before the consideration of their limited numbers; and they thought it better to try the Scots still, divided as they were among themselves, and glean from them whatever they could, than venture into the open plains of a broad country and among a united people.

Landing, accordingly, at the mouth of the Esk, their rapacious legions soon over-ran the coast country. Robbery and rapine had its full sway for a time: the unresisting people fled before the invaders, who spread terror and desolation wherever they went; and harried and burnt all the towns and villages from Bervie in Forfar to the Frith of Tay. It was not until the invaders were within a few miles of Perth, which they had determined immediately to carry by storm, as well as to gut and pillage the old palace of Bertha, that the army, hastily collected by the Scottish king, were able to offer some check to their progress.

When the Scots came up, they found the Danes in a crowded encampment on the face of a hill, near a village by the Tay, in the parish of Redgorton, in Perthshire, and still — though known chiefly in the neighbourhood as an extensive bleaching-ground — well remembered in history by the name of Loncarty. When the Danes saw the Scottish array approach, and the latter descried the formidable legions of their invaders, pitched rank behind rank on the face of the height, a solemn pause took place between the armies, as if both felt that the fate of their existence or that of their country was almost too much to be put to the risk of a single engagement.

But we must now, short as the chapter is, turn over to the immediate subject of our tradition.

CHAPTER II.

On the edge of a hollow, on a branch of the stream, near which the armies lay, there lived at this time an industrious "landwart man," of the name of Hay, or La Hay, or Haya, as some of the ancient records spell the name, who, notwithstanding the terrors of invasion, peacefully prosecuted the labours of the field. Athletic and powerful, though not very rich, this farmer had two sons as brave as himself, yet by no means as peaceably inclined, or on an occasion like this so disposed to their labours, when war and ravage were almost at their door.

The farmer had doubtless many desires for the settlement of his children, and his sons had many ambitions for lands and lairdships; besides, each had his sweetheart whom he dreamt of o' nights, and whom he was doubtless exceedingly impatient to marry. When, therefore, the blast of war blew almost at their ears, and the cry of the coming foe began to be shouted along the valley of Glenshee, the hearts of the young Hays beat high at the sound; they looked on their father's ploughings with youthful contempt, and murmured and muttered, as young men will do, that no one would lead them to the forthcoming battle.

"Why should we labour here," they said, "on this cold sterile spot, while there are rich lands on the Tay from Errol to Kinnoul, which the king has to give to his brave defenders? The Danes are come to the very hill of Loncarty, while we roost here over our plough, like base louts of the field. Will no one give us a sword or hauberk, that we may strike a stroke for Scotland and the king?"

"Hooly, boys, hooly," said the cool landwart man, "the maiden does not dance till she's bid to the floor, and the piper does not pipe till he knows who hires him. The lands, to be sure, are broad in Strathtay, and rich in Gowrie, but every cheese must keep to its own chisset, and every man to his own trade, till fortune

comes to buy him lands that his father never
paid for. So keep your valour till you get the
word, and hold your plough irons to defend
your own heads. Up! the sun is high, let us
go to the ploughing."

With reluctant steps the youths followed to
their labours, but the sough of war rose up
through the glen; the boom and buzz of distant
squadrons disturbed their industry and swerved
their attention, the shrill note of the pibroch
came fitfully on the blast to make their hearts
bound with stirring thoughts, and crowds of
stragglers hurrying down the valley unsettled
their minds to their lowly toil. — But we must
now return to the king's camp in the neighbourhood, and speak of the great things that
were doing in the war.

The armies were now ready for the onset,
the Danes descending to the foot of the hill,
and the Scots in lines on the little field below.
Malcolm Duff, " Prince of Scotland and Lord
of Cumber[1]," led the right wing, Duncan,

---

[1] See Note B, at the end of this Tradition.

thane of Athol, the left, while the king himself, with his principal nobles and best men, took charge of the centre. The anxiety of the Scots monarch for his kingdom and his existence was shown by the pains he took to animate his army. "To move his nobles with courage and spirit," says the old chronicler Boethius, whose graphic account of this engagement we cannot hope to equal, "King Kenneth discharged them of all malise and duties to him for five years to come, then promised, by open proclamation, to give ilk man that brought him the head of ane Dane ten pund, or else land perpetually." When this was done, the worthy king "made orison to God to send his cause gude fortune."

"The armies stood long arrayet," continues the able chronicler, "while at last the Scots, too fierce and desirous of battle, came with incredible shower of dartes, arrows, and ganyes[1] on the Danes, who, impatient to sustain the invasion of Scottis, came forward with great nois." No corresponding shout, however, was

[1] See Note C, at the end of this Tradition.

set up by Kenneth's army, who joined in battle without even a sound of trumpet, and both " fought so fiercely that nane of them might sustain the preiss of the other."

But soldiers are mercenary like most others, and Scotsmen (like Englishmen) seldom forget their individual interests ; so the " ten pund " that the king had promised, so ran in each man's mind while he fought, that the heads of Danes, with a view to their value, were the chief thing that all aimed at, to the great detriment of the general battle. Thus, whenever a Scotsman killed a Dane, his great care was to cut off the man's head, and carry it, for safety, dangling in his hand, or else to run with it to the rear to secure his *ten pund*, and leave the victory to take care of itself. The consequences of this preponderance of individual interests were soon manifest ; and when the Danes observed it, says Boethius, picturesquely, " they cryet out with a schill voice, either to have victory," over such a head-cutting people, " or all at once to die." So, incontinent, they rushed with such propellant forward, that both the wings of Scottis were put to flight."

" Nochtless," however, continues our quaint historian, " the mid battle resisted valiantly the haill press of enemies. Now stood our army in great danger, for mony of the Scottis fled" (head in hand), " and were cruelly slane by the Danes."

The Hays, meantime, kept coolly labouring at their plough, although the noise and havoc of the distant battle sorely tried the self-denial of the young men. When the bruit arose, however, that their countrymen were beginning to flee, they could stand it no longer, and taking their coulters in their hands, for want of better weapons, away they set, at least, to have a stroke at the dastards of their own people, who now began to run across the fields near them. Proceeding onwards towards the army, they came to a narrow pass in the rear, through which the retreating Scots were rushing to get out of the danger.

Fired with indignation at this increasing cowardice, while they saw their country now at the mercy of the invaders, although the king still fought with the centre division of his men, "naked of both the wings," the gallant countryman and his two sons, "thinking nought so honourable as to die valiantly among sae mony noblemen," placed themselves in the gorge of the passage, "nocht far fra the battal, where gret numbers of Scottis were slane miserably fleeing," and slew both Danes who pursued and Scots who fled; saying, that all men deserved to die who turned their backs upon an enemy.

This noble conduct had an instantaneous effect to stay the panic, as our worthy chronicler most picturesquely states. So "ane certain number of Scots, who were right valiant and forcy, cryet out with schill voice, 'All gude Scottis men, return and renew battal, for defence of your king and realm, and avise now, whether it is more honest to jeopardy you with gude chance, in defence of your prince, than to be shamefully murdert in your fleeing!'"

Whether this cogent speech was made by the Hays themselves is not stated, but what by exhortations, and what by heavy blows with the yokes of their ploughs, the gallant farmer, assisted by his family, " constrained the Scottis whilk were fleeing, to return with him to battle against their enemies." They did so, and the Danes " astonest by their returning, and trysting" that this was " some new army coming on thar backs, left the chase of Scots, and returned to their folk. Then the Scots (whilk were vanquished afore), were raised with new spirit and courage, rushed fiercely on their enemies and put them to flight." Great slaughter was made in the battle, but more in the chase. " So the Scots," continues the chronicler, " gat this day ane glorious victory," particularly creditable to the perseverance of the mid wing of the army ; " yet, maist honourable to Hay and his valiant sons."

So unexpected was the advantage, after so disastrous a morning, and so complete and final was the discomfiture of the invaders, that the joy of the victors was almost as boundless as the king's gratitude to the patriotic individuals, who had been the means of achieving so glorious an adventure. The night after the battle was passed in the Scots camp " with singing and dancing, and incredible blitheness," and the succeeding day was looked forward to with pleasure, that the nobles and men who thus rejoiced might witness the honours given to Hay and his brave sons.

But the spoil was so considerable that had been taken from the invaders, — their ravages through this part of the country having been very productive while it lasted, — and the occasion so important of awarding its distribution, that the king, returning to his castle of Bertha, there commanded the valiant farmer, who had been the means of his glorious achievement, to be arrayed in cloth and splendid apparel, and forthwith brought before him.

The good man, however, nothing desiring the offered splendour, and considering that he had done nought but his duty to his country, " came with his sons in their auld and rusty habit, still sprinkled with the dust and sweat of battall," and modestly waited the king's pleasure. It was a brave sight to see his ma-joy in the midst of his nobles, awarding to each soldier his portion of the spoil, while crowds of people rent the air with acclamations, as Eric and his sons came forth into the midst. "What wilt thou have, brave man?" said the king, "and how shall I content thee for what thou hast done for thy country and for me?"

"I have done but my duty, honourable liege," said the farmer, "and it is not for myself that I would ask a reward; but my sons have maidens that they long to wed, and there are rigs of land from Errol to Kinnoul, that bear a crop of richer promise than the watery pastures in the Spital of Glenshee."

"Thou hast said right and modestly withal," answered the king; "and thy gallant sons shall have such rigs as a willing maiden may not refuse. To-morrow, make proclamation in our good city of Perth," he added, turning round to his attendants, "that we meet with our court at the Stone of Errol, and as far as the hawk shall fly, from our own hand, and until the spot where he alights again, if that shall

extend over a shire of our kingdom, these lands
shall the Hays have in full perpetuity, for the
service they have rendered ns on the field of
Loncarty."

Accordingly, after a day of acclamation and
joy, in which Kenneth and his army went in
procession through his good city of Perth, the
admiration of the people being more given to
the gallant Hay and his brave sons than to all
the nobles then in the monarch's train; the
whole assembled at the Stone of Errol, amidst
a gay crowd of lords and ladies, that the king's
award might be honourably given.   The gay
company was that morning set like hunters in
the greenwood.   The falconer was ready, and
handed his best bird to the king, while all the
nobles stood round, and envied the honours
done to Hay and his sons.

The hood was taken off the impatient bird,
it rose like an arrow off the king's finger; and
while it mounted high in air the people gave a
shout that made the welkin ring, and could
almost be heard at the hill of Kilspindie. Away
galloped the horsemen forth into the plain,

that they might see and give witness where the falcon should fly.

Away went the bird out of all men's sight, and it flew and flew and never stopped, until it began to draw near to the town of Ross, which is not far from " bonnie Dundee." Then it poised itself, and began to descend, until it lighted down on " ane stane," which is still pointed out to the traveller in these parts, and called the Falcon Stane until this day; and so when the messengers returned the king gave to Hay all the lands over which the falcon flew, between Tay and Errol, " quhilk lands are yet inhabited by his posterity." [1]

" Attour," saith Boethius, " that nane of his valiant deeds should perish, but aye remain in recent and perpetual memory, King Kenneth gave him three red shields in ane field of silver, to bear in manner of arms in place of the yoke, to signify that he was promoted from small and obscure lyneage, to great honours, riches, and lands."

[1] See Note D. at the end of this Tradition.

So this is the origin of the great family of the Hays, which hath spread itself over every part of the united empire; and this became the beginning of the many honours deservedly heaped upon the numerous descendants of the valiant farmer, from the day of Loncarty until the present time.[1]

Nor is our excellent tradition without a moral. Nay, indeed, it contains a double induction, which is more than can be said for many a longer tale. For, besides the prominent one so creditable to the Hays, its chief pith lies, after all, in the following maxim,—that no king, when he goes forth to battle, ought to offer a reward of "ten pund" for the cutting off of heads in the heat of the fray.

[1] See note E.

NOTES

TO THE TRADITION OF

THE HAYS, AND THE FIGHT OF LONCARTY.

NOTE A, page 1.

PRIDE of country is only an extension of the principle of pride of descent, and frequently takes the same direction. It was this that made Buchanan so zealous in raking up from all the monkish chronicles the names of so many *kings*, of which he makes this Kenneth to be the eightieth, although he " rang," as the Scots call it, as early as towards the end of the tenth century.

As we have alluded to those chief characteristics which have made this monarch remembered, it is to be observed, that since the *exposé* of the border thieves and highland robbers, by the late Sir Walter Scott, the two extremities of this ancient kingdom, where they principally made their depredations, have had a bad name, while the people of the east and west centre have plumed themselves upon their superior historical honesty. But though the worthy lieges of the western shires are known to be perfectly just men in our own day, it appears that in King Kenneth's time they must have been rather worse than their neighbours; for, in commencing his proceedings against the swarms of depredators with which his realm was almost eaten up, and essaying to make a circuit round the kingdom, he thought fit to begin in Lanarkshire, and set himself down in that ancient county. Here, as the reader knows, he summoned all the leading men in the west; but so deeply were the lairds and barons of that neighbourhood implicated themselves and by their relatives in the crimes that the king wished to punish, that scarcely any of them attended; so his majesty could do nothing at that time, and was obliged to put a smooth face on the matter, and to fly to an honester part of the country, namely Galloway, to consult what was best to be done. The state of matters seems to have been too bad for him to know how to apply a remedy; and it was only by getting together his barons at Scoon by a sort of stratagem, and overawing them when assembled by an ambush of armed men, that he got them to consent to reform themselves first, and then to give him their aid in punishing the most "notour" thieves of his kingdom.

But James the Fifth, five centuries afterwards, was, of all the Scottish monarchs, the most active personal hunter of the professional thieves of his good realm; at a time when the king bare upon his individual shoulders the weight of governing both his barons and his people, and was looked to as the personal dispenser of justice and punisher of crimes. It was on one of those travelling circuits, as the reader knows, that he hanged the celebrated Johnnie Armstrong and his men, near the border, a proceeding at which the latter were exceedingly astonished.

Though the old principle of man's preying upon his fellow is rooted in the same soil and evolves itself still by the same unceasing efforts, it can seldom now go so direct to its object, and requires a longer apprenticeship to the world, to master the complexities of society and make sure of its victim.

NOTE B, page 11.

It may be hardly necessary to remind the reader that Cumber, or Cumberland, was considered part of the Scottish kingdom; and the kings of that country gave their eldest sons the title of princes of it; in order, no doubt, that they should prize it more because it was debateable land, and usually claimed by the English, to which after many "just and necessary" wars, it was, of course, ultimately ceded.

NOTE C, page 12.

Ganyes were a sort of heavy dart or javelin, thrown from some engine, probably of the cross-bow character, which some speak of as "ane irone gunn." These machines were much used in ancient times, must have been very useful for destruction, and were probably accompanied by some machinery. Douglas thus speaks of them, in his translation of Virgil :—

> " So thick the ganyeis and the flanys flew,
> That of takles and shafts all the field was strew't."

Note D, page 20.

During the times when, from the similarity of appearance on the field of battle which the wearing of mail armour gave to men, it was customary for each clan or name to wear a particular badge in the helmet or bonnet, generally a sprig of some plant, the Hays adopted the mistletoe for theirs. There was formerly, as we are informed by Mr. Hay Allan, whom we shall hereafter have further occasion to quote, in the neighbourhood of Errol, and not far from the Falcon stone, a vast oak, of an unknown age, and upon which grew a profusion of the plant. Many charms and legends were considered to be connected with the tree, and the duration of the family of Hay was said to be united with its existence. It was believed that a sprig of the mistletoe, cut by a Hay, on Allhallowmas eve, *with a new dirk*, and after going round the tree three times sunwise, and pronouncing a certain spell, was a sure charm against all glamour or witchery, and an infallible guard in the day of battle.

A sprig of this plant, gathered in the same manner, was then often placed in the cradles of infants, and thought to defend them from being changed for elf-bairns by the fairies. It was also an ancient prophecy, that, when the root of this oak had perished, " the grass should grow in the hearth of Errol, and a raven should sit in the falcon's nest." This, like many other traditional prophecies, has never been exactly fulfilled, although the oak has disappeared for many years, unless the passing of the lands of Errol from the family may be thought to help out the anticipated catastrophe.

NOTE E, page 21.

Mr. Chalmers, the author of the "Caledonia," and others after him, do not believe in our tradition, notwithstanding all the *proofs* that remain in existence of its perfect authenticity. It is very uncivil of any prying antiquarian not to believe a good story. For our part, we believe every thing that is pleasant to read or tell, and *shall* believe it; and the *will* is the better part of faith, as all men know. Besides, to elevate the argument above the occasion — for all moral or pleasurable purposes, *impression* is the thing; and impression, when once made, is little affected one way or another by questions as to fact, when the mind is satisfied; especially as it is so often found that fable and fancy are better and more agreeable than hard-featured truth.

We are not willing to part with the tradition of the Hays; and we therefore argue, with the annotators of Buchanan, and with even Mr. Chalmers himself in another part of his book, that tradition is always founded *on something;* that where it is feasible, and supported by existing monuments, it is likely to be true; and that, if we reject it, we reject the chief foundation of early history. That there was a battle fought at the place called Loncarty, is proved from the tumuli still observable on the field, and the quantities of human bones mingled with spear heads and other remains of ancient weapons that have been from time to time dug up among these tumuli. And the truth of the story of the falcon is pretty well attested by the existence of the stone on which it is said to have alighted, and the transmission from age to age of an incident which is little likely to have been the invention of a rude people.

The genealogists, however, copying from one another, assert (the more positively that they know nothing on the matter); that the Hays did not come into Britain until the twelfth century, along with the followers of William the Conqueror, although Chalmers only uses a "probably" in speaking of this; and, on the authority of an old charter, sets down, that the first of the name *appearing on Scottish record* was William de Hay — or, as Douglas spells it, Haya — who was settled in Lothian, and became *pincerna domini Regis* — king's butler, or cup-bearer to Malcolm IV. This William died about 1170, but having married a sister of Ranulph de Sules, Lord of Liddisdale, his office, of pincerna passed into the Soulis family, although his eldest son inherited the joint lands.

The heir of this baron, called also William de Hays, carried on the direct line of the Hays of the middle parts; but it was his brother Robert from whence sprung the earls and marquesses of Tweeddale, as well as the ancient lords of Yester, and the Hays of Locherart. The second William, chief of the house, was the frequent companion of William the Lion, and had the honour to be one of the hostages for him, upon his being liberated from an English prison by Henry II. in 1174.

During this period, however, says Chalmers, " there were *other Hays* in Scotland;" and we take leave to argue, with some authorities, in defence of our tradition, that the Hays first proprietors of Errol were originally a Dutch family, and that the name was probably Haig (or as like it as may be), from the town of that name. Chalmers, however, on the authority of his charter, makes

William the Lion give Errol with its pertinents in the carse
of Gowrie, to William de Haya, the second above mentioned; although there is no reason why that property
might not have been in the family before, or the present
might merely be a confirmation of the right.

Antiquariarns and peerage writers have little reason,
however, to dogmatise upon the subject of the origin of
this family, as appears from various documents which
have by enquiry come into our hands, but which can
hardly be noticed here. To a book of poems, but little
known, published some years ago by James Hay Allan,
Esq., a highland gentleman of talent, and considerable
acquaintance with the manners and antiquities of the
North, there is appended some curious notes, among
which is one giving such an account of the real origin
of the Hays as is well worthy to be put against the *ipse
dixit* of the antiquarians. This account purports to be
taken from a MS. history of that family to which he
refers, but where he found it he does not inform us. We
extract the note entire, as he gives it, for the information
of such as take an interest in these enquiries : —

" Mac Garadh," he says, is the ancient name of the
Hays. It is of genuine Gaelic origin, and was given first
to the family in allusion to the celebrated action by which
he raised himself from obscurity. It is very expressive
of the circumstance : its literal signification is a dike or
barrier, and was given to the ancestor of the Hays for
his conduct at the battle of Loncarty, when he stood
between the flying Scots and the victorious Danes like
a wall or barrier of defence.

" The reason of the loss of the original appellation in
after-times, and that it was not perpetuated in the sub-

sequent surname of the family, must be sufficiently evident to those who are acquainted with the history of hereditary designations. Surnames did not come into use in England before the time of the Conqueror, and their introduction in Scotland was at a date a little subsequent. The name of Garadh was given to the ancestors of the Hays about one hundred and fifty-six years before, and had not, therefore, been subsequently retained by his descendants as an individual designation, but was only used generally as the name of the whole race, as Clann na Garadh, and particularly as the patronymic of the chief, who was designated Mac Mhic Garadh Mor, and Sgithan Dearg, the son of the son of Garadh-of the red shields.

"At the time, therefore, of the adoption of surnames, the appellation of Garadh had grown into antiquity, and there were also other reasons which still more forcibly actuated in its neglect. In the reign of Mac Beath, there were but two brothers of the direct descendants of Garadh; and during the troubles of that tyrant's usurpation, the younger 'being right bald and stalwarth of heart,' went into Normandy, where he married the daughter and heiress of one of the barons of the dukedom.

"Surnames had by this time become partially in use on the Continent, and in his domiciliation in Normandy, the descendent of Garadh was desirous of adopting a name which should conform to the language and usage and language of the country, and at the same time perpetuate the memory of his origin. For this purpose he assumed the name of De la Haye, which is a sufficiently literal translation of Garadh; the first signifying a hedge or fence, the latter a dike or barrier.

" In the reign of Malcolm Cean Mor," continues the same authority, " the son of the first de la Haye was one of the warriors who accompanied William of Normandy into England. Some time after the Conquest, he made a journey into Scotland to visit his uncle, the chief of the Clan na Garadh, then grown to a very advanced age, and without children. During this visit the old chief died; and there being no other heir, De la Haye was declared his successor. From this time he abandoned the service of William, residing wholly in Scotland; and having refused to return to the English dominions during the subsequent quarrel with King Malcolm concerning the protection of the Saxons, he incurred the resentment of William, and was forfeited of all his Norman estates. From this period the name became hereditary to the descendants of Garadh, and the old appellation dropped into oblivion."

The further account given by this gentleman of these early times, may be thought by many important; and is succinct and well-expressed as matter of history. To the civilising policy of this Malcolm, and still more afterwards of David the First, in inviting into Scotland so many Norman chieftains, whose fathers had come to Britain with William the Bastard, and which chieftains became the founders of so many of our great Scottish families, we shall hereafter have occasion to allude. " But the Gaelic having," continues Mr. Hay Allan, " been neglected at court, and broken by the vast intercourse of foreigners, gradually wore into disuse, and was at length entirely superseded by the Saxon. The ancient Celtic names fell with the language in which they had arisen; the fashionable appellations of foreigners obtained without rivalry; and nearly at the same period appeared the De Champbells, the De la Hayes, the De Bruces, the De Ruthvyns, the Frasiers, the De Boyds, and many others, who either adopted in a foreign country a foreign appellation, or sprung by one side of the house from the adventurous warriors of the continental chivalry.

" The destruction of the Scottish records by Edward I.; the dispersion, at the Reformation, of the Carthusian library in Iona; and the loss of the Stirling papers carried into England by General Monk, have deprived us of all deeds or other documental evidence of the family of Hay while it bore the name of Mac Garadh; and for this reason *their legal and chartulary history is confined to the Saxon records;* and, as these are no older than the Conquest, this, coupled with the French construction of the surname, gave rise to the erroneous belief, expressed by Douglas and others, that the family was of *Norman* and *Italian* extraction.

" The same accidents and the same fatality have injured the history, and obscured the origin, of the Whymses, and several other houses of Celtic derivation."

But though Mr. Hay Allan omits to tell us in whose possession the MS. history now is, we cannot doubt of its existence; for he has printed in his book a war-song of the family, called " The gathering of the Hays," which, he says he copied from an odd leaf or fragment, which he found pasted into that history. The slogan song begins in the following stirring manner, and the whole, accompanied as it was on the bagpipe by the pibroch of the clan, gives a good idea of what must have once been the effect of such words and music :—

> " Mac Garadh ! Mac Garadh ! red race of the Tay,
> Ho ! gather, ho ! gather like hawks to the prey :
> Mac Garadh, Mac Garadh, Mac Garadh come fast,
> The flame's on the beacon, the horn's on the blast.
> The standard of Errol unfolds its white breast,
> And the falcon of Loncartie stirs in her nest :
> Come away — come away— come to the tryste —
> Come in, Mac Garadh from east and from west."

The picture of the charge is almost terrific :—

> " Mac Garadh is coming ! like stream from the hill,
> Mac Garadh is coming, lance, claymore, and bill :
>   Like thunder's wide rattle,
>   Is mingled the battle,
> With cry of the falling, and shout of the charge;
>   The lances are flashing,
>   The claymores are clashing,
> And ringing the arrows on buckler and targe !"

The transcriber of this song states that some stanzas of it, as the above, &c. are very ancient, and others are quite modern — that scraps of it he has heard sung by old people in Perthshire — and that the old war-cry of the Hays was " Haleu Mac Garadh !" — See *Bridal of Caolchairn, &c. by James Hay Allan, Esq.* Note, p. 334, &c.

But to return to our own historical sketch :—

It was during the glorious struggle of the deliverer

Bruce, that the Hays who lived in his days distinguished themselves for noble patriotism for their depressed country, and romantic attachment to their heroic king; Gilbert de la Haye having been appointed one of the regents of the kingdom during the minority of Alexander III., and Nicholas de la Haye, then of Errol, being one of the nominees of Bruce to the throne of Scotland. Gilbert and Hugh, the sons of the latter, being also at his romantic coronation by the Countess of Buchan, and following him in his efforts to resist Pembroke and Percy, who had now marched as far as Perth; at the brave and disadvantageous struggle of Methven wood Hugh de la Haye was taken prisoner by the English, and Bruce, with his remaining followers, was driven to the mountains.

Here, along with the Earl of Athol, the young and gallant Sir James Douglas, Sir Neil Campbell, Edward Bruce the brother of the king, and many others, as well as several ladies who chose to share the danger of their lords in this wild hiding-place, Gilbert de la Haye, the remaining brother, encountered with his king and his brave companions all the perils and toils of that remarkable campaign. Not to dwell upon the details of these stirring times, it was for his services during Bruce's struggle for independence that the grateful hero raised Gilbert de la Haye (as the name was then spelt) to the dignity of hereditary high constable of Scotland, which is held by the Earls of Errol until the present day.

It was James II., however, who, for services rendered, created Errol into an earldom, adding that title to the office of constable united in the head of the house; and from this noble stock, says Chalmers, spring the Hays

Earls of Kinnoul, Hay Lord Becolie and Earl of Carlisle, Hay of Leyes, Hay of Pitfour, Hay of Renfield, Hay
of Inchoch, and many others.

This sketch must necessarily take in but few facts, and
omit altogether any notice of the subsidiary branches of
this family.   Francis, the eighth earl, adhering to the
catholic religion, as did most of the heads of the ancient
families, joined with the Earls of Crawford, Huntley, and
Bothwell, in a rebellion against James V.'s government
in 1589, and in 1592 Errol was committed prisoner to
the castle of Edinburgh on a charge of " papistry " and
a treasonable correspondence with Spain.   See Pitcairn's
Criminal Trials, Part II.   Notwithstanding that the Earl
and Huntley were released from this trouble, refusing to
decamp from the kingdom, they raised a formidable army
of their adherents, and defeated the royal army of 7000
men at Strathaven, commanded by the Earl of Argyle.
The circumstances of their case of rebellion, however,
must have been peculiarly excusable; for, on the king's
advancing against them, he granted them permission to
go abroad, upon their giving security that they should
neither return without his licence, nor engage in any new
intrigues against the protestant religion, or the peace of
the kingdom.

This earl, who was married to a Douglas of the Morton
branch, as also to two Stuarts, one the daughter of the
then Earl of Athol, and the other of the celebrated
Regent Moray, appears, notwithstanding his rebellion, to
have been a man highly regarded both by his king and
his own dependants; and the former gave him permission
to return to Scotland after an absence of only two years.
Afterwards, in 1604, he was one of the Commissioners
nominated by Parliament to treat of a union with Eng-

land. " He was," says Sir Robert Douglas, " a truly
noble man, of a great and courageous spirit, who had
great troubles in his time, which he stoutly and honourably carried; and now, in favour, died in peace with God
and man, and a loyal subject to the king, to the great
grief of his friends." One act of this earl ought not
to be passed over. Dying at Slains, his noble castle in
Aberdeenshire, which stands on a picturesque precipice
overhanging the sea, he gave directions, on his death-bed,
that, instead of the gorgeous funeral intended for him, he
should be buried privately in the church of that place,
and that the calculated expense of a showy " earthing up"
might be distributed to the poor and needy of the neighbourhood. This was done amid blessings and prayers
for his soul, and his memory is held in corresponding reverence even until this day.

The son of this nobleman, who acted as high constable
of Scotland at the coronation of Charles I., though bred
up in the protestant religion, appears to have been of a
very different disposition; for, pleased with show and
expense, he lived in such splendour, that he involved
himself in debt, and was obliged to sell his ancient pa-
ternal lordship of Errol, granted to his ancestors, says
Douglas, " by King William the Lion, and the lands
thereunto annexed." The son of this nobleman, namely,
Gilbert, the tenth earl, having no male issue, the title and
property fell in to the Hays of Killour; and in the early
part of last century, the title devolving on a female,
namely, Mary, Countess of Errol in her own right, who
married Alexander Falconer, of Newton, second son of
Lord President Falconer, the countess, at the coronation

c 6

of George II., claimed to act by deputy as high constable of Scotland, and the Duke of Roxburgh was appointed to officiate for her ladyship on that occasion. Lady Margaret Hay, who succeeded this lady, having married James, fifth Earl of Linlithgow and Callendar, and that nobleman *going out* in the fifteen, his estates were attainted; so Lady Ann Livingston, the surviving daughter, having obtained a lease of her father's attainted estate at a low rent, married William Boyd, the celebrated Lord Kilmarnock, who was beheaded in 1746, for his attachment to the house of Stuart.

The history of the latter unfortunate nobleman is well known; and if it be true, as is generally alleged, that he was induced to "go out" in the forty-five chiefly by the instigation of his lady, as well as that of his grand aunt, the old Countess of Errol, wife of President Falconer, then alive, the case is remarkable of a house being divided within itself; for, while the father and his *second* son, namely, the Honourable Charles Boyd, were engaged for the young Pretender, his eldest son, namely, James, Lord Boyd, held a commission from George II. in the twenty-first foot, and William, the third son, was in the royal navy, and on board Commodore Barnet's ship, at the period of his father's execution. His brother Charles, above-mentioned, after the battle of Culloden, fled into Arran, the ancient territory of the Boyds, and among its wild mountains managed to conceal himself for a whole year. Fortunately finding a chest of medical books, the refugee occupied himself in the study of them so effectually, that he acquired considerable skill in physic; and, escaping to France, is said to have practised medicine on the Continent for twenty years, after which he returned to Scotland, and, living for a time in the family castle of Slains, in

Aberdeenshire, died at Edinburgh, in 1785, after marrying a lady of the name of Haliburton, daughter of an Edinburgh citizen.

James, Lord Boyd, above mentioned, claiming his father's forfeited estate, the claim was sustained by the House of Lords, in 1751: in 1758, he succeeded his grand-aunt as fourteenth Earl of Errol; and in three years after, his lordship officiated at the coronation of George III. as hereditary high constable of Scotland. Of this there is an anecdote that is worth recording. Neglecting to pull off his cap on the king's entrance into Westminster Hall, some of the bystanders gave him notice of his duty: on finding his error, Lord Boyd confusedly pulled off his cap, and apologised to the king for his unconscious negligence and seeming disrespect. But the good-natured monarch entreated him to be covered as before, and condescendingly intimated that he looked on his presence at such a solemnity as a very peculiar honour.

The personal appearance of this nobleman, particularly when dressed in his constable's robes, is described as remarkably handsome and imposing. "His stature," says Dr. Beattie, in a letter to Mrs. Montague, "was six feet four inches, and his proportions most exact. His countenance and deportment exhibited such a mixture of the noble and graceful, as I have never seen united in any other person. He often put me in mind of an ancient hero; and I remember Dr. Johnson was positive that he resembled Homer's character of Sarpedon;" and Sir William Forbes, who introduces the above into his Life of Beattie, adds, " Were I desired to specify the man of the most graceful form, the most elegant, polished, and popular manners which I have ever known in my long intercourse with society, I should not hesitate to name James, Earl of Errol."

But when the qualities of the mind and the virtues of the heart and disposition corresponded with such an exterior, what a truly noble personage we have before us! His manners, says the same authority, were " wonderfully agreeable;" he was " a most affectionate and attentive parent, husband, and brother; elegant in his economy; somewhat expensive, yet exact and methodical. He exerted his influence as a man of rank and a magistrate in doing good to all in his neighbourhood. In a word, he was adored by his servants, a blessing to his tenants, and the darling of the whole country;" and his death, which took place at Callendar House, in the 53d year of his age, is spoken of as " a great loss to his country, and a matter of unspeakable regret to his friends." Such a character, united to such high station, forms altogether a picture of human nature truly enviable.

Two sons of this nobleman were successively Earls of Errol; of the latter of whom, William Hay Carr, the present Earl, is the second son. The Earl is, therefore, the sixteenth Earl of Errol, and twenty-first high constable of Scotland.

On the privileges and estimation of this latter peculiar title, the reader may possibly have some curiosity. We therefore, subjoin the following observations, professionally given by Philip Wood, in his " Annotations on Sir Robert Douglas."

" As constable of Scotland," he says, " the Earl of Errol is, by birth, the first subject in the kingdom, after the blood royal; and, as such, hath a right to take place of every hereditary honour. The chancellor and constable of England do, indeed, take precedency of him, but these are only temporary honours, to which no man can lay claim by birth; so that, *by birth*, the Earl of Errol ranks, *without a doubt*, as the first subject in Great Britain, next to the princes of the blood royal." — Vol. i. p. 556. note.

*   *   *   *   *

Of traditionary poetry illustrative of the history of the Hays, we have met with little besides the known ballad, beginning —

> " Errol is a bonny place,
> It stands upon a plain," &c.

And although, in ancient times, ladies of the highest rank busied themselves in employments which those of modern times would not deign to superintend, or even to have it supposed that they had any knowledge of; yet we doubt if the ballad poet was well acquainted with his subject, when he puts the following lines, however interesting for their quaint descriptiveness, in the mouth of any of the countesses of Errol. The lady, as the ballad states, is sadly discontented because she is childless; and, in her vexation, is supposed to murmur thus : —

> " What needs I wash my apron,
> Or drie it upon a door?
> What needs I eek ? my petticoat
> Hangs even down afore.

> " What needs I wash my apron,
> Or hang it upon a pin ?
> For lang will I gae but and ben,
> Ere I hear my young son's din."

But if the Countess of Errol could wash an apron for herself, and hang it upon *a door*, it is to be remembered that Queen Penelope was an industrious weaver; and the daughter of Jacob, who was, at least, a prosperous Palestine *laird*, could go to the well herself to draw water. But that was in the good old times, when ladies were of some service; and the countess would not have grudged her work if she only had had a son to give her more to do. So, being " very unhappy, indeed," she totally ran off from her lord; or, more literally speaking, *deserted the diet*, notwithstanding a daily invitation, as in the Aberdeen rhyme : —

> " Seven years on Errol's table
>   There stands clean dish and speen ;
> And every day the bell is rung,
>   Cries, Lady, come and dine."

*   *   *   *   *

One of the most remarkable men of the Hays' name was the celebrated favourite of James I., who created such envy of the Scots among the English nobility.   This was James Lord Hay, Baron of Sawley, in England, first advanced to his baronage *without* a seat in the House of Lords.   He was made master of the king's wardrobe, and afterwards created Viscount Doncaster and Earl of Carlisle, and sent ambassador to the French and other courts.

The chief reason of Lord Hay's being employed on these embassies, was, besides his acknowledged abilities, his fine person, and extraordinary disposition to magnificence in dress and style of living. " He was," says Granger, " princely in his entertainments, magnificent in his dress, and splendid in his retinue."   The story of his having his horse shod with silver, when he made his public entry into Paris, is well known. "It is probable," adds Granger, in referring to the fact, "that the shoes were purposely slightly fastened, for the more ostentatious display of his vanity, especially as a smith went in the procession with a bag of horse-shoes of the same metal, for a supply."

Nor was it merely by the richness of his apparel, and the pomp of his retinue, that the Earl of Carlisle excited the envy of the English and French nobles of his time. His entertainments were on a scale commensurate with his exterior grandeur, for he had pies baked full of perfumed meats, of such extraordinary size and richness as to excite the wonder even of the luxurious French. It was part of the boasted kingcraft of the cunning James to endeavour, by means of the ostentatious vanity of this lord, to dazzle foreign courts into respect for his government. But they are seldom successful who calculate too far on the meaner passions of human nature; so the ambassador, with all his splendour, was often treated with studied contempt. Prince Maurice, for one, as is related, having received intelligence that the English "ambassador and his retinue were to dine with him, called for the bill of fare, which was intended for the ordinary course of his table that day. Finding a pig, among other meats, and knowing the Scottish aversion to that animal, the prince ordered two pigs to be dressed instead of one, without any other addition. This was an intended affront, as well to the king as to his ambassador; for James's hatred to swine's flesh was proverbial. The opprobrious pig was, therefore, the occasion of much laughter at this time."

The profusion of James, in the embassy alluded to, is astonishing, when his own poverty is considered. The dresses of this nobleman were the theme of ample description by the writers of the time. How he supported this extravagance is not well known, saving that James, in order to uphold him in it, procured him for his wife the only daughter and heiress of Lord Denny, the greatest match, as we are told, of that time. The Earl of Holland was the only man about the court who could vie with the magnificent Earl of Carlisle; and when the two, as appointed, espoused Henrietta Maria, then Infanta of Spain, in the heyday of the Potosi mines, they were each " clothed in beaten silver."

Aside from this peculiarity, however, the Earl of Carlisle was an able and sensible man. His passion for dress and feasting continued almost to the last moment of his life, even when he knew that he was given over by his physicians. He died on the 25th of April, 1636.

One of the most gallant and accomplished cavaliers of this family, however, was the well known Sir Francis Hay, of Dalgatie. A faithful follower of Montrose in his unfortunate career, he was taken prisoner with him at his last fatal battle, and condemned to the same terrible fate. Refusing, on the scaffold, as a good Roman catholic, the attendance of the presbyterian clergy, he was not permitted the consolations of his own form of faith in his dying moments; and yet he kissed the axe of the headsman, avowed his fidelity to the king, and died like a soldier.

Several persons of this respected family have distinguished themselves even in antiquarian literature. The MSS. collected by Father Richard Augustin Hay, once a canon of St. Généviève, at Paris, and prior of St. Pierremont, and afterwards of Drumboot in Scotland, an intimate of the well-known Lord Auchinleck, at the beginning of last century, were thought an acquisition worthy of purchase for the Advocates' Library in Edinburgh, where they now are. Father Hay is also author of some curious particulars regarding the Templars, some collections in family history, an account of churches, monasteries, and " devout places," and other works. There is also Alexander Hay, the well-known historian of the antiquities of Chichester; and William Hay, the translator of Martial's Epigrams, &c.

*   *   *   *   *

What branch of the Hay family settled in the south of Ireland we have no means of knowing; but they being still strongly attached to the catholic religion, the first of them probably took refuge there during the troubles that preceded the Reformation in Scotland. One of the most prominent of them, of late years, was the well-known Edward Hay, long secretary to the Catholic Association : a better-tempered man, or one who could imbibe a more capacious skinful of claret or whisky punch, never stretched a leg under Irish mahogany. Mr. Hay, however, was almost too good-natured and open of mind for some of the society with whom he was associated; and, though his elder brother had been hanged in the troubles of 1798, was neither so violent nor so wild as several of the others. There is a story, however, of another brother of Mr. Hay's, who, although the whole family lay under the heavy ban of government suspicion, was then on service against the rebellious part of his countrymen, as a captain in a dragoon regiment, that probably deserves to be told here, though partly narrated in several of the publications of the time. It is this : —

During the sanguinary skirmishes that took place in Ireland, upon the first assault of Wexford by the rebels, the forward bravery of Captain Hay led him into circumstances which ended in his being made prisoner by the enemy.   At this period quarter was seldom given or taken, at least for more than a day, on the part of the rebels, and only then that they might despatch their prisoners with more aggravation of cruelty and degradation. From the manner in which Captain Hay's family, however, was regarded in the neighbourhood, his life was spared; and this circumstance, together with what afterwards followed, became the cause of a charge of treason against him.

When the captain got back to his troop, he became one of the gallant band who so bravely defended the town of Enniscorthy; but the approaches of the rebels, in the celebrated battle of Vinegar Hill, had been so regular, and their tactics so superior to their ordinary proceedings, that it was broadly suggested by some of the loyal yeomen that their plans must have been given by Captain Hay, and that, in fact, he must have been their willing prisoner. For these suspicions a court martial was appointed to try him for desertion and high treason, the fatal proceedings of which were only suspended by the bloody attack on the town immediately after.

Agitated by the various terrors of these circumstances, Captain Hay had little care for his own life, compared with that of one in whose fate and safety he was deeply interested.   This was a Miss Moor, daughter of a merchant in Wexford, to whom, with all the gallantry of a soldier and the warmth of an Irishman, the captain had become strongly attached. Fleeing from her native city, during the horrors of these times, accompanied only by a Mrs. Ogle, wife of the member for the county, the ladies, unattended by any protector, took refuge in the town of Enniscorthy; Miss Moor, in particular, thinking herself safe in any place where the captain was near.

Enniscorthy, though once one of the strongest places in the south, where the English, under the redoubted Strongbow, originally established themselves, is now without fortification; and, beautifully situated on the banks of the Slaney, forms almost the base of the celebrated Vinegar Hill, which rises, round and picturesque, out of the plain behind it. The horrors of this frightful time were only beginning; for, led by the celebrated Father Roche, the priest, the rebels, with wild shouts, came close to the town; and a succession of scenes took place, perhaps unparalleled in history for obstinate valour and ferocious barbarity. No quarter was given or taken on either side: the rebels, with their green flags, came up in confused masses, and with wild cries, on the English troops; and as often as they were repulsed, and made to run, Father Roche, a man of great height and proportionate muscle, in a squalid dress, covered with blood and the mud of the field, and with a countenance described as ruffianly and terrific, rallied them again and again, and with blasphemous appeals to the God of battles, brought them afresh to the charge.

The comparative handful of royal troops fought long and obstinately; but at length, overpowered by numbers, and wearied with their persevering charges, they were ultimately forced within the town; and now a scene took place whichwell might appal stronger hearts than those of the poor ladies, who all this while suffered unspeakable terrors. As soon as the rebels got into the street, furiously seeking for lighted brands, they not only massacred the fleeing wretches, but set fire to the town in every direction, in order that the relics of the royal troops who were hemmed in beyond it might be completely destroyed.

The feelings of Captain Hay, all this while, and in particular when he saw the street in which his beloved and her friend had taken refuge fired on both sides by order of Father Roche, it were not easy to describe. The moment was the last, and the case was desperate. Having a powerful horse, in which he could trust, he leaped upon it, dashed through a crowd of savage incendiaries into the midst of the burning street, determined to rescue her, or perish with her in the flames.

But how to leave his horse while he sought his friend, as the terrified animal reared, and snorted, at the objects of its fear, he could not decide. Jamming it, at length, in a narrow passage, he managed to fasten it, and soon found the ladies fainting in distraction, and giving themselves up for lost. There was no time for expressions of joy when hurrying them down to the street : he begged of them, for God's sake, to be cool, and exert all their energies, while he should try to save them : but what was he to do ? for there were two of them besides himself, and here he had but one horse, their only hope, while the flames from both sides of the street were fast approaching them, and the savage shouting without told too well what was going forward. Lifting Miss Moor in his arms, he at once set her on the shoulder of the animal : conjuring her to hold firm, he next lifted Mrs. Ogle on behind the saddle, while he sprang on also between them ;

and thus, three on one horse, he determined, if possible, to make his way through the fire and the rebels.

When they got again among the smoke and the heat, the burdened animal refused to go forward, the sight in front was so truly appalling : but it was now life or death to them all ; and the gallant Hay looked forth into the flames with determined bravery, only still exhorting the ladies, who clung to him, to be firm and courageous. Thrusting the spurs into the very ribs of his horse, he dashed into the flames, while the fire and smoke almost blinded him, and the heat was so intolerable that the foaming animal stood still at one point, trembling with terror, and again refusing to move. The ladies screamed, feeling the scorching fire, yet the determined captain still urged the horse forward, while the hissing flames twined round their heads, and the choking smoke almost rendered them insensible ; but it was the falling brands of burning timber, and large sparks of hot flame, that was most dreadful to the ladies, and most terrific to the poor animal, as they struggled through the fire. At length, by incredible efforts on the captain's part, and great resolution on that of his fair charge, they cleared, though severely scorched, the burning town ; and when the rebels at that part saw a horse gallop out from the midst of the flames, carrying three persons, with looks of terrified excitement, they gave way on every side, and even set up shouts of admiration at so much bravery.

The joy and gratitude of the ladies, to their gallant deliverer, when they found themselves safe, though severely scorched, may be partly conceived. They and their friends loaded him with blessings; and that he married Miss Moor afterwards, we have no doubt, if it were for no other reason but to make the drama complete. On this latter point, however, we have no information; but we know that Captain Hay's bravery, on this occasion, removed all the suspicion to which he had been subjected, and he was restored to the full confidence of his regiment, and had the applause of all.

THE PRIORS OF LAWFORD;

A STORY OF THE DOMINIE.

CHAPTER I.

ONE long summer's day I had been travelling on, in my usual pedestrian manner, through a series of sweeping yet solitary valleys, such as may be found, as he goes, by any by-road topographer, towards the eastern and southern extremities of Scotland. The country was sufficiently romantic to interest the fancy of a wanderer like myself; but as the sun declined towards evening, I had plodded on for several miles without seeing a human face, and I began to long exceedingly to meet with some habitation, where I might enjoy a little comfort and rest. In this part of the world I was a perfect stranger, and now began to get uneasy; for I was spent and weary, and even the song of the blackbird, which still echoed through the woods, failed to bring its usual refreshment to my spirit.

Much farther I had not proceeded, when, buried " cosily " among the upland woods, and partly straggling down a green slope, a sweet romantic village came unexpectedly into my view, and delighted my fancy with pleasing ideas of what I might find within it. As I drew near, the small dwellings seemed so quaintly built, and huddled together with a look of such simple sociality,—the place seemed altogether such " a rest and be thankful " station, for those who, like myself, chose to wander to and fro in the world, to see what it might contain, as well as to chase away sad thoughts, that the contemplation brought me involuntary comfort, from the impressive conviction, that, bad as the world is, there is still to be found in it much peace, purity, and happiness.

As I came on towards the village, the hour of eight struck sonorously from the bell of the tower, and presently it began to toll an even-

ing chime, which broke pleasingly the surrounding stillness, and sounded away among
the valleys, with a musical and murmuring
tinkle. This was a gracious sound to my
reviving spirit, as I musingly entered within
the long street, and observed the youngsters
come out from the doors up and down, to enjoy the outside sociality of the summer's night;
for, in truth, every thing had a happy and
contented look; and I thought that even the
jolly red face of the Marquis of Granby, that
was painted on the sign-board of the decent
inn, seemed .to grin upon me a hearty and
inviting welcome.

I was soon within the old-fashioned hostelry,
and, seating myself in a large arm-chair of a
comely parlour, I drew a long breath, and
looked upwards, giving thanks for the mercies
thus pleasantly and conveniently thrown in my
way. At the same instant I was attended by
a clean-looking woman, namely, the landlady
herself, who came to offer me her best refreshment. A single glance showed me what sort
of person the landlady was; and, in five minutes

after, my mind was made up to pass a whole day in her house, perhaps more, to get acquainted with this interesting village of Hillington.

" Who are the principal people about this neighbourhood, mistress ? " I enquired of the curtsying landlady.

" The principal family hereabout, sir," she answered, kindly, " live down the water in Lawford Holm; but it would be a long tale to tell you all about them," added the woman, mysteriously.

" And who preaches in that fine old church of yours, mistress ? "

" That 's just what I wish to tell you, sir," said the woman: " Mr. Kinloch, the old minister, seems to have but a short time to live; but his successor is so much beloved, that his name is in every one's mouth here.   May be, sir, as you are a stranger, you are come to the placing."

" What placing, mistress ? I have not heard of it."

" Mr. Bannatyne, the new minister, is to be

placed on Wednesday, and this will be a great doing in Hillington."

" No doubt. But who lives in that ill-made square house among the trees, that I observed on the left hand, as I came into the village?"

" The laird of Glaunderston, sir,—and his daughter is ———"

" The laird!" said I, surprised—" is an old acquaintance of mine: I was not aware that he lived here. But what were you going to tell of his daughter?"

" She is spoken of as the wife to be of the handsome young minister that's about to be placed in Hillington kirk—but, indeed ———"

" Indeed — what, mistress?"

" Oh, sir, she is a coarse creature."

" Nothing remarkable in that, mistress," I said: " coarse and fine are often spun together, in this world, for wiser reasons than I can make out. Marriages, they say, were once made in heaven, but that must have been long before my time."

" You are an observable man, sir," said the

woman: " I wish you could stay to see the placing."

" Why to see that, mistress ? "

" I cannot tell you, sir: but there is a lady ——— "

" Very likely. There is always a lady in every thing that is interesting. And what lady is it ?"

" The lady of the Holm, sir. It's not for me to talk to a stranger about her; but, perhaps, you may hear something concerning this lady from the laird of Glaunderston. An observable man like you should not leave this country side without knowing something about the Priors of Lawford."

" Prior ? that will be the name of a family. An English name, I think it is."

" Yes, sir. A strange, and yet an admirable old family it is, and ever has been, long before the remembrance of living man; although I cannot tell you about it what I would, at this present talking ; and then, sir, there is the young minister. I'll tell you what it is, if that young gentleman ever couples himself with

Glaunderston's coarse daughter—but ye'll excuse me, there's a bell ringing in the wee parlour, and I'll be wanted;"—and with this, tripping out of the room, after a slight curtsy, the tantalising woman left me to ruminate over this imperfect information.

All the addition to her hint that I could afterwards obtain was, that Mr. Bannatyne, the said minister, was expected at Glaunderston House on the following day; and thither I determined to walk, shortly after breakfast next morning; for my mind was awakened about something, I knew not what.

Upon going to the laird's house, he was exceedingly pleased to see me, and introduced me to the old minister of the parish, whom he had hospitably invited to meet Mr. Bannatyne. The latter *did* arrive, just as the old gentleman and I were talking. Of the latter, however, to wit, the Reverend Mr. Kinloch, who had been minister of the parish for nearly forty years, I must first say a few words.

Contrary to what experience had taught me to expect in a common country clergyman, I found the senior to be a man of general information and a gentlemanly spirit; one whose comparative want of knowledge of the world, of which he was himself sensible, was well made up by the quality of his reading, and great natural shrewdness and sagacity of mind. I was just rejoicing inwardly over the value to his parish of such a man, in the character of its pastor, as well as to the inexperience of him who was to be his successor, when a coach stopped at the door, and Mr. Bannatyne, of whom we had been talking, accompanied by another clergyman, alighted, and joined our company.

The first glance I had of this remarked person, even his walking across the room, showed me that he had one advantage, of value both to himself and his charge, to wit, the birth and rearing of a gentleman; and his conversation soon indicated that his mind set him above the usual peculiarities of his calling. But he was not a mere youth: his age might be four and twenty; and his looks were certainly all that the talkative landlady of the inn had described.

Involuntarily he interested me, and I soon saw that here, as well as in the village, he was the idol of the general women, and the grand object, in particular, of the laird of Glaunderston's red-haired daughter. This discovery I grudged at exceedingly, knowing that the unequal yoking together of the coarse and the fine in the world is none the better for its being often done, and becomes a root of bitterness from which grows up many bad shootings.

Though far from being troubled with itching ears, to make me a runner after popular preachers, yet, the obviously superior character of Mr. Bannatyne gave an interest to the ceremony of his being inducted, or "placed," which determined me to attend it on the following day. I had also a curiosity to see the assembled people of this romantic neighbourhood, and to observe in what manner a youth who had interested me so much would take upon himself so important a charge. In the morning, accordingly, I made ready in time; but before the ringing out of the second bell,

remembering the hints and half sentences of
the talkative landlady, my curiosity was awakened to know something further, if possible,
regarding the particular family of whom she
spoke.   When I called upon the good woman,
however, I found, to my surprise, that her
mouth had been completely closed to my enquiries, from some sudden consideration of
publican prudence, in consequence, no doubt,
of my taking up my abode with the laird of
Glaunderston.

"I'm in a public way, sir," she said, "and
it's by the public I live : so it is not for me to
keep a waggling tongue in my head, about the
worthy gentles of this canny neighbourhood,
among whom I earn my bit and my sup; but
as you are an observable man, sir, and about
to go to the placing, when you set yourself
down in the laird's seat, just observe you a
young lady in the green pew fornent you, wi'
the broad scutcheon of arms on the pillar above
her head."

"I'll mind what you say, mistress," replied
I; "but tell me now, whose are the arms that

you speak of, and what is the reason of all this mystery."

" There is the kirk bell begun to ring, sir," she said, " and I must be going, although ye *be* a man of interrogation. But if ye would know what I wish you of this remarkable family, look at the lady that sits beneath the scutcheon. Ye'll ken her, sir, by her pretty fair face, and her skin as white as milk, an' her dark swelling eye that's never off the minister."

" Go on, mistress," said I, peremptorily, " speak out, if you be a woman."

" Then, sir, just do you watch the lady's face at the placing, and see how she looks at the trying questioning, and the denunciation, and the laying on of the hands, and the apostolic benediction, and the confirming prayer,— just observe the countenance of Rebecca Prior, and if you have an eye for a woman's thoughts, and can read the changes of a bonnie face, when the soul within kindles up under the cheek, and the heart beats because it daurna' speak, ye 'll think of what I say."

The word of my reply was not ready at my tongue's end, when I looked up, and, behold, the woman was gone.

The church bell now sounded, as I wandered forth, with romantic effect over the neighbouring hills, and echoed away through the valleys below the town; so I joined the sober crowd that issued from the houses, and soon entering by the kirk stile, and passing the monuments of the ancient graveyard, I placed myself comfortably in the laird of Glaunderston's pew, anxious to witness the ceremony of the placing.

As the church filled with people, there entered by the door opposite to me, a tall, dark, remarkable-looking gentleman, accompanying a lady aged about twenty; and as she came forward in the passage, even before she had entered the seat under the scutcheoned pillar, I knew that she was the one whom I was given to watch.

There never was a female more worthy of observation, or one more likely to excite that sort of interest which belongs to the finer species of sexual character, and which is "above and beyond" mere personal beauty. I do not mean to describe so well known a ceremony as the "placing" or consecration of a Scottish minister, after the austere forms of the Genevan presbyters. I intend only to speak briefly of what I observed regarding this peculiar lady, and in the demeanour of him who was the subject of the ceremony, on whom, at least, in the character of her spiritual instructor, and with all a maiden's modesty, were the eyes of the female intently riveted.

Her features, I could see at a glance, might be said to be perfect; and, what is more, they indicated that mixture of the lofty and the sentimental, which is always so interesting, and sometimes so awful, in the female character. Her skin was beautifully delicate; there was but little colour in her cheek; and though her hair tended to fair, her eyes were deeply dark and sparkling, their large pupils contrasting strikingly with the somewhat pallid, yet healthy, hue of her skin. But I had not yet seen her as I did before the ceremony was finished, nor was I able for a considerable time, fully to understand the meaning even of what I saw.

Mr. Bannatyne demeaned himself during the whole of the ceremony with that modest good sense which, from previous observation, I certainly expected. But he did not go through this day's trial like one of the timber pillars that supported his pulpit. He did not hear and answer to the affecting charge of St. Paul to the elders of Ephesus, without being moved, and that deeply, with the serious nature of the duties which he was now taking upon him. But it was the lady——the pale, poetical-eyed lady, that riveted my attention more and more. As I watched her during the exercises of this morning, I could have sworn that there was love for the man, burning at her heart, which mixed with, and received elevation from, her admiration of the pastor. Whenever, therefore, his speaking eye indicated that he was moved by the solemn things that were addressed to him, or that his own tongue uttered, she, who gazed in his countenance throughout, as only a woman can look into the soul of the

man whom she admires, seemed ready to bur
out into sobs of audible emotion; but, pressir
her lips hard together, to confine her feelin
within her own breast, she only suffered t
large drops to stream down her pale cheeks,
to stand like crystals glazing over the da
pupils of her eyes.

It was not to be supposed that, on a day lil
this, the look of the young minister should i
dicate any thing of reciprocity with the evide
emotions of the lady. By the time, howeve
that the ceremony was finished, and that I h
seen and heard all, my curiosity and intere
were wound up to the highest pitch, to kno
something more of the two individuals, both
whom, in their supposed relations to each oth
and the world, had already made a deep ir
pression on my mind. All was soon ende
and I went forth with the crowd, convinced,
well from what I observed, as from the hints
the landlady, that there was something to l
known of no common nature regarding pe
sons who severally so much interested m

but of whose character and the peculiarity of their circumstances I was yet ignorant.

It was during my further sojourn in this secluded neighbourhood, and my subsequent journeyings to these parts, that I was enabled to pick up the particulars I have to tell regarding the old family of Lawford.

CHAPTER II.

On the side of a rising ground, which slopes down into a pleasant hollow, or rather holm, as such a spot is named in Scotland, only a short mile from the village of Hillington, stood, at this period, an old-fashioned picturesque building, which, overlooking from the midst of the wood with which the slope was covered, the small streamlet or burn that meandered down in the hollow, was known from time immemorial by the name of the mansion of Lawford. The streamlet was also called by the same name, which, as its etymology intimates, eventually served to designate the whole neighbouring estate; and this ancient property has been, for more generations than could easily be traced, in the possession of a family who originally came from England, but who had long been familiarly known in the country by the general designation of the Priors of Lawford.

Of this ancient family, once pretty numerous, only two persons at this time remained to claim direct and near connection with it; and these two were somewhat strangely and, with respect to the world, solitarily situated. The one was a maiden, the only daughter now living of the last married male of the family. The other was the only brother of that person, who had died about a year ago, and of course the uncle of the maiden, still, also, unmarried; and these two persons lived together, in much seclusion, in the stately old mansion by Lawford burn. Neither the young lady nor the elderly gentleman were common characters, as was well known to such of the people in the neighbourhood as had sufficient perception to observe this; and it need not be added, that it was the niece of the tall dark-visaged gentleman who had so strongly interested me on the day of the placing.

There was not, probably, another person in the parish who had had the sagacity to observe what the landlady of the inn had observed and pointed out to me, in regard to some supposed

sentiment of Rebecca Prior towards Mr. I
natyne, the minister. As for the young cle
man, he was perfectly a stranger to the exist
of any thing of the kind, and very much s
the lady herself; for, though he had before
period once sat in her company, she
scarcely exchanged a word with him ; and
behaviour had been so silent, and timid,
peculiar, both on that occasion and when
had noticed her among others in her pe
church, that she seemed to him more li
vowed and pledged nun, who had renoun
the world and its pleasures, than " any mo
mixture of earth's mould," who lived and d
amongst us.

It was not from any romantic exaggeratio
her beauty — which, in truth, needed no
aggeration — that Mr. Bannatyne took up
notion. It was simply an impression of c
racter, regarding a lady of whom every
spoke in terms of the deepest respect, and v
whom he had few expectations of making
acquaintance. At times, indeed, he felt a str
wish to have some intimacy with her and

uncle; for when he came to be settled in the parish, the society he found, male or female, was extremely limited; and curiosity itself, with something like awe of the nun-like female, gradually heightened that sentiment. She seemed, however, to have taken, as he thought, something like dislike to himself; for, in subsequently meeting her at Lawford House, in consequence of her uncle's hospitality, her reserve became almost more marked than good breeding would warrant, until he began to fancy that she even tried to avoid him. Yet, at other times, afterwards, when she *did* enter into some distant conversation with him, her observations were so judicious and so tasteful — her very language indicated so much mental accomplishment, such unassuming refinement; and he thought her words were at times so penetrating in their meaning — even her voice seemed so musical — that he became interested concerning her to absolute absorption, and was momentarily flattered into an idea that she almost took a pleasure in his society.

Mr. Prior himself had taken an evident partiality for the minister; and in the subsequent visits of the latter at Lawford House, as he involuntarily watched the countenance of Rebecca, she would again, at times, become unaccountably silent, as if she was careful to eschew further direct communication with him.   But anon, as he talked to her uncle, her large eye would sparkle while watching his words; then she would gradually offer some remark, and join them, as if giving way to her feelings; when afterwards, suddenly checking herself, so soon as the conversation became serious or interesting, she would, upon some slight excuse, rise and leave the room.

This conduct, so unusual for one of her agè, very much astonished Mr. Bannatyne. " What could her meaning be?" he often enquired of himself; for this was repeated several times, and under modifications of manner and circumstances so various, that he knew not what to think. Sometimes it deeply provoked his pride; and at others it excited feelings of a very different kind : for more than once the transient look that she cast on him — her full expressive eyes, as she rose to leave his company, had a meaning in their glance so despairingly sad, that it almost affected him to tears; and on these occasions, if eyes could speak, he thought hers seemed eloquently to beg of him to excuse her manner, to forgive her, and to take no offence at her behaviour. But, at such times, after Mr. Bannatyne was left alone with her uncle, the conversation of the worthy old gentleman appeared to him so tedious, and he himself became so abstracted, that both gentlemen would sit and observe each other for a time with a look of indefinite but subdued mystery.

Still the minister could not stay from the house, and the same scene was acted over and over again. The same dread of something unexpressed, seemed to be over all; and yet they could not live separate. Expressions occasionally dropped from the old gentleman also, and looks were exchanged between him and Rebecca, which filled the minister with a feeling so painful, that it was almost terrifying to himself; and yet, he knew not what was its exact meaning, or to what it tended. Sometimes now, as he sat and looked at them both, a sort of vague dread would come gradually over him, which he could not define, and which was associated with some notion or suspicion, for which there seemed to be no expression. Even the solitary and antiquated mansion of Lawford seemed now to his fancy to have something mysterious, if not terrific, about it; and as he went down thither in the winter evenings, the stream in the holm, as he crossed it, appeared to meander dark and dreary down the hollow, and the wind to moan sadly through the woods, as if warning him of some dismal tale that he dared not be told. At length, some slight incident occurred between him and Rebecca, which alarmed his pride, while it affected his feelings; and as he crossed the stream that night, on his return home, he determined, whatever it might cost him, to absent himself henceforth from this strange though fascinating family.

But now again, as he sat at home over his books after this, in his dull lodging in Hillington, he found that by staying away entirely

from his secluded friends, he was punishing
himself much more than, in the moment of
alarmed pride, he could have suspected; and
began, like all candid minds, to think that there
might be something in himself, or in the position of the lady, or in the nature of the case
altogether, more than he knew of, which might
form a good reason for that manner, to him, of
which he complained.   But even the society
of Mr. Prior was of itself so desirable in this
dull neighbourhood, that it was too much for
him to deny himself the pleasure and advantage he might derive from it, on account of
any unexplained fancy   regarding a female
living in his house, whose manner to himself
might be perplexing, but of which there was
no reason that he should take any particular
notice.   Besides, with Mr. Prior himself he
felt that he was not yet half acquainted; and,
as for the lady, though she did no more than
pass out and in as they talked, her simple
smile at her uncle's joke, and the penetrating
gaze of her large dark eye (should she never
deign even to speak to him), were, as he thought,

a positive delight, compared to the obtrusive chatter and freedom of the coarse daughter of M'Gilvray of Glaunderston.

"And more than all this," he added, to himself, as he paced the floor of his solitary study, "young men, as my venerable predecessor says, are disposed to be rash in their judgments, and dictatorial in their decisions, before they have time to know what is hidden under the external surface of things. Doubtless, I am to blame, in presuming to set up my own inexperienced pride, against the invaluable advantages, at my age, even of the instructive evils, that may arise out of intercourse with wise and accomplished people. It becomes me, as a teacher of others," continued he, "to feel, that I also am liable to misapprehension, to error, and folly. I will, this very evening, arise, and, in the repentant spirit which manly candour has often to exercise in life, seek one other interview, at least, with the venerable proprietor of Lawford."

Pursuing the train of the minister's reflections, it must here be added, that there are few things more puzzling to sensitive persons in early life, than the occasional *manner* towards them, of those, whose good opinion they are anxious to deserve. This Mr. Bannatyne strongly felt on his new visit of the same evening at Lawford, particularly with reference to Rebecca Prior; for, though he had persuaded himself, that it was her uncle only he had gone to converse with, and that her behaviour, or notice of him, was of no manner of consequence; he found, to his uneasiness, that, whether it was curiosity, or whether it was pride, not only the words she addressed to him, but her minutest look, were now matters of increasing solicitude. Yet he would not seem to regard her, he thought; for, in fact, her presence was of no importance to him; and this ridiculous watching of the countenance, and pondering on the motives of a strange girl, would wear off as his curiosity came to be gratified; for, as to any more serious sentiment, that, of course, was out of the question.

The character of both these persons, as they appeared at this time to the anxious young pastor, require, perhaps, a word of explanation. That of Mr. Prior, in particular, appeared to the young man odd and unaccountable in several respects. With a sportiveness of fancy, which seemed evidently to fit him for social enjoyments, and which occasionally showed itself through his habitual seriousness and taciturnity, he yet seemed systematically to seclude himself from the world, and to look with jealousy upon any intrusion into his habits, although what he called an intrusion was yet evidently felt to be a real relief. On some occasions, in the society of Mr. Bannatyne, Mr. Prior's conversation became, to our youth's surprise, even humorous and caustic; and when he contrasted this lightness, with the general strain of profound and didactic thought in which he usually indulged, and the instructive, though gloomy, speculations upon the condition of humanity, which made the staple of his earnestly delivered aphorisms, he was convinced that there was something hidden under all this, which it would require more than ordinary penetration to find out or appreciate.

As to Rebecca, however, the minister observed, that whatever was peculiar regarding her, beyond her habitual expression of simple and resigned melancholy, consisted entirely in her behaviour to himself; for her conversation with her uncle was easy and sensible, besides maintaining a tone of graceful humility that was extremely seductive; and every movement of hers, and every arrangement of the household under her charge, indicated the most perfect taste and propriety.

Had the minister had less dignity of character, and used more freedom with others in the neighbourhood, the prying tattle of a country parish would' soon have furnished him with certain particulars regarding the Priors of Lawford, which might have served as a cue to the explanation of all this. But, as it was, he could only trust to his own observations, and as these became more acute, and had more to feed upon, they became still more absorbing to his faculties, and their subjects more interesting to his feelings. He saw an elderly gentleman without wife, child, brother, or sister, living in almost total seclusion, with no companion or society, but that of a thoughtful maiden of nineteen, the daughter of his deceased brother; who, in the very spring-time and beauty of youth and health, seemed also generally to abstract herself from all society but that of a gloomy and eccentric uncle, and to shrink from coming in contact with a world which would have hailed her presence with joy, and fed upon her smiles with rapturous admiration.

"What can be the meaning of all this?" he still enquired: "it is not natural for age to refuse honour, or beauty and youth to eschew admiration. There must be some fearful cause that compels the old to avoid society, that solace of life, and the young to choose pensiveness rather than joy, at the very period when the heart beats quick, when the blood is warm, and the romantic fancy travels over bright regions of imagined and anticipated felicity."

It was in vain for him to strive against the increasing anxiety of his curiosity, or whatever else the feeling might be called, which induced him to watch over Rebecca's manner in the way he was constrained to do. He saw, also, that she was aware of his constant and sensitive observation of her; and this seemed still more to increase his embarrassment; for whenever she caught herself joining the discursive conversation between her uncle and him, until she perhaps echoed some sentiment that Mr. Bannatyne had uttered, or joined her judgment to his with animated approbation, her countenance would again assume a strange expression of mental agony, as if she suddenly recollected some painful apprehension.

" There is some mystery of sorrow hanging over this family," he still murmured to himself, as he walked solitarily home from Lawford House, one night, in a mood of unusual gloom, " which all my observation cannot penetrate. In this world of strange mysteries, of various and hidden sources of sorrow — this darkling pilgrimage, wherein we still grope in such un-

certainty as to many deep enquiries concerning ' being's end and aim,' I know that it is too
true, that, in spite of appearances, and of all
the coveted appliances and means which fortune
seems to collect around her greatest favourites,
for the momentary elation of the youthful
heart, and for the strengthening of the decep-
tions of tantalising hope, still there will be
found, according to the sombre meaning of the
Italian proverb, to be ' a skeleton in every
house ' — a concealed cause of regret or of
dread in every habitation, or in every heart.
What can be the nature, or what the history,
of that remorseless phantom that lurks among
the recesses of the mansion of Lawford, and
which cruelly poisons the cup of life to these
gentle hearts? What can the name be of the
skeleton fiend whose bare bones ever and anon
seem to rattle some sound of dread or of horror
to check the risings towards enjoyment of the
sorrowful spirits in this secluded house? or
whose fleshless arm points to some fearful index
in nature, of some reserved woe in the future
destiny of the family? By heavens! this

maiden shall draw aside to me the dark curtain
that covers this terrific object, that I may be a
sharer in her sorrow myself, or at least be enabled to bear some portion of her burden ! "

About this period one or two trifling incidents took place between the minister and
Rebecca, such as *will* happen in the course of
an intercourse now becoming so constant,
which had the effect of fairly drawing his attention to the state of his own feelings, and of
opening his eyes to what he could no longer
disguise from himself.   It perhaps need hardly
be added, that simple curiosity was now no
longer the feeling of his mind regarding her.
Admiration — increasing and deepening admiration — was, by this time, united to a more
touching sentiment.   Unsuppressable passion
increased deep interest for its object, and rendered sympathy so intense as to be almost
painful, until Rebecca Prior became the idol
of his spirit, and the charm that awakened him
to another existence.   Still there was the secret,
the apparent mystery, unopened, unsolved.
Bannatyne had determined that she should

remove the curtain, and disclose the skeleton that caused her melancholy, and his own. But he had not yet the courage to ask her to do so. He was happy in her society each evening, and yet he was most miserable. Such is love !

CHAPTER III.

By this time, there was not a man (at least there certainly was not a woman) in the whole parish of Hillington, but whose mind was perfectly made up as to the present intentions, immediate measures, and whole future history, of their beloved young pastor. That he was shortly to be married to the heiress of Lawford had long been clearly seen: that he had fairly disappointed the laird of Glaunderston's daughter was matter of no regret; and that he was to get such and such lands and plenishings with the last remaining daughter of the house of Lawford, was all fully understood and settled.

All this, however, was much more than a matter of mere gossip to the honest laird of Glaunderston, and the female part of his family. The laird was disappointed, he was almost indignant; the lady was wroth, and thought herself wronged; the daughter was in a pet, and would have complained, only that no one in

Scotland ever prospers who dares to say ill of the minister.

But, in truth, had not the laird been a man whose expectations were formed more from his own wishes than the nature of things, he might have seen, from the first, what was seen by every body else around, that, though naturally anxious, like every well-meaning father, to obtain a comfortable settlement for his favourite daughter, yet the simple fact of Mr. Bannatyne's coming to be assistant minister in the neighbourhood, and accepting, for a time, the hospitality of his house, formed little ground for so extravagant an expectation as that he was shortly to have, in such near relationship, the fastidious and gentlemanly junior minister of Hillington. We can seldom, in this world, receive a gratification to ourselves, without, whether conscious of it or not, giving pain or offence to some other person; so the interesting visits of our clergyman to Lawford House were, without his suspecting it, carefully observed, and enviously felt, by the angry and disappointed family at Glaunderston.

The idle gossip of his parishioners, however, had far outrun the truth, as to the prospects or the intentions of their pastor in the quarter where he visited; for, instead of the common-place process of wooing and wedding, such as the ordinary world experience and expect, his mind, even amidst the pleasing excitement of passion, was, as before hinted, plunged into a sea of cares and fears, with which all who seek to enjoy the higher emotions of our nature seldom fail to be painfully tried. When he came to see fully into the state of his own mind, and to conclude, in candid self-examination, that, reason as he might, from this time forth earthly happiness and Rebecca Prior were with him inseparably connected, he, in the spirit of manly sincerity, resolved at once, that, in spite of all considerations arising out of their respective conditions in life, and in the face of that inexplicable manner which at times had given him so much uneasiness, he would declare to her the passion he no longer could control, and would learn from her own lips all that he so anxiously wished to know.

But, no sooner had he come to this ultimate determination, and sought to end his anxiety by carrying it into effect, than he found that Rebecca had, with all a woman's tact, long penetrated his intention; for she avoided every thing in the shape of an opportunity for his meeting her out of the presence of her uncle, and, when accidentally left with him, she would look round her, for an instant, in apparent alarm; then, rising and excusing herself, would steal out of the room, as if some sudden dread had just come over her. And yet she did not scruple to converse with him as she had done at the more early period of their intercourse; indeed, so evidently pleased were her uncle and herself always to see him, and so warm were the constant invitations of each to favour them with his society, that he seemed to be now almost one of the family, and could converse with both upon every subject but the one that was nearest to his own heart.

Now, also, the reserve that Rebecca had at first shown to him had in a great measure died away, or had at least assumed a different cha-

racter; but still the opportunity — the wished-
for and yet dreaded opportunity of speaking to
her that one word — of asking her that one
question — was always denied him, so that the
very pleasure which her society gave him was
almost a torture in his present uncertainty. As
he farther thought of the possible result of
such a communication, after all these happy
evenings, the idea at times tended to deepen
his distraction of mind, and make his per-
plexity almost intolerable.

This state of mind at length could not longer
be borne, and, going down to Lawford House,
one afternoon, he determined that *that* night
should not pass without his obtaining some
determinate satisfaction.

The time seemed favourable in several respects, and Mr. Bannatyne hoped that the
careless eccentricity of the old gentleman
would, at some part of the evening, afford him
the wished-for opportunity of saying a few im-
passioned words in private to Rebecca. As he
sat with them both in the evening, conversing
as usual, he even thought that Rebecca seemed

in a mood more than commonly favourable to his purpose, while the uncle was, this night, peculiarly taciturn and abstracted. Thus, the two young persons being left very much to the obligation of direct conversation, the clergyman's delight was evident in his countenance, even in the midst of his fever of watchful anxiety.

Mr. Prior had a way of rising from his seat and walking about, during familiar conversation, talking as he walked ; and it was not uncommon for him to open the door during a pause in their discourse, and to go out and down stairs; when, having taken a short turn in the open air, he would quietly come back, and, taking no notice of what might have been done or said in his absence, would proceed with the conversation or discussion, resuming it precisely from the point at which he had left it.

This night he was, as I said, more than ordinarily absent and taciturn, until, the conversation between Mr. Bannatyne and his niece turning accidentally upon the subject of the remarkable facts furnished by the infinite diversity in human character, he seemed suddenly roused into eager attention.   Lewis Bannatyne, observing this, pursued the subject warmly and eloquently, maintaining his favourite doctrine, that, viewing them philosophically, mankind were not so bad and wicked as they were often called, either by querulous misanthropists who did not sufficiently consider the position in which the poor race of Adam were generally placed, or by gloomy expounders of divine revelation who refused to open their eyes to the whole of the subject.

" There is truth in what you say," said Mr. Prior : " man is not, after all, a very bad sort of being ; he is merely contemptible — contemptible even in his virtues, for they are either hardly worthy the name, or are overstretched until they become the plague and the bane of virtue itself ;—contemptible also in his vices, which, while they also often scarcely deserve the name, are yet the bane of his happiness, and the world's constant curse.   And yet," he continued, " I have known some, and the world has preserved the history of many, who were as thoroughly and purely wicked as even fiction has pictured, or as hell itself could furnish."

" And I have met with several," said the clergyman, looking across to Rebecca, " who, as far as I can judge, are as purely virtuous, gentle, and good, as ever poet painted as belonging to humanity; and on whom Heaven itself can only confer greater purity, or higher elevation of spirit, by divesting them of the clay that as yet ties them down to mortality ! "

" I even agree with you also in that," said the uncle, getting animated, " and I admire the man who can see this much in mankind, and who rejoices, as you seem to do, in the pleasing truth. But did you ever observe, Mr. Bannatyne, how much mankind seem to run, as to disposition and character, in distinct races, possessing and maintaining a specific series of family characteristics? This is the fact, not only with isolated tribes, as among Indian nations, but even in our artificial and refined state of society; for single families have often, for ages and generations, evinced a spe-

cific and characteristic individuality. I need
not now refer you to the history of some of
the chief families who figure in the annals of
our country, for the distinct characteristics by
which they were known in their own times, or
are known to us who live after them, as far as we
can trace some degree of purity in the lineage,
nor need I instance to you the Stuart family,
which has passed away; nor most of the other
prominent families which now fill the different
thrones of Europe. A slight attention to their
several histories will prove the truth of what I
contend for, which is, perhaps, of more importance than is generally thought."

" The subject is somewhat curious, sir," said
the minister, thoughtfully, " and no doubt important, as a general enquiry."

" It is important also as a *particular* enquiry,
Mr. Bannatyne," said the other, with peculiar
meaning.

" " Perhaps it may, sir, but I have not as yet
thought of turning my attention to it."

" It is the duty of every one to know character, that he may not blindly contribute to

swell the black current of evil which deluges the world. It is the process of nature, that man forms connections in life, and thereby some particular race is continued. But what race would a wise man choose to continue? Shall we be, in this particular, less wise than the beasts that perish? Does not the gentlest dove mate with the most gentle of her kind? Does the blood courser unite his fiery nature with the sluggish breed of the Pays Bas? Are there not, among men, whole families which, like the birds of the boughs, belong to what may be called a good or an evil nest? and shall the reason of men be less useful for their own happiness than the common instinct of the beasts of the field?"

" What mean you, sir?"

" It is of the last importance, my dear sir," said Mr. Prior, emphatically, " for those who wish to form connections in life, to know those with whom they unite, both with reference to their own after-happiness, and that of the posterity that may be the result. And, if you wish to know me, or any man or woman, in a deeper sense than can be obtained through the conventional mockeries of social intercourse, enquire the history of the family from which I have sprung; ascertain the peculiarities of the nest to which the bird may belong with which you would offer to mate for life. Trust me, the qualities of the heart, the peculiarities of the blood, and the great considerations of the disposition and bias, are with much certainty transmitted through families, and are matter of inheritance from the male or female branches of a house."

Having risen and continued walking while he said this, the old gentleman, almost before Mr. Bannatyne was aware, had left the room; and the minister had become so absorbed in the sudden reflections caused by this conversation, that he did not notice Mr. Prior's absence, until he heard the echo of his footsteps as he passed through the hall below.

The moment was now come for which Lewis had so long watched: Rebecca and himself were left quite alone, and seated opposite to each other. She smiled faintly, and seemed about to continue the conversation; but, as she looked across to him, her tongue was arrested by observing the expression of anxiety depicted in his countenance. For a few moments he also attempted, in vain, to utter a word, while the silence seemed so intense and so painful, that the lovers thought they heard the beating of each other's hearts.

At length Lewis was able to get out the single word " Rebecca."

She started at the word; but, instantly recovering her breath, as if relieved by the sound of his voice, she smiled sadly, as usual, while he proceeded.

" Rebecca," he said, " I see you perceive my anxiety to say a few words to you. Do not, I pray you, think of moving, but hear me. I have long waited for such an opportunity as this. Nay, listen to me, Rebecca; for the state of my mind is now such, that —— "

" Some other time, Mr. Bannatyne; do not speak now ! " she exclaimed, interrupting him. " Do not, my esteemed friend !—I know what you would say — I have dreaded this. Do not say any thing to me, but what may be spoken in my uncle's presence — and, hark! there he is returning again."

"No, Rebecca," he answered, after listening a moment, "it is only your fancy that thus alarms you: but now, for the sake of Heaven," he added, solemnly, "grant me an interview for five minutes only, at some time and place where I may speak to you without witness or interruption; for I have that to say to you which is of the last importance to me, both as it regards my peace of mind, and even my future usefulness as a minister. Rebecca, what alarms you thus?"

"Oh, Mr. Bannatyne, do not—do not speak of such a thing!"

"What on earth can you mean, Rebecca?"

"I cannot tell you, Lewis — I cannot; why should you ask my meaning of me? I conjure you, as my friend — as my minister, whom I wish to hear weekly in public without distraction —whom I wish ever to honour and reverence ! not to seek from me any further explanation regarding my family, or my own unhappy state ; and, above all, that you will not offer to speak to me differently from what you have till now done."

" Rebecca !" he exclaimed, " I cannot bear this. This strange mystery, where my happiness is so deeply involved, will drive me distracted. I must be suffered to express what my own breast can no longer contain. I must be satisfied from your own lips, or —— "

" Or we must never meet more," she said, calmly : " that, Lewis, is the only alternative. I have foreseen all this for some time ; but my own weakness, and the pleasure I have enjoyed in your society, as well as love for my uncle, who, I saw, was also refreshed by your conversation, has made me put off the evil day : but it has come at length, and too soon. Lewis, it will be better for us both that, from this day forward, we meet no more."

" And not one word of explanation of this mystery, Rebecca ? "

" There is no mystery, Lewis, — none whatever; it is merely duty that compels me. Oh! do not look so. I cannot bear it!"

"And will you not meet me, to hear what is bursting in my bosom? Will you not speak to me one word for the satisfaction of my feelings?"

"Do not ask me, Lewis. I entreat of you do not ask me, — for I cannot." And, so saying, she hurried out of the apartment.

He threw himself back into his chair, in a state of stupefaction, from what had just passed. In a few minutes afterwards, however, he was aroused from his stupor, by the *soft* tread of footsteps, and, looking up, perceived the slender figure of Rebecca glide softly into the room; and, coming forward, she again placed herself in the chair she had formerly occupied, quite near to him.

"Forgive me, Mr. Bannatyne," she said, after a moment, and breaking the painful silence. "I ask your forgiveness; for I already repent me of the determination which I have just expressed; and, though I know not well what further I shall have strength to say to you, yet I am aware there is something more than I have yet been able to speak due to your feelings. I have resolved, therefore,——resolved, in spite of the painful delicacy of a subject which is bitter to my thoughts, and in spite of all a maiden's pride, to give you, out of my own mouth, a most sad explanation. It is no romantic fancy that has caused this reluctance to meet you on a seeming mystery; but there are reasons for all this, which you will understand when you come to hear them. In one word, I will meet you this night, even before you sleep, in the little conservatory at the east angle of the mansion. Wait for me there, after you have parted from my uncle. And do not, Lewis, put any unkind interpretations on my conduct, either now, or hitherto. I will meet you alone, as I would my brother," she added, passionately, clasping her hands together; " I will speak to you as my minister; I will unlock the secret of my sorrow to you, as my adviser, as my friend, perhaps for the last time we may ever dare to talk in private. But, hark ! here comes my uncle."

It was a weary half hour that Lewis spent after this, when, at length, taking leave of Mr. Prior for the night, he sprang forth to the park without, to wait, at the angle of the mansion, for his interview with Rebecca.

CHAPTER IV.

" WHAT a large portion of our time in this life is wasted in mere *waiting!*" exclaimed the minister to himself, as he paced anxiously up and down, within view of the place appointed ; ten, fifteen, twenty minutes having already elapsed, and still the conservatory was dark and dull. " Waiting," he went on, " for *something* that seems necessary for our happiness, and the want of which prevents us from enjoying the present hour, — the hour that for the time we think so long, and which afterwards appears so short, and so barren of every thing but the torture of impatience — but there ! at last I see a light."

As he hastened towards the conservatory, he saw, through the glass, the figure of Rebecca moving inside, and looking anxiously around her. Presently he was at the small door which opened into it, under a porch of creeping plants, which she unlocked, and he stood before her.

She seemed to hesitate a moment as he gazed in her face, while she stood partly shaded by the plants of the conservatory, the habitual melancholy of her countenance amounting at this moment to an expression that was almost tragic ; and yet, as her dark eye beamed on him, he thought he had never seen her appear so charming.

" I am most grateful for this condescension, Rebecca," he said, " more grateful than I can express."

" Alas ! Lewis," she answered, mournfully, " you will not say so before we part. This stolen meeting between you and me looks romantic, but, assuredly, it will end in being only common-place, barren, and sad. I would not affect to be blind to the sentiment that burns in your eye, my friend, nor is this meeting, I confess, without feeling on the part of one even in my hopeless predicament. But we meet not, Lewis, on this painful occasion, as those meet who have words to say, that must never pass my lips, and emotions to indulge in, that I must never feel ; or that I must smother

within the struggling bosom where they rise.
But do not reply here; it is fit that our communication should take place in that part of
this ancient mansion where the very walls
around us may tend to the illustration of what
I have to say. Come, I will be your guide:
follow me."

They trod lightly along several passages
with which Lewis was quite unacquainted; then,
mounting by a back stair until they came to
the upper part of the building, she opened a
door; and they entered with some hesitation a
square lofty room with a carved and painted
ceiling, like an old saloon, and the walls hung
round with old family portraits.

"I do not bring you here, sir," she said,
as she observed him fix his eyes upon the
heavy carved ornaments of the chimney-piece,
and seeming to feel almost uncomfortable, while
he glanced around at the range of painted
faces which appeared to gaze on him from
within their frames,—"I do not bring you into
this unfrequented apartment from the impulse
of any romantic fancy, or that I myself have

any pleasure in entering a place which can impress me with nothing but associations deeply humbling to my spirit; but simply from the reason I have already given, and that here, at least, we have little chance of being interrupted or overheard."

They seated themselves on two old carved chairs, covered with rich but faded damask; and she gazed for some moments, in melancholy silence, upon the row of portraits on the walls, until painful emotions seemed to be struggling in her bosom.

" Rebecca, you seem strangely moved," he said at length: " speak, I beseech you! what mystery is this that you still delay to disclose?"

" There is no mystery, Lewis; I tell you again there is nothing remarkable in what I have to speak of, although every one feels his own sorrows most deeply. Nay, do not look upon me thus, Lewis. It is no sin of mine or my father's that I have need to be ashamed of. It is simply that there is a judgment of Heaven upon our house. But doubtless it is better to fall into the hands of God than into the hands of men: and I submit. Alas! do not look so piteously upon me."

"Rebecca, I am distracted for you! and you will not put even sympathy towards you in my power, by at once disclosing what you have to tell me. And yet you have undertaken to——"

"Well, Sir, I know I have promised. Alas! that this horrible statement should come from my own lips. Observe you these portraits around you, Mr. Bannatyne: some of these are grim and stern, like the men of their time; others, as you see, are mild and melancholy of look, particularly those of latter generations. But, to begin with my father,—my poor, sad, interesting father; that is he with the black robe and the pale countenance, so like my uncle whom you have just parted from. I wonder how I can bear to enter this room after what I know. It was here he chiefly lived of latter years; and see you that small door in the recess, under the large picture?"

"Yes, I see it: but what then?"

" That door opens into the small closet in which he died; and for two years before his death he never left that room, although generally in good health. Heard you never his history?"

" No, Rebecca, no : but why go into this unnecessary train of allusion to the history of your ancestors? Nothing that you can say shall prevent me declaring that I love — tenderly, passionately, love ! Nay, it is to speak this one word that I have anxiously sought to meet you in private ; and nothing that may have impressed your pure and delicate mind shall prevent me from suing for that hand, for that heart, without which I feel that I shall never know happiness. Why do you thus shrink from me, and look so fearfully. What can this mean?"

" Oh, Lewis, your passionate words distract me ! why will you not listen to the tale that I am about to tell you?"

" I see what it all tends to, Rebecca: some of these grim carles have, in the person of your father, engaged you under some impious, some

rash, some unnatural vow, which you ought
not to keep. Every feeling of the heart, every
consideration of life, love, hope, Heaven itself,
seem to conjure you to break it, and to preserve
the peace and happiness of your ancient house.
Will you do so, Rebecca, for my sake — for
your own, will you break this accursed vow ?"

" Your impatience misleads you, Lewis,"
she answered calmly : " there is no vow, no
engagement ; and why will you still speak to
me of love ? I must not answer your im-
passioned language. On that subject, as I told
you at first, my lips must be sealed for ever,
even to you."

" Then you are betrothed to another — I
must not speak to you of the sentiment that
absorbs my heart — that heart that I ought to
devote to the service of the sanctuary, but
which irresistible passion has made to swerve
in favour of one who is icy cold, and cruel as
cold, or you could not tantalise me thus."

" Oh ! not cold, Lewis — not cruel; you
wrong me sadly when you say so ! " she exclaimed, clasping her hands together, while her

voice quivered with rising emotion. "What would you have me to say? would you have me to speak as it becomes not a maiden to speak, to him whom she would love, does love, but dares not! Oh, Lewis, pity me! I am a wretched doomed girl. The hand of Heaven is upon me. The joys of a wife, the tenderness of a mother, I must never know: I must wear out my life in maiden seclusion, and go down to the grave, the last and saddest of my race, without a relative to weep over me when I am gone. Ah! Lewis, it is you that have made me feel my weakness" — and a burst of tears stopped her utterance.

"What can be the meaning of this dreadful distress!" he said, as he watched her while she sobbed beside him: "I will not again open my lips until you disclose to me the mystery, or whatever it is, that places you in this unhappy situation, and causes you this grief. Rebecca, have pity on me, and tell me in two words the cause of all this."

"I will, I will, when I am a little composed. Heaven will give me strength to speak of the sad misfortune of my family, even to you. But can you not save my feelings, by surmising what I mean? Have you never learned any thing remarkable about my ancestors? Have you never, Lewis," —and she fixed her large eloquent eyes on him as she spoke,—" observed any thing peculiar about my uncle or me?"

" No, Rebecca; I have heard nothing; I have observed nothing."

" Alas! that I should have to undergo this additional trial," she added, mournfully: " then know, Lewis, that — bring your ear to my lips, while I speak the dreadful words — there is *madness* in my family!"

" Yes, now you must hear all! I am doomed by the blood that runs in my veins to be yet a raving maniac! — nay, start not, for it has been the fate of almost all those, my ancestors, whose pale faces now look sadly upon us by the dim light of this single taper, and several of whom passed years in that state, the most humbling that Heaven permits to afflict poor humanity, in that very closet within the recess, where also

my poor father died in the melancholy insensibility of total derangement ! Now, Lewis," she
added, standing up, and looking down upon
him with despairing energy, " what do you think
of your poor Rebecca now ?   If ever, then, or
whenever that heavy hour arrives, surely you
will come and try to soothe me in my sorrow,
without despising me ; but yours I can never
be in this world.   Now, farewell ! the bitter
words are spoken, and I am relieved."

For a few moments, the minister sat and
gazed upon her, unable to speak.

" This is a sad tale, Rebecca," he at length
said ; " but yet you may in some degree be deceiving yourself.   No, it cannot be ! your sensibility perverts your reason.   Believe me," he
said, starting up, " this is nothing but delusion,
and you are yet to be mine."

" Lewis ! " she exclaimed, " do not terrify
me, by the mention of a supposition, the fulfilment of which might entail upon me and
yourself incurable sorrow and guilt.   Listen !
remember you the dreadful penalty of the Roman law for such an impious act as you now

dare to hint at ? [1]   Ah ! well may you start at
the thought.   And, how could you bear to
think of my doing as my grandmother did, many
years ago ?   Observe ! see you this portrait of
that dark-eyed lady ? how pale she looks, and
yet how benign !   What a sheeted effect that
plain white drapery has, in contrast with these
black glossy curls that wave over it!   Alas !
how can I look at her — my unfortunate ancestress !   You are still incredulous.   Come
hither, and I will convince you," she added,
opening the shutters of a long Gothic window
which overlooked the woody height at the rear
of the mansion: "see you that," she went on,
pointing to a small sheet of water, spread out
on the height, upon the bosom of which the
moonbeams now shone brightly, and from the
further end of which fell into a chasm below,
the cascade that formed the source of Lawford
streamlet."

"Is it not a beautiful spot, quiet and lovely ?
and yet it is never visited nor mentioned by
any of us, from the sad associations connected

[1] See Note A. at the end of this Story.

with it; it is only seen well from this room and the closet within, and has always been called the Lady's Linn, from the time that that unfortunate lady threw herself into it one day, when the evil spirit of our house was upon her, and parted with her suffering maniac existence at the cold bottom of that ominous lake."

"You shudder with horror, Lewis," she went on, after a pause, "and well you may, though far less than I ought, at past misfortune and future doom. But this is not all, and you do not believe still, although I have my own father to instance. Ah! my poor, sad, unhappy father — I think I see him this moment, as he placed his cold hand on my head, in that very closet beyond the little door, and said that I was fated to be yet — hark! did you not hear some one within. Heavens! who is this coming upon us here? Look, Lewis, the door opens! Can this be my dear father again!" and she fell on her knees before the figure which now entered from the closet, wrapped in night clothes, bearing a light, and looking angrily upon them both, as they stood in astonished confusion.

" What means this?" said the intruder. " How are you in this room, Rebecca? and what do you here again, sir?" he added, addressing Mr. Bannatyne: while both, having recovered their momentary terror, now recognised the voice of Mr. Prior, who, having heard a noise, had followed it to this deserted apartment.

" It was from *my* earnest entreaty, sir," said the minister, stepping forward, " that Miss Prior consented to this meeting."

" And in this room, Rebecca? was there no place but this for your midnight assignation?"

" Mine is the fault only, sir; and be *mine* the punishment, if there is to be any," said Bannatyne, warmly.

" Do you interrupt me, sir?" said the aroused gentleman, with a very unusual expression. " Ha! I see how it is. It will be necessary for you, young man, to discontinue your visits at this house."

" That may be, sir," said Mr. Bannatyne,

with dignity; " I must request, however, that you draw no unfavourable conclusion respecting your niece, at least, from what you now witness.   Only be considerate towards *her*, sir, and I obey you from this moment;" and he ended by taking two or three strides across the apartment.

A change now came suddenly over the face of the old man, as he stood looking at both of the young persons, — the countenance of Rebecca wearing an expression of inward agony; and, stepping forward hastily, he caught the clergyman by the arm.

" Nay, Mr. Bannatyne," he said, much moved, " you will not go from my house in anger, if you are here for the last time.   The wrath of Heaven, that has pursued my family until the tenth generation, is enough for me and my poor solitary niece to bear.   Forgive me, my friend.   I might have known that it would have come to this, and am myself to blame; but if we must lose even *your* society for ever, take a kind farewell of my poor Rebecca. There is *my* hand, too!   We have spent many happy evenings together; but I see no happiness remains for our doomed house, on this side of our final resting-place.   Heaven bless you, sir, and preserve to you the happiness that must never be ours!" and, laying his hand on the arm of Lewis, and looking sadly in his face as he pronounced this benediction, he then lifted up his taper, and turned to leave the room.

" Sir, this is evident delusion!" said Lewis, detaining the uncle in his turn, "a mutual, a fatal, deception of yourselves.   It is but the melancholy fantasy of voluntary misery that is destroying the happiness of this worthy family, and is now tearing asunder warm hearts, that are already knit indissolubly.   It is parting for ever this dear lady and me, not as even the grave parts friends and lovers, but making a separation which must be a living death. You shake your head at what I say — you still look round at these solemn faces on the canvass, and forth from the window on that cold moonlit lake.   Great Heaven above!

keep us all from the frightful delusions of insanity!"

Clasping their hands, as their young friend spoke these words, the old man and Rebecca threw a look upwards, as if they would have penetrated to Heaven, and the ardent *Amen!* that rose from the bottom of their hearts, seemed to be echoed back like the whisper of the dead, from the pale figures that looked down from the walls around them. The old gentleman, now catching hold of the minister's hand, wrung it with a meaning look in solemn silence, then turning away, departed slowly through the small door of the adjoining closet.

We may not dwell upon the ultimate parting of Lewis and Rebecca — reason is great against the weakness of passion, and the virtuous heart suffereth many trials.

CHAPTER V.

It is not every day that one meets with any thing that interests them : for the world is a dull world, and the heart a barren thing ; and it is seldom that even the pains of life are of sufficient dignity to excite a moral reflection.

But *I* was excited, and my heart was interested about the singular situation of the Priors and their visiter ; for one pang or throb of deep-seated feeling — one genuine manifestation of the noble self-denials of resolute virtue, does more to reconcile us to our " low-thoughted " species, than the thousand varieties of selfishness and stupidity.

And so I kept the matter of these young persons much in my mind, and thought over all that they might have thought, and fancied in my sympathy what they might have felt ; and, as soon as the summer came round again, I determined to wander towards their part of the country.

Away then I set in the early part of the year, and I thought to get to Hillington by the end of the week ; for, although I am no great saint (as the world had better know), I hate your Sunday stragglers and busy idlers, who cannot enjoy the solace of religion and of rest. But the week's journey was long, and the weather was blasty ; and, being unusually fatigued on the road, by the time Saturday night came, I was fain to take up my quarters at a very indifferent inn, with a great flashy sign, about four miles from Hillington.

Having rested my weary limbs there for the night, I rose, refreshed in body and pious in spirit, on the dull Sunday morning, proposing to walk forward, and be into Hillington in time for the kirk service : but, whether it was carnal laziness, which is apt to come over me on that particular time of uprising, or whether it was the solacing sweetness of the road that made me muse and dawdle on the way, I know not ; but it was long after the congregation had collected in the old building, and somewhat towards the latter end of the service, that I found myself within the precincts of the town, and pondering my way through the sweet and solemn old churchyard.

This morning was exceedingly different from the pleasant evening when I had first entered the town. It was drizzling rain, and heavily dull. The sun waded sullenly through the thick vapours; dark clouds of streaming mist lingered in the valleys as I came along; and by the time I got into the churchyard of Hillington, feeling ashamed of entering the kirk at this late hour, I sat down on a tombstone, languid and sad. The people within were singing a psalm; and the old melody, which came over my ear in the distance, was so quaintly plaintive, and was drawn out, as I thought, with such melting simplicity, that it seemed to me like a requiem for the obscure dead who lay in the graveyard around me, so that, in my present mood, it almost melted me into tears.

I rose, however, and entered the kirk, in order still to catch a remnant of the pious inspiration of the morning worship, and haply to make such observations as, from the long interval which had elapsed since my former visit, should now occur to me. After I had slipped myself stealthily into a back pew, as became a late interloper upon the sanctity of the service, the very first look I got of the face of the young minister showed me that something was wrong with him, and had taken effect upon his mind,— that something had happened, in my absence, to damp the glow of his natural enthusiasm, and to cloud his spirit with serious melancholy. I was still more convinced of this, from the strain of the prayer which he was now offering up to Him "who seeth not as man seeth, and who trieth the hearts and the reins of the children of men." It was not yet two years since I had been at his placing,— and yet a change had evidently come over his character: for the very tones of his voice were quite altered. Even his congregation, as was natural from the affection they bore him, had been infected by his spirit, and, musing upon the deep reasonings and sad inferences which the state of his mind led him to draw from what he observed in the world, his people went and came, every seventh day, to their solemn old church, with a pervading and inexplicable gloom.

After some time, I had a glance also at the face of Miss Prior, to whom my attention had from the first been directed; but the look I obtained of her was with some difficulty; for, though there she sat, beside her grave and reflective uncle, in the family pew, under the moth-eaten scutcheon, as on my first seeing her; she did not now, as before, look once with admiration in the minister's face, but sat during the whole time in one position; her face shaded with her hand, and her large dark eyes, when I could get a sight of them, preserving the same striking expression which they had ever done, but contrasting strongly with the paleness of her face, as if profoundly steeped in melancholy.

When the service was over, I was obliged to go home with the laird of Glaunderston, who had noticed me in the church, considerably against my own inclination; for I would much

rather have taken up my quarters with the
blithe landlady of the inn, where I should undoubtedly have learned something regarding
those whose history now interested me.   Being
at this time ignorant of what had taken place
to Mr. Bannatyne, I tried to get something out
of the laird and his family; but I might as
well have consulted the clumsy posts which,
under the name of pillars, upheld the *dignity*
of the front entrance to his house: for the
laird was one of the worthy people, of which
three fourths of the world are composed, who
can tell you readily where the most advantageous things are to be got to eat and to wear,
and how this man made money, and the other
man lost it, but never take the least notice of
any thing of higher import, or which might be
of interest to a wandering observer like myself.   All I could learn from him was, that
the new minister had considerably disappointed
many good men in the parish; that he had
not used him or his daughter altogether well,
but had gone about a strange reserved family,
who lived at a place called Lawford, until there

had been some falling-out among them; for that now he seldom was seen to go there, and yet was still unmarried, and was, in short, a man that few could understand.

Next day, when about to walk down into the village, I learned, by mere accident, that the good and sensible senior pastor of the parish, Mr. Kinloch, was now confined to bed, and had for some time been thought to be dying. This news was impressive to me, from the opinion I had formed of his judgment and information, on my first meeting him in this very house; and, in short, I was greatly minded to step over to the manse, and see the old man; both from the respect I felt for him, and because I had a curiosity to know what he would say regarding the present state of mind and character of Mr. Bannatyne, his successor. The thought was no sooner a matter of musing in my mind, than the knock of a stranger was heard at the laird's door.

This circumstance giving me an excuse for leaving Glaunderston House, I immediately departed, to visit, by his couch, the dying old minister. I mounted the creaking stairs to the chamber of the sick, and sat myself down by his bedside. "How sad a thing is death!" I thought; "how pathetic to look upon and talk to a living being, who is so soon to be 'for ever hid from our eyes!'"

"Your visit, my friend," said he, "is a refreshment to me. Sit down by me, and let us commune together. If I am not mistaken, you witnessed the placing of Mr. Bannatyne, my successor."

"I did," said I; "and great is my concern respecting him. To say the truth, many a weary foot I have travelled, and many a hill I have climbed, in this upland neighbourhood, until I was breathless, for little other earthly end but to hear, from time to time, how he lived, and what was his history, and that of the strange family of Lawford, in the hollow."

"I wish I could see him now," said the dying man, solemnly: "I feel that my time is not to be long; and I have much to say to him

before I depart. I fear me that his mind is
unsettled. Oh, that I could see him while I
have strength ! "

The old man had not the words well out of
his mouth, when the servant announced that
Mr. Bannatyne wished to be admitted.

I thought that this was a providential opportunity for me, and waited anxiously to hear
and see what might pass on so serious an occasion. In another minute Mr. Bannatyne was
bending over the bed of the dying man.

I was affected upon observing the evident
change in his appearance. The thoughtfulness
of five and forty was already on his brow,
though twenty years had yet to run their
course before he should have arrived at that
age. I saw that a death-bed advice was going
to be delivered to him; and my ears were open
to its solemn import. After a few preliminary
sentences, the dying man, settling himself up in
bed, thus spoke : —

" It has been matter of satisfaction and
thankfulness to me, Mr. Bannatyne," he said,
" that Providence has been pleased to ap-

point over my beloved people of this parish, to succeed me as their pastor, one possessing the mental qualities and endowments of which you are well entitled to boast. I confess it would have caused serious reflections at such a time as this, and might have deeply embittered my dying day, had I had to leave my simple yet intelligent people in the charge of many of those raw youths, who, springing up from among the lower orders, are yearly issuing from our cheap universities, and who, placed in the important position of religious and moral instructors, by the simple forms of our Genevan church, — under circumstances very frequently when they are below the level of the generality of the people, in all that constitutes valuable applicable acquirement, — serve so effectually to perpetuate prejudices, of which the age is justly ashamed, and cruelly to hinder the natural struggles towards improvement of a great portion of our intellectual countrymen.

"It is not for me, however, at a time of this kind, to expatiate upon so well known a disadvantage which attaches to our popular pres-

byterian ecclesia, and our pious nation; further
than as a ground for congratulation to myself
and my people, that I am leaving over them
(you cannot suspect me of flattery at this hour)
a man of capacity, who, with the education suitable for his office, is possessed of the general
knowledge and intellectual advancement which
form the characteristics of a gentleman; and
who, while he builds up his people in their holy
faith, will deal out to them, from time to time,
rational principles to provoke and to assist
their own thinking, upon subjects suitable for
them; and who knows how, by making them
wiser, to make them better, men.

" Yet a few things I would take leave to say
to you, Mr. Bannatyne, as I am about to be
taken from you, which, whether, with your
good sense, you may need them, or not, may
not be thought impertinent from me, as the
result of some experience, both as a minister of
religion, and an observer of the world. Some
of these things you may think somewhat common-place; in truth, I think them so myself:
yet the daily disregard of them shows that they

are either less understood than you and I would suppose, or that their importance is not admitted until after the usual disappointments of experience, and the incurring, and propagation, perhaps, of much real evil.

" The most common error of young men of some natural assurance and readiness of speech, and whose necessary isolation from the world, and *set-up* position, as religious teachers, is so apt to give them a false opinion of themselves, is the vulgar ambition to become *popular* preachers, and so to get the empty portion of the world, for a brief period, to run after and admire them. I need scarcely tell you that the low artifices and feverish strivings of this sort of ambition are far beneath a man of real talent or true worth; and that it holds with preachers of the Gospel, as with other men who address the public, that the quiet approbation and hearty respect, as well as steady friendship, of *one man* of sound intelligence and worth, is to be prized above all the unstable shoutings of the giddy multitude. Besides, no man will ever gain extensive popularity, at least he will never retain it, upon so debateable a subject as religion, by sincerely speaking the truth. He must study the character and flatter the prejudices of the itching-eared portion of his people, exaggerate what they delight to hear exaggerated, cloak or suppress what is likely to offend, and, in short, become a pander to the eternal errors and hypocrisies of the vulgar.

"What is the usual end of all this? That, after the feverish excitements and ungodly triumphs of his brief day shall have passed away, and the inflated fool has scared away from his acquaintance every wise man and estimable friend, he dwindles down and sinks into unwelcome isolation, harassed with vain endeavours to please the low-minded and the vacillating, whom he first condescended to flatter, but who now, tired of his bombast, begin to suspect his motives, and traduce his name; and it will be well if the whole does not terminate in the bitter inveighings of disappointed vanity, and the impotent complainings of merited neglect.

" With respect to the character of your instruction to a mixed people, I cannot suppose
that any aberration into a weak enthusiasm for
particular theological views, which are ever
varying with the fashion of the age, or the narrow conceit of individuals; or any mistaken
attempt to propitiate a clamorous party, will
ever lead you into the common error of the
more ignorant of our cloth, of worrying your
people constantly with puzzling reasonings upon
mere *doctrine*, and ringing constant changes upon such words as ' faith ' and ' grace,' or at least
upon what may be contained in one or two simple propositions. This wretched system, which
frightens from our churches so many of the
best informed and most valuable men in society,
and which makes religion itself so often treated
with sneering and contempt, is in general re-
sorted to from mere paucity of intellect and information, by those who find it much easier
to fill up their tasked hour with the unintelligible rubbish of cant and quotation, than with
those applicable views of human life, Scripture,
and duty, which require in the preacher some

thinking and observation, and his failure in which show too glaringly his real ignorance and incapacity.

" Believe me, sir, this is a most serious evil, both as respects religion and morality, and has the most extensive effects even upon our national character. Do you not observe, by comparing one place with another, and our own nation with others under a different system, that it is this priestcraft-jangling of words and names, this early and incessant harassment of the intellect, with doctrinal mystification, while the practical self-denials of a truly religious spirit, the great subjects of justice and mercy, honour and honesty, between man and man, under the names of virtue and morality, are neglected, or even sneered at, as ethical and heathenish ; and thus, by the habitual setting up of doctrine and dogma, above, or even in opposition to, what is tangible and practical in conduct, systematically forms the character of our charged national hypocrisy ?

" I need not further show you that all this arises from the great preponderance, in Scotland, of the lower order of mind, in that important matter, public instruction; for the very literature in our book-shops, and which is devoured in such quantity by the class that have public influence, would alone prove it. I sincerely rejoice, however, that you will be one among the few loftier intellects, who will fairly devote yourself to the noble task of restoring the natural union between a modest piety and that enlightened sense of obedience and of duty, that is at all times more apt to do, than to teach — to make men less ready to babble and to argue, than to show their faith by *their works*. Thus religion, instead of being an uneasiness and almost a horror, as it is frequently taught; you, by interweaving it with those practical views of social life, feeling, and experience, which its genuine operation makes so truly interesting, will show it as designed to be, not only the corrector of the vices and waywardness of the human heart, but the consolation and the staff demanded by the weakness of humanity. Consider, sir, in this respect, the deep importance of your office, and how much good you may do among your people, by giving them a key to the understanding of their own characters, by detecting and exposing to them the intricacies of unchristian selfishness, as well as the delusions of blinded self-love; so that, teaching them habitually to attend to their own motives, in connection with duty, some rational foundation may be laid for true Christian benevolence.

" In connection with what I have said regarding doctrine, however, I would not advise you to abstain entirely from abstract reasonings, if your subjects are chosen not for the purpose of showing yourself off, which I know you to be above, but for the communicating of applicable *practical* instruction. Indeed, a certain quantity of what is called pulpit logic upon debateable subjects is perhaps indispensable, in accommodation to the taste of the common people; for our national character is somewhat metaphysical, and it being a characteristic of those who have little knowledge, to delight in subtlety and ratiocination, it is to his preacher that the poor man naturally looks for the chief part of his necessary mental entertainment. Beware, however, of leading your people too far for their previous knowledge, and be careful not to say much upon subjects which are purely theological. If you, by an injudicious use of controverted subjects, teach your people to argue, instead of to act; if you once make them conceited and puffed up with their fancied knowledge, you will raise up to yourself a hundred enemies, you will thin your congregation, and divide your parish into endless sects of squabbling disputants; and you will ultimately find, that, instead of being the minister of peace, you have been the minister of confusion.

" One word more, I must say, with more particular reference to yourself. I learn, with regret, that your sermons have of late assumed more of a tone of melancholy than is strictly consistent either with your known good sense or your time of life. This I sincerely regret, because to me it is an evidence of some internal suffering on your part, with the cause of which it does not become me to intermeddle. But, permit me to say, that, although it is very natural for any public instructor to mix his own present feelings with what he delivers to others, any peculiarly gloomy view of human life is unphilosophical and injurious. It is unphiloso- phical, because, whatever may be the present sorrows of individuals, such a view of things does not agree with common opinion and ex- perience; for I need not remind you that hu- man life is neither a state of entire happiness, nor the contrary, but is as the mind happens to view it; and the views of the mind on this sub- ject are with many in a state of much oscillation, although generally on the side of cheerfulness and comfort. What I allude to is often ex- ceedingly injurious, especially in this end of the island, — for the Scots are a people predisposed to gloom; and the cruel and vulgar system of exaggerating the terrors of death and judg- ment, and even drawing terrifying pictures of future horrors, is never practised by men of sense, but by popularity-hunting fools, to catch the applause of the vulgar.

" Mr. Bannatyne," added the old minister, seriously, after a long breath, " I must say, fur- ther, that I could wish much to live still to see you married. A minister of the Gospel should not be long without a companion in his home, that he may not be subject to the distractions of passion, or those wanderings of the heart, that belong to the solitude of the virtuous bachelor. But forgive my freedom; it is dictated only by anxiety for your usefulness and happiness.

" Finally, my friend," he continued, after another pause, " never let your aims, in any respect, *descend*, tempted either by the clamorous applause of the base, or scared by the vituperation of the ignorant, which few of the wise can at all times escape. Seek constantly the approbation of the highest and the best, along with the approval of your own mind, and a sense of Divine favour.

" Forgive, and yet think of, this long advice. I feel myself growing weak, and see, in the filmy dimness of earthly organs, that death is drawing fast near. Give me your hands, my friends; — nay, look not so sad, for my hope is good, and I am well content.

" Heaven bless you ! Heaven make you happy ! "

Why should I dwell upon the death of the righteous ? I saw and was conscious that the living had laid it to heart !

CHAPTER VI.

IT was some time after this my second arrival in Hillington, and even after the Rev. Mr. Kinloch was laid in the grave, ere I was able to come at such authentic particulars regarding the young minister, and the much talked of Rebecca Prior, as satisfied the craving curiosity which had been raised in me concerning them.

I found that after the shock had somewhat passed off, which Mr. Bannatyne's mind had received by the disclosures at that painful scene, sketched two chapters back; and he was able to think calmly, and to endeavour at some degree of resignation, that he had again ventured down towards Lawford House; and though his announcement had a startling and almost terrifying effect upon the solitary Rebecca, both herself and her uncle felt a relief from his visit.

" I am come yet again to see you, sir," said Lewis, as the old gentleman kindly offered him his hand, " if you will receive me, at least once more, as a well-wishing friend and your minister; for, to say truth, I feel that I cannot all at once wean myself from society in which I have enjoyed so many happy hours."

" Mr. Bannatyne, you are welcome!" was all that Mr. Prior said; and he spoke the words emphatically, and with some emotion, as he shook the young clergyman by the hand.   He then stood still, and gazed involuntarily as the latter turned to address Rebecca, as one does upon an experiment, of the result of which he is anxiously uncertain.

That meeting between the two was certainly sad and embarrassing; for, in spite of the trembling pleasure that was after all experienced by both, on finding themselves again in presence of each other, the sense of humiliation, and something like dread, on the part of Rebecca, was so acute during the whole time they were together; and stifled feelings so mingled with compassion in the breast of the minister, that a few guarded sentences was all that either would venture to utter.   This proceeding had, however, by no means a deceiving effect; it was but like the rainy haze, that, excluding from view the April sun, serves, instead of concealing, to add the charms of awakened fancy to the pure brightness and warmth which glows in the heavens; and which, though it cannot be seen through the streaming obscurity, is felt and known to be burning behind it. In this spirit Lewis sat with her for a brief space of time; and, after exchanging a few enquiries and observations, chiefly with her uncle, he rose to take his leave.

"It will be a happiness for us to see you at Lawford still, *sometimes*," said Mr. Prior, looking with solemn meaning in his face, "as you seem to understand the footing upon which even our minister must be received into this solitary mansion."

Mr. Bannatyne bowed respectfully, as he pressed the old gentleman's hand, but made no reply. He then turned to Rebecca, and took her trembling fingers, while the uncle walked to the window, that he might not seem to observe them.

" I could wish you to come again to us, Lewis," said Rebecca, in the half whisper of suppressed feeling. " Come *sometimes* still as —as my uncle's friend and mine. The pale tenants of the cloisters themselves, in former ages, who, like me, had no hopes but towards another world, might, at times, as we read, be permitted a distant correspondence with those on whom their thoughts had once dared to dwell,—those, at least, who ministered in the service of Heaven. But, may I beg—— "

She withdrew her hand hastily, without finishing the sentence, as if the touch of his fingers, and her increasing emotion, had suddenly alarmed her; and, turning upon him a melancholy glance, as formerly, the two, without further speech, sadly separated.

These visits were repeated at intervals of some distance, and became again, to both, a sort of dubious and dull consolation ; for it was long before they could get accustomed to each other's society; he obliged to view her in this new and melancholy light, and she with the consciousness that he, on whom her thoughts involuntarily dwelt, must think of her only in association with the most humiliating calamity that can afflict humanity. Yet did not mutual admiration at all abate, but seemed rather to increase, with increasing experience of each other's disinterested resignation. But then as the smothered flame of affection burned purer, and more intensely, a kind look, or a tender word, would often kindle feelings which were almost too trying for mere humanity.

A laborious attention to the duties of his ministry became now more than ever the consolation and the refuge of the unfortunate Bannatyne; and the solemn last words of his sage predecessor seemed yet to sound in his ears like the voice of inspiration. His people, and particularly his wealthier parishioners, while they held him in veneration, beyond what his years demanded, yet looked upon him almost with something like wonder. He now lived so secluded and companionless, a bachelor still, in the large empty manse, of which he had taken possession on the death of Mr. Kinloch; and his deportment was so serious, yet his address was so mild; he was so reserved, except upon matters of duty; and his comings and goings to and from the solitary hollow of Lawford seemed accompanied with such sadness, if not mystery, that, even while he was reverenced as the best of men, he was looked upon with a species of undefined sympathy.

Meantime, his acquaintance with Rebecca became more affectionately unreserved, as time and intercourse strengthened their own minds and increased their mutual confidence. Endeavouring to regard each other as brother and sister, their tenderness was unspeakable; and even the good and venerable Mr. Prior himself seemed to delight in witnessing their more than earthly affection. But though they were all in all to each other, even in this strange situation of consented celibacy, anxiety and dread regarding what might happen hereafter, would often throw a damp over their warmest feelings, that still contended against the constant restraints of their watchfulness over themselves.

The peculiar predicament of these two interesting persons began now to be partly surmised by the people of the neighbourhood, and the very rustics, who lived among the hills above, as well as the villagers of Hillington near, would watch them curiously as they were occasionally seen together; for the prying whisper of rustic interest, as well as of sympathetic feeling and respect, had prepared every one who passed them, for some understanding of their strange situation. It was thought melancholy to see two persons, so young and so formed for happiness and for each other, walking distantly together as the tenderest and the most constant of friends, yet relatively so placed; — as they went on heartlessly towards the village, on occasion, the grave uncle of Rebecca stepping on in solemn taciturnity by their side; or as they might sometimes be observed from the high road above the hollow, on any quiet lowering evening, " in the gloaming," with looks of disappointed yet resigned affection, taking their lingering stroll by themselves, on the low level sod by the black rippling streamlet of Lawford.

" Surely, Rebecca," he said to her, one evening, as they wandered together, "surely it is at least possible you may be deceiving yourself regarding this dread malady of your family, and that you may be thinking of it too seriously? Nay, pray do not stop me this once, for it is seldom we have such an opportunity of conversing unwitnessed; and we are sufficiently intimate now, methinks, to reason this subject with calmness."

"Believe me, Lewis," she replied, earnestly, "you will find that it would be much safer for us both to avoid a subject of such painful delicacy: I could wish that you had not even now hinted at it. But think you I could have decided upon treating you as I did, from your first coming to Lawford — that I could afterwards have strung up my resolution to drive you from our house, by making a disclosure that was to be the means of separating us for ever? Think you that I could have determined upon degrading myself in your eyes, and giving up all that is dear to a woman's heart, and that I could have lived so long this sad life, to end but with the grave, having neither present joy nor future hope, without having passed many an hour of heavy reflection, upon all that I know of the past, and all that I dare not think of in the future; or without a sore struggle with the feelings of nature? It is better, my friend, much better, for us never again to speak upon this subject."

" And yet, Rebecca," he replied, in the subdued tone of sadness which was now become habitual to him, " as I walk for hours together in my solitary apartment in Hillington Manse, pondering on the sad circumstances of our peculiar fate, I sometimes think that we may be all this while deceiving ourselves by imaginary terrors, and that the time may come when we may conclude that we have been needlessly suffering under a scaring delusion. When I reflect, Rebecca, on the superiority of your mind, as daily evinced in the delightful conversations we have enjoyed together, I cannot think that such a heart and such an intellect should ever become wrecked under so awful a visitation. Pray allow me to go on : my thoughts are awakened by my own experience of you. No,

Rebecca, I will not continue to believe that such a fate can ever be in reserve for so gifted a mind as I have found yours to be."

"My dear and valued friend," she said, her voice trembling from her feelings, "do not, by your persuasion, try to unsettle my thoughts. Would you have me to confess to you, with an unguarded tongue, what mine own heart feels when you are absent from me, and when the leaden spirit of solitude and seclusion comes with dead oppression over my sinking heart? Would you have me, Lewis, to speak of a woman's feelings, whose own bosom is unable to carry her bursting affections?"

"I pray you calm this emotion, Rebecca, and let us still discuss this matter, painful though it be. My mind misgives me upon the subject of your apprehensions, from every day's observation; and I may not lightly encourage you in a fancy so exceedingly serious, if it bears the slightest appearance of delusion."

"And think you, Lewis," she continued, "that, during the long progress of this sore trial, I have not meditated upon the melancholy cases of my ancestors, for ten generations bygone, and reasoned upon every view of the painful subject, until my heart became faint with the intensity of my own reflections; and yet I could see no way of escape from the sacrifice required of me; but by a weak reliance upon a bare possibility, or a wilful dereliction from that principle, by which, in the strength of Heaven, I trust I shall always be guided. But I am the last, and I *shall be the last*, of an unhappy race! alas! unhappy, indeed!" she repeated, her voice sinking again into its former tone of re- flective pathos; " for the amiable and the virtuous have become involved, through me, in the meshes of our private calamities. Forgive me, Lewis: I know that it has been my fate to be the destroyer even of your peace; I am aware that you will hereafter say, it had been happy for us had we never met. Had that been the case, I might have borne my private regrets with comparative resignation."

" Rebecca, you may be bearing griefs which Heaven has not laid upon you. I would, and will, bear with you myself — bear with you, and share with you whatever sorrows it may please Providence to cause you to suffer, in reality and in truth — but this sad anticipation of evil, this prospective grief, is, forgive me, Rebecca, it is wearing you to the grave."

"Oh, my friend, do not insist upon this fancy! you are wandering from the point about which I would speak to you. I know my own situation: I am resigned to my fate — a fate which, sooner or later, is as sure to be mine as it has been of my ancestors — but you, your path of duty is different. It is now fit, Lewis, that you should, from henceforth, consider me as I am, and as I am to be; and seek for yourself another destiny."

"What strange language is this, Rebecca?"

"It is proper language, Lewis; these are the words of truth and soberness. Listen to me: why should two be miserable when the hand of Heaven is laid only upon one? Why will you voluntarily extend the afflictions of Providence farther than God himself has designed them to extend? Nay, patience, sir, and I will explain. Since you and I can never be united, oh, my friend! let your thoughts of tenderness be turned to some other object; consider your duty to yourself, to God whom you serve, to the people of whom you have taken the oversight. Lewis, do not look so, but think of this — think of it for my sake; and were you — were you once united to one who might be worthy of you, should the unhappy malady of my family at any time overtake me, and my weak reason give way under the decree of Heaven, I might receive from you, as my minister, the comforts and consolations of the gospel of peace. Will you not speak?"

"Rebecca! do I really hear aright? am I to receive this torture from you?"

"I beseech you, my friend, to think seriously of what I say. Do not suffer yourself to be thus unhappy in your youth, because *I* am unfortunate: I appeal to yourself, to your sense of duty, and your opportunities of usefulness — I appeal to the religion that you teach, and the God whom you have undertaken to serve. I charge you, in the name of the souls of which you have taken the charge, and for whom you must give an account at the day of judgment!"

"Rebecca, for mercy's sake, do not speak thus. Can you expect the heart to tear itself asunder by its own act? Think you that even Heaven expects what is inconsistent with the weakness of human nature? Rebecca, my dear Rebecca! promise me not to speak of this subject again."

"I will, Lewis, I will speak of it!" she exclaimed, drying the tears that rained down her cheeks: "I am convinced it is the straight path of duty for us both; and obedience to duty always brings calm to the mind. Think — think of this."

This unexpected proposition — this noble disinterestedness — this sacrifice of self beyond human capability, deeply affected his elevated mind.

A passionate reply was on the minister's tongue, when the approach of Mr. Prior put an end to this scene of agitated excitement.

CHAPTER VII.

ANOTHER long winter had about this time passed over, and again I crept out from my wearisome solitude of Balgownie Brae; for the weather was becoming soft and mild, the green herbage of the field was sprouting lively up from the holms of Clydesdale — the spring sun had entirely melted the snow which had so long rested on the bald summit of Benlomond, and now glinted pleasantly at e'en o'er the fells of Strathblane; for the last blasts of Yule were forgotten in the valleys, and the time of the singing of birds was come.

It was pleasant to me to hear the rejoicings of nature, as, with my leathern wallet again on my shoulder, and my staff in my hand, I once more " took the road," and, humming to myself some pleasant madrigal as I went along, or chanting, like the singing-birds around me, some cheerful and commendable chant, I wandered forth to see my old friends here and there in the world, and to gather up the gleanings of my former adventures.

But not being particularly hurried for time, I, as was my besetting fashion, so lingered about this place and the other; and had, in truth, so many hands to shake, and healths to drink, to this body, and the next body, on my way; that, in spite of my original intention, it was far towards summer before I passed the high road that overlooked the green hollow of Lawford, and the foliage beyond interrupted my view, so that I was almost within the streets of the town, before I had a peep of the romantic old steeple of Hillington.

" Ye're welcome, sir," said the sonsie landlady of the inn, curtsying long before I drew near her door; " I'm glad to see you in Hillington again, so just step in here to the garden parlour, for I ken you like to hear the birds, and to look out at the bonnie blue hills of Duneiroch. Now, sir, just set ye down in your ain leather chair, while I get the supper ready, for I hae mickle news to tell you about the gentles of this country."

I had hardly swallowed my broiled chicken, and three fourths of a sweet fresh trout that was set before me; and was just nibbling at a bit of crumpy oaten cake to give a *goût* to my cheese and my dram of brandy, when in came the landlady again, and bustled about me in the kindest manner, expecting that I would give her the pleasure of telling me all the circumjacent gossip which she had been hoarding for me ever since I had formerly left the neighbourhood. It suited my humour, however, by assuming at first a grave taciturnity, to coquet for a time with her evident incontinence of womanly clishmaclaver; but my nature was not so made for cruelty as to continue this long, so at length I allowed her to open upon me all that she had to say.

The first great event which she had to inform me of was, that the Laird of Glaunderston's red-haired daughter had actually got a husband at last, and was now fairly married and off; which was a great relief not only to the old man and all the family in Glaunder-ston house, but even, in one sense, to the whole village itself; "for," said my landlady, "I have been maid, wife, and widow myself for many years, and I know what it is perfectly weel; but I never heard such a moan and a lament-ation for the want of a husband in the course of my life, as was made about the weary disappointments of Miss Nelly M'Gilvray of Glaunderston. But, thank God, she 's married now, and that 's a blessing."

The other part of the landlady's news was, that there had lately come to live in the neigh-bourhood a very extraordinary and kentspeckle gentleman, whose presence was likely to have more than common influence in certain quar-ters in the parish, and who, in short, had some-how been known to Mr. Prior of the holm; but, at all events, he had already, more than any of their neighbours, their minister alone excepted, got a footing among the secluded family at Lawford.

My landlady gave me a very strange account of this gentleman, such as made it difficult for

me, for a considerable time, to judge what his
real character actually was, and what were likely
to be the effects of his increasing intercourse
with persons so reserved in their habits, and generally so retired as both the Priors and their
friend Mr. Bannatyne were well known to
be. But what the worthy woman said of him
amounted to this — that he was a long-headed
and a travelled man; "for he had been," she said,
"far abroad, at Seringapatam, and the Cove of
Cork, and such like remarkable places — had
seen the burning hills all the way in Mesopo-
tamia, and elephants carrying castles on their
backs over the great mountains of Amsterdam!"
Whether this gentleman had once been a
voyager with Captain Cook, or travelled with
the great Baron Munchausen himself, was not
clearly determined; but certainly he must have
seen a deal of killing and slaying abroad, for
he talked of the taking off of heads, and the
destruction of whole cities, with extraordinary
coolness and complacency; and hardly less so
of the unfortunate inmates of the various prisons

and magdalens on the Continent, which it had been also his fortune to visit in his time.

This was a sort of information, however, that it had often been my fortune to be obliged to unravel; and thus much I, at least for the present, was able to conclude;—that this Mr. or Dr. Heywood (for that was the name of the new resident) was no common person, at least for his information and his opinions. I gathered, further, from the whole tone of the landlady's remarks, that his presence had a decidedly favourable effect upon the spirits of those for whom I felt so much interest.

Dr. Heywood, as I afterwards found, had actually practised as a physician abroad; but having, on his return, made choice of this hilly and romantic parish for air, had now retired to live in it upon the fortune which he had acquired. The family of the Priors was too conspicuous and remarkable for him to remain long unacquainted with whatever was known regarding their character and history; and, having procured first an introduction to the minister, he was soon enabled, through him, to form some acquaintance with a family about whom his curiosity, from what he had learned, had been strongly excited.

Hearing that the secluded family at Lawford had at length added this gentleman to the narrow circle of its acquaintance, I took some pains to ascertain his character; especially as a manifest influence over all became the result of his visits. I thought him at first too much of a theorising philosopher, who made his information subservient to those fancies which the very benevolence of his disposition had led him to indulge. Upon getting into some intimacy with him, I found, however, that he had only accustomed himself to reason too generally; to view human beings too much in masses; and to draw grand conclusions from the comparisons of surfaces and the computation of numbers. He seemed to me to think too highly of what frail man could do in shaping the intricate course of his destiny, and in guiding the helm of his own happiness. His mind, occupied with the sum total of conclusions, rested little on individuality, and was impatient of detail; so, though his information was undoubtedly great, and his purposes noble, he had seen so much of mankind, that he could hardly be said to see clearly *a man.*

The singular situation of the minister and Rebecca, which was now no secret in the neighbourhood, had so impressed Dr. Heywood, that the excessive delicacy of the one subject, and the evident shrinking from it of all concerned, could not hinder him from gradually approaching it. Mr. Prior was at first almost offended with his freedom; but as the Doctor began by referring to the common opinions regarding different races and tribes of men, and gradually slid into observations upon the peculiarities which have been observed to run in families, until they assumed very decided characteristics, the old gentleman became interested, and, to the alarm of Rebecca, seemed even to encourage the discussion. Subsequently the Doctor ventured to throw out some remarks upon the cases of several former members of the Prior family, which astonished the old gentleman, both from the acquaintance which the former showed with its history, and the use he made of the facts adduced. One of these facts was, that not every one, but only a majority, of Mr. Prior's ancestors had been afflicted with the fearful malady of his house; and that it never, except in two cases, had appeared throughout the female line.

The effect which the mention of some of these things, and of the hints that followed them, had upon Rebecca one evening, when, in presence of Mr. Bannatyne, the Doctor proceeded to urge them, was such as instantly to put a stop to the conversation at that time. Lewis, however, and even Mr. Prior himself, began to awake as from a dream; and, though Rebecca remonstrated strongly with her uncle, against again disturbing her tranquil melancholy, by the discussion of a subject upon which she dared not think with the least hope, the very night following was appointed for talking it over with the anxious physician.

CHAPTER VIII.

THERE never was before seen, in the fruitful month of September, so peculiar a day as that which followed the one on which was made to Rebecca the unexpected communication recorded in the last chapter; for who would expect the gusty blasts of March, or the shining showers of April, in the teeming season of autumn, or to see the clouds and storms of dreary winter sweeping athwart green meadows, and shaking the trees in the woods of Lawford, while the birds of summer yet sang in the boughs, and the foliage had not yet taken the painter's tint, which renders it more interesting while prognosticating its speedy decay?

It had been the habit of Mr. Prior, in watching over the mental health of his beloved niece, whenever he saw her in any unusual state of spirits, to drive off to some distance, exploring all the cross-roads and long valleys within twenty miles, and lingering only where nature was most attractive, but seldom visiting the great towns, or mixing with any offered society. On the morning of this day, he observed that the equilibrium of her spirits was evidently disturbed. She confessed that she had rested ill through the night; for hope, in spite of all the efforts of her reason, had begun to intrude with flattering *perhapses* into her fancy, and her inward dread was, of allowing her thoughts to be further troubled by wishes and reasonings which might only end in adding bitterness to a fate to which she had thought herself quite reconciled. But the variegated scenery of a favourite part of the country, through which her considerate uncle judiciously brought her, together with his own cheerful conversation by the way, tended materially to refresh and settle her mind; and even the strange changeableness of the autumnal day, and the picturesque drifting of the occasional storm along the speckled plain spread out beneath her, had that grateful effect upon her excited thoughts, which the everlasting language of pure nature has ever had upon minds of great sensibility.

They had proceeded a considerable way by a route that was rather new to them, and were returning towards home as the day advanced, when, as they proceeded slowly down a narrow entangled lane, into which Mr. Prior, who prided himself upon his knowledge of localities had led them, their conversation was interrupted by the coachman stopping short to inform them that the road on which they were was no thoroughfare, and terminated, as he could see, in a private property in front of them ; that, in fact, they had lost their way ; and that he could not even turn the carriage conveniently, without proceeding forward, and getting within the gate of this unknown demesne.

" We cannot possibly take such a liberty," said Mr. Prior, with his habitual reserve and delicacy.

" I dare not attempt to turn here, sir," said the man.

" Know you the name of the property before us ?" said Mr. Prior, looking out.

" I think it must be Bicknel Hill, sir," said

the man, " owned by Mr. Dryburgh, that is, Dryburgh of Bicknel."

" Surely I have heard that name," said Mr. Prior, repeating it. " Rebecca, my dear," he added, turning to his niece, " is not that the name of the person whom we heard had some-time ago married the daughter of our neigh-bour M'Gilvray of Glaunderston."

" It was some such name," she said : " but, for Heaven's sake, sir, do not let us go within a mile of such people. That horrid woman will be sure to fasten herself upon us in some way, if we enter within the gate."

" Let not that trouble you, Rebecca," said Mr. Prior, good-humouredly ; " the lady's father and I are old neighbours. Drive on, John ; " — and in five minutes after they were stopped by a small lodge, out of which issued an old grumbling man, who, with some diffi-culty, admitted them through the rickety gate into the old avenue of Bicknel Hill.

When within the gate, they found the ill-kept road so narrow, and the elm trees of the straight avenue so close, that it was impossible

for them, with either decency or safety, to turn
and go back, without proceeding to the very
door of the old mansion; and this, of course,
required Mr. Prior, in spite of the dread of
Rebecca, to send his compliments to Mr. Dryburgh, of whom he had a slight knowledge,
to apologise for his intrusion, and to enquire
his way.

As they proceeded forward, however, both
found their attention arrested by many objects
around them, which they could not possibly
have expected to find in any civilised country-
gentleman's property. Such a tampering, by
abused art, with graceful nature, appeared in
every thing they saw, that the assemblage of inanimate objects, when taken together, assumed
a positive expression; and, in spite of Mr.
Prior's grave disposition, he could hardly for-
bear laughing aloud at the *tout ensemble* of the
laird of Bicknel's house and property. The
scene into which they had thus accidentally
been introduced was certainly an unlooked-
for diversion to both : such an *olla podrida* of
whatever was useful and ornamental, natural

and artificial, graceful and ridiculous, all hidden among the leafy luxury of nature, or staring out in the pedantic elaboration of art, as appeared in the grounds of Mr. Dryburgh, never, perhaps, was before seen. The place was all wild, and yet it was all garden, and park, and plantation : still it was neither; but a confusion of clumps, hedges, gates, grottoes, whale's jaw-bones joined like Gothic arches, wooden lions grinning at the gates, with black painted eyes and red mouths, shooting Cupids, and brawny figures that ladies dared not look at, summer seats and bowers such as never was before seen or invented. How the man could have got together such a collection of absurdities, in this inland quarter of Scotland, as encumbered and made ridiculous his unfortunate grounds, was perfectly astonishing; but, from the figure-head-like objects that were stuck on the ends of an old wall that flanked the garden, as well as the mast-like flagstaffs, and ropes, and twirling vanes, that shot up from among the foliage at the end of the stables, the proprietor might have been taken for a retired port-admiral, while the judgment was again disconcerted by numbers of wooden men and women, standing in various attitudes, at the angles and entrances, reminding one of the painted Neptunes and shameless Venuses who adorn those delectable retreats of elegance, the tea-gardens of the metropolis.

Nor was the house itself, a tall, old-maidish form of a building, much less laughable. It seemed perfectly riddled with small holes of windows, which seemed to grin down upon the beholder up and up to the very slates of the roof. And then, when the eye turned itself aloft so far, a crowd of long toppling chimneys appeared, bristling up into the very clouds, and filling the spectator with alarm lest every blast of wind, where wind was no rarity, should cause these ill-formed giants, who carried their heads so high, to precipitate themselves down, through the roof, upon the unfortunate tenants of this dangerous mansion.

But, as if the building were not already sufficiently ridiculous, the present laird, on the occasion of his marriage, had caused to be placed, in front of the door, two stumpy round pillars, of the composite order, and other absurdities, by way of a porch, which entirely darkened several of the small windows, and had united at the foot of each gable end two low hulking round houses of a different-coloured stone to the rest of the building, which he chose to call wings, but which, as the wings of Mercury were placed at his feet, seemed to have the same congruity with the tall figure above them.

The sight of these various *outré* objects was so amusing to Rebecca, as well as to her uncle, that it quite put her in a gay humour, and made her almost wish for, instead of dreading, a sight of the newly-married couple within, who owned so odd a wilderness of monstrosities.

Yet, when they arrived at the entrance, and she observed the bustle that their approach had created within, and Mrs. Dryburgh already planted at one of the port-hole windows, and afterwards at the entrance, she felt some of her former dread at the idea of the officious familiarity of such a horror.

" Bless me, Miss Prior, who could have thought to see you coming of your own accord to visit me and my husband, at Bicknel Hill!" exclaimed the lady, coming forth in person, and speaking from between the stumpy pillars of the porch: "really it is such an honour. But, to be sure, when one is married, they have a right to expect —— "

" We are most happy to see you, madam," interrupted Mr. Prior, politely; "but, on this occasion, the visit is somewhat accidental, for, in truth, we had lost our way, when we found ourselves in the lane leading to your house, and, at this hour in the afternoon, must be contented with enquiring for your health, and the shortest way to Lawford, without doing ourselves the pleasure of alighting."

" It 's not possible, Mr. Prior," said the lady, with true Scotch vulgarity of tone, " that ye 're going away from my door in that manner, without coming in and wishing me weel, now when I am married. The laird, my husband, would tak it quite as an affront, sir, as weel as your old neighbour, my father, the laird of

Glaunderston, if he were to hear of such a thing; and look you," she added, "holding out her hand, elegantly, to catch the rain drops, "there's another shower coming on. Ye must really come into my house, and see what like my gudeman is, Miss Prior. John! Jenny! Jamie!" she screamed to the staring servants, "what do you stand there glowring for? Run, this moment, an' seek the laird. Ye'll find him, nae doubt, on the Parnassus mount, up there beside the nine Mooses, putting up that long-legged image o' the blind 'Pollo."

The servants scampered off different ways; and Mr. Prior, finding it vain to argue with the classical lady, who, as she said, would take no denial, now, as she *was* married, alighted with Rebecca, and, following their hostess into a small old-fashioned apartment, lighted with seven or eight holes called windows, were soon after gratified with a sight of the tasteful Mr. Dryburgh.

"This is my gudeman," said Lady Bicknel, introducing the classical laird, in the person of a rosy-cheeked, fair-haired, lively man, with a short neck, round shoulders, and arms that reached almost to his knees, and altogether as unclassically formed a being as ever offered to set up a graven image in honour of the ancients. The elegant admirer of Phidias and Praxiteles was economically dressed in fustian and corduroy; an orange-coloured cotton handkerchief, rolled like a bell-rope, served to fill up the space between his chin and his shoulders; leather leggings, bespattered with mud, encased his brawny limbs, and these were shod by a pair of enormous brogues, which increased the height of the wearer by at least an inch.

"Hoo are ye, Mr. Prior?" said the bluff laird, with a genuine Scotch bow; "and how do ye do, Miss Prior: dear me, mem, I never could get a sight of you, except it might be in Hillington kirk; an' ye 're aye sae mim an' sae mute, that I little thought to hae seen you stepping across my floor-head at Bicknel Hill, although we are sic near neighbours, as my gudewife says."

"Deed, gudeman," said Lady Bicknel, "it's my fault entirely; for I should hae renewed acquaintance wi' Miss Prior; but really when folks get married, they have no time for any thing: but will ye not be seated, Miss Prior? Na, na, ye must stay and take a snack: here, John! Jenny! Geordie! what are ye standing there for? bring in the luncheon this moment. Ye 'll excuse me, Miss Prior, ye see I 'm a plain woman, an' we 're a' plain country folks here at Bicknel Hill."

There is nothing that qualifies the manifold afflictions from country kindness, from persons that are in general a *horreur*, but the disarming consideration that it is well meant; and in this spirit did Mr. Prior and Rebecca suffer themselves to be set down upon long-backed chairs, having leathern seats, with a lunch placed before them, principally consisting of a large dish of coarse cold boiled beef, which would have served as a pic-nic for a dozen squires of the Caledonian Hunt; and the pressing solicitations to eat and drink, by the laird and lady within, seemed to be seconded by the noisy voice of the storm without, which, by this time, began to batter against the windows, and to whirl about among the lofty chimneys of the rocking mansion.

" Take another wing o' the pullet, Miss Rebecca," insisted the lady : " the storm frae the hills makes people hungry. Dear me, I declare ye're doing nothing !   Now, that was just the way with me before I was married : but now, bless you, Miss Prior, I have aye such an appetite, I'm quite ashamed o' myself.   Laird," she cried, across to her husband, whose mouth was too full to answer her, " I'll just take another striffen o' the beef: really Bicknel Hill is a hungersome place."

" What did you think of my grounds as you came along, Mr. Prior?" said the laird, after a most polite hob-nob with the old gentleman, which helped materially to clear his own mouth.   ·

" You have certainly contrived to introduce considerable variety into them," said Mr. Prior, politely.

" But don't you think, sir," said the lady, striking in across the table, " that my gudeman there is rather too much given to graven images

of heathen idolatry, whilk you may have seen
sentinelled about the grounds up and down? I
assure you, Mr. Prior,— since we married ladies
may be allowed to speak among you learned
gentlemen, — that it's a real calamity, that I
cannot take a walk in my own policy, or turn a
corner wi' safety, but up starts a great houghy
fallow at the back of every bush; some Hector
or Keelis, wi' hardly a tag to cover his naked-
ness, holding a great swurd or spear threaten-
ingly o'er my head, as if he meant to fell me:
it's really dreadful."

" These are purely matters of taste, madam,"
answered Mr. Prior, hardly able to suppress
laughter.

" And don't you think, sir," added the lady,
" that these statue men, and image makers
should, for decency's sake, be more liberal of
garments to their gods and goddesses, heathen
though they be; for I have read in Rollin's
Ancient History, that the heathens themselves,
before the flood, did not go so perfectly mother-
naked?"

" Hush—sh, my dear," said the learned

Theban of a laird, with an overawing shake of the head ; " it does not do for women to talk so freely of men's affairs."

" Na, deed, laird," said the outspoken lady, " ye need na fash to shake your head at me, for ye mind what a fright I got that moonlight night, coming hame frae the laird o' Libberton's in the howm, wi' naething but Nelly and the lantern. Ye see, Mr. Prior, Nelly and I had crossed the fields for shortness, and got into the grounds through a stile just aboon the auld monument that was bigget for the laird's great-grandfather, and were holding on by the moonlight through among the birks, as canny as kittens, when, just as we turned the dark elbow of a rowan-tree copse, up gets a great Roman gladiawtor between me and the moon, the light whitening him like a sheeted ghaist, and his weapon thrust into our very faces. Lord ! my heart jamp into my mouth, and I scrieght like ane wud ; for, ye see, sirs, I had never seen the image before, and I actually thought the muckle thing would hae jumped down aff the stane, and worried us, that is, poor Nelly an' me. Na, ye needna laugh, gudeman, for there's Mr. Prior's a considerate man, an' he kens perfectly weel that it's no for married ladies like me, ahem! to be exposed to thae untoward images."

The laird good-naturedly promised that the matter should be considered: but the rain being now over, he would not suffer Mr. Prior to depart without being shown more fully his grounds and gardens. Having, therefore, persuaded the old gentleman to accompany him without, Lady Bicknel and Rebecca were left together.

A momentary feeling of uneasiness came over the latter, when the gentlemen had departed; for which, however she blamed herself, when she contrasted her own character with that of her hostess: still, in order to prevent any unpleasant allusions, she adroitly tried to engage her in conversation about the tasteful beauty of the grounds at Bicknel Hill.

But people like Rebecca are far less artful than they think themselves, when brought in contact with such as Mrs. Dryburgh, who had too much of the woman in her to suffer such an opportunity as this to pass, without the enjoyment of a little female triumph over her serious neighbour, in the good fortune of her own marriage. After a few passes of fencing talk, accompanied with a look of extraordinary sweetness and kindness, she thus began upon the sensitive Rebecca : —

" And hoo is your health noo, Miss Prior? ye 'll excuse me; but although my father, the laird of Glaunderston, or my husband, the laird of Bicknel, canna just hold up their heads wi' the Priors o' Lawford, yet, as a neighbour and an auld acquaintance, Miss Rebecca, I 've had a great concern for you ; an', dear me, we all thought that ye would have been *married* long ago ; but there 's nae signs o' that, that I can hear of. Noo, ye see, there 's me, that 's married, an' in my ain house, an' likely to hae a family o' my ain, ahem ! — dear me, Miss Prior, but ye 're looking quite auld-like, as I may say; ye 're surely no' in gude health — an' hoo is Mr. Bannatyne ?"

" Mr. Bannatyne, madam?" said Rebecca,

her face colouring at the other's hypocritical impertinence — "I don't understand you."

"Hoot, ye understand me weel enough, Miss Prior, an' ye'll just excuse my freedom, but ye ken I was aye a plain-spoken body, an' really I canna help speaking to you about the minister, for he does not do by you as I thought he would. Does he still come to see you now and then?"

"I think, Mrs. Dryburgh, you might have more delicacy and good senset han to ———" Rebecca could not proceed.

"It is nothing but concern *for you*, Miss Rebecca, that makes me speak, so ye need not take it the least amiss," said the lady, looking with piteous kindness on the agitated girl; "an' really the minister appears to use you so — but I would not say *a word* ill of a minister; yet Mr. Bannatyne has so long — ye'll excuse me, Miss Prior, but I am a married woman now, and have a right to speak to young folks. Dear me, how ill you look! — but you had always a pale face — take half a glass o' wine?"

I 4

" If you have any thing to say, Mrs. Dry-burgh, let me hear it at once ! "

" I see ye 're flurried a little, Miss Prior," added the coarse woman maliciously, and en-joying her revenge on Rebecca for rivalling her successfully with the handsome minister of Hillington — " but, ye see, us married women *ought* to give advice to young inexperienced ladies; and really Mr. Bannatyne, although he was once a sort of joe of my own, is so long about this marriage — if he *mean* a marriage — that, if ye would take my advice, Miss Prior —— "

" Mrs. Dryburgh," interrupted Rebecca, while she strove to master her feelings, " I know not why you should make observations to me about Mr. Bannatyne : he visits Lawford as my uncle's friend and mine ; and any advice regarding him, or his conduct, addressed to me, is unnecessary and inapplicable."

" Weel, that 's very sensibly spoken, Miss Prior ; quite sensible, as I am happy to perceive — an' certainly ye must ken better than I do ; but, ye 'll excuse me — the world is an observable world.   Indeed, after the talk that has been talked about you and the minister ——— "

" What talk? — what is your meaning, Mrs. Dryburgh?"

" Why, ye ken, Miss Rebecca, people *will* speak: but I have aye maintained, on your part, that although your forbears the auld Priors o' Lawford — that is, your father, and grandfather, and great-grandfather, maybe, as I've heard my ain father tell, fell rather into a demented way, yet surely the minister — dear me, your face is grown like a sheet again — I hope ye're no gaun to faint in my house. Is there naebody there?" screamed the lady — " John! Jenny! Geordie!"

" I'm better — I'm better now: do not call any one!" urged Rebecca, recovering herself by an energetic effort — " it is only the consequence of my long ride. Now, Mrs. Dryburgh, say, in one word, what you mean by these hints."

" There now — I'm glad to see you come to yourself again," said Lady Bicknel, also recovering — " an' ye speak very sensibly — I aye said ye could talk as sensibly as *I could ;* an' that that could never be the minister's reason for standing aff an' on in that strange sort of way — meaning, Miss Rebecca, by hints? Noo, ye need na be the least flurried ; just put that mouthful of wine over ——— "

" Mrs. Dryburgh, " said Rebecca, indignantly, and pushing away the offered wine, " this indelicate freedom with me and my family is what I cannot excuse."

" Odsake, Miss Prior, dinna speak sae sharply," said Lady Bicknel, astonished at Rebecca's scornful energy; " ye'll remember that I'm a married woman, and all I have to say is, that, if ye take my advice, ye'll just tell the minister yourself, plump an' plain, suppose he *be* a minister — that although, as the folk say, you may be rather ——— "

" Mrs. Dryburgh, what are you aiming at? It is not fit that I should listen to language like this ! " — and, rising as she spoke, while her eyes flashed with scorn, she was proceeding to leave the room.

" Sit doon — just sit doon, Miss Rebecca

— odsake but ye're proud an' pettish. I beg your pardon a hundred an' fifty times, although, being a married woman, ye might take my advice when it's all for your gude. But now set ye down, an' smooth your face, for there's your uncle and my gudeman coming back. Odsake, if the laird ken'd that I had wagged a tongue at ony o' the Prior family, I would never hear the last o't. Noo, just forgi'e me, an' let us be friends — ahem! What a fine afternoon it's turned out !"

As the good lady spoke the last sentence, Mr. Prior and the laird entered the room, to the great relief of Rebecca; and the old gentleman, seeing at a glance that something had been said to ruffle his niece, managed to get off; and in a few minutes they were again driving rapidly towards their own pleasant valley at Lawford.

CHAPTER IX.

THE autumnal day, hitherto so variable, had, as has been said, brightened into unusual beauty, as Mr. Prior and Rebecca rode on towards their home. The richness on the landscape, of the afternoon tints, was heightened and enhanced by the shining freshness which the departed storm had left; and the clouds, having cleared away over the nearest range of hills, appeared rolled together in the far distance, and, mixing in contrasting masses with the partial lights shining on the blue summits of the mountains, gave a picturesque grandeur to the still stormy horizon.

As they were driven along, Mr. Prior, as usual, pointed out to Rebecca every peep of nature in sky and landscape that seemed grand or interesting; but he remarked, with concern, that the mind of his niece had been disturbed to a much greater degree than she would confess; for the wide range of " meadow green

and mountain grey," now lying gay beneath
them, had lost all charm for her, and every
effort of his failed to arouse her from that
tendency to abstraction, which experience had
taught him to regard, in any of his family, with
a sympathetic and apprehensive anxiety. The
habitual delicacy, however, with which her
good uncle had always treated her, prevented
him, at this time, from touching upon the cause
of her disquietude; and they arrived at home
individually brooding in secret over the painful
idea, that the world had rejected them as social
beings, and already talked of them as ultimately doomed to the melancholy seclusion
of mental alienation.

The expected visiters did not come to dinner: but this, so far from being a disappointment to Rebecca, seemed to be a relief to her;
for she evidently looked with dread upon the
further discussion of a subject with which she
thought hope could never be associated. At
length a carriage was heard to proceed down
the avenue; but, by this time, Mr. Prior was left
quite alone, for Rebecca had retired for some

time, and, when the gentleman arrived, was nowhere to be found. As it was on her account, chiefly, that the meeting had been appointed, Mr. Bannatyne, in particular, felt much disappointed at her absence, and at the evident gloom upon her uncle's countenance.

The servant who had been sent to request the attendance of Rebecca now returned to say, that she was neither in her room, nor any where else in the house. Mr. Prior felt strangely at this intelligence, and rose and walked hastily about the apartment. Doctor Heywood was disconcerted, and knew not what to think; Mr. Bannatyne rose also, walked to the window, and, drawing the curtains aside, looked abroad upon the lawn, upon which the early moon was now shining dimly. A thought struck him as he gazed down the woody hollow of Lawford, and traced the sinuosities of the streamlet that here and there reflected the watery rays of the moon; and, taking his hat, he was soon in the lawn behind the mansion.

Some impulse led him to take the road towards the height beneath which was the dark chasm into which gushed the streamlet of Lawford, from the solitary pond above, called the Lady's Linn. Rebecca seemed always to have avoided this spot, and *he* had never been so near it before. The rain of the early part of the day had swollen the waters of the linn, which tumbled with a heavy and saddening sound into the rocky chasm below. Lewis was moved, and contemplated the place as the mysterious emblem of some hidden destruction. But this, he thought, must be fancy only, and the fancy oftener deludes poetical minds into imaginations of sorrow than of joy.

Leaving the falling waters boiling with a hollow sound beneath, Lewis mounted the height to see the linn ; but, though the evening was delicious, and the idea of Rebecca had led him abroad, the hope had left him of finding her so far from home as this. He could not resist the impulse, however, of visiting the linn, now as it was so near. The trees that crowned the height were scattered and irregular, and the spot had altogether a neglected appearance ; but its very wildness made it more picturesque to Lewis, when, emerging from among the bushes, the open expanse of this hidden lake, made light by the reflection of the moonbeams, now burst upon him.

The solitude of the place was perfect : even the hum of the falling waters below, deadened as it was upon the ear by the intervening thick trees that bordered the lake, seemed to deepen the idea of absolute seclusion ; and the still small voice of Nature alone was heard to echo through the woods around. Lewis was absorbed, as, threading his way among the trees, he traced the green margin of the lake. He had forgotten every thing but some vague and melancholy associations with this holy place, when, as he proceeded musingly forward, he found himself suddenly grasped by the arm, and, looking round, after the start that such an encounter gave him, he perceived the pale features of Rebecca, her person wrapped in a mantle, and her dark eyes gazing on him with unusual animation.

" What seek you here, Lewis ? " she said,

quickly; "who taught you the way to the Lady's Linn?"

" Rebecca, this is strange," he replied : " why do I find you wandering on this ominous spot?"

" Do not be alarmed, my friend," she answered, calmly; " there is nothing remarkable in an outcast like me loving to brood, in solitude, over sad thoughts, particularly when my mind is disquieted by this coarse world, and my fancy wanders towards another state of being. But I am glad you are come — very glad it is you that have come to me at this moment;" and, as she earnestly spoke, she grasped closely his arm.

" Then come home with me, Rebecca," he said, kindly, and returning her pressure; " they wait for us at the mansion."

" Not yet, my friend, not yet: let us discourse here an instant. Tell me candidly — tell me, Lewis — did ever a thought come across you — a temptation — to — to suicide? Nay, start not. 'Tis not so uncommon. Death, *as such*, may not be an evil. *Life*, we know, often is."

" How can you talk thus, Rebecca? Let us leave immediately this solitary place."

" Why should we fear to talk of any thing? See you that small stream that murmurs at the upper end of the linn, how it struggles and foams through obstructing and dividing rocks; how it leaps and bubbles and brawls in its short course; and how quiet it is when it reaches the depths of that placid linn, on the smooth bosom of which the clear moonbeams now sleep so sweetly. 'Tis the old tale, Lewis — struggling time, and quiet eternity."

" You are melancholy to-night, Rebecca; you are not as usual; and here the air is cold. Let us hence to the house."

" You will not, surely, like the worldling, run from me, because I am sorrowful ! " she said, mournfully. " Is not our friendship, our *more than* friendship, cemented and strengthened even by melancholy? Nay, let me speak to you, Lewis, as I have always spoken when the sadness of my heart comes upon me. What do you think of the world, which would not allow me to have you, even, for *a friend ?* "

" Dear Rebecca, do not encourage these melancholy reflections. *Do* come home with me! There is something awful in this wild spot just now. See you, the moon is under a dark cloud — the trees round these waters assume strange shapes in the gloom; and the chill breeze begins to moan in the woads, and to sweep up the hollow past us. I know not how you can linger here, for the cold black depths of that still linn make me shudder when I look into it."

" It is you that are fanciful, Lewis, and apt to be uneasy, and scared by this gloom and solitude. Now, as for me, it does me good, when my heart is disquieted, to gaze upon these dead waters; and when I sit here in the deepening twilight, thinking of the empty idealisms of life, and the numerous disappointments of warm-hearted youth, — of the penalties connected with that very reason of which we think so highly, and the sadness that mingles even with truth itself; — I obtain resignation to an anticipated state that the obtuse world abuses with its pity ; nay, I feel almost a happiness in my hopeless

equanimity, which is only disturbed by such
vain discussions as was this night intended; and
when, on this spot, I have solemnly made up
my mind to the sacrifice of every tender hope,
my prayers to Heaven for mental tranquillity
mingle with the roar of the falling waters, as
they tumble heavily into that chasm among the
rocks, — prayers sincerely addressed to the
High and Lofty One, that, in my hour of aberration, when reason shall have abandoned *this*
helpless tenement, He will not desert me; —
then, then, my friend, the spirit of my unhappy
ancestress, who gave up her struggling soul *to*
her Maker beneath the cold waters of this linn,
seems to join in my petition for resignation to
the sad fate of my fathers, and to point a ghostly
hand, over these woods, towards the heaven
above us, where that blessed moon, and *the*
stars that twinkle beside it, cannot hide the glory
that is beyond; and where there remains a rest
for the frail victims of earthly calamity."

Lewis stood for a minute, unable to answer;
and then, taking her gently away from the margin of the linn, he said, as they went slowly

down the slope, " This is a mournful subject, Rebecca, and these are thoughts which I did not expect you to be occupied with this night : but the mind, I know, is a riddle — I feel it in myself; perhaps the highest minds are the most difficult to understand : but allow me to remind you, that, with all supposable acquirements, and all its intensity, the mind is often its own worst enemy, and hugs, with the prejudice of a determined melancholy, the galling chains of its own misery."

Ob, Lewis ! " she said, and by this time the tears were streaming down her cheeks, " your very reproof is a pleasure and a blessing to me : but my weakness — my poor — "

" Do not speak of weakness, my adored Rebecca," he exclaimed, now melted with her emotion ; " we never love those who have no weaknesses. Is it not weakness that causes the close embrace of the twining tendril and its supporter, — which, if they must bend under the blast, bend together, — yes, Rebecca, and rise together when the storm is over, and grow together, and bud and blossom together, and rejoice together in the richness of summer, and shed their leaves together, when winter approaches, and wither together at last, Rebecca, — and die together ! ”

Tears, and broken sentences, and intruding hopes that were too bright, and apprehensions that were too sad for the contrast, occupied the lovers until they reached the mansion, where the approaching discussion was now involuntarily looked to, as that which was to decide their fate for the rest of their lives.

CHAPTER X.

"You would not have me, sir," said Dr. Heywood, addressing Mr. Prior, when all were seated round him, "begin a formal lecture upon so delicate a subject; particularly as I pretend to advance nothing either very new or recondite, but simply to apply what is known regarding a specific malady to the case, in particular, of this young lady. Ask me, therefore, if you please, what questions you think proper, and I will answer them to the best of my ability."

"There is one great principle regarding this point, which, you say, has been universally admitted of late years," said Mr. Prior, "which, I confess, has made a deep and even hopeful impression upon my mind; and that is, that insanity is essentially a bodily or functional derangement only, and so liable to be treated medically, like other maladies. Yet, doctor, you will excuse the scepticism, perhaps of

ignorance, if, accustomed to the terms of metaphysics and the impressions of the world, I
attach to the notion of the thinking principle —
of that essence which, like the great Being who
created it, ' no man hath at any time seen nor
can see,' *res ipsa*,— an idea so abstract and mysterious, as to make the ministering effectually
to a *mind* diseased, a thing hardly consistent
with human skill, particularly if, like any other
mental peculiarity, it may have been transmitted through several generations."

" I sympathise with your doubt, sir," said
the Doctor, " and with the feelings that give
rise to it : yet, as gout and scrofula, the most
inveterate, perhaps, of the other hereditary
disorders, have been much overcome by scientific treatment, so has even *manie hérédité*,
as Esquirol calls this dreadful malady. But
though I by no means flinch from the consideration, so important in the case of this
family, that such an affliction may be inherited ;
knowing that in all exclusive tribes, as the
Jewish people, the Quakers, Moravians, &c.,
as well as in clanships, and among aristocratic

families accustomed to invariable intermarriages among each other, such predisposition has been and is transmitted; yet allow me to say, that persons supposed to be in this unhappy situation are by no means the best judges of the application of any general rule to their own cases; and least of all can they, before such predisposition may have actually manifested itself, be supposed to understand either the doctrine of transmission as likely to affect themselves, or the mode which experience has pointed out of aiding benevolent nature in her usual efforts to free herself from the constitutional derangement to which accident or vice may have, through a series of generations, subjected her."

"Proceed, sir, if you please," said Mr. Prior; "we are all attentive."

"Without troubling you at any length upon so wide a subject," continued the Doctor, "permit me to observe, that, from several facts that have come to my knowledge, in the history of the cases of several individuals of your family, I am obliged decidedly to conclude that the professional friends of your house, Mr. Prior, and even yourself, have made some capital mistakes, both as to the nature of the malady supposed to be manifested in former generations, and as to the actual danger of your family from it, at the present point of its dreaded transmission. In the first place, allow me to urge upon you, that *mania hérédité* does not invariably proceed in a direct course, as the history of your ancestors will prove, nor even *per saltum* in the second or third generations, as some have maintained; nor is there, indeed, any general rule of transmission that can be relied on as applicable, by anticipation, to the cases of individuals in whom no manifestation of it may yet have taken place, and who may have safely passed the period of majority. It is worthy of consideration, however," added the Doctor, addressing Rebecca, " that this malady, madam, never but in one instance appeared among your ancestors in the female line; and then was associated with circumstances of nervous temperament and worldly trial, that make it by no means decisive as to its belonging to the hereditary character. But there is another consideration, applying to yourself individually, Miss Prior, to which I attach great weight in this enquiry. That consideration is, that, in the general history of *mania hérédité*, there is hardly a more decided symptom *à priori* of the predisposition in question, nor a more certain precursor of a sudden manifestation of it, than the attempt to conceal, and even the strenuous denial of, such a predisposition, with a uniform reluctance to advert to its history; for I have constantly observed, that craft and deception applied to self and others, is strictly an attribute of insanity, both symptomatic and confirmed; so that the readiness of this lady, sir,"— he addressed her uncle, — " to confess, and to dwell upon, so humbling a calamity, her very dread of its manifestation, and her anxiety to avoid any risk of it, is to me a very strong proof that she is in little danger of its ever breaking in upon the happiness and tranquillity of her accomplished mind. Besides all this, be it observed, — if you will excuse me, madam, for speaking of you in the third person, in your own presence, —— that it is circumstances of trial, always apt to disturb the reasoning faculties, or to take from us the command of our own minds, —— that commonly bring into action the hereditary disposition ; and I hesitate not to affirm, in presence of you all, that few females of her years have suffered patiently, and with noble resolution, as Miss Prior has done, a severer trial to a youthful heart, than I know she has endured before this day."

" Heaven bless you, sir ! " exclaimed Mr. Bannatyne, with unconscious emotion, as he hung with increasing interest upon the Doctor's words. " You delight me by giving the sanction of your opinion to a consideration which has dwelt upon my mind more than I can now express."

" Proceed, sir ! pray proceed ! " was echoed by all, not even excepting Rebecca.

" Upon the disposition to this malady generally, since you are pleased thus to listen to me," continued the Doctor, " allow me further to remark, that there are several peculiarities remotely symptomatic of it, which are by no means scarce in the world, and of which most people are little aware. The chief are those unaccountable and fanciful freaks practised by some, which we usually designate by the mild name of eccentricities, and of which, from the physical obliquity in perception and judgment whereon they are founded, those who practise them are unconscious in themselves. Although these absurdities of conduct are generally only a matter of laughter in the world, yet, if unnoticed and unchecked, they have a tendency, in time, to ripen into positive insanity. The seriousness of the circumstances in which you are placed, madam," he added, looking to Rebecca, " obliges me to refer even to this remote and indecisive characteristic of what you dread; but which, so far from having been evinced by you, up to this moment you have shown a consistency and a firmness, in circumstances of trial, that indicates any thing but weakness or obliquity of mental constitution. Nay, further — (since you have placed me in the lecturer's chair, you must hear me out), — even that disposition, so common in sensitive and intellectual constitutions, which, if indulged in, makes the nearest approach to some kinds of insanity, namely, a tendency to brooding over favourite themes, to fanciful abstractions, and the building up of idealisms, poetical or profound, has, if at all existing in Miss Prior's mind, already withstood, as before observed, such trying circumstances, that I should have little fear of its operation in future, if her abiding good sense enables her to watch over it as a dangerous tendency; and particularly if her situation came to be so changed that the natural feelings of her heart may find their exercise and their repose upon those objects that are applicable to the gushing affections of a woman, and which, excuse me, madam, I give it as my opinion, that it would be as dangerous as it is cruel longer to suppress."

A pause of nearly a minute followed this speech, during which no one had the courage to interrupt the perfect silence. At length, Rebecca, lifting up her head from the position which her state of feeling had caused her to assume, and fixing her dark eyes upon the Doctor, in a tone of solemn earnestness, said : ——

" Sir, there is one point more, to which you have not yet adverted, which, for aught I know, may come to overturn all you have advanced, and which, in the effect it has uniformly had upon my thoughts, is of too much importance for me to suffer even delicacy itself to prevent me from mentioning, placed, as I am, in the midst of my dearest friends. Is there not, in the very look of those who are hereditarily disposed to this sad affliction, something which the experienced can read with ease, and which as surely indicates the fate that is in reserve for them, as the hazy glare surrounding the watery moon foretells the storm that is brewing in the sky? Now, sir ——" she was unable to finish the sentence.

" Be explicit, madam ; not only your happiness, but that of all present, depends much on the issue of this discussion."

" Oh, sir, satisfy me only on this one point," she exclaimed : " does not your long experience

among the bereft of reason, enable you to see
in my very eyes that peculiar expression which
distinguishes the individuals so doomed, as it
surely indicates the malady of our unhappy
house?—I see, sir, I perceive by your hesitation,
that upon this important point you hesitate to
answer me ; " — and, as she spoke, her large
eyes, now sparkling from her emotion, began
to fill with tears.

"You are quite mistaken, madam," replied
the Doctor, a little staggered by her manner and
the pointedness of the enquiry, "in supposing
that I am unwilling to answer you upon this
point also ; although, from the nature of the
case, I confess, I could have wished you to
rely less upon inference from a fact so liable to
fallacy or abuse.   I do not mean to deny that
there is, to my apprehension, in the eyes of
both yourself and your uncle, *something* of that
indescribable expression, which is known, to
those accustomed to observe it, to accompany
the hereditary predisposition to mania.   But I
have never contended that you are in your
generation entirely free from a certain degree

of that *predisposition*, or that you are not,
therefore, more *in danger* on account of it, than
if nothing of the kind existed.   I have already
stated to you the grounds of my opinion, that,
admitting a certain degree of that predisposition to exist, it is in your case neither so decided in itself, nor so alarming in its contingent
indications, as to warrant the present sacrifice
of your happiness.   And as to the indication
in the eyes, I must say, at a time too solemn for
the passing of a mere compliment, that in you
it is so blended with the fascinating expression
of personal beauty, and the speaking glance of
poetic intellect, that I can scarely detect a
single distinct trace of that nameless glare,
which, in many that I have seen, was to me so
decisive."

Another silence ensued, after the doctor had
finished, which was, after a few seconds, broken.
with a striking effect, by a deep and struggling
sigh bursting from Rebecca, as if at that moment a heavy load had just been removed from
her heart.

   " And may there, indeed, be no real danger?" she at length exclaimed. "May this awful calamity never, probably never, overtake me? Oh, sir, do not deceive me by raising hopes too flattering to me to think of, after all I have suffered. Dear uncle, dear sir, tell me what you think? Are *you* also convinced, by what seems too delightful for me to listen to?" and by this time she had stepped forward, and was kneeling at her uncle's feet.

"Rise up, my sweet Rebecca, and be not thus agitated," said the old gentleman, much affected: "your feelings are too sharp and powerful for your own tranquillity; but I trust the time is at hand, when this painful consciousness is about to be removed. Be seated, Rebecca, for we have somewhat more to say, and let us calmly come to a conclusion in this matter. Mr. Bannatyne," he added, addressing the minister, who, little less agitated, was by this time standing beside the chair of his Rebecca, — "Mr. Bannatyne, can you forget for a moment your feelings as a near and dear friend to my niece and myself, and tell me, as a man and a minister of the gospel, as dispassionately as you can, what is your own opinion of the facts and reasonings which our medical friend has just offered to our consideration?"

"You will excuse me, gentlemen," said Mr. Bannatyne, recovering himself, "if I am unable to express myself, at this moment, before a man of science, in terms becoming the serious nature of this enquiry. I must say, in a word, that I am entirely convinced by what the Doctor has advanced, and neither from reason nor feeling can offer one caveat to the qualified and yet decided conclusion to which he has come. There is but a single point to which my reason, from what little enquiry I could make upon this subject, would seek an answer; and the answer I should like, with Doctor Heywood's permission, to receive from the lips of Miss Prior herself."

"Name it, Lewis, name it!" said Rebecca, aroused again into something like alarm.

"It is simply," he replied, "that it has been observed, as I believe, that one of the conscious experiences of those who have eventually been lost in the oblivion of insanity, has been an occasional strange rapidity of thoughts, over which they had no power, and a wild association of them which they could not resist, with an exaltation of the ordinary qualities of the mind, which was delightful at the time, like the dreams of the opium-eater; and yet, from the restlessness and anxiety with which it was accompanied, was painful, from the intruding consciousness that it was morbid or unnatural. Rebecca, dare I ask you, if at intervals your experience has been such as this?"

"Alas!" said she, mournfully, "I think it occasionally has been somewhat thus with me. Indeed, that hurry of thought which you describe, I feel at this very moment. And yet, I cannot say——"

"My dear sir," said the Doctor, "a moment's consideration will convince you, from analogy, that the very terms of your question are more calculated to create such symptoms, than to explain those that exist. Need I say, that that rapidity and elevation of thought, which is undoubtedly a general precursor of insanity, is so near akin to the ordinary workings and elevations of mere high intellect, that, were we to take the one for the other, every man of genius might, at times, make such a confession, as in this way would lay him open to the charge of insanity?"

"Then, sir, does this really amount to nothing?" said Rebecca, with another sigh of relief and hope.

"Your own answers prove it, madam," said the Doctor, taking her kindly by the hand. "An intellect like yours is to be guided, not goaded; and feelings like yours are to be allowed to gush forth towards those you love, lest they burst the bosom in which they cannot be confined, and take captive the reason which would check them in vain. Heaven bless you, madam, for you ought to be blessed," said the Doctor, becoming almost affected as he looked at her, — "blessed with all those domestic endearments that are suited to the cravings of female affection."

A pause of some minutes here occurred; for the parties concerned seemed to anticipate the result of the whole, and were overpowered with astonishment at the change of prospect that had burst so suddenly upon them. The silence was broken by the old gentleman, on whose countenance the others' looks were now involuntarily fixed.

" My dear children, as I may now call you," he said, " Providence has at length, in an un-expected way, relieved all our hearts of a heavy burden, and shown us clearly what his will is. I know well your thoughts now, for I have long witnessed your ill-smothered feelings. You have had, indeed, a weary and a sad pro-bation; but Heaven, at last, puts a happy end to it, I trust,—for it calls you, at last, to be man and wife. Stand up, my sweet Rebecca; come forward, Mr. Bannatyne, while I join your hands; and may Heaven above make you abun-dantly happy; for the dark clouds of sorrow and dread have now been dispelled, and the sun of joy will yet arise, to prevent the extinc-tion of my ancient house."

Mr. Bannatyne and Rebecca stood for some moments, their hands joined together, but un-able to speak. A tumult of joy at the idea of yet being a happy wife to her beloved Lewis so burst upon her, that she seemed completely overpowered; till, looking in the faces, first of her uncle, and then of the minister, she gave a short sob, and was relieved by a gush of tears.

When Rebecca had been assisted to her seat, and the others present had shed their irrepressible tears in silence beside her, they found that something more was wanted to give relief to their feelings, and that relief they found in a quarter, to which the pious and virtuous usually have resort.

Mr. Bannatyne, giving the tone to what each one of them felt, stretched forth his arms towards heaven, when the company had stood up around him, and, in an address of grateful thanksgiving to the Deity, poured forth those aspirations, in the name of all present, which the world can neither give nor take away.

CHAPTER XI.

WHAT a change now took place in the hitherto dignified and dull seclusion of the venerable mansion of Lawford! The excitement of anticipated novelty of circumstances, and the cheerful bustle and business of preparation, is always a pleasing relief from the dull *ennui* of plenty and lack of care; but it is only once in one's life that any can properly experience the unequalled delight of preparation for their own wedding.

The change in Rebecca's circumstances and prospects was almost beyond her own sober belief, and at times was almost too much for the tranquillity of her spirit. But occupation, cheerful and interesting occupation, that panacea for so much of the evil of life, and antidote to the eating poison of great mental activity, prevented the excess of her happiness from injuring the tone of her sensitive mind. Who shall describe all that is to do in a decaying mansion, which seemed to have been doomed to pass into new hands, by the melancholy event of the extinction of the family — its owners for centuries; but which, as its reinstated occupants, is suddenly restored to the joyful prospects of the continuation of an ancient line, to be its lords in many future years? — or who shall adequately speak of all the bright and happy feelings which connect themselves with such events, in minds like those of the gentle Priors of Lawford.

Artists of the cabinet, and artists *du drap* now occupied the busy Rebecca from morning to night, for some weeks prior to her marriage day. Her uncle was not less engaged with architects and decorations; for the old mansion was of course not only to undergo a thorough repair, but to be made to assume a splendour against the time that the happy pair should return from their marriage jaunt, such as was fitting to enhance joys and prospects so pleasing, and of late so unexpected, and to celebrate an event which formed a new era in the family history. The good old gentleman seemed now to be entirely a new man, as Lawford House seemed like a new place from bustle and expenditure, and the very servants flew up and down stairs like fools in their stir and their joy, and made twenty errands into the talking village of Hillington, or to the houses of the numerous small lairds in the neighbourhood, to indulge country gossip, and reciprocate delight in the great event of the approaching marriage.

That marriage in due time did take place, with more general excitement and rejoicing than had been known in the neighbourhood for many years. The whole people of the village of Hillington seemed determined to take a part in it, and in some way did so when the day arrived; for the Priors of Lawford had been from time immemorial so highly respected, and their young minister was by his parishioners so deeply beloved, that himself and his interesting bride, who had so long been observed wandering sadly together, under the strange restraint of their own principles, were regarded with an almost worshipping admiration. The bald marriage ceremonial of the Scottish church was performed in Lawford House by the nearest neighbouring clergyman, and was gone through by the trembling Rebecca with a comparative tranquillity of mind and a leaning of her feelings upon the affectionate attentions of her husband, which delighted her anxious uncle, and greatly assured all present as to the real stability of her powerful yet sensitive mental constitution.

As the carriage in which Rebecca and Mr. Bannatyne, now man and wife at last, which soon drove off with them on their marriage jaunt, passed through the main street of the village of Hillington, the shouts of the waiting people were only subdued by their profound respect; and long after the happy couple had left the town behind them, the noise of the firing of fowling-pieces, which was then the practice at popular weddings in the country, continued at intervals to remind them, by irregular echoes among the hills around, of the affection of the people, who had long watched and talked of their abiding regard. The pair proceeded first to Edinburgh, and thence to visit the more picturesque districts of Scotland; an indulgence which Mr. Bannatyne's fortune, as well as his arrangements in his parish, enabled him to take along with his bride; and, in the mean time, Lawford House was left entirely to the tradesmen employed upon it.   Soon after the departure of the bridegroom and bride, Mr. Prior and Dr. Heywood took a sober and comfortable tour by themselves, to visit several old places, and see sundry old friends, who might enhance their cheerfulness, by reminding them of the pleasures of former times, and interest them by talking of the changes of years, and of the sweets and bitters of the days that were past.

It is usual to end a tale with a marriage or a death, because men are fond of representing life as a drama, of which all the events tend to one point of happy termination, or to one decisive and woeful catastrophe.   But this dramatic form of the events of destiny is seldom found to correspond with actual experience; and life itself, if fairly represented, may in many cases happen to furnish passages of genuine interest

to those who are tired of the obvious common-
places which can scarcely at this day be avoided
in the artificial arrangement of hackneyed incident. Be this as it may, my tale is not ended,
because I have brought it to the time when
those whom I knew and loved were made man
and wife; nor have I found, from actual observation, that all sorrow and solicitude, all hope
and fear, are entirely at an end with the most
interesting couple on earth, when they come
before the minister, and he has lifted up his
hands over them in the presence of many witnesses, and declared them to be from that
moment " married persons."

CHAPTER XII

Years and months had passed away since this, and the harvest had been got in which followed Lennox's marriage, and stern winter had come and gone, with its long nights of comfort by the parlour fire, and its blustering blasts heard sweeping over the woods of Lawfell without, and howling and thudding against the windows of the mansion. A new spring had also arisen to "clead the birken shaw," and even the soft showers of "summer again" fell warm yet refreshing over the green valleys of Scotland, before I took my tramps once more abroad from the solitude of Balgownie Brae, to see what friends the grave had spared me over the face of this changeable world, and what tears might have wetted the cheeks of those whom, in sundry places, I remembered with concern; for I was acquainted with many a thoughtful soul, to whom laughter itself was not always a pleasure, nor the natural alternations of softening sadness always a pain.   Up hill and down dale, therefore, I wandered once more, and saw many a kind body, and heard many a comforting tale; but there were few of all those who at this time interested my thoughts, that I was more anxious to hear of, or more blithe to see, than the amiable family of the Priors of Lawford.

But surely, thought I to myself, as I plodded on, I must be getting to be an old man; for I feel the roads becoming long, and my breath becoming short; the wading of brooks does not agree with the stiffness of eild, and the day is always far spent now, before I can win to the end of my journey.   The time was, when I could keep up, foot for foot, with the cleverest lass that ever tramped to market with her basket of eggs; and when the prettiest who was ever wont to look in my face as we padded over the dewy ground, saw nothing in it then to prevent her making me her confidant of all the love that had ever at any time kept her from her sleep.   But, alas! I say to myself, surely the days of man are as the grass, and as the flower of the field he withereth; "for the wind passeth over it," saith the Psalmist, "and it is gone, and the place that now knows it soon knows it no more."

It was on a dull, dropping, drizzling evening, at the latter end of August, when I found myself at length drawing near to the sweet village of Hillington. I had that day travelled towards it by a different road from that to which I was accustomed; and whether I had wandered out of the straight way, I know not, but it seemed to me unusually long, as well as lonely and dreigh. The mist that had crowned all day the lumpish hills on my right was not disposed in shadowy and floating wreaths of grey white, screening poetically, as I have seen it, the rich purple colour which the hills wore at this season; but lay in dead clouds of sad obscurity all round, limiting the dreary prospect to the watery fields on the lower grounds, and the dull sky in which the sun seemed ashamed to show his face.

· The quaint old steeple of Hillington Church, which now shot upwards between me and the fading light, began to relieve me; but, somehow, it and the gothic windows of the building beneath it, reminded me also of age and mortality, into which my thoughts had now taken an unusual turn; and I entered the empty long street of the town with a sadness over my spirit as if Providence were preparing me, as it often has done, by an inward impression, for the sudden surprisal of some evil tidings. I almost mistook the door of my own inn, although I had known it so long and so well ; for no one stood at the entrance to welcome me, as had always been the case aforetime, and I saw no other but strange faces in the passage. Although, in going in, I made nought to do, but entered my accustomed room as usual, I soon saw that some change had taken place within the premises. The respectable square-looking high-backed arm-chair, which had hitherto been my favourite resting-place in the little parlour, and which I sometimes thought seemed almost to know me, and to stretch out its bowed arms on my arrival with a look of welcome, was now nowhere to be seen, and its place was supplied by a newfangled figmaleery affair of red mahogany, the very shape of which was a grievance to me to look at.

I deposited my little wallet on another new acquaintance among the furniture, and gladly disposed of myself into a resting position ; but I had rung the bell three several times before any one appeared to do the services of the hostelry as I should command, and then, instead of the sweet little fairy of a girl that used to bring me my comforts, and light me to my bed at night, there was a red-elbowed, shock-headed kimmer came blattering in at the door, without the least respect, and impudently asked me what it was I wanted.

The first words I was able to address to this ill-boding apparition were by no means worded with my usual circumspection, and consisted of short-spoken enquiries into the meaning of this topsy-turvy state of the head inn of Hillington, and why it was that my old acquaintance the landlady had not on this occasion chosen to wait on me as formerly. It was little to be expected that I should get much satisfaction of the brazen cutty who now stood before me; but I was able to draw from her one piece of news which shocked me not a little in the mood I then was; to wit, that my blithe and kind landlady had been some time dead, and that the inn and its furnishings had, of course, passed into quite new hands.

The reflections that this simple event called up, entirely took away my appetite for the ill-regulated supper that was now set before me; for I felt, in spite of my worldly reasonings, that I had lost a friend who used to cheer me in one of my most interesting rounds; and I remembered with apprehension of further disastrous intelligence, the vile forebodings that had haunted my spirit all day, as I wandered alone by the wayside, and thought with sorrow of the progressive narrowing of the circle of my ancient acquaintances. I further learned, that my old friend, the laird of Glaunderston, was also no more; having been cut off shortly after my last departure from the neighbourhood by an hereditary inflammation; and that his son-in-law, the laird of Bicknel Hill, was now reigning

L 2

in his stead over the numerous ugly figures which he had contrived to transplant, and to set up all round among the clipped bushes of Glaunderston plantations.

But, of my interesting friends the Priors of Lawford, I was at length enabled to learn many particulars which had occurred among them since Rebecca's marriage; and the relation of which had various effects upon my own feelings. I stayed, with but little personal comfort, for a few days in the inn at Hillington, to gather together my own thoughts, as well as the different details I was able to pick up. I did not think them altogether satisfactory, but, such as they were, they enabled me in my own way to proceed with my story.

The happiness that fell to the lot of Rebecca Prior and her husband, for a considerable time after their marriage, can only be judged of by those who have themselves tasted what tranquil bliss *may be* enjoyed in the state of well-assorted wedlock; and who can enter into the appreci- ation of that intense sense of felicity, which is experienced by minds and hearts such as were

those I speak of, now as they were in circumstances so much to their wishes, and with the
enhancing recollection of so much previous
suffering.   If in the world the happiness of
mortals were permitted to be long without alloy,
assuredly theirs would have been so from their
marriage day forth.   But though troubles
spring not out of the dust of the earth, nor
does sorrow gush, says the sacred murmurer,
from the ground we tread on; though a man
look towards the east, and all is serene brightness, and towards the west, and there appeareth
no enemy; yet, above or around, or from
within or without, a canker worm shall arise
to eat into his joys; or the very winds of
heaven shall bring to him on their wings, their
commissioned portion of the world's evil.

And yet, to Rebecca, there came nothing
outwardly for many a day, to break the pleasing
spell of her well-enjoyed happiness.   She and
her fond husband, and her cheerful and revived
uncle, enjoyed their dream of conscious felicity
in the tranquil domesticity of their hearth at
Lawford, amidst the regard and respect of all

who knew them.   The only thing that could
be said to trouble Rebecca's thoughts was, the
occasional stealing intrusion of that apprehensive conviction, so natural to minds capable of
enjoying very highly any earthly good, that her
present felicity was too unmixed to be lasting;
and a shadowy presentiment shot, at times,
through her mind, that, though neither she nor
her Lewis could at present see where it was to
come from, some event was not far distant,
which would at least cause a ripple upon the
tranquil surface of their sea of happiness. Her
long indulged dread, too, of the family malady,
had taken too fast hold upon her mind to be
altogether eradicated, even by the joyous events
that had so lately taken place; and although
such a thought was now banished as often as it
intruded, her very felicity made her at times
still turn to this point in the index of possible evil, with a disturbing feeling of nervous
anxiety.

The keen eyes of affection enabled Mr. Bannatyne at length to perceive this, and the prospect of an heir being speedily given to the

family having increased the joy of all, while it deepened the interest in every thing that concerned Rebecca, he immediately consulted Doctor Heywood, whether some additional society, in the shape of female attendants, might not be likely to banish from her mind what remained of this troublesome though vague dread. The doctor at once agreed in the propriety of the arrangement; observing, at the same time, that it had always been a peculiarity of the Lawford family, that they had kept themselves too much in a state of seclusion, chiefly from their own sensitive refinement of mind, and their too lofty conceptions of what was becoming in human nature. But as Mrs. Bannatyne was, as they knew, too fastidious to admit too much familiarity of such female society as was furnished by her own neighbourhood, if a gentlewoman could be found, possessed of an intellect that should render her worthy to be Rebecca's companion, while her circumstances placed her in the situation, in some degree, of a dependant, such a person might at all times, and particularly at the forthcoming crisis, be a most valuable member of the family at Lawford.

On consulting Rebecca concerning what the gentlemen had concluded for her, she was quite pleased with the idea of what she called so agreeable an indulgence, particularly as the adding such an attendant to the establishment at Lawford, would likely be the means of making comfortable some deserving, and probably unfortunate, person. An application having been at once made to a friend, extensively acquainted in Edinburgh, a gentlewoman was soon introduced to Doctor Heywood, who seemed to be perfectly suited to the wishes of all concerned; and was soon after installed as a permanent inmate in the family of Mr. Bannatyne. Strange as it may appear, however, the only person who entertained a shadowing doubt regarding any part of the high character which this lady had received, was the one principally concerned, namely, Rebecca herself; who, when Mrs. Chapman was introduced to her, thought, that what a first impression enabled her to judge of the stranger, being involuntarily less favourable than description had made her anticipate, ought to be dismissed from her thoughts, as an unworthy and fanciful surmise. But the part that the new inmate at Lawford was destined to play, may excuse a little particularity in my account of her, and of her previous history.

Mrs. Chapman was a widow, now about twenty-eight years of age, a member of a family of some antiquity, though not wealthy, but who, having made an imprudent marriage in her youth, had greatly incurred the displeasure, though she had not lost the good opinion, of her friends. Her husband, as usual in such cases, had used her barbarously; but this she bore so well, and she withal discovered, while he lived, such prudent conduct, and such decision of character, that the displeasure of her relatives turned into sympathy, and they did all they could to alleviate the difficulties into which her husband's early death, as well as his general improvidence, had plunged her. What principally recommended this lady as a companion to Rebecca was, that she was a woman of " strong sense," as well as general intelligence, who had seen not a little of the world, and suffered, with a fair character, not a few of its trials. Her person was ladylike, and her full blue eyes had that peculiarity, that they could express in an instant the various transitions from modest humility to something like boldness.

The constant society of Mrs. Chapman, although it was occasionally felt, both by Rebecca and her husband, to be somewhat of a restraint upon them, yet was, upon the whole, an agreeable accession to their domestic enjoyment; and, ere long, she became a great favourite with every one, high and low, in the mansion. The gentlemen seemed to be particularly taken with the gaiety of her manner, and her powerful good sense in conversation; and whenever, in process of time, a suspicion crossed the mind of Rebecca, that her companion seemed to take more pains to show off the admitted goodness of her understanding, than was exactly suited to her own situation, and the respect she owed to her (Rebecca) as the lady of the house and her protectress, she repressed carefully every unfavourable suggestion, and turned the suspicion back upon herself, from a candid dread of indulging any thing like the mean feelings of female envy towards a person in Mrs. Chapman's dependent situation. This suspicion of self, and benevolent tendency to her own crimination, rather than allow of blame upon another, had very much become a rooted habit of Rebecca's mind, and partly arose from her lofty conceptions of virtue and purity, but more from that terror of discovering any thing like perversion of intellect, or the most distant symptoms of the malady of her house, which had haunted her from the moment when she was first made acquainted with the dreadful truth.

Time went on, however, and no incident occurred materially to disturb the smooth stream of happiness which was enjoyed by all who dwelt in the mansion; and the safe birth of a son to bless the delighted parents and family, and to heir the ancient property and name of the house of Lawford as well as Bannatyne, was succeeded by rejoicings such as never had been witnessed in the vicinity of Hillington. Although the recovery of Rebecca was somewhat tedious, her feelings, on finding herself at last occupied with the endearing duties of a mother, and as she often contemplated her own sweet babe, while the infant lay asleep on her knee, seemed almost too acutely delightful for the strength of her mind to bear with sobriety, weak as her accouchement had evidently left her. But the mental wanderings not unusual at periods of weakness, although Rebecca had experienced her full share of them, she did not suffer to fill her with any material alarm, until an evident peculiarity in the manner, *to* her, of Mrs. Chapman, when she conceived her strength almost completely recovered, aroused her to enquiries and suspicions exceedingly unfavourable to her quiet of mind.

What this peculiarity consisted of, it was not very easy either perfectly to identify or define: it was one of those things in the address and manner, to us, of others, which implies or makes us *feel* a real degradation, but which is yet too nice in its shadings, and too much blended with kindness and apparent respect, to prevent us from suspecting it of being more or less the creation merely of our own fancies : but it was of such a nature, in Rebecca's case, that she could not, consistently with her own dignity, consent to herself to ask for any explanation concerning it; nor was she sure that, even although she should bring herself to condescend to this, she should obtain an answer on which she ought to depend.

This feeling was the more painful to the private thoughts of Rebecca, as the thing she complained of seemed, at times, to be participated in by her dear Lewis himself; and even his extreme tenderness and caressing kindness, during the progress of her recovery, were, in part, attributed to this new sentiment with which she fancied that she began to be regarded. That sentiment, which seemed at first to take the shape of a humiliating, yet kindly, condescension, to her weakness, as if of mind as well as body, when she was perfectly recovered, became, as she thought, of a more decided and expressive character, filling her with alarming cares and enquiries, and again turning her attention intensely inwards. She now observed that often when she spoke at table, Mrs. Chapman would assent studiedly to what she said, as one will do to the idle babble of a child, with whom they would not condescend to argue.

Notwithstanding the respect that she had for Mrs. Chapman's understanding, this was conduct which she was determined to take an early opportunity of effectually checking; but it was not easy to do it, without either, in some degree, compromising her own dignity, or incurring the suspicion of being actuated by motives the very idea of which she held in the highest disdain. She did speak to her, however, on an occasion of peculiar provocation, and in the presence of Mr. Bannatyne and her uncle; and though this was done with that mixture of raillery and seriousness, which bespoke the considerate delicacy of a mind anxious to convey with tenderness a merited reproof, the colour that rose into the face of the widow, as she observed the surprise that Rebecca's remark excited in Mr. Bannatyne, and the flash that instantly shot from her eyes, indicated, besides a consciousness that the reproof was a just one, sentiments which, at the moment, seemed far from amiable.

The old gentleman, after an embarrassed remark of Mr. Bannatyne, turned off with a laugh this little spurt between the ladies; and before they rose, Mrs. Chapman put on such a look and manner of humility and penitence, that Rebecca was not only completely mollified, but, in the considerate candour of her spirit, retired to rest in a mood of self-accusation, from the suspicion that she might have, after all, unmeritedly wounded the feelings of a destitute woman and a dependant. On speaking of the matter afterwards, privately, to Mrs. Chapman, and comparing the strange looks and guarded replies of that lady, with sundry tender questionings and soothing remarks of Mr. Bannatyne, the thought at once struck home to her heart, that, by something unknown to herself, in her speech or manner, she had been exhibiting, to the alarm and consternation

of those around her, some distant symptoms of
the dreaded malady of her family.

When this horrid idea took possession of
her mind, it is not to be expressed what she
felt in private, as she brooded over the fancy
with apprehensive despondency; and yet she
thought, upon the most rigorous examination
of her own mental experience, that, if there did
actually exist the surmise that she suspected, it
must be founded on a mere mistake of over-
watchful anxiety concerning her; for, if her
own judgment weighed any thing whatever in
such an enquiry, she could find no ground for
coming to any such distressing conclusion: but
the insane, she knew, were always deceivers of
themselves; and though she would have given
worlds to know precisely what her Lewis actually thought concerning her, so sensitive was
she upon this dreaded point, that she could not
bring herself to disturb his mind with the most
distant enquiry upon the painful subject.   Unfortunately, at this time, Doctor Heywood was
in London, or on the Continent, whither he had
gone of late to live for a season; and in this

state of painful self-observation and uncertainty, the happiness of the married life of the unfortunate Rebecca, was now disturbed and poisoned by the internal struggle and distraction of a nervous anxiety, about what might be evinced by her manner and conversation.

And yet there was something occasionally in the manner of Mrs. Chapman, particularly in her argumentative or playful conversations in presence of Mr. Bannatyne, that, while it challenged her admiration of that lady's talents and tact, excited, unwillingly, flashes of thought across her mind of a nature exceedingly distressing to the feelings of a doting married woman. But again there seemed other things inconsistent with these obtrusive imaginings; and when Rebecca, when alone with the minister, observed his completely artless, and truly affectionate, almost adoring, conduct to herself, she was inclined not only to blame herself for suffering the intrusion of such unworthy and painful fancyings, but seriously to suspect that such thoughts were too surely symptomatic of that malady which was at once, perhaps, her

companion and her curse. And then, to confirm
her in these unhappy suspicions of herself, she
observed, along with the humble and deferential
manner to all, of the talented widow, that, sometimes, when she (Rebecca) had uttered a sentence, Mrs. Chapman seemed to regard her
with a look as if of mingled sorrow and compassion; and, turning her large eyes next upon
Mr. Bannatyne's countenance, would playfully,
and without noticing what Rebecca had said,
proceed with the thread of her own absorbing
conversation.

The reader has, by this time, probably, seen,
in the conduct of Mrs. Chapman, the real
meaning of all this; but which the unsuspicious
benevolence of Rebecca's nature would not
allow her, in any case, to conclude. To be
short, if Mrs. Chapman was a person of " strong
sense," she was also a woman of strong passions;
and a week had not elapsed from the day of
her arrival at Lawford House, before her eye
was fascinated, and even her feelings absorbed,
by the handsome and unsuspecting minister of
Hillington. Nor was this guilty admiration

unknown to herself, as such a thing might have been, for a time, to a more simple, or, in plain terms, a more modest woman; but, though fully aware of all the danger and all the wickedness of indulging a sentiment of this sort for a married man and a minister of religion, with that recklessness of consequences which has ever been the characteristic of the most abandoned of her sex, she at once gave herself up to the influence of her vicious passion; and, without any precise design or planned purpose, found her only pleasure in fishing for the admiration and striving to seduce the affections of the youthful minister. Had Mr. Bannatyne been as practised as *she* was in the ways of the world, he soon could have read the meaning of the alluring arts of the widow: but the feeling of suspicion is the penalty only of the experimental knowledge of evil; and so the single-hearted clergyman was, as yet, perfectly blind to all that Mrs. Chapman dared to show to attract his regard.

CHAPTER XIII.

DURING all this time, Mrs. Dryburgh, who now lived much at the old-fashioned mansion of Glaunderston, near Hillington, made several attempts to impose herself anew upon the acquaintance of Rebecca, now as the latter was, as she said, a " married woman." In these efforts she was not entirely unsuccessful, particularly after the introduction of Mrs. Chapman into Lawford House; for, as Rebecca's good nature was fully a match for her own shrinking reserve, her crafty dependant easily managed to favour the visits, from motives of her own, of the talkative lady of Bicknel Hill.

One day, Rebecca, having been somewhat discomposed by her own reflections upon something that had occurred at the breakfast table in the morning, had thrown herself upon a couch in her apartment, and, indulging for a time the feelings that oppressed her, insensibly fell into a dreamy sleep, while Mrs. Chapman sat by in professed attendance. She was awakened by the noise below of some one's entrance; but, hearing the voice of Mrs. Dryburgh in the hall, she feigned to be still asleep, as Mrs. Chapman passed out of the room to receive her visiter, in order to avoid the personal annoyance of the former lady's present society. Although, in doing this, she had, as she thought, given sufficient indication to Mrs. Chapman that her slumber was feigned, she was surprised to find the latter return on tip-toe, leading in Mrs. Dryburgh; and the two, seating themselves beyond a light curtain or screen, commenced conversation in her hearing, under the seeming supposition that she was asleep.

"An' hoo are ye, Mrs. Chapman?" began Lady Bicknel, as Mrs. Dryburgh was usually called by the country people, "weel, hoo are ye? Dear me, but I'm quite happy to meet you just by yoursel, Mrs. Chapman, for I've often been wishing for a quiet word o' you, about Miss Prior — bless me, I never can call her any thing else but Miss! for really I never thought to ha'e seen her a married woman; an' I'm greatly concerned about her — but are ye sure she's fast asleep?"

"Quite sound, Mrs. Dryburgh," said the other; "besides, she lies off at a distance from us, and cannot possibly hear."

"Weel, ye see, Mrs. Chapman, I would just like, as I say, to hae twa words wi' you about Mrs. —— Mrs. Bannatyne — dear me, I never can get my tongue about her married name — for I wonder hoo she is since she was married, puir dear lady, an' how she's getting on, an' hoo she's doing with the baby, an' if her head, ye see, is just quite right; for ye know, Mrs. Chapman, that marriage is a trying thing, an' ye have been a married woman yoursel, Mrs. Chapman, and I would just like to ken — but are ye sure she'll not hear us?"

"There is no fear of that, if we do not speak any louder."

"Weel, Mrs. Chapman, does your lady, do ye think, just appear aye fair an' square i' the head? — because, ye know, the Prior family was aye an odd family: an' does the puir lady never take ony bits o' tirrrivees, or ony kind o' queer symptomatics, or hysterics, or —— eh ? "

" Ye know, Mrs. Dryburgh," said the widow, with a demure and wise look, " that it would not be becoming in me to let the least word pass my lips that would look like a disclosure of family affairs; and I need not tell a woman of your experience, Mrs. Dryburgh, that in every family there *are* matters that —— "

" I am perfectly aware of that, Mrs. Chapman, an' it 's a most wise and sensible observe of you ; because I 'm a married woman myself, an', as you say, in every family there *are* little affairs — but as to this lady, there is something in her look — but I may be mistaken, Mrs. Chapman ; an' noo, as we are by ourselves, I would just like to hear your breath about her, puir thing ; for if she were ever losing her reason, an', as I say, she has sometimes a very strange look with her — God help her puir young family ! an' the minister himself would gang clean crazy after her. But what do ye think ? "

" I think, Mrs. Dryburgh, that — but it 's not to seek what I would say."

" Hech sirs ! but ye may tell *me*, Mrs. Chapman, for I jaloused as much. An', really, ye maun hae a kittle place o' 't amang them a'; for it 's so hard to know what to do wi' a daft body: ye'll excuse my plain talk — odd, I hope she doesna hear us ! "

" No fear of that, madam."

" An' she'll whiles talk quite odd, an' as it were silly ? "

" She does talk very strangely sometimes."

" Hech ! hech ! its just beginning on her."

" One would really at times almost think so."

" And imagines every thing she says, quite gude sense and perfect gospel ? "

" You know that is the nature of that unfortunate state of mind."

" Perfectly the nature o' 't; and ye'll no dare to contradict or argue wi' her, whatever she may say."

" It would be of no avail ; besides, it would be somewhat cruel to the dear young lady, — an' so I just give a look to the minister or so, and say nothing."

" O but ye're a sensible, wise woman, Mrs. Chapman! what a treasure you must be to that puir demented leddy ! "

" Hush — sh !   But you must not suppose, Mrs. Dryburgh, that I have mentioned to you any thing particular; Mrs. Bannatyne is a sweet young creature, an' the minister is such a dear kind —— "

" Oh, is n't he a fine-looking gentleman, the minister ! he's a full head an' shoulders above Mr. Dryburgh, my stumpy gudeman — but, talking of men, Mrs. Chapman, Mr. Bannatyne should never have been a minister wi' a black coat, he should have been a grand dragoon offisher, wi' a red coat an' a swurd, — that's aye what I say."

" He would have looked just to my mind in the cavalry dress, certainly," said the widow delighted with the thought: "but hush — speak low ; it is likely Mrs. Bannatyne will shortly waken, and it would be as well, Mrs. Dryburgh, that you were not found here alone with me."

VOL. II.   M

" Ye say right, Mrs. Chapman," added Lady Bicknel, rising; " an', dear me now, what ye tell me about your lady, is just what I was afraid of, whenever Miss Prior became a married woman."

" Remember, I have not told you any thing particular, Mrs. Dryburgh," continued the widow, looking wise; " for family affairs are what I shall never speak of."

" You are a discreet woman, Mrs. Chapman, I see that; but just trust to me, for I ha'e more sense, after all, than ye may be would expect, when ye come to find me out."

" It is evident you have a deal of sense, ma'am," said the widow, slily, " and it's a great blessing, Mrs. Dryburgh," she went on, in a louder tone, " to be possessed of one's senses; for if the mind is any way astray, and the reason out of joint, what a chaos does it not make in the whole system of our mental comprehension!"

" What a beautiful style of language you have in your speech, Mrs. Chapman!" exclaimed Lady Bicknel, with a flattering sweet-

ness of manner, which was exceedingly enchant-
ing to the knowing widow, only she could with
much difficulty preserve herself from a burst of
laughter.

" Before I was married, *my* style of language was allooed to be uncommonly elegant,
for my father had me at Mrs. Deyelle's boarding-
school, which, ye know, was the very first rate ;
but, when a woman gets *married*, Mrs. Chapman, an' especially in a country place, why, ye
see, we forget our lair, an' our parley-vous, an'
every thing. But farewell, mem, an' just give
my kind regards to Mrs. Bannatyne, an' say,
that I could not think of disturbing her, when
I heard she was taking her *bon repos*. Ah,
Mrs. Chapman, what a pity it is to see sae
pretty a young creature as that — hush —
getting quite out o' her mind. But that was
the state o' her puir father before her, wha died
demented, an' that is the curse o' the whole
Priors of Lawford, as I've heard my father
that's dead an' gone often say. What a blessing it is to be in possession of one's sound
senses ! You and I ought to be thankful for

our wits when we look at that unfortunate leddy ; an' then there's the baby too.   I 'm feared to think what it's likely to come to yet.   Oddsake, mem, do ye think that she could be hearing us all this time? "

CHAPTER XIV.

THE truth contained in the fable of the Boys and the Frogs, that what is but sport to some is death to others, is oftener applicable than those, at least, who are in the habit of looking only for sport, are, in their thoughtlessness, ready to admit: and so it was in the case of Rebecca and Mrs. Chapman, as detailed in the preceding brief chapter. To the unfeeling widow, however, it was more than sport, as has been already hinted, to work as she was doing upon the sensitive mind of the young wife; and her success was equal to the depth of her craft and the singleness of heart of her unsuspicious victim.

Rebecca, compelled as she had involuntarily been, to be an eves-dropper to that which was destructive to her own peace, had only heard distinctly a part of the conversation between the two women; but the widow, having taken this method of making her indirectly acquainted with what she desired might be believed to be her sentiments, took care to give sufficient voice to that part of the talk which she wished her lady to hear; and the way in which it was spoken, and the whispering indistinctness of the remainder, conveyed an impression to the unsuspicious Rebecca, even more deep and decided than the crafty Abigail could have anticipated. Along with that impression, the few words of caution and seeming reluctance to allow her own sentiments to escape, uttered by Mrs. Chapman, in the early part of the conversation, conveyed to the amiable mind of her lady the notion, that the widow was more her friend than, from some other indications, she had been ready to suppose; and, making allowance for the natural talkativeness of her sex, that she was a very prudent and considerate person. Whenever a suspicion contrary to this crossed her thoughts, she only treated it as a further proof of that obliquity of mind which belongs to insanity, and into which she now feared, or rather concluded, in her dread, that she was fast merging.

From this hour there was a decided change in the conduct of the unhappy Rebecca, while her doting husband (her uncle having in the mean time gone to spend a few months in Edinburgh) was obliged to notice in her what filled him with such alarm and distress of mind, as, in delicacy towards the old gentleman's peace, he was actually afraid to make the subject of any communication to him for the present. Yet what he could remark in the changed lady of the mansion was not of that nature to enable him to come to a very decided conclusion. Her obstinate yet unwilling taciturnity; which, in fact, arose from her nervous dread of saying any thing which should confirm her own and his suspicion of any aberration of mind, though, at first, set down by Mr. Bannatyne to that cause, became, at length, by the insinuated representations of Mrs. Chapman, to be considered as a proof of something even more intolerable to him than the mental affliction; namely, alienation of heart from himself. What else could it be, he thought, that made her now appear studiously to avoid him; and, dwelling only over the constant contemplation of their infant, instead of being much with him as formerly in their days of happiness, to answer him with suspicious hesitation when he met and addressed her, and even palpably to shun his society?

On her part the change was even more deeply distressing, forasmuch as it centred chiefly in distrust of herself. And yet, with the most rigorous examination of her own thoughts, all the self-humiliation that candour had reared upon extreme modesty could not lead her fully to conclude that a real aberration had actually manifested itself in her mind. But by this time the widow had contrived to turn her suspicions partly into another channel; and the fortune and connections of the minister, leading him, of late, into occupations of a public nature, which took him occasionally from home, the wily woman, with her usual art, contrived, by degrees, to insinuate into the mind of the secluded Rebecca, that Mr. Bannatyne was no longer the man he used to be; and to render her even more guarded than ever, in her behaviour, when in his presence, by the broadly asserted suspicion, that, in consequence of the mental imbecility that she had lately shown, his mind was beginning to be quite estranged from her.

And yet, sometimes, she thought, he looked kindly, and, as she imagined, with compassion, upon her, and addressed her inquisitively, yet with an expression of anxious affection ; but this very manner, again, threw her mind back upon her suspected aberration, and she dreaded to reply to him, lest she should further betray something of the malady of her family. But malady, the actual malady, seemed now undeniably to be coming over her, as she would sit wistfully contemplating her slumbering baby in her chamber, the fruit of the love between her and her Lewis, in days when as yet her mind was sound and his affections were to her all in all. And then, when her chosen solitude grew irksome to her, she would steal up to, that shut-up chamber, where the portraits of her ancestors, who had died in that dreadful state, glared melancholy around upon her from their dusty frames, and seemed to look piteously down to another hapless daughter of a hapless house, who, with fatal infatuation, had made herself another link to continue the chain of their misery to future generations.

" Is Mrs. Bannatyne not coming to-day also, to meet us at dinner, Mrs. Chapman ?" said the minister, one evening, as he sat down with the widow to their solitary meal. " Truly, this is very sad and uncomfortable."

" She bade me excuse her again, sir," said the widow, mysteriously ; " besides, she complains of being ill."

" What am I to think of this ? And is Mrs. Bannatyne really so ill ? I will go and speak to her."

" Indeed, sir, excuse me," said the widow, " but it were better not."

" Why, Mrs. Chapman ? did she say she would not see me ?"

" Something to that purport, sir. But not by any means these words. Excuse me, sir ; but I have already said all I could to Mrs. Bannatyne."

" But she seemed obstinate."

" I do not say, obstinate, sir. Mrs. Bannatyne seems to be ill."

" How unfortunate it is that Doctor Heywood is not here ! alas, what a case am I in ! "

" Shall I go and speak to your lady again, Mr. Bannatyne? I would do any thing to see you happy, sir."

" I know you would, Mrs. Chapman. My obligations to you are infinite. I cannot express my sense of your attention to my poor Rebecca. But you need not go to her again. It might irritate her mind. Heaven will enable me to bear this trial ; and time and patience may yet bring her to herself and me. Excuse me, Mrs. Chapman, but I cannot partake of these viands : " and, seizing his hat, the distressed Lewis rushed forth, to seek calm to his mind in the woods of Lawford.

He saw Rebecca at night, but only for a few moments, although the crafty widow was constantly in his way. In two days after, he was preparing to depart for Edinburgh, to attend the meeting of his presbytery, his fortune enabling him by this time to have an assistant in his clerical duties; and his communications with Rebecca being now chiefly through Mrs. Chapman, he sent for that lady to enquire if it would be agreeable for Mrs. Bannatyne to see him, that he might take his leave.

"Your lady will see you, sir," said the widow, with seeming joy, after making the enquiry; "but it might be advisable to say but little to her at present, and, above all, not to ask her any particular questions."

"I will attend to your suggestion, Mrs. Chapman," said the minister: "but how will you entertain my poor Rebecca during all the time of my absence?"

"Ah, sir, she will not be entertained, that is the misfortune. But I will do all in my power, and there is Mrs. Dryburgh visits her occasionally."

"Mrs. Dryburgh! and is my Rebecca reduced so low as to take pleasure in the company of Mrs. Dryburgh! Alas! But as for you, madam, I cannot express what I owe to you for this self-denied attention to my poor wife — I trust her entirely to you."

When he entered her chamber to take leave as permitted, he found Rebecca bent over their infant, and her eyes gleamed with joy as she rose to meet him. But she pressed his hands in silence, and looking up in his face, seemed ready to burst into tears.

" How are you, Rebecca? How are your feelings to-day? I am sorry to see you look so pale."

" Are you really sorry for me, Lewis? "

" Truly I am, but —— " here a look from the widow admonished him to say little.

" I am going to part with you for some time," he went on ; " but I leave you with good attendance in this worthy lady."

" Going to leave me, Lewis — and never told me till this moment? "

" *I* told Mrs. Bannatyne, sir, but she forgets," said the widow, with a nod to the minister.

" You told me? How can you say so, Mrs. Chapman?" said Rebecca; a slight flush of indignation passing over her pale countenance

mured to himself as he rode, musing on his solitary way, leaving behind him his beloved village of Hillington. " I wish I had said something more to my poor Rebecca, she looked in my face so sadly, as if something oppressed her. Can it be possible that I am deceived? I feel a strange dissatisfaction with myself, I can scarcely tell why. But yet I might have spoken more to her — I thought she looked disappointed; and my own heart yearned to caress her as I used — but that unhappy malady! What if *I* have been to blame in increasing her sorrow! I could almost go back this instant, to enquire further concerning her, and judge for myself. But in two weeks I must return to Hillington, and surely by that time her state of mind will he more decided."

With such reflections as these, Mr. Bannatyne pursued his solitary journey to Edinburgh.

CHAPTER XV.

I⊤ was a melancholy time to Rebecca, that, while Lewis was from home, and she was left entirely to the brooding abstraction of her own thoughts, and to the constant society of the crafty Mrs. Chapman. "Oh if I could but see my uncle," she would sometimes say to herself; "and now another month must surely bring him to Lawford. But yet I am almost afraid to see him, if this horrid despondency be indeed that unhappy affliction which has been the misery of our house — I have not courage to write to him, to hasten his return."

"Yet surely," she would think within herself, as she sometimes took an airing abroad in the carriage, "this sadness cannot, after all, be decided insanity, for the breeze of heaven seems as delightful to me as ever, and the fragrance of the hills comes refreshing to my senses; the woods of Lawford look still lovely and green, and the birds on the branches pipe sweetly as

I pass. There is not a flower that "adorns the green valleys," but I know and delight in as the silent friend of my youth; and the broom that grows yellow on the braes of Greenwood speaks a language as solacing to my poetic apprehension, as does the pretty spire and solemn burying-ground of the old church of Hillington, to the heavenward aspirations of my wounded spirit.

"But I will not be positive in that difficult judgment which is founded merely on my own consciousness; and if the affections of my husband have not yet deserted me, the malady of my family may never come upon me in that full and frightful measure, that shall destroy that reason which preserves my responsibility to Heaven that is above me — the great and merciful Heaven, — which does not disdain to watch over the wanderings even of a heart like mine."

But heavy clouds and shadows of despondency would again come over her reflective spirit, as she sat solitary in her chamber; and thoughts would arise in her weary abstractions, which almost convinced her that it was indeed no misrepresentation, that she was really astray in her mind. And then, as she watched the nursing of her beloved infant, and her heart was lightened by his interesting playfulness, she would look through the obscure vista of future time, to the days when the babe might be a man, and the proprietor of Lawford — till the portraits of her ancestors in the deserted chamber seemed, in her thoughts, to prophesy of the child's after-destiny; and the dreadful imagination of his yet being a raving maniac before he left the world, to carry forward to another generation the fatality of her house, would close with anticipated horrors the fancies that oppressed her.

Nearly three weeks had passed away since Mr. Bannatyne left Lawford, and the sacrament Sunday at Hillington church was now at hand, and still the minister had not yet come home. It was a long and sad period to Rebecca; but at length, as the sacrament week advanced, the minister did arrive, in company with another clergyman, one of his intended assistants in the ensuing solemnity.

" Where is Mrs. Chapman? how is my

Rebecca?" were the first questions h
on stepping once more into the hall
ford.

" Mrs. Bannatyne, I am sorry to say,
very peculiar state," said the widow, w
already in the way.

" Let me see her; I wish to speak t
said the minister, eagerly.

" Pardon me, sir, but it might not
all at once to break in upon your poor
the state she is."

" What state is she in, Mrs. Chapma
form me quickly, for this is worse
had imagined."

" I am no physician, sir, and I can
scribe her state in a way that, perhaps, yo
well understand. But, sir, she is ver
and low. I have, however, got Mrs. D
to visit her sometimes, and that lady is v
now."

" And may I not see her, as well
Dryburgh ? "

" Certainly, sir, if it is your wish — b

" What would you say, Mrs. Chapm

" You know, sir, that it is a peculiarity of those who have unhappily fallen into that state, that they have a distaste at those whom they formerly loved the most, and that the very sight of them irritates their disorder."

" Gracious Heavens ! and has it come to that with my poor Rebecca ?"

" I do not absolutely say so, sir ; but from some expressions she has used ———"

" I understand you, Mrs. Chapman, and perceive the considerate delicacy by which you are actuated. Alas ! and this is, at length, the state of my adored wife ! "

" But I will hint to her cautiously, that you are come home, sir," continued the widow, happy at the success of her diabolical insinuations, " and see if it would be at all safe for you to see her ; and surely she will consent to meet you. Then, if you take no notice of what she may say, you may see the dear lady for a few minutes with little danger."

" God bless you, Mrs. Chapman, do what you can to enable me to see her without aggravating the state of her mind. And in the mean time, pray say to Mrs. Dryburgh, that I should be glad if she would step this way."

" I feel for you much in this affliction, sir," said Mr. Bryce, the clergyman, whom he had brought with him, when the widow had withdrawn. " But as, in this world, we require oftener to be reminded than instructed, allow me the liberty of reminding you of the necessity now for exercising the much talked of virtues of fortitude and resignation."

" I thank you for your counsel, sir," said Lewis, sadly; " but do you think I am right in giving way to the judgment of this woman, in abstaining from seeing my poor wife in her affliction ? "

" The lady speaks sensibly, and with much apparent reason," said the stranger clergyman ; " and, certainly, I have heard of cases wherein the patients could not bear the sight of those who once were the most dear to them : but I would have you to make enquiry of the other lady who visits Mrs. Bannatyne, and if she confirms the opinion of this Mrs. Chapman, no private feelings which you must naturally have, ought to be gratified at the risk of aggravating the disorder of your unhappy wife."

Lewis agreed, with a sigh, to the opinion of his friend: and, as they were talking, Mrs. Dryburgh entered the apartment.

"I am obliged by your attention to my unfortunate lady, madam," said Lewis, as she came forward; "and, pardon me, Mrs. Dryburgh, but as you have had opportunity of seeing her often in my absence, may I ask you if you think that she is so ill, that my seeing her now might be injurious to her tranquillity?"

"I am much afeard o' 't, sir; and, indeed, it would be a black danger and detriment the way the puir lady is in," said Lady Bicknel, having received her cue from the widow: "and, mair than that, sir, as I was saying to that worthy woman, Mrs. Chapman, if ye would take my advice, ye would take away that bonnie bairn of yours frae her, or at least watch her very carefully anent it."

"What mean you, Mrs. Dryburgh?"

"If ye had heard, sir, what strange talk she was talking to the infant, one day when she thought I was not hearing her; and she looked at the dear bairn wi' such eyes! Lord preserve us, sir, but I could na but think o' that dreadfu' story o' Lady Belldowie, that ye may hae heard of."

" What story do you allude to, madam? this is strange talk."

" Did you never hear of Lady Belldowie, sir, that lived at the Point o' Garnoch, by the sea-side, in the next shire. The puir woman, sir, went clean out o' her senses; for, ye see, it was in the family, and she actually murdered her ain bairn!"

" Mrs. Dryburgh," said Lewis, with a look of more than horror, " I hope you did not tell this story to my unhappy wife."

" Ne'er a bit, sir; but she *did* hear it, and that when I could na hae thought she was minding me telling it to Mrs. Chapman; an' if ye had just seen, sir, how she scream'd, as it were, into hersel', an' wrung her hands the-gither fearfully!"

Mr. Bannatyne rose, and paced the room, in dreadful agitation.

" But have you heard Mrs. Bannatyne talk in such a manner of me, madam — you will excuse me," said Lewis, stopping, and fixing his eyes on Mrs. Dryburgh — " as to induce you to suppose, as Mrs. Chapman does, that I ought not to see her for the present ? "

" I have never heard the puir lady talk much at all; an', indeed, she 'll hardly speak to me: but I see plainly that the least iota would put her clean into the hysterics, an' I would advise you, sir, not to go near her until Mrs. Chapman, who understands her far better than I, give you permission."

" I think that advice is safest, sir, under all the circumstances," said the stranger clergyman, " however painful it may be to your own feelings."

By such reasoning was Mr. Bannatyne — after despatching letters to her uncle and Dr. Heywood, requesting, if possible, their instant return to Hillington — restrained from visiting his unhappy Rebecca, until the following Sunday morning; when, just as he was preparing to go to his church, to attend to the solemn ministrations of the sacrament, he found his mind so depressed, and uneasy with himself, that he intimated his determination to risk a short interview with her, having learned that she was already up, and engaged in her devotions, and he requested Mrs. Chapman to prepare her for his coming.

The widow, somewhat alarmed by the minister's determined manner, did prepare Rebecca, agreeably to what she had so carefully insinuated since his return ; and soon Lewis, accompanied by Mr. Bryce, his friend, found himself once more in the presence of his spouse.

Rebecca did not rise as he entered, although she gave a slight start upon first setting her large liquid eyes again upon him, as if the sight was almost too much for her now ; but immediately observing that he was accompanied by a stranger, she turned her face towards the book that was before her, and appeared to take no notice of his presence.

" Rebecca ! — Rebecca, my love ! " — he said, drawing near, " will you not speak to me, which, as my anxiety for you, I have at last come to pay you a visit?"

"I cannot imagine a visit of ceremony from you, Louis, as my husband," she said "and this, I perceive, is perfectly such; as besides the incivility of announcement, you have, I observe, come to me with a suite behind you."

This speech was so sensible, both as to its matter and the tone in which it was spoken, and the reproach in it was so reasonable, upon a supposition of her sanity, that Mr. Bannatyne was perfectly thunderstruck. But, fearing to give a direct reply, until he saw further into her state of mind, he only said, —

"I wish you were sensible how much it is the contrary of what you say, Rebecca. But you are scared for going abroad. Are you really well enough to venture forth this morning?"

"I would be ill indeed," she replied, "if that prevented me from attending the Hillington sacrament. It is good for those who are broken in spirit to go up betimes to the Lord's house, for he spreads a table in the wilderness, even for those who are left without comforter; and the deeply depressed under the world's sorrows he strengthens, and raises up from the depths of despair, and fills their mouths with songs of deliverance."

" Rebecca," said Lewis, more and more astonished, " I did not expect to find you in this placid spirit. There is always hope for those who turn to Heaven in their sorrows, for the consolations of religion are neither few nor small."

" And *it is* consolation I am in need of, Lewis," she said, hardly able to articulate; " since I have lost your affection."

" I cannot bear to hear you speak thus, Rebecca. I am under some delusion. For Heaven's sake do not give way to this emotion."

" You have been four days at home without coming to speak to me, Lewis. I am an outcast and a spectacle in my own house !—but go away to the table of the Lord. Dispense with your own hands the sacred symbols of affliction and

N 2

humiliation. It well becomes you, after the sorrow you have brought to my heart."

"You must not allow yourself to be thus agitated, sir," cried Mr. Bryce, as the distressed young clergyman smote his forehead, and looked wildly, first at Mrs. Chapman and then at Rebecca. "Remember the duties that you have this day to perform, and there is the Sabbath bell already sounding from Hillington kirk. Postpone, I beseech you, this trying matter, at least, until the services of the day are ended." And saying this, Mr. Bryce, along with the now rallied Mrs. Chapman, succeeded in withdrawing Mr. Bannatyne from his wife's apartment.

CHAPTER XVI.

IT was with a sad and perplexed spirit, on the same quiet Sabbath morning, that the Reverend Mr. Bannatyne proceeded to Hillington kirk, and mounted his pulpit to commence the public worship of the day. The reasoning of Mr. Bryce, on their way to the village, benevolently intended to calm his mind regarding his conduct to Rebecca, by urging, in extenuation, the deceptive nature of the malady with which she was suspected to be afflicted, and the probably ignorant zeal of Mrs. Chapman, by whom he had suffered himself to be persuaded, had but little effect against the cutting conviction of having caused suffering to her whom he loved above all objects on the earth, which now stung him with a thousand almost intolerable regrets.

Never before had the beloved minister of Hillington begun the solemn duties of a sacramental occasion with such an uncomfortable and disturbed mind. There may have been some cause, he thought, for the representations of Mrs. Chapman; but, at least, Rebecca had had reason enough left to feel bitterly the systematic cruelty with which he appeared to have treated her; and, if she were now returning to perfect mental health, he was conscious of having caused her, perhaps, irreparable misery, at a time when he ought to have been her comfort and her stay. 'T is true, his regret was in some sort needless, as applying to what could not now be recalled; but when, in the course of his preaching, he unavoidably cast his eyes to where she now sat, as formerly, looking up in his face, and drinking in the word of Divine consolation from his lips, as she had ever done, his heart yearned towards her, as the best beloved of his soul; and he could have gladly undertaken any personal suffering, if that could make up for one pang that he had unwittingly caused her to feel.

What Mrs. Chapman had, by degrees, insinuated into Rebecca's mind, to string it up to the pitch at which it was on this Sabbath morning, it were tedious now at any length to parti-

cularise.   But, with all the understood weakness
and softness of her sex, the very intensity of.
her feelings upon a subject so precious to her,
and so interwoven into her heart, as her husband's affections, gave her mind a strength, or,
at least, a tension, upon that particular point, of
which her Lewis could have had no idea.   She
heard, therefore, his discourse this day with
all the piety which the subject matter of it was
calculated to promote ; but, instead of yet reading his compunction in his countenance, every
thought that he uttered, that she was constrained to admire, only sent, with the approbation of it, an additional pang to the core of
her heart, from the feeling that she had alien-
ated and lost the regard of so admirable a man,
and so deeply beloved a husband.

When the sermon was ended, she felt an ex-
haustion coming over her, and pressed forward,
on the opening of the tables, to take the sacrament on its first dispensation, in order the more
speedily to retire to her home.   By this time
her mind was in a strangely excited state, and
while the people sung the preliminary psalm,

she was pressed forward among a few others, who were filling up the upper end of the tables, just at the time when Lewis was descending from his pulpit to preside at the first, after the manner of the Scottish church; and, from the politeness of those around, or some chance cause, she was placed at the head almost beside her husband, and next to Mr. Bryce, who was, after the pastor, to officiate at the tables.

When Mr. Bannatyne took his seat at the upper end of the tables, and found his Rebecca, whom he had been considering as a lunatic, and with whom he had had so unsatisfactory a scene in the morning, seated so near him at this ordinance, his feelings were such as it would not be easy by any words to convey a just idea. A series of events, very unlooked for, had made his wife and himself, who had for so long been to each other like the apples of their eyes, almost perfect strangers for several weeks; and the pleasure that he felt in seeing her thus recovered, and seated beside him at this sacred ordinance, was strangely dashed by what he knew was the state of her feelings with regard to himself. But the long extempore prayer was immediately proceeded in, and the abundance of the heart of the deeply-impressed minister gave forth things, in his fervent address to the Deity, which took their tone much from the emotions that struggled in his bosom with reference to her, whose case lay now so heavily on his spirit.

It was no common prayer offered to the Father of mercies and the God of all grace and consolation, which now ascended up to Heaven from the burning heart of the pious minister of Hillington. It was an unbosoming of himself, and on the part of his people, to the Deity, which touched the hearts of all present, with an unction and a fire almost beyond utterance. He knew he was praying both for Rebecca and himself, as well as for his beloved communicants around, now also deeply affected; but what *she* felt at every word that he uttered while standing trembling, under the influence of her feelings, almost by his side, it would not be easy to find language to express.

The assembly sat down; and the bread was

broken and distributed to the disciples, while
the whole congregation was melted in tears,
and all thought they never had witnessed such
deep feeling in their minister. But not a tear
would come from the eyes of Rebecca, although
the crowding emotions which struggled for
vent in her bosom were mounting fast to something surpassing the mastery of human infirmity. Continuing speaking to the communicants the words of consolation, while the elders
went down the passes with the elements, as is
the manner of the Scottish church, Mr. Bannatyne next " took the cup," and gave one to
the clergyman on his right; but, in handing
the other to his left, he was so strangely overpowered and confused in his thoughts, that,
instead of giving it to Mr. Bryce, who was the
person next to him, he handed it at once to
his own beloved wife.

Rebecca, who was looking up in his face at
the moment, took the cup from his hand, and,
putting it to her lips, drank of the symbolic
wine, under the influence also of overpowering
and absorbing feelings, which prevented her

from being sensible to any impropriety, while the elders, who stood looking on, and the other people near, were quite struck with this strange and unexpected communication.

To both, this was a peculiar and an awful moment. It was a solemn communion of both with their Heavenly Father; but it was also an involuntary communion between husband and wife, expressing thoughts and feelings which language could not evolve. " He whose death we are now commemorating," went on Mr. Bannatyne, in his exhortation at the time to the communicants, " who was himself deeply touched with a feeling of our infirmities, enters into the closet of our inmost spirits, and draws the poison from the wounded mind; for, knowing our frame, and remembering that we are but dust, he forgiveth all our wanderings and healeth all our sorrows; and when heart and flesh do faint and fail, he has promised to be himself the strength that we need and our comfort for ever; that comfort and support, which all who love Him ought, also, in this world of trial, to be constantly to each other."

At this moment the still solemnity of the communion was broken by a scream, which appalled every heart, to the outermost aisles of the church; and the people simultaneously rose to look round them for the cause. The scream was from Rebecca; and what must have been passing in her bosom, while her Lewis uttered these words, no language can describe; but her cry was so loud, and yet so mournful in its expression, that every heart was pierced as with a sharp instrument, to the very extremity of the assembly, and all were horrified at the suspicion of what could have taken place to the lovely wife of their much-regarded minister.

It was, indeed, a sad moment for him, and an awful interruption of the solemn services of the day. The working emotions of Rebecca, which she had mastered in her solitary chamber at Lawford, and borne up against during all the time of the supposed alienation of her husband's affections, proved too strong for the cutting conviction that she had on that morning been blaming him wrongfully; and thus, all that was favourable to exciting the malady of her family, meeting together in her breast at the moment of their mutual communion, over-powered that reason, at last, of which she had so long been jealous; and the unhappy Re-becca was obliged to be carried out of Hil-lington church, now evidently, at length, in the masterless paroxysms of insanity.

CHAPTER XVII.

IT was a strange tale that was told from mouth to mouth through all the parish of Hillington, that the minister's lady had gone out of her mind on the sacrament Sabbath day, and had screamed out in the kirk at the very communion table. It was a sad event to all but one within the walls of the ancient mansion of Lawford.

Every suspicion regarding her, which had been infused by the crafty widow, and which the affectionate minister had so deeply repented of indulging, was now fully confirmed, to Mrs. Chapman's infinite gratification, by the manner which the unhappy lady evinced, during the frightful insensibility of madness. The experience of the past would not from henceforth allow Mr. Bannatyne to absent himself from her: she now exhibited a general alarm whenever he came near her; and when, in particular, he spoke to her with kindness, she seemed ready to hide herself in the very stone of the wall, in her maniac anxiety to flee from his presence.

Rebecca now, with the wild but pathetic obstinacy of the peculiar state of her mind, took up her abode in the chamber next to that deserted one before alluded to, which contained the portraits of her line of ancestors, most of whom had spent the last days of their unhappy existence in that very apartment to which she from this time would cling and claim as her own. In the mean time, letters with the painful intelligence of what had occurred had reached her uncle, and, in three days after the event, the old gentleman had returned to Lawford, in company with the valued friend of the family, Doctor Heywood.

It was a sad sight for the worthy Doctor, who had taken so much interest on behalf of Mrs. Bannatyne, to see her as he did on his arrival at Lawford; and it was a sadder meeting which took place in that ominous chamber between her and her excellent and grieved uncle. Yet she was perfectly tranquil, and even wildly sensible.   Her face was pale and her eyes were dilated; and though she said little, and looked bumbled and sad in their faces, there was a touching pathos in the tones of her voice, which melted the hearts of her visiters with sorrow.

" Uncle, good uncle," she said, caressingly hanging on the old man, " how long is it since I have seen you?   Many a weary day have I spent in Lawford since you left us; and are you really come back to see me at last?   Bless you, uncle! but I am happy to see you!   Yes, I am very happy.   I am quite happy now! for I always knew it was ordained I should come to this little room at last.   And here I shall remain by day and by night, until the ladder is let down for me to climb to heaven by; and then I shall mount—mount—aspire and struggle: —how finely saith the poet,

> ' Oh, the pain — the bliss of dying!'

What makes you look so sad, sir?"

" I am sad for you, Rebecca.   I wish you would leave this room, and come down stairs again."

" Oh, no, no, dear uncle ! are not these all our ancestors' pictures in that next room, that I am so well acquainted with ? Did not my father and grandfather live in this room, and look out at this little window, till the day of their deaths ? Did not my grand-aunt live in this room — and see you there abroad — is that not the Lady's Linn on the height, where she drowned herself, poor soul ! when the evil spirit mastered her ? I will not leave this room, sir — never till the last ! "

" God help her, poor heart !" said Mr. Prior, turning away his head, and wiping off the tears which started into his eyes.

" And I am happy to see you too, Doctor — good Doctor," she continued, smiling with melancholy wildness in that gentleman's face, as she clung to his arm, " and I love you — love you much, Doctor Heywood, for you were the man that got my Lewis and me married. These were happy days, Doctor ! but Lewis has quite changed, and hates me now ; does he not, goody ?—'you told me so," she said, with a bitter expression, as she turned towards

Mrs. Chapman. "But I thought he had made it up with me one Sabbath day in Hillington church, when he gave me the red wine to drink, out of the silver cup, with his own hand, and the tables were covered with a white linen cloth before me; but a darkness came across my eyes, and a ringing rung in my ears, and the owls seemed to scream from the rafters of the kirk, and voices sounded from the hollows of the steeple, and the minister and all left me alone at the Lord's table, and I 've never seen him since. Alas, for me !"

The gentlemen descended, much affected, to the room below, where the melancholy minister waited to receive them; and a serious and lengthened consultation took place as to what was to be done in regard to the unfortunate lady.

One of the first things that struck Doctor Heywood, on his entrance once more into Lawford House, and especially on his ascending to the apartment which Rebecca had *chosen*, was a palpable error in his own management in regard to her who might now be called his patient, and which arose from the character of his mode of philosophising upon insanity, as was briefly hinted at several chapters back. The Doctor had accustomed himself so much to generalise the application of principles which he understood with perspicacity, that he overlooked those details of practice and those considerations of exception and individuality, which so essentially change the bearings of many general conclusions. Had he attended, as he ought, to the *history* of the *maladie héréditaire* of the Priors of Lawford, he would have seen at once the great effect of the constant presence of those objects which handed down to each generation a crowd of associations, calculated to keep constantly before the mind all the sad circumstances which that history furnished; and, in venturing to advise the marriage of Rebecca, he would have carefully withdrawn her, from that moment, from the scene of the afflictions which had almost destroyed the house of Lawford.

There were other things that occurred to him, in consequence of what fell from Rebecca

as well as from what was related by the minister
himself, that made him resolve carefully to sift
the conduct of those who were much in the
way of his patient; but, before he could obtain
opportunity of any other than a general conversation with Mrs. Chapman, he heard with
surprise that the latter lady had talked of
giving up her charge, for what cause he could
not learn, while, in the mean time, chance threw
him in the way of a very familiar and unexpected *tête-à-tête* with Mrs. Dryburgh. Having,
besides, perceived something in the manner of
Rebecca, which quite cheered him as to what
could be done for her, and having found little
satisfaction in what he could learn from Mrs.
Chapman, he was well pleased, for the present,
to encourage the communicative spirit of the
loquacious Lady Bicknel.

"Weel, sir, dear me, Doctor," said the lady,
"but it's a pity that ye ha'e gi'en up the doctor
trade; ye'll excuse me, for I hear you so much
roosed up for your skill an' sense, an' ye hae
sic a notion of the women's complaints, and sic
a handicraft about them, Mr. Heywood, that it

maun be a perfect pleasure to see you lay your finger on a pulse. But I'm thinking the minister's wife is in a state that's beyond your skill. Ae, but she's a heavy handfu' to the puir minister, an' she never was a wife for the like of him. Noo, if onything was happening her — which would be a great relief, nae doubt, frae the way she's in — I'm just thinking what the minister would do, the dear gentleman : — what think ye, Doctor?"

" Really, Mrs. Dryburgh, I have formed no opinion ; but what makes you talk upon such a supposition ?"

" Oo, sir, it's no a'thegither my suppose — it's Mrs. Chapman's suppose, too ; for the puir demented creature canna live lang in yon way, for she eats just nothing. Now, if ought were happening, I ken somebody that would jump at the minister. Od, but I maybe shouldna tell you, sir."

" Why not tell me, Mrs. Dryburgh, if I'm such a man about the women as you say ?"

" Deed, sir, as you're a jocose sort o' man, an' likes a crack, I can tell you that, that

sneck-drawing widow would gie the very eye
out of her head for the minister's little finger, if
that dowie creature the present Mrs. Bannatyne
were awa', an' I dinna see but ye might speak
a gude word for her yoursel, Mr. Heywood (if
onything should be likely to happen), an' if
she got an inkling o' that, I'm sure the very
thought o''t would gar her wait on this demented
lady, till see what might turn about."

A light flashed across the mind of Doctor
Heywood, at this conclusion of the speech, that
raised thoughts and suspicions on the instant,
the bare idea of which almost took his breath
from him.   But, suppressing any indication of
the ideas that had struck him, he merely said,—

I've certainly heard of such things as
parties speculating about prospective marriages
in this way, but, having no skill in match-
making, I cannot pretend even to form an
opinion upon the subject: but now, Mrs. Dryburgh, allow me to ask you, if, in your intercourse
backwards and forwards with Mrs. Chapman,
and as far as you had opportunity of observing
Mrs. Bannatyne, before the period of her

screaming out in the church, you witnessed any particular repugnance, on her part, to the company of her husband?"

"Why, sir, as to repugnance, ye see, sir, I canna just say, Doctor; but if you would make your meaning a wee thought clearer, and not use such lang-nebbed words, I would answer you to the best o' my pith; for, to tell you the truth, although I was weel brought up at the buirding schools, an' the tip-top masters, I have not what ye ca' much dictionary learning."

"Have you ever observed, madam," said Mr. Heywood, with some shortness of manner at the dawdling talkativeness of Lady Bicknel, "that Mrs. Bannatyne seemed to have a dread to meet with her husband, or did you ever hear her express alarm at the idea of his visiting her?"

"Why, sir, to speak the honest truth, I never heard her speak much at all. But Mrs. Chapman told me that she was quite against his seeing her, which I thought very unnatural. And yet, one day, now when ye remind me——"

"Well, madam?"

"I thought it very odd after that; for I heard her say, sae pitiful, to Mrs. Chapman, 'Does my Lewis never offer to come to see his forlorn Rebecca?' that was the very words, and the puir young lady looked sae wistful. But then ye ken, sir, she was not hersel, an' quite maunered in her mind."

"And what did Mrs. Chapman say to that?"

"I didna hear ony reply, sir, an' I think the widow only shook her head."

Doctor Heywood rose hastily, and began with long and rapid strides to pace up and down the room.

In a few minutes after, he was out and through the house, looking for an opportunity of speaking privately with Mr. Bannatyne.

"Have you attended to my wishes, sir," he said, somewhat abruptly, on meeting him, "not to go near your lady's apartment, since my return to Lawford?"

"I have never seen my poor Rebecca since your arrival here, sir," said the minister, with a melancholy expression, "and your injunctions are exceedingly painful: besides, were it not for my confidence in you, I should be strongly inclined to doubt of their wisdom."

" You speak, as most men do, from your feelings and wishes only, and little from reason, my dear sir," said the Doctor : " you must give me your entire confidence, Mr. Bannatyne; for this is the physician's first requisite for success : have I it, or not ?"

" You have it unreservedly, sir," said the minister; " for Heaven's-sake do as you will in my house, only restore to me, if it be possible, my beloved Rebecca."

" Then, sir, remain where you are until I return," and without another word the Doctor left him alone.

But a few minutes elapsed, in painful mental suffering, when the Doctor again entered the room, accompanied by Mr. Prior.

" I have brought you together, gentlemen," he said, " in order that you may both judge of the result of a conversation I have just had with that viper, Mrs. Chapman. You start, as all good men do, at unexpected treachery ; but had you seen as much as I have of the baseness of the base, of the cruelties practised upon those who are least able to bear mental pain, and that on the convenient plea of their insanity, you would be no way astonished at what I have now discovered.   In two words, I am convinced that this woman, whom we all trusted, whom I was the means of recommending to this respected family, has been practising on the mind of her unhappy lady, for the purpose of sending her ultimately to the grave, with the presumptuous hope of one day sitting in her own chair at the head of Mr. Bannatyne's table!   Well may you be astonished, sir, living as you have lived, and occupied as you have been.   Even *I* would be incredulous, after all I have seen, did I not know that the whole struggle of selfishness in this world consists in one species of mind taking advantage of another,—the cunning deceiving the upright and virtuous, — the coarse fattening upon the sufferings of the fine, — the obtuse and cruel making a prey of the sensitive; until the capacity to feel is justly regarded as a misfortune, and one half of the world is almost driven to insanity by the oppression of the other.

" Your astonishment silences you," continued the Doctor, after a pause, " and you wish to be further satisfied ? You *shall* be so, fully, else I am mistaken, if you will observe the result of my communication with this person, and the representation she is likely to make to her most injured lady. This you shall soon do, if you will condescend to place yourselves where you can overhear what they say. You consent? Then follow me. We can get, unobserved, into the recess, immediately contiguous to Mrs. Bannatyne's apartment."

They all proceeded towards the chamber : but while the minister expressed the relief that Doctor Heywood's opinion had given to his mind, he almost feared when he reverted to the painful scene in the church, that the surmise was too joyful to be true ; and put further questions as to the likely nature of the disorder, as well as to the necessity of such a mode of satisfying themselves, as they now were unwillingly about to adopt.

" Did you know, sir," said the Doctor, " how many persons have been persuaded that they were insane, or actually made so by others, when under the influence of strong feeling, you would not spare any pains to get at the bottom of the character of those who are chiefly about the person of your lady. My suspicion now is, that mere desponding hypochondriasis, which may be transient in its duration like a fit of passion or of sorrow, is all that at present divides her from her family, and has been entirely brought on, I conceive, by the cunning arts of this horrid woman. But haste, and we shall speedily ascertain."

When the gentlemen had mounted the stairs, and placed themselves where they could plainly hear what passed between Mrs. Chapman and Rebecca, the low murmuring tone of plaintive sorrow, in which the latter spoke in answer to the widow, struck upon the heart of Lewis with such affecting impression, that he was with difficulty prevented from rushing at once into the room.

" To leave me again, did you say?" said Rebecca, her voice rising as she seemed to meditate upon the widow's words; "you cannot mean so, Mrs. Chapman! Not, surely, without seeing me and his child."

" I heard no wish of the kind expressed," said the widow: " truly, madam, I pity you deeply.   She who has outlived the affections of a husband that she loves has little inducement to prolong a neglected existence."

" What a change has come over the spirit of my life !" said Rebecca, resuming her plaintive tone: " even this very morning I rose unusually refreshed, for my dreams were of Lewis and my lovely baby, and the thoughts that used to hang like a heaviness on my heart seemed to have vanished before some unusual sunshine.   But now all is gone again, and I am weary, weary of my life.   Neglected ? — lost the affections of my husband ? — was not that the word you said, Mrs. Chapman ?"

" Yes, madam, that was the word ; and before *I* should be so used, I would — would do some rashness — I am a strong passioned woman, but ——— "

" Why don't you say it all ? "

" I would slip out of this room when the

glooming came down, and end my life and my
wrongs at the bottom of that linn there on the
height among the trees."

" What frightful temptation is this coming
over me?" said Rebecca, with a shudder.
" Woman, what is this you hint at? I see
something horrid in your face."

The widow merely looked at her, and shook
her head.

" Surely, Mrs. Chapman, you are not ad-
vising me to take away the life that God hath
given me! And have I not a baby — a lovely
baby, and my Lewis will not come and see him
or me? Neglect! pity! what words are these
that I have been hearing of late? and from
you? Your pity, woman! that art eating my
bread, and ought to comfort me under my
trials. What is this? Can this be called
insanity? Am I a maniac because I love my
husband? Woman, you are imposing upon
me: answer me one question — did Mr. Bannatyne really say he would not see me?"

" Not exactly, madam; but I told him —
that ——— "

" Wretch ! there is guilt in your face ! your tongue falters, and your eye quails at my questions. What thought is this breaks upon me ? Now I remember the horrible insinuations you uttered to that ignorant creature, Mrs. Dryburgh, while I lay on my sick couch. Now I see it all ! You have made me contemptible in the eyes of my beloved husband ! You have persuaded me against my own convictions almost into madness itself. When I think of all that I can now recollect, a crowd of horrible suspicions rises into my brain, that I can hardly attribute to humanity. Out, vile woman ! that speaks to me of the drowning pool of the lady's linn, and hast put evil and alienation between me and my husband ! "

What an impression there is in talent ! what a majesty in truth ! As Rebecca spoke, her delicate figure seemed to tower upwards into the size of an incensed queen, while the quailing widow sunk lower and lower, until, overwhelmed with confusion that the other had penetrated her, she at last sunk in supplication at her feet.

o 4

" You wrong me, lady," said the alarmed
widow; " your own mind is wronging us both.
If Mr. Bannatyne was as before, surely ———"

" I will not hear you, widow! You are deceiving me about Lewis. He loves me still: I know
he does; for, when we sat together at the table
of the Lord in Hillington church, I myself saw
the affection that beamed in his eye: and he
prayed for me—I know it was for me, until
the big tears rolled down his trembling lips,
and he gave me the cup with his own hand. I
will go down this instant and humble myself
before him. I will confess that my poor mind
has wandered, and that my temper requires
indulgence. Give me my shawl. Nay, attempt
not to prevent me—for a woman's affection is
strong as death, and mighty as the grave—
as the grave, woman! where it only can be
ended."

Voices were now heard in the adjacent
apartment:—" Stand back—come forth!" said
Mr. Heywood, as the panting minister came
forward, eager to receive into his arms his distracted wife; and, as they retired a few paces

into the large ante-room, the door burst open, and Rebecca, followed by the widow, issued hastily forth.

Her start at the sight of the three gentlemen was neither so sudden nor so alarmed as that of Mrs. Chapman.   Standing stock-still for a moment,   while no one had as yet the power to move, she gave a slight scream of joy, and threw herself forward into her husband's arms.

"I knew you would come to see me!   I was sure you would not quite desert me!   Oh! Lewis!" she said, looking piteously in his face, as she held him round the neck, "forgive and pity the wandering and the weakness of your poor Rebecca."

"I have been deceived, Rebecca," he said, at length, as he dried his eyes, while Mr. Prior, and even the physician, were also affected to tears.   "I have been abused.   I have been misrepresented.   I never wished to desert you. I will watch over you myself from hence, and be a stay to you in all your wanderings; for you are my wife—my valued,   my adored wife.

Now, come down with me, and away from that detestable woman, and this day shall be a day of rejoicing at Lawford."

" And my uncle, too !" she said, grasping hold of his hands — "my dear uncle: surely I am not quite astray in my mind, or I should not so feel the joy of this happy moment. And has this woman been deceiving you too? Alas, widow, it was cruel of you to vex the hearts of those who loved as we have done."

" Hence, cockatrice ! " exclaimed Doctor Heywood, swelling with indignation, as he looked on the abashed and confounded widow. " Woman, you are not fit to *live* in a world where there is already so much misery, when you could have the heart to drive to temporary madness such a sweet spirit as this ! "

Why need we tell further what more happened at Lawford, to the joy and pleasure of all the kind hearts who dwelt far and near in the parish of Hillington? Whatever distraction of the mind had happened to Rebecca was soon dispelled by the affectionate conduct and constant society of her husband, and the judicious attention of Doctor Heywood; the latter, after Mrs. Chapman was disgracefully dismissed, insisting upon an entire change of scene to Rebecca, and that she might be taken from beside the unpleasant associations connected with the history of her ancestors. The health of her mind was fully completed by an easy excursion to the capital, and was insured by an ultimate removal entirely from the old mansion of the family.

Months and years, since these events took place, have now passed away, and Rebecca is still the beloved wife of Mr. Bannatyne, without experience, or dread, of any mental aberration; living in tranquillity and happiness, mother of a numerous family of promising sons and daughters, who, the uncle having died at a good old age, have since grafted the name of Bannatyne, with good hopes and prospects, upon the ancient designation of the Priors of Lawford.[1]

[1] See Note B to this tradition.

NOTES

TO THE TRADITION OF

THE PRIORS OF LAWFORD.

NOTE A, page 109.

THE ancient governments, considering the children of their citizens as belonging to the state, were more watchful upon the subject of marriage, for the obtaining of a healthy progeny, than seems to be thought necessary in modern times: and the Romans, recognising from experience the principle of mania being hereditary, passed the severe law, that, if persons dared to marry in the consciousness of this taint, they were to be punished with the same severity as was vestal incontinence; namely, both parties were to be buried alive, that so frightful a disorder might not be propagated.

NOTE B, page 299.

The names and local allusions in this story, as in that of Lady Barbara of Carloghie, are entirely imaginary, and we abstain from all particulars, for reasons which must be obvious to the reader. That in forming a connection so interesting as marriage, however, attention should be given to many enquiries of the deepest importance to individuals, both for their own sakes and that of generations of posterity, will be evident from a little consideration of what experience has ascertained, and physiological enquiries have set forth. This is indeed the true moral of many painful cases of the sort we allude to, that have come within our personal enquiries, and which we have endeavoured to illustrate in the Dominie's tale.

The facts illustrative of the well-established doctrine of the transmission from generation to generation of peculiar qualities, both physical and mental, are not only most curious and interesting, *philosophically*, but deserve a much greater degree of attention *practically*, than they usually meet with from a thoughtless world, unwilling to learn what is most important for it to know, and constantly swayed, upon such a subject, by some predominating motive or passion, which, for the time being, is all in all.

That, in the transmission of life, both animal and vegetable, every thing is uniformly *after its kind*, is a rule of nature observed from the beginning; and to its extreme importance to ourselves and our posterity in the formation of unions, and the entailing of existence, we would do well to take heed. Hence the decided characteristics observable in families, not only in bodily form or strength, but for virtue or for vice, for feebleness or for capacity, especially where their position obliges them much to marry among each other. " In this way," says Dr. Gregory (not to speak at present of the obvious mental qualities by which many of the prominent families of Europe are distinguished), " parents frequently live over again in their offspring; certainly children are born similar to their progenitors, not only in expression of countenance and form of body, but also in the character of their minds, in their virtues, and their vices. The imperial Claudian family, for a long time, flourished at Rome, brave, fierce, proud : it produced the cruel Tiberius, who was a most gloomy tyrant; it numbered among its members a Caligula, a Claudius, an Agrippina, and at last, after a duration of six hundred years, terminated in Nero himself." — *Gregory Conspect. Medicinæ Theoreticæ*, p. 4. Edin. 1815.

Not only are the mental qualities very generally transmitted (though rarely to all their extent of *power*), but also the peculiar conformations of the person.

" It appears to be a general fact," says Dr. Prichard, " that all connate varieties of structure, or peculiarities which are congenital, or which form a part of the natural constitution impressed on an individual from his birth, or rather from the commencement of his organisation, whether they happen to descend to him from a long inheritance, or to spring up for the first time in his own person, — for this is perhaps altogether indifferent, — are apt to reappear in his offspring. It may be said, in other words, that the organisation of the offspring is always modelled according to the type of the original structure of the parent.

" On the other hand, changes produced by external causes in the appearance or constitution of the individual are temporary, and, in general, acquired characters are transient ; they terminate with the individual, and have no influence on the progeny."

This transmission, through families, of original conformation, applies not only to external form and peculiarities of shape, &c., but to the *type* of character and disposition, or even to some malformations of the mind or constitution, usually denominated disease. Of the former sort many curious instances are on record, as the case mentioned by Maupertuis and adverted to by Prichard, of two families in Germany which had been distinguished, for several generations, by six fingers on each hand, and as many toes on each foot. The instance of the family of Jacob Riche, the surgeon of Berlin, belonging to one of these, is curious, who had the twelve toes and fingers. He inherited this from his mother and grandmother: the latter was married to a man of the ordinary make, to whom she bore eight children, four of whom had only the ordinary number of these, like the father, and the other four had the long and short *sires* like the mother.

There are even instances of similar peculiarities running through families mentioned by Pliny. The Philosophical Transactions record an instance where the writer had known of the transmission of supernumerary fingers and toes for four generations; and in the Edinburgh Medical and Surgical Journal, vol. iv., is an account of a family at Iver who for nine generations had transmitted a peculiarity of this sort, in general only through the women. The imperial house of Austria has had transmitted through it, for many centuries, as we learn from Archdeacon Coxe, a singular thickness of the upper lip, which is believed to have been originally introduced into the Hapsburg family by an intermarriage with the ancient house of Jagellon.

But it is a singular and wise provision of Nature, that

though she transmits, until accident terminates them, these *her own original formations*, she never transmits the external mutilations or alterations performed *by men*, as in the case of cutting off of limbs or splitting of ears, or docking of the tails of animals. Were she to do this, human caprice, fancy, or fashion would soon throw all nature into monstrous confusion.

But the liability of the peculiarities of the mind, and even of some of the more rooted diseases interwoven into the constitution, to be transmitted and entailed upon one's posterity, deserve a degree of attention which the subject seldom receives even from the more thinking part of mankind.

" It is well known to medical practitioners," adds Dr. Prichard, " that (the doctrine of transmission) equally applies to those minute varieties of organisation which give rise to peculiarities of habit or temperament, and *predispose* to a variety of morbid affections, as deafness, scrofulous complaints, and the whole catalogue of disorders in the nervous system. Even those singular peculiarities termed *idiosyncrasies* are often hereditary, as in the instance of a remarkable susceptibility of the action of particular medicines, such as mercury." — *Prichard's Researches into the Physical History of Mankind*, vol. ii. p. 539., &c.

Insanity, as a disease, like other diseases which, being inwrought into the physical constitution, is transmissible, would seem, from its connection with the brain, to partake of the hereditary qualities both of body and mind. Upon the general subject, however, we have been favoured, since the foregoing story was written, with a communication from our respected friend, Sir Andrew Halliday,

of Hampton Court, M. D., formerly physician to his
Majesty, when Duke of Clarence, then living at Busby,
and himself author of some tracts on insanity, — which
we consider peculiarly valuable. Sir Andrew, speaking of
the admitted effects of families constantly intermarrying
among each other, or, in the language of farmers and
jockeys, in reference to cattle and sheep, " breeding in
and in," says, " that breeding in and in deteriorates the
race, is a fact known to all men ; and that diseases accidentally engendered very soon become hereditary, is
equally well established ; and insanity, as a bodily disease, is one of those that are easily continued from one
generation to another. Yet the fact seems not so well
known, or is not attended to as it ought, that it is the
physical qualities of the *male parent*, whether good or
bad, that are chiefly formed in the offspring, and the
mental endowments of *the mother :* that is, a strong
healthy father will have a strong healthy son, even though
the mother may be so diseased or delicate, as not to survive the birth ; but a puny father will never have a healthy
progeny, even though married to the finest woman in the
nation. If you want to have good lambs," adds Sir
Andrew, characteristically illustrating his position by the
example of domestic animals, as he understands farming,
" never regard the condition of the ewes, but take care to
provide good strong healthy tups.

" Insanity," he goes on, philosophically, " arises from
physical causes, that is, *weakness* or *irregularity* in the
construction of the instruments of the mind. The
healthy strong energetic father gives the *instruments*
which, when cultivated in earliest infancy, by the *sound
mind* of a superior mother, forms the man of talent ; and

nothing else will do it. The males of a family in which the predisposition to insanity exists, should all be emasculated, but the females may be allowed to marry as they please; for though they may become deranged themselves, they will not taint their children. This I hold to be a fact, as I have ascertained beyond a doubt."

The extensive observation of Sir Andrew, both at home and on the Continent, as well as his sound natural sagacity, entitles his opinion, on such subjects, to the highest consideration; and had these important conclusions been as widely made known as it is our wish to make them, many painful cases of family distress, from the apprehension of insanity, which have come under our own observation, where sensitive and high-minded females were the sufferers, might have been greatly mitigated, or rather, as we believe, entirely saved.

With regard to the effects of particular families marrying for many generations continually among each other, considered to be so deteriorating to any race, which forms such an objection to hereditary honours, and which furnishes such men as the late President Jefferson with his republican sneer against the sovereigns of Europe, we have met with many facts that we consider curious and interesting, but none so little known or so applicable as two for which we are indebted to the same authority. When the first De Bruise, grandfather of the Scottish hero, of whom we have hereafter to speak further, obtained from David I. the lordship of Annandale, north of the Tweed, the Celtic inhabitants, whom he found on his new property, were too proud and independent to do any menial labour for a Saxon, as Bruise originally was; consequently, when he planned his castle of Lochmaben, he was obliged to import from England all his domestic establishment to do the work of building. These he located near him, and as they increased he formed them into four divisions, founding for them towns, which are known to this day by the names of the Four Towns of Lochmaben. The people who formed this English colony were, by the natives around, so despised, that they were shunned as if they had been lepers, and obliged constantly to marry among themselves : they have long formed a distinct race, and are called by their common appellation, although all the reasons that originally made them so have for centuries ceased to exist. These people are so evidently inferior to all around them, that no one has ever risen up among them who has shown any qualities to remove the stigma by which they are known. They are even lower in stature than the usual standard of Scotsmen ; and Sir Andrew thinks they have less than common physical strength, besides being known in the neighbourhood as " *a quarrelsome and litigious race ;*" — characteristics certainly bespeaking no enlarged capacity.

The other instance is to be found in the small island of Lismore, in Argyleshire, where a colony of English was originally planted by the Bishop of the Isles, under similar circumstances. These foreigners being despised and avoided for the menial services they performed for the priesthood, and forced to continue intermarrying among themselves, became so deteriorated in every manly quality, as to obtain the local soubriquet of *the Lismore sheep ;* and, to cry " *baa,*" like that animal, in the presence of a native of this island, is so mortal an offence, that, during the American war, when some of them had enlisted in the army, bloody quarrels were often the consequence of this trick upon the Lismore men. Some other instances of similar effects from colonisation in the isles are given, as we believe, by Colonel David Stewart, in his " Sketches of the Highland Regiments."

MACDONALD OF GLENCO,

AND

JEANIE HALLIDAY OF ANNAN;

OR,

THE ORIGIN OF THE FAMILY OF JOHNSON, OR JOHNSTONE, LATE MARQUESSES AND EARLS OF ANNANDALE.

CHAPTER I.

IT was about the beginning of the ninth century, or, perhaps, a few years later, that the Craithnæ, a tribe of the ancient Celts or Britons, finding their banishment into Ireland irksome, or the boundaries of Ulster too confined for their numbers, determined to retaliate upon their latest oppressors, the Saxons, and, if possible, to recover some of the pleasant valleys of Britain, of which they had not as yet lost altogether the recollection. To this they were urged on by the bards of their tribe, who yet chanted in the halls of their chiefs the glorious days of Fingal and Ossian, and told of the battles that had been lost and won by the sons of the Gael in the years of their oppression.   It may be, too, that some pleasant accounts of the indolence produced by security and of the petty wars among the Saxons themselves, had reached the Green Isle; and that the Celts saw the facility of considerable conquests upon the outskirts of their empire.

However this may be, true it is, as the industrious Chalmers has proved, by authentic documents carefully preserved in his " Records of Caledonia," that about the period we have referred to, a large body of Celtic warriors crossed the channel, that divides Ireland from Scotland, and in a few months drove the Saxon outposts once more within the English border ; and having thus conquered, kept possession of the whole peninsula between the Clyde and the Solway Frith, even extending as far east as the river Esk.   The hilly lands (now fresh and blooming) of Eskdale-muir formed then the barren desert that separated them from Berwickshire and the Lothians; or the whole was more pro-

bably a forest, and impassable.   The leaders of
the Celtic host had the country partitioned
among them, and it was peopled anew by their
brave followers.

The chief to whom our story more immediately relates received as his portion the vale, or
dale, of the river Annan, then, as the chronicles
tell us, one immense and almost impenetrable
forest of oak and pine ; and the buck or the
wild boar, that was roused from his lair at the
foot of Hartfell, could be followed to the mouth
of the Annan Water, a distance of some thirty
miles and more, without ever emerging from the
shade of the grove.

Here, to the source of the stream which gave
its name to the vale, and in the bosom of the
mountains from which the Tweed and the
Clyde, as well as the Annan, take their rise,
the chief of this Craithnæ tribe fixed his residence, and built himself a strong tower, known
as the castle of the Corehead.   As his people
multiplied, and manners changed, surnames
began to be assumed, as distinctive marks of
a better civilisation; and thus the marauder of

Annandale became known by the name of Halliday.

This appellation arose, as tradition affirms, from the circumstance of the chiefs being accustomed to call his *foray*, or *plundering excursion*, into England " Holyday work ; " and when he intended to make a " raid " over the Border, he intimated to the clan, that the day so appointed was to be kept as a " halliday." However this may be, the mountain that commands the best view of the counties of Cumberland and Westmoreland, and from which the blaze of the war-beacon could be seen all over the vale, — has, from the earliest times, and up to the present moment, been always known as the *Halliday Hill*. Here the people assembled, and here the banner of the chief was unfurled. These were the happy times, when a stout fellow on one side of a stream or a mountain could appropriate the goods and gear of another beyond it, with the greatest freedom and propriety ; and when a strong arm and a light foot were of more importance to the making of a man's fortune than the tedious accomplishments of learned reading and writing.

And pleasant work it was for gallant fellows to knock a neighbour on the head and drive away his cattle. The chief of the Hallidays had contrived to reside at the Corehead, and to hold undisputed sway in the vale of Annan Water, for more than two centuries, when King David the First, of crafty memory, invited to his court and his country a host of Norman adventurers (the poor sons of England's nobility), who could either claim kindred with his queen, the heiress of Huntingdon, or had been his companions while at the court of his brother-in-law, Henry I.

Among the numbers that crossed into Scotland at this period, our Scottish history has much to do with a certain "Robert de Bruis," son of a Norman baron, then Lord of Cleveland in Yorkshire. This young hero received from the Scottish king a gift of the whole vale of the Annan, — not as it had been made over to the Hallidays, by right of conquest, and as the reward of manhood, but by a *feudal charter*, a *parchment* holding, as it was called ; a system that had lately been introduced into Europe, and was now the fashionable mode of making the subjects a little more dependent upon the sovereign.   To this De Bruis there was conveyed the " allodial " country of the Hallidays, to be held by him of *David the King*, as the charter, bearing date A.D. 1134, says, "*per jus gladii.*"

When land was plenty and men few, this feudal chief would find no difficulty in securing a spot whereon to build a strong dwelling-place ; and, accordingly, De Bruis, having selected a piece of land, which juts into a lake of considerable extent in this neighourhood, and close to the ancient burgh of Lochmaben, began to build ; and by the help of artificers from England soon completed a castle that was sufficient to bid defiance to all the Celtic power in Scotland.[1]   Though no longer the independent chief of the district, Halliday still continued in repute, as " the Laird of the

---

[1] See Note A, at the end of this Tradition.

Corehead," and was venerated as the chief of all that remained of his clan.

But the warlike habits of this people, their detestation of the Norman yoke, and their religious enthusiasm, had led the greater number of them to join the Earl of Huntingdon, the grandson of King David of Scotland, when he became the lieutenant of the gallant Richard of England (Cœur de Lion), and marched under his banner to the Holy Land.   Their chief, after this, A. D. 1250, had married a sister of the renowned Sir William Wallace; and their son and heir, *Tam Halliday*, of Corehead, was a devoted follower and favourite captain of his gallant uncle.   Thus it was to this young chieftain's valour, and the aid of a hundred of his " Annandale men," that Wallace confessed he owed his famous victory over the Southrons at Biggar.

When Scotland's hero was betrayed to his enemies, Tom Halliday followed his unfortunate uncle to the Tower of London, received his last sigh, and returned to Annandale breathing vengeance against all who wore the livery

of Edward I.   He next became a warm supporter of " the Bruce," and commanded a part
of the body-guard at Bannockburn.   In his
lifetime Wallace having made the old chief, his
brother-in-law, governor or keeper of the castle
of Lochmaben, he still occupied this charge,
when the English army under Edward marched
on to the celebrated siege of Caerlaverock.[1]

*   *   *   *

It was about the commencement of the fourteenth century, that the laird of that time found
himself left with no heir to his house, save one
only and much beloved daughter, yet spoken of
in Annandale by the name of " the beauty of
Corehead."   Jeanie Halliday was a blithe and
comely damsel, with all the warm-hearted good
nature characteristic of her people, and all the
romance of a wild country maiden, confined to
the indolent seclusion of a rich Scottish vale.
But having no brother or sister, nor any companion near, but an old wisdom-talking nurse,
by eighteen she began to appear restless and
brooding, and to feel strange longings to go

[1] See Note B, at the end of this Tradition.

abroad somewhere, just to see what sort of a place the world might be.   Her nurse said this was folly, and belonged to the natural discontent of happiness; but the young lady differed entirely from this opinion, and said, that if there was no pleasure in seeing towns and houses where the king lived, there was, at least, a delight in looking upon mountains higher than Queensberry or Orickstane, and rivers broader and grander than the Annan or Moffat Water.

It was one day, while in one of these plaintive moods, that she descried from the narrow window in the square tower of Corehead the dark tartan and ruddy-brown face of a stranger, who was approaching the outer gate of the castle.   The traveller was quite unattended, save by a couple of Highland stag-hounds, that ran at his heels; yet he marched up to the entrance with a bold bearing, and by the quick voice of her father, and the bustle she heard among the gillies below, there appeared to be considerable pains taken to receive him. Had not the nurse duenna had as much curiosity as the laird's daughter, she would not have allowed her charge to descend from the tower to get better sight and knowledge of the stranger. But being noway behind in this female characteristic, she indulgently acceded to her lady's wishes, and both were soon placed in a situation where they were at little loss as to what was now going forward.

" And what 'll be your name and quality, sir stranger?" enquired the Laird, observing that, because he had not moved his own bonnet, the young man still carried his, with jealous Highland dignity, cocked somewhat tastefully with a declension towards the right ear, showing the thick-curled light-brown locks, that clustered over a bronzed brow and well rounded head.

" I come from the northern airt, whence your own race rose, Corehead," answered the youth : " it 's a good country for a manly heart, where the red deer in the forests require a light foot, and the capercailzie on the cliffs a sharp eye. Ye have heard of Macdonald of Glenco?"

" Ye are welcome, youth," said the Laird, with a grasp and a shake of the hand; " welcome is a Macdonald to a Halliday of Corehead.   But from the pleasant coiries of Glenco you did not come to the Lowlands without a mission or a heraldry ? "

" A bet hallan is ill to bear," said the youth, " and an angry father ill to face.   I come to seek a refuge with the Hallidays of Annandale, until my father's wrath shall be overpast."

" Never shall a true Scot of my name refuse sanctuary and safety to the fleeing stranger," said the Laird, " if no limmer deed, such as a Macdonald could not do, has provoked the just wrath of a parent."

" Ye shall know the deed in a breathing of words," said the youth.   " A minion gilly of my father's following went with me to the forest; for the deer is now scarce, and the hunting is long in the bare wilds of Glenco; and the red beasts have taken to the great coverts of Athol.   Three days we stalked, and little we got; at last a noble buck fell under aim of my own mark, but the distance was far, and the animal trailed a space with the bullet deep in his body. The minion was forward, and ran to the spot as the dogs brought down the prey. Presuming on the favour of my partial father, the serf had not patience to give his master the honour that he had won; and, flourishing his dirk, gave the animal the death with his own hand, just as I came up to finish my own work. To my indignant challenge for this insult, the villain replied with a provoking word and a saucy look. Was I a man or a chief's son, that I was to bear this?—I spoke to him again, to keep my wrath from boiling over. He muttered between his teeth, in dark Highland sullenness, some insulting words, that he might have taken back, but no man that ever wore the eagle's plume could endure the reckless defiance of his vassal eye. My blood was up in my throat; my naked dirk was in my hand, for I had drawn it to slay the fallen buck. Into the fellow's body it went, with lightning's quickness,—and ten inches, well planted, are enough to kill even a Macdonald of Glenco. Yet we treated the fellow with decency, and buried him in the wood in his plaid, as if he had been a born chief. This is my deed, and this its provocation."

"Foogh!" exclaimed the laird of Corehead, "is that the feud? A common accident — a trifle for a gentleman. A father to put his son to the angry horn and all for the life of a villain gilly,—'tis a monstrosity!"

"But my father, the laird," said the youth, "likes to kill his gillies himself, or to hang his villains at his own door, with a solemn decency and a pronunciation."

"No doubt, no doubt — it 's a dignity for a gentleman to be so minded," said the laird; "but if there 's nought in the fray but ten inches of fair steel in the wame o' a rascally gilly, that 'll ne'er be a mote in the marriage o' your father's son, young man: and so, lads, let us in to dinner."

CHAPTER II.

THE introduction being thus satisfactory between the Laird and his refugee visiter, Jean Halliday and her companion had sufficient opportunity to make their observations on the young stranger.   At first the lady did not precisely like him, because, coming to her father's castle as he did, and seeking there an asylum from a father's anger, it was natural to expect that he ought to have been a hero.   But ladies' heroes are not every day to be met with; and though Glenco challenged admiration in several particulars, he was upon the whole different from what her imagination had painted of that sublime character.   Though light and athletic like a roe on his own mountains, he was neither very tall of person nor had he a heroic or melancholy look; and though he spoke and often acted, in reference to his beloved mountainsports, with all a Highlander's warm enthusiasm, there was a common-sense sagacity in his ordinary conversation, which was fatal to the high illusions of that romantic abstraction.

Nevertheless, when Ion began to talk still of his own glens in the north, and to describe with discrimination those town wonders of the Scottish court, and those bright deeds of Scottish bravery, which had so highly inflamed Jean Halliday's fancy, the penetrating fire of his light hazel eye began to be felt with power in her inmost spirit, and growing admiration of the active-minded youth took its root in the solid foundation of heartfelt esteem.   When first they met, they were not particularly taken with each other, and had almost resolved individually against any thing like love.   But virtuous feeling and its adjuncts are deeper and surer, after all, than the unsteady blaze of passion; and many months had not gone round, ere he had completely won Jean Halliday's heart.

It is a property and part of the delight of that pleasing dream, to dwell in secret enjoyment over its delicious illusions, and to conceal itself if possible from all the world, but particularly from the stern prudencies of a father. They had courted, and consented, and made wedded vows, and were living, by the connivance of the nurse, together under his roof, agreeably to the peculiar custom of the times,—when Jean Halliday became impressed with delightful anticipations, for she knew that she should soon become a mother.[1]

But wedded joys bring wedded cares; and now unwonted anxieties began to becloud the face of the mountain stranger, and intrusive apprehensions to disturb the peace of the Laird's daughter. Strange men from the Highland hills came secretly at night to the castle of Corehead, and stranger reports of broils and blood were brought out of the peaceful valley of Glenco. The tenderness of Macdonald for his Lowland love seemed to increase with his growing concern regarding her; but to all her entreaties, as to the cause of what troubled him, he would as yet give her no satisfaction. At length, one morning, she awakened late from the oppression of a repeated and terrific dream, and the first news she heard was,

[1] See Note C, at the end of this Tradition.

that, long before the dawn of that inauspicious morning, Ion had departed secretly and stealthily from Corehead, and was by this time far on his way towards the bleak hills of the north.

The Laird came in from his morning's hunt, and found nought as usual in the hall of the castle. "What means this desertion of every one here?" he said to the old nurse, whom he met in the passage; "and what noise is this I hear booming above my head, that sounds like the wail of woman's lamentation?"

"It is your daughter Jean; and weel she may wail," said the woman, "for ye've brought a serpent into the house, to sting to the heart the heiress of Corehead; and now when the deed's done, and the ill's wrought, he's off o'er the hills to his ain kin, and left her to sorrow, a vowed wife but a shameful mother."

"Confound you, lassie! have ye done this?" exclaimed the Laird, as his weeping daughter, rushing in as they spoke, now threw herself distracted at her father's feet: "have ye dared to make love and handfast with a land-louping

Highlander, and never a word of consult with
your own father.   Ho there ! Rob, and Jack,
and gilly Tam, where are ye all ? Go, sound the
horn from the castle top; for if there 's a Halliday on the Annan Water, I 'll have the villain's
blood or his body ere three days' suns set behind the hills of Galloway."

In vain Jeanie entreated to spare her lover's
life.   The old man's hot blood was highly up,
and ere another hour had sped round the dial, she
saw him and his following of hardy Hallidays
sweeping off from Corehead, with their faces
towards the north, and climbing the then almost
perpendicular ascent of the Orickstane Brae.

Three days, however, run quicker round than
occurs at the moment to an angry man ; and so
it was the last of these ere the Laird and his
men found themselves approaching the small
town of Callander, whose well-known situation is
at the mouth of the gorge of the great pass that
leads into the Highlands at Lochearn.   At that
time it consisted of but a few straggling houses,
or huts, scattered with little regularity on each side
of the stream ; and the chief " change house,"

or hostelry, which stood out in the centre of
the clachan, was by no means commensurate to
the accommodation, either as to respectability
or number, of a Lowland laird, and his saucy
following, even of that day.

" What'll ye want here ?" said a red-headed
Highland wench, answering with tardy reluctance the bold knock of the Laird's gilly at the
door.

" A bed an' a braxy for the Laird himsel,
an' a brochan an' down-lying for his honour's
following," said the man, proudly : " stand out
o' the gate, ye jade, an' let his honour in."

" The house is fou, an' there's nae room,"
said the wench, no less peremptorily : " gang
awa' wi' your Lowland Laird to some ither
door."

" Deel's in the limmer," said the disappointed Laird, pushing past her ; " what other
door is there here for mense or shelter in your
hungry clachan ? "

A glance within convinced him, however,
that the wench had spoken truth ; for the ample
kitchen and chief apartments were completely

filled up with great brawny Highlanders, who, crowding towards the narrow passage, laid their hands on their ready dirks, to defend their possession.

The Laird went back for an instant to consult what was to be done; and as he talked with the landlord, who now made his appearance, he observed the little hole in the thatch, which could hardly be called a window, cautiously opened, from which a grey head and hard-featured national face was next thrust out, as if to reconnoitre who sought admittance. A beckoning sign from the Highlander in the thatch at once withdrew the landlord back into the house; who soon, however, returned, and, by his cautious questioning and manœuvring parley, showed some disposition to grant the Laird some accommodation.

" But who'll be the lead of this brave following?" enquired Corehead, retaliating in his turn their Highland suspicion.

" She never speers wha eats her bread an' drinks her broust if they pay their shot like a shentlemans," said the host; " but since his brave honour frae the hills offers a condescension to the Lowlander, she 'll tell her ain name if she likes it, an' if no, she 'll haud her whisht."

" But what accommodation can you give to all these men?" said Corehead.

" Hoogh! isn't there a gude brochan to stay their stomachs, an' an usquebaugh to make a sauce an' a savoury, forbye a lown hill-side to lie on, ahint the house? and what would his honour hae mair? But be sure the Lowlanders take care o' their tongues afore the mountain men, when the drink warms, or, faith! there 'll be red blood the night in the town o' Callander."

Things being thus satisfactorily arranged, the laird was let in, and forthwith introduced to a stately old Highlander, the same who had put his head out from the thatch. A suspicious civility passed between the strangers; but as, in this country inn, they were both in the condition to want congenial society, they sat down to see what each other was made of.

A few turns of the honest usquebaugh, however, helped greatly to soften down their original caution, and to induce the lairds, by degrees, to talk allusively of their own affairs. But, though they sidled, and hinted, and fished for each other's words, and moralised, as Scotsmen will do, about certain partly revealed vexations, they still avoided saying any thing direct; although each became more interested in the conversation of the other.

" They 're vile bodies, thae women," said the Lowland laird, gloomily generalising moralities in his drink; " an' it 's a hard hap for an honest gentleman to hae naught to heir his fair estate but a witless lassie, that takes up and takes on wi' every land-louping villain that seeks a hiding frae his kin in her father's castle."

" Naught ava ! a perfect nothing !" exclaimed the Highlander, " to having a set of godless sons that involve a shentleman in brulzies and broils, until he hardly kens the safety of his ain throat.   And they kill, and are killed, till heir and heritor, sib and son, are buried awa in the black yird.[1]   Ohon — honerie ! that I could catch a sough of my last remaining boy !"

[1] Earth.

To this unexpected pathos of the stalwart laird, Corehead replied by a corresponding groan; and both gentlemen could say nothing, for a little, but swallow down their griefs in simultaneous gulps of the comforting liquor.

"If *I* e'er had a bonnie daughter wi' a pawkie ee," said the Highland laird, drily, and speaking in the usual style of Job's comforters, "no land-louper man or wild loon, that couldna agree wi' his ain kin, should e'er ha'e been trusted in my castle, to abuse and bamboozle a lassie's heart—so, may be, gudeman, ye just got what ye deserved."

"The speech is o'er true, though rather saut in the hearing," said Corehead, penitently. "But if the deceitful villain comes within my clutches, I'll hae his blood or his body, though Glenco himsel should set on against me!"

"Glenco!" cried the Highlander, half rising from his chair. "Deevil damn! friend, what is 't ye say?"

"I just say, since I've spoken the word, that if auld Glenco, when I win to the hills, doesna help me to a reparation on his ill-doing son, the Macdonalds and the Hallidays will hae a tulzie that will show what Lowlandmen will do to them, who would put an insult on their chief's daughter."

The old man, starting up, almost overturned the table and the bladder of whisky,—for bottles were unknown in those days, — in his eagerness to embrace Corehead, and to thank him for the news, crying out, " I 'm Glenco! I 'm Glenco! Deevil! I wonder what blinded my bleered een, that I didna ken a Halliday of Annandale from a common cowardly Sassenach o' the English border."

The lairds now sat down to talk in the greatest cordiality, explaining many things on each side that greatly tended to justify the conduct, and even to raise admiration of the spirited youth, of whom they found they were both in search; and, some key being now found to his latest movements, Glenco agreed to return with Corehead into the Highlands in search of Ion; for his eldest son, having been just killed in a broil with the Grahams, the former was now sole heir of his lands.

Next morning the two lairds were just ready to set forth together, having finished an enormous Highland breakfast, when a stranger from the hills was announced as seeking to speak with the laird. Glenco had hardly given his consent, when Ion, his son, pale and halting as if from a long journey, rushed in, and threw himself at his father's feet.

The explanation and the reconciliation was more than cordial; it was moving — it was enthusiastic: for a father easily forgives his only son, and the son had nothing to pardon in the father.

"But what made you run from my house, Ion," said Corehead, shaking him next by the hand, "with such a sudden mystery, and a suspicious presumption?"

"I had not leisure for old men's advices and women's tears, when a brother's blood was to be avenged," said Ion, a brave feeling flushing up his pale cheek: "but now I *have* avenged my brave brother! I *have* upheld the honour of my name and clan ; though not, indeed, without a shedding of my own blood that has reduced me to this weakness;" and, saying this, he sunk exhausted into the arms of the Macdonalds, now all gathered round.

"Thou shalt not suffer for this, my brave son," said the Highland laird, "thou must back to the mountains to show thyself to the clan, for thou art now *Tanister* and heir to my name and house; but, after that, thou shalt again to the Lowlands, to marry afore the priest the choice of thy heart; for a Halliday shall never have to complain of a Macdonald of Glenco."

It was a pleasant journey that Ion had, with his father's band, in marching back to his mountains and his people; and a still more joyful day for Jeanie Halliday, when she saw, from the top of Corehead tower, the Macdonald and his hardy followers come winding down by "the De'il's Beefstand," and bounding across the pebbly stream of the Annan. The horn sounded loud to call the Hallidays out; they came forth from every cleugh and glen, like a rushing stream, and, soon flocking together round their happy chiefs, joined their shouts to the loud screams of the Highland bagpipe in praise of the fair heiress of Corehead and the brave and hardy titular to the name of Glenco.

In a very few days the young pair were married; and, when the priest of Moffat had said the holy words, the laird sent round the usquebaugh as plentifully as water, to the great rejoicement of every Highland heart. When the feast was over, the lads and lasses danced merry reels on the level grass, until the screed of the bagpipes echoed up the glens of the Moffat water, and even as far as the Kinnell, until the sun sank behind the towering summits of Hartfell, Saddleback, and Orickstane.*

It only remains to be told that the old man built a house for the young couple near to where the castle of Lochwood afterwards stood; that the eldest son of this union became laird of Glenco, and the second got the lands of Annandale; that the former was the ancestor of the chief and his kin, who were murdered in the famous massacre of 1690, and the latter, as

> ¹ See note D, at the end of this Tradition.

Ion M'Ion, or son of John, being thence usually named Johnson, became the laird of Johnston, and the founder of a name well known in that quarter, which long bore many honours, and is widely spread in Scotland at the present time.

NOTES

TO THE TRADITION OF

MACDONALD OF GLENCO, AND JEANIE HALLIDAY OF ANNAN.

NOTE A, page 319.

THE ruins of De Bruis's Castle are of great extent, and worthy of a visit from the architect or antiquary. When the great grandson of the first De Bruis succeeded to the crown of Scotland, Lochmaben Castle, in Dumfriesshire, became a royal palace, and such it has continued; the Lords of Annandale being generally hereditary keepers. Mr. Hope, who, in right of his mother, succeeded to the Johnstones of Annandale, and has assumed their name, is keeper of the royal palace of Lochmaben. But all the property in and about the ruins belongs to Lord Mansfield, as representative of the Murrays, long Earls of Annandale, and the descendants of Randolph de Moravin, made Earl of Murray by his nephew Robert I. A. D. 1313.

For the materials of this tradition, as well as the historical particulars appended to it, we are indebted

Q

to Sir Andrew Halliday, of Hampton Court, formerly mentioned, known as an intelligent and industrious antiquarian and himself author of a genealogical history of our own royal family, the house of Guelph, and other important works.

NOTE B, page 321.

Robert the First, even after he had gained the crown of Scotland, was still designated Lord of Annandale; being created such by Alexander III. A.D. 1273; but he subsequently gave this lordship to his brother Edward, in 1306, and at *his* death, in 1318, to his uncle Randolph, Earl of Murray. Still the Laird of Corehead held considerable property in the stewartry of Annandale, and was esteemed a chief of the most ancient descent.

NOTE C, page 329.

From the prevalence of the Salic law, or customs, in Scotland, under the Celtic dynasties, arose a strange practice, sanctioned by their laws, and approved of by their morals. The strictness of Scottish entail is well known; and, also, that most of the old tenures were " *male fiefs.*" Hence, in Dumfriesshire, and all over the kingdom, it was common for people of condition to " *hand-fast*" their children, especially their eldest sons; that is their parents agreed that the heir of A. should live with the daughter of B., as her husband, for twelve months and a day. If, in that time, the lady proved with child, or, became a mother, the marriage was good in law, even though no priest performed the ceremony (the church rites were seldom omitted); but if there was no appearance of issue, the contract was ended, and each was at liberty to marry or "handfast" with any other lover. Hence arose the well-known case of legitimising, by subsequent marriage, children born in Scotland out of wedlock.

There is, at this day, a custom prevalent among the Dutch at the Cape of Good Hope, not dissimilar to this, and well known to English gentlemen who make a stay there on their way home from India. The lady is *adopted* without any ceremony, and if fruitfulness is not the consequence, the matter rests where it was; the gentleman goes home to his country, and madam looks out for another lover. But if there is a child to seal the bargain, the roving gentleman is *held fast* by church and law, and the two are henceforth, as the Highlandman would say, " one beef."

Note D, page 340.

Queensberry is a famous high mountain, that bounds the Annandale horizon. Orickstane and Orickstane-Brae hang, as it were, over the Corehead; and Hartfell, the highest hill but one in Great Britain, Shawfell, and Saddleback, are mountains of note close around the " auld biggin." " The Devil's Beefstand" is one of the most remarkable dells in the world, and situated at the head of the Annan, and near the top of Orickstane. From the last elevation you have a view of the whole vale of the Annan, from its source where you stand, to its entering the Solway Frith. From Halliday Hill, which is at a short distance from the foot of Annan Water, you have a view, again, up to Orickstane, as well as over into Cumberland and Westmoreland, bounded only by Skiddaw, Stanmore, and Penrith Fells on the south, and by Queensberry, Orickstane, and Hartfell, to the north and east, and by Criffel and the Galloway Hills on the west.

The Hallidays of the olden time were tolerably "notour" robbers and marauders, like the other border clans, as we learn from the ancient ballad of "The Outlaw Murray," a good version of which is given in the first volume of Sir Walter Scott's "Border Minstrelsy." The ballad details the particulars of an expedition of the king (probably the fourth James) to bring into subjection that famous chieftain, who had "a fair castelle, bigged wi' lime and stane," and a "royal companie" of five hundred men. In this affair, Halliday, laird of Corehead of the period, and his son, figure along with Sir James Murray of Traquair, Andrew Murray of Cockpool, and other free-living neighbours of the worthy outlaw, to whom he sent for help against the inconvenient intrusion of the monarch.

There were most cogent reasons for this anxiety on the part of these chiefs, as quaintly told in the ballad: so, when Murray heard the news, nothing daunted, he boldly met the emergency:—

> " ' I mak a vow,' the outlaw said,
>   ' I mak a vow, and that trulie ;
>   Were there but three men to take my part —
>   Your king's cuming full deir sall be !'

" Then messengers he called forth,
    And bade them hie them speedilye;
  ' Ane of you gae to Halliday —
    The laird of the Corehead is he.

" ' He certain is my sister's son;
    Bid him come quick and succour me!
The king comes for Ettricke Foreste,
    And landless men we a' shall be.'

" ' What news! what news!' said Halliday,
    ' Man, frae thy master unto me?'
  ' Not as ye wad, but seeking your aid;
    The king 's his mortal enemie.'

" ' Ay, by my troth,' said Halliday,
    ' Even for that it repenteth me;
For gif he lose fair Ettricke Foreste,
    He 'll take fair Moffatdale frae me.' "

It was no wonder the old gentleman was alarmed; but
he was a man of spirit, and had something in his power,
for he immediately adds —

" ' I 'll meet him wi' five hundred men,
    And surely mair if there need be;
And ere he 'll lose the Foreste fair,
    We a' will die on Newark Lee!' "

The other lairds were not less zealous; and, having
met together, the chief of Ettrick further addressed
them, on their common danger, proposing that four of
them should form a regular deputation : —

' " Auld Halliday, young Halliday,
    Ye sall be twa to gang wi' me ;
  Andrew Murray, and Sir James Murray,
    We 'll be nae mae in companie.'

  " When that they cam before the king,
    They fell before him on their knee,
  ' Grant mercie, mercie, nobil king !
    E'en for His sake that dyed on tree.' "

To this pathetic petition his majesty returned an exceedingly austere answer ; talking of nothing less than hanging them all " on gallows hie." But the nobles who stood round adding their arguments to the bold threats of the outlaw and his friends, and the latter going through the feudal formality of giving up the keys of his castle, the king was pleased to think better of his sentence, and, in short, not only returned him the keys, but made him sheriff of the Forest of Ettrick, the first who had the office, which the family held for many years.

THE END.

LONDON .
Printed by A. Spottiswoode,
New-Street-Square.

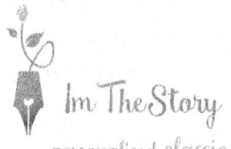

CPSIA information can be obtained
at www.ICGtesting.com
Printed in the USA
BVHW060551280819
556854BV00001B/109/P